The Heritage of Heinlein

CRITICAL EXPLORATIONS IN SCIENCE FICTION AND FANTASY
(a series edited by Donald E. Palumbo and C.W. Sullivan III)

1 *Worlds Apart? Dualism and Transgression in Contemporary Female Dystopias* (Dunja M. Mohr, 2005)

2 *Tolkien and Shakespeare: Essays on Shared Themes and Language* (ed. Janet Brennan Croft, 2007)

3 *Culture, Identities and Technology in the* Star Wars *Films: Essays on the Two Trilogies* (ed. Carl Silvio, Tony M. Vinci, 2007)

4 *The Influence of* Star Trek *on Television, Film and Culture* (ed. Lincoln Geraghty, 2008)

5 *Hugo Gernsback and the Century of Science Fiction* (Gary Westfahl, 2007)

6 *One Earth, One People: The Mythopoeic Fantasy Series of Ursula K. Le Guin, Lloyd Alexander, Madeleine L'Engle and Orson Scott Card* (Marek Oziewicz, 2008)

7 *The Evolution of Tolkien's Mythology: A Study of the History of Middle-earth* (Elizabeth A. Whittingham, 2008)

8 *H. Beam Piper: A Biography* (John F. Carr, 2008)

9 *Dreams and Nightmares: Science and Technology in Myth and Fiction* (Mordecai Roshwald, 2008)

10 *Lilith in a New Light: Essays on the George MacDonald Fantasy Novel* (ed. Lucas H. Harriman, 2008)

11 *Feminist Narrative and the Supernatural: The Function of Fantastic Devices in Seven Recent Novels* (Katherine J. Weese, 2008)

12 *The Science of Fiction and the Fiction of Science: Collected Essays on SF Storytelling and the Gnostic Imagination* (Frank McConnell, ed. Gary Westfahl, 2009)

13 *Kim Stanley Robinson Maps the Unimaginable: Critical Essays* (ed. William J. Burling, 2009)

14 *The Inter-Galactic Playground: A Critical Study of Children's and Teens' Science Fiction* (Farah Mendlesohn, 2009)

15 *Science Fiction from Québec: A Postcolonial Study* (Amy J. Ransom, 2009)

16 *Science Fiction and the Two Cultures: Essays on Bridging the Gap Between the Sciences and the Humanities* (ed. Gary Westfahl, George Slusser, 2009)

17 *Stephen R. Donaldson and the Modern Epic Vision: A Critical Study of the "Chronicles of Thomas Covenant" Novels* (Christine Barkley, 2009)

18 *Ursula K. Le Guin's Journey to Post-Feminism* (Amy M. Clarke, 2010)

19 *Portals of Power: Magical Agency and Transformation in Literary Fantasy* (Lori M. Campbell, 2010)

20 *The Animal Fable in Science Fiction and Fantasy* (Bruce Shaw, 2010)

21 *Illuminating* Torchwood: *Essays on Narrative, Character and Sexuality in the BBC Series* (ed. Andrew Ireland, 2010)

22 *Comics as a Nexus of Cultures: Essays on the Interplay of Media, Disciplines and International Perspectives* (ed. Mark Berninger, Jochen Ecke, Gideon Haberkorn, 2010)

23 *The Anatomy of Utopia: Narration, Estrangement and Ambiguity in More, Wells, Huxley and Clarke* (Károly Pintér, 2010)

24 *The Anticipation Novelists of 1950s French Science Fiction: Stepchildren of Voltaire* (Bradford Lyau, 2010)

25 *The* Twilight *Mystique: Critical Essays on the Novels and Films* (ed. Amy M. Clarke, Marijane Osborn, 2010)

26 *The Mythic Fantasy of Robert Holdstock: Critical Essays on the Fiction* (ed. Donald E. Morse, Kálmán Matolcsy, 2011)

27 *Science Fiction and the Prediction of the Future: Essays on Foresight and Fallacy* (ed. Gary Westfahl, Wong Kin Yuen, Amy Kit-sze Chan, 2011)

28 *Apocalypse in Australian Fiction and Film: A Critical Study* (Roslyn Weaver, 2011)

29 *British Science Fiction Film and Television: Critical Essays* (ed. Tobias Hochscherf, James Leggott, 2011)

30 *Cult Telefantasy Series: A Critical Analysis of* The Prisoner, Twin Peaks, The X-Files, Buffy the Vampire Slayer, Lost, Heroes, Doctor Who *and* Star Trek (Sue Short, 2011)

31 *The Postnational Fantasy: Essays on Postcolonialism, Cosmopolitics and Science Fiction* (ed. Masood Ashraf Raja, Jason W. Ellis and Swaralipi Nandi, 2011)

32 *Heinlein's Juvenile Novels: A Cultural Dictionary* (C.W. Sullivan III, 2011)

33 *Welsh Mythology and Folklore in Popular Culture: Essays on Adaptations in Literature, Film, Television and Digital Media* (ed. Audrey L. Becker and Kristin Noone, 2011)

34 *I See You: The Shifting Paradigms of James Cameron's* Avatar (Ellen Grabiner, 2012)

35 *Of Bread, Blood and* The Hunger Games: *Critical Essays on the Suzanne Collins Trilogy* (ed. Mary F. Pharr and Leisa A. Clark, 2012)

36 *The Sex Is Out of This World: Essays on the Carnal Side of Science Fiction* (ed. Sherry Ginn and Michael G. Cornelius, 2012)

37 *Lois McMaster Bujold: Essays on a Modern Master of Science Fiction and Fantasy* (ed. Janet Brennan Croft, 2013)

38 *Girls Transforming: Invisibility and Age-Shifting in Children's Fantasy Fiction Since the 1970s* (Sanna Lehtonen, 2013)

39 Doctor Who *in Time and Space: Essays on Themes, Characters, History and Fandom, 1963–2012* (ed. Gillian I. Leitch, 2013)

40 *The Worlds of* Farscape: *Essays on the Groundbreaking Television Series* (ed. Sherry Ginn, 2013)

41 *Orbiting Ray Bradbury's Mars: Biographical, Anthropological, Literary, Scientific and Other Perspectives* (ed. Gloria McMillan, 2013)

42 *The Heritage of Heinlein: A Critical Reading of the Fiction Television Series* (Thomas D. Clareson and Joe Sanders, 2014)

43 *The Past That Might Have Been, the Future That May Come: Women Writing Fantastic Fiction, 1960s to the Present* (Lauren J. Lacey, 2014)

44 *Environments in Science Fiction: Essays on Alternative Spaces* (ed. Susan M. Bernardo, 2014)

45 *Discworld and the Disciplines: Critical Approaches to the Terry Pratchett Works* (ed. Anne Hiebert Alton and William C. Spruiell, 2014)

The Heritage of Heinlein
A Critical Reading of the Fiction

THOMAS D. CLARESON *and*
JOE SANDERS

Foreword by FREDERIK POHL

CRITICAL EXPLORATIONS IN SCIENCE FICTION AND FANTASY, 42
Series Editors Donald E. Palumbo *and* C.W. Sullivan III

McFarland & Company, Inc., Publishers
Jefferson, North Carolina

The senior author, Thomas D. Clareson, died in 1993,
having written three chapters of this study. Joe Sanders
continued the work, writing the remainder of
the text and editing the orginal chapters.

LIBRARY OF CONGRESS CATALOGUING-IN-PUBLICATION DATA

Clareson, Thomas D.
The Heritage of Heinlein : a Critical Reading of the Fiction / Thomas D.
Clareson and Joe Sanders ; foreword by Frederik Pohl.
   p.   cm. — (Critical explorations in science fiction and fantasy ; 42)
[Donald E. Palumbo and C.W. Sullivan III, series editors]
Includes bibliographical references and index.

ISBN 978-0-7864-7498-1
softcover : acid free paper ∞

1. Heinlein, Robert A. (Robert Anson), 1907–1988 — Criticism and
interpretation.   2. Science fiction, American — History
and criticism.   I. Sanders, Joseph L.   II. Title.
PS3515.E288Z57 2014   813'.54 — dc23   2013045117

BRITISH LIBRARY CATALOGUING DATA ARE AVAILABLE

© 2014 Thomas F.R. Clareson and Joe Sanders. All rights reserved

*No part of this book may be reproduced or transmitted in any form
or by any means, electronic or mechanical, including photocopying
or recording, or by any information storage and retrieval system,
without permission in writing from the publisher.*

On the cover: Poster art for the 1950 film *Destination Moon*, loosely
based on several Heinlein novels (Eagle-Lion Films, Inc./Photofest)

Manufactured in the United States of America

*McFarland & Company, Inc., Publishers
Box 611, Jefferson, North Carolina 28640
www.mcfarlandpub.com*

To Alice Clareson
*(original dedication prior to
Alice Clareson's death in 2012)*

Table of Contents

Foreword by Frederik Pohl   1
Preface   11
A Note on Texts   15
1. A New Calling: *For Us, the Living*   17
2. Early Professional Writing   23
3. Transitions   53
4. The Juveniles for Scribner's   62
5. The "Classic" Period   108
6. *Stranger in a Strange Land*   132
7. The Final Period   140

Summing-Up   197
Appendix: Nonfiction   215
Works Cited   217
Index   219

Foreword
by Frederik Pohl

When it comes time to write a foreword to a work as soundly wrought — and as thoroughly introduced by its own authors — as this one, a problem arises. The problem for a prospective introducer is simply to try to think of what he should say to encourage the reader to get on with the reading. Much of the time the solution will of course depend on the circumstances of the reading. For many, the book may be read as an assignment in a class on "Writings of R. A. Heinlein 101," and if that is your case you will be able to count on a sound class with a cheerful instructor, because this book has made his work of teaching it so much easier. For others, perhaps they may already have come across a Heinlein story or two and would like to know what else there is to look for. Or, if they are adults who don't care to read stories written for children, perhaps what they need is reeducation on what a story ostensibly written for teenagers could be like when its author was Robert A. Heinlein.

Unfortunately, Messrs. Clareson and Sanders have done their very good bests to meet all those needs already, so that all that is left for me is, perhaps, to tell you a little bit about why I am here.

Mostly, I think, that is because I was one of the earliest of Bob Heinlein's editors. Not *the* earliest, of course. John W. Campbell, editor of what was then still called *Astounding Stories,* was the unchallenged Number One in that department. But for one reason or another an occasional Heinlein story didn't meet Campbell's needs. (There were in fact four such while I was editing the two magazines.) Those came back to Heinlein in California, who immediately sent them to me, as the teenage editor of a pair of salvage markets, *Astonishing Stories* and *Super Science Stories.* I also immediately sent him a rather small check for the right to publish the stories in one or the other of those magazines.

Fortunately for my readers, Heinlein was not the only science-fiction writer whose Campbell rejects went straight to me. Another was my good fan friend and fellow member of the fans-who-would-be-writers club, the Futurians, Isaac Asimov. Indeed, that small club was the mother lode of nascent writing talent in those years, since it included Damon Knight, Cyril Kornbluth, Richard Wilson, and four or five other blossoming sf authors. Nearly all of them gave first look for whatever they wrote to Campbell, not only because his magazine was clearly the class of the market, but also because it paid the most. And when those stories came back from Campbell, as they almost always did, it was a no-brainer to give the next look to me. That wasn't because I was second-highest payer after Campbell, or anywhere near it, but only because submitting them to any third party required making an investment in postage stamps, whereas offering them to me often meant no more than tossing them across a room.

I can't claim that *Astonishing* and *Super Science* were really good magazines. I was too wet behind the ears and my budgets too puny for hopes of that. But because of the Futurians — and Robert Heinlein — they were a lot better than they had any right to be.

My status as Number Two market, following *Astounding,* gave me more benefits — exceeding the mere access to better stories — than I deserved. Whenever Isaac, or any of the others, came back from a visit to Campbell's office they were sure to be a-bubble with stories about what John had said or done. I listened with a highly attentive ear, because whatever John Campbell did in the course of editing his magazines, I copied as quickly and as completely as I could in editing my own.

You will note that the four Heinlein stories that Campbell rejected and I snapped up have barely been mentioned in the text of this book by either of the collaborators. The names of the stories, in the order in which I did the snapping, were "Let There Be Light" "Beyond Doubt," "Pied Piper" and "Lost Legacy," and I can tell you why I bought them. I bought "Let There Be Light" on its merits. It wasn't a great story, but neither were the commonalty of Heinlein's early pieces. "Let There Be Light" wasn't rejected by Campbell solely for a lack of those merits, I'm pretty sure. It was quite as good as many of the early works that John did buy, and I believe that what doomed it was an off-color joke Heinlein had included in the text. John Campbell's chief and only editorial assistant, Kay Tarrant, who did all the copy-editing, was known for her relentless censorship of anything that, say, might offend an elderly spinster all of whose brothers were priests. In any case, it was not merely on their aforesaid "merits" that John bought almost all of the early Heinleins. It was to keep the stream of submissions flowing in the hope of better work before long, which is what I too was doing on my much smaller scale. We both got what we paid for. John, after a much bigger investment, got all those great Heinlein serials, and I got the deeply felt novelette "Lost Legacy."

Unfortunately, however, I must add at this point that in the world of publishing pulp magazines justice is not always served. Sometimes even a really good story can be brutally maimed by a heavy-handed editor. This happened to "Lost Legacy." My Uncle Sam had finally issued his invitation to reclothe myself in air force blue — or rather, because the first stage would be basic training, in fatigues. If I had known what was going to happen to "Lost Legacy," for which I signed the purchase order the day before I left the company, I could easily have stalled around for a day or two, long enough to do the job myself. I didn't, though, and whoever did the copy-editing turned out to have many creative ideas for changes and "improvements" that I wouldn't have made on my worst day, and that Heinlein himself truly hated. (Fortunately, when the story was reprinted Heinlein was able to restore the originals.)

One last comment about this world of Heinlein's beginnings, and mine: Years later some of Heinlein's personal correspondence began to show up in the hands of science fiction's fans and collectors. One letter was something he had written to a New York writing colleague, and it concerned me. "If Freddie" — that was the first time I had any suspicion that among his intimates he called me "Freddie"; he never dared it to my face — "is getting a raw deal from those higher-ups I want to know about it. I'll never sell them another word, and I'll try to make sure none of my friends do, either."

I was really touched. I was pretty sure that Robert respected me as an editor — why else would he ask for suggestions for changes, and then even make the changes, despite my beggarly word rate? But I had had no idea his loyalty would go that far.

How a Legend Begins

Robert Anson Heinlein was not born with the gifts that would entertain and delight generations of readers in countries all around the world. The gifts he was born with would do no more for him than to let him set down on paper matters about which he felt strongly. They would do nothing about causing any other party than, perhaps, his mother and his then-current girlfriend to read what he had written. Writerly skills were simply absent.

So Heinlein's first story that he intended to be professionally published was a novel called *For Us, the Living*. We know that he intended it for professional publication, because he himself shipped it off to two different publishing companies. They, for their part, shipped it right back as a reject. As well they should, for the manuscript, by an unknown author and displaying none of the storytelling craft that Heinlein taught himself a couple of years later, would have been a prime candidate for rejection by any publishing company that stays in business longer than a week. The manuscript was lost for years, apparently because Heinlein himself wanted it to be. Then, unfortunately, it was found again and signed for publishing under the imprint of publishers who knew that any manuscript of book length signed by Robert A. Heinlein would be bought by at least some fraction of his fandom, since so many such books already had.

I said earlier that prospective readers owe the authors of the present volume a debt for having written it. So you do, all of you, simply because Thomas Clareson and Joe Sanders, having read *For Us, the Living* and then told you what it was like, have now insured that you never have to read it yourself.

The (Relatively) Big Money

Heinlein, rejected at every turn in his plea for an active commission in the navy, had at last settled for spending the war in a small and unusual research facility in the Philadelphia Navy Yard, along with old friends Isaac Asimov and L. Sprague de Camp and a newly met one, Virginia Gerstenfeld, who was a lieutenant (junior grade) on active naval status and thus the superior officer for Ensign Robert Anson Heinlein (Ret.). What the fruits of their researches were is unclear. They apparently published nothing, although that could be said of almost any military research performed during the war. Still, the team took their charge seriously enough that Heinlein found time for little or no fiction writing until the nuclear bombs on Japan and the Red Armies racing south from Siberia set them all free. Then, after some months of analyzing and trying to teach himself how to mimic the work of successful magazine short-story writers, he eased himself back into the life of a professional writer of science fiction with a few short stories.

That is when he very quickly discovered that one and a half, even two cents a word, was not necessarily the limit of a writer's financial dreams.

The fact of the matter, not always understood by writers, is that there isn't any measurable qualitative difference between a really good pulp story and a really good story that sells to a higher-paying market — to, that is, the magazines that in those days were called the "slicks." I myself was taught that lesson at a party when the fiction editor of *Playboy* took me aside to say, "You know, Fred, I would have bought at least three or four of those stories you've been running in *Galaxy*." I had to learn painfully, by the accident of a chance conversation at a cocktail party, the truths about selling to the slicks. Heinlein was luckier.

His new literary agent, Lurton Blassingame, had known them all along, and when "The Green Hills of Earth" came out of Heinlein's typewriter the agent correctly judged that *The Saturday Evening Post* would like to buy it, as they did. The ice once broken, Heinlein went on to write four more short stories for the *Post*. Three of them sold there. One of them did not, and I would like to register my opinion that that one, "Jerry Is a Man," is the best of the four.

When I said there was little difference in quality between the pulps, or at least a few of them, and the slicks, the truth I was trying to express was that stories sent by their authors or agents to a slick-magazine editor could be rejected for many reasons the pulps didn't have to worry about.

One of these was "being political," and I think that was the factor that doomed "Jerry Is a Man" for the slicks. The question of race relations in America was very much in the public mind in that period—a thought which I have no doubt was in Bob's mind as he was writing it as well. That is precisely the sort of thing slick editors do not want to publish, or at least don't want to publish unless the story can be publicized as a sort of litmus test of feelings usually concealed. I don't know whether or not the papers of Heinlein's agent, Lurton Blassingame, have been collected already in some university library. If they have, and if the rejection letters for "Jerry Is a Man" can be located, I predict that they will be found to contain the words "too preachy."

Now you may ask, "Why are the slicks so timorous?" And the answer is, "The pulps and the slicks nourish from quite different revenue streams." A pulp magazine is a perishable commodity because of the date on its cover, and it is sold like any other such. Let us pretend that a copy of a pulp magazine costs 50 cents to manufacture, is sold at that price to local "distributors" (think of them as like wholesalers of canned goods) who sell them to neighborhood 7-Elevens (for 60 cents), who, finally, sell them to some person who, with his or her family, is the consumer who pays full price. (And, as perhaps I should have warned you a few sentences earlier, you must not trust my numbers. All the costs of making, selling and buying magazines have changed so much and so erratically that all these numbers, as well as any I might predict for the future, are now fantasy.)

But the principle is right, and now we come to the fundamental difference between slicks and pulps, which is how they are sold, and how that affects everything they do. By and large, pulps are sold one copy at a time, purchased in person and off a newsstand by someone who expects to read them. Slicks, on the other hand, are primarily sold by subscription and thus by mail, each subscription covering the twelve monthly issues of one year The form of the order for the subscription is generally a bind-in or blow-in coupon in an earlier issue of the magazine itself, or in a mail-order subscription appeal sent from its publishers. The appeal may not be anything the buyer might consider a "good read." It is more likely to offer useful recipes, interesting fashion news, titillating scandals, practical health or diet tips, and, most important, a dazzlingly cheap subscription price. If there is any fiction at all in an issue it may be as little as a single story in a 160-page magazine. And here's the core of the difference between slicks and pulps: The pulp publisher may spend as little as 25 cents an issue to cover all costs of preparing and publishing the issue that they will sell to the distributor for 50 cents a copy. The slick publisher's comparable manufacturing costs are much higher—say, $2 instead of 25 cents for preparation and manufacture—*plus* an item which, if ever itemized in the cost of getting a pulp magazine out, will rarely be higher than a sum somewhere in the range between very little and nothing at all. That item is sales promotion, which covers many things, including assorted forms of adver-

tising, but especially selling subscriptions anyway they can. That promotion may take any form you like, but is seldom cheap. Slick magazines, you see, don't make their money on what readers pay to get their magazines. They make it on what advertisers will pay to include their advertising. And the amount advertisers will pay per page of advertising is where all the profits, the sometimes very high profits, of slick publishing come from. So if a magazine publishes a story that alienates readers, it has lost far more than the customer will pay to read it. (Disclaimer: in my younger days I spent nearly a decade in a rather enjoyable job as the chief copywriter of sales promotion for both *Popular Science* and *Outdoor Life*.)

Through the good offices of his agent Heinlein discovered the existence of still a third class of magazine, the out-of-category pulps. Those are the magazines with such a long history of reader-pleasing fiction that, although they are true pulps in almost every way, their by-the-word pay to their writers was better than that of the average specialized pulp western, crime, or love story magazine. *Argosy, Blue Book* and one or two others are the exemplars of this class. There are also some fairly well-paying magazines which went to members of a specific group, the *American Legion Magazine* and *Boy's Life* being the most important to Heinlein. He even ventured outside of the familiar pastures of science fiction and fantasy once or twice, in *Popular Detective* and in — of all things — *Calling All Girls*.

How to Revise a Life

Up to this point our authors, Thomas D. Clareson and Joe Sanders, have had little to say about Heinlein's personal life. That is as it should be. This book isn't a biography. It concerns his writings, not the events of his personal history. But in that history there was a noteworthy change in the immediate postwar period which could not help but have an effect on his thinking, and thus his writing.

That began at war's end, when Heinlein said good-bye to his comrades at the Philadelphia Navy Yard and then left Philadelphia to join his wife, Leslyn, in California. Lt. Gerstenfeld had said her own good-bye to him when he was leaving, but it didn't take. She apparently had some afterthoughts, because the day after Heinlein got home there was a knock at the door of his California home, and when it was opened there stood Virginia Gerstenfeld, her baggage around her. I don't know what her exact words were, but the sense of them was that she had decided to come in order to help Robert. She doesn't appear to have said exactly how she proposed to do it.

It is an enormous temptation to speculate on the events of the next couple of weeks in the Heinlein house, but I am going to resist it. Heinlein's biographer, William H. Patterson, Jr., has probably done all that can be done about describing that period, but much the greatest part of his information comes from only one of the participants, Virginia Heinlein. It's a pity this is so. What is clear is only that Heinlein's marriage to his second wife, Leslyn, had been in worsening trouble for a long time, apparently largely because Leslyn was unhappy. At some point Virginia aided Robert in filing a divorce suit against Leslyn. The two then fled the home, living in cheap motels and the like, until the divorce was granted. (In all later discussions, Virginia repeatedly stressed the point that there had been no sexual activity while they were on the run.) Then the two rejoined human society and in 1948 were married, Lt. Virginia Gerstenfeld becoming Mrs. Ginny Heinlein.

Coincidentally, Robert's political viewpoint went from left of center to right — eventually far right — of center.

The Well-Oiled Machine

Once they succeeded in getting married the pair stayed that way. Heinlein had entered his golden years, writing easily and well — and very profitably, the fruits of his writing having been estimated as rising to something like seven figures. As a writer, Heinlein became the very model of an editor's he-never-misses-a-deadline contributor, whose works always sell. That meant a new book every year for the juvenile (but not really so juvenile in the telling that many thousands of adults didn't wholeheartedly enjoy them) series he wrote for Scribner's. At the same time there was a new serial almost every year (generally the magazine publication of one of the Scribner's novels) for the delight of his core readers in the magazines *Astounding*, *Galaxy* and *The Magazine of Fantasy and Science Fiction*, usually referred to simply as *F&SF*. All the books were well reviewed and sold well, but three of them stand out.

The first of these is *Starship Troopers* (1959), which Heinlein wrote specifically to demonstrate what a properly organized political system should be — in particular, conferring the right to vote only on those who have served in its military. The book is also popular, even with readers who are not very interested in being instructed, as a first-rate future action adventure, seen as such especially after the film version was released in 1997. Then, in 1973 *Stranger in a Strange Land* appeared, and Heinlein, who had been becoming increasingly well known, was converted into a true May-I-Have-Your-Autograph-Sir celebrity. This was in part because of some of the elements of a religion that Heinlein had written into the book — including cannibalism on the flesh of departed loved ones — but perhaps even more to the scandalous report that was circulating asserting that Charles Manson, leader of the pack of murdering young women who had Hollywood terrified, had got some of his ideas from Heinlein's book. The rumors certainly enhanced the book's sales, but seriously angered its author, who did not allow them to be discussed in his presence.

Then there was *The Moon Is a Harsh Mistress*.

I had been asked to take over the magazine *Galaxy* when Horace Gold, the editor who created and shaped it, became too ill to continue. I enjoyed the work — I compared getting the editorship with a young boy's Christmas gift of a giant set of electric trains — not least because it gave me the chance to publish most of Heinlein's new book-length works as serials in my magazines.

I must say that this was not always a shrewd editorial decision. Heinlein, after a string of winners, had hit a soft patch. I think of it as "the Podkayne period," because it represented a time when Heinlein seemed to be writing novels of kinds he had never tried before, just to see if he could do them. The exemplar of that period was his novel *Podkayne of Mars*, told from the point of view of the young girl Podkayne. I published it not in *Galaxy* but in my second-string magazine, *If*, which I think hinted to my readers the suggestion that I didn't think it was Heinlein's best work. I took my own feeling as a longtime Heinlein fan to probably apply to many of my subscribers: Having had so much pleasure from reading Heinlein's work for so many years I wanted to read everything he was writing now, if only just to see what the old man was up to. The reader mail seemed to bear that theory out.

When I got the manuscript of *Farnham's Freehold* from Lurton Blassingame, the opening was pure political oratory that put me to sleep. I called Lurton and told him, "I'd like to buy it, but I don't want to do that to my readers, so how about if I buy it as is, at its present length, but amputate the first two or three thousand words before I publish it?" Lurton chuckled and said, "Sure."

But he never told Heinlein, who called me up as soon as he saw the first installment, furious. He simmered down when I told him I'd got Lurton's permission, but insisted that the book edition carry this line on the copyright page: "A short version of this novel, as cut and revised by Frederik Pohl, appeared in *Worlds of If* Magazine, 1964 — RAH."

Fortunately, Heinlein didn't hold a grudge against me, and not long after that the payoff for my patience came.

A novel-sized envelope appeared in my office in New York, with the return address of Lurton Blassingame's agency — a Heinlein novel, no doubt. I began reading the contents in the hope that this one would be more like Heinlein's old masterpieces, or at least a little less like poor little Podkayne or longwinded Hugh Farnham. And indeed it was all those things. By the end of the first page he had me hooked. By the completion of the first scene — a dialogue between a half-Russian computer mechanic who lives on the Moon and his biggest computer, which — or who — refuses to speak to him — I was beginning to think of cover art. When I finished reading it, on the train home and long past my bedtime, I scribbled a note on the purchase order for *The Moon Is a Harsh Mistress* as I was signing it: *I guarantee a Hugo for this.*

In due course we published it and, yes, it did win that year's Hugo for Best Novel, I am sure in the process giving my magazine, *Worlds of If*, a big boost for the Hugo of its own that it then won as Best Magazine for the year. With all his novels, Heinlein scored the Hugo for only four of them. My personal vote — recognizing that the book is up against some truly stiff competition — is that this is the best of them all.

How My Favorite Island Did Bob Heinlein In

In the spring of 1978, worn down to a nubbin by an assortment of high-priority work demands and some wearing family matters, I decided to treat myself to a couple of weeks of South Sea Island decompression. I told no one where I was going but my secretary-assistant, warning her in ferocious terms to tell no one else, and booked two weeks in an imitation little grass shack (though furnished with working electricity and plumbing), on the island of Moorea, next-door neighbor to the more famous Tahiti. It was all I had hoped for. Not (of course) a drop of rain. Skilled French cuisine in the restaurant out over the water. A *maitresse d'* and a Polynesian serving staff that let me practice my meager French on them, coconut palms dropping their fruit just outside my door, and skin-diving in the warm, gentle lagoon a few steps farther — well, I'll stop. I'm not selling tickets. But I had a rented car at my call and freedom to explore the island — which, like so many of the South Pacific islands, was nothing but the top of some old underwater volcano that had poked its way through to the surface of the sea, then stopped erupting. What was left of the volcano was a really king-sized mountain in the middle of the island, which I could have climbed at least partway if I had wanted to, but didn't.

And then it was time to go home to my family and my duties, and I hopped on the little puddle-jumping plane that took us across the channel to the Tahiti airport, the one with the bizarre name of F.a.a.a. And as I was crossing the airport floor to the four-engine French jet that would carry us to California I heard my name being called: "Fred! Hey, Fred! Why the devil weren't you at the Heinlein party last night?"

* * *

Well, it was all easy to explain, though a cause for real regret. Bob and Ginny had treated themselves to some South Sea sun, just as I had, only their comfy little cabin was on a good-sized cruise liner. Ginny had equipped herself with a list of names to call for a party at every port of call. Ginny not being telepathic, my name wasn't on the list.

I happened not to cross paths with them then for, I think, more than a year, Bob being reported not feeling well. But then time passed, he had become well enough to be granted an honorary doctoral degree in Michigan, and Bob and Ginny invited me and my light of love, Dr. Betty Hull, to watch it happen. When we got to the room on campus where a sort of pre-degree party was going on we found forty or fifty friends already there, munching canapés and sipping drinks. After a bit, Ginny took advantage of tidal currents among the guests to join us in a corner. "Robert and I are going to cut out of here in a little bit," she said. "We've got an early dinner date, but we'd like it if you'd come to our place down the road for some friendly conversation around eight?"

"You bet," Betty Anne said, and then, glancing at the card Ginny had handed her, "But this place is a good ten miles away! Weren't there any rooms closer?"

"All too many," Robert told her, grinning. "But there'll be some sort of a party after the ceremony, and we didn't want it to be in our hotel room. Don't forget, now. Eight o'clock!"

And at eight o'clock, decently fed, we were knocking at their room door. Robert let us in. By the time we were seated and supplied with drinks, Bob tending bar and Ginny delivering the glasses, I remembered what I had wanted to tell them. "I don't know if anybody ever mentioned it," I said, "but a year or so ago, when you two were on a cruise ship that stopped at the island of Moorea—"

I stopped there, because the look on her face had abruptly darkened into anger. She almost dropped the Canadian-and-ginger she was handing me. "Moorea!" she snapped. "That little pipsqueak of an island almost killed my Robert. I never want to hear that name again!"

* * *

Heinlein completed the story for us. They had parked the car at the steepest rise they could find and got out for a look. "I tried to see the top of the mountain," Heinlein said. "I tilted my head back as far as it would go, and then something went *spoing!* inside my skull. It was as though a thermite bomb had gone off in my head—fiery hot, exploding, unbelievable pain. And then it got worse."

What it was, the doctors said, was something called a transient ischemic episode. The important word in that name was "transient," as it indeed was, though "transient" does not mean "maybe a weekend, and then it would pass" or anything like it. It did have an end, though—but then there was something else and then some other thing else, for almost ten years of life-threatening medical crises.

But those, too, passed. And then he almost was his old self, and stayed that way long enough to write five new novels: *The Number of the Beast, Friday, Job: A Comedy of Justice, The Cat Who Walks through Walls* and *To Sail Beyond the Sunset*. As a group these are five ambitious attempts to transcend all that had gone before. But—and I cannot tell you with what sorrow I say this—time, age and, above all, the ravages of illness had deprived Robert of the ability to set ever-higher challenges for himself and to meet them all.

And something else had happened. He had lost his editor.

Here I don't mean to refer to any specific human being, simply some human being who can read a clutch of pages and say, "You're not getting through to your reader here, Bob. What are you trying to say?" That is, someone to challenge the author as an equal.

I think almost every writer needs an editor just to keep him on his toes. I don't think Bob Heinlein would have come up so far and so fast if he hadn't had John Campbell challenging him, or that his Scribner's juveniles would have held to that level of excellence without Alice Dalgliesh's vigilant eye. Heinlein really disliked her querying and arguing style, but I think it helped him more than is generally realized. And then, for those last five books, he had no one.

An editor's real job, you see, is to provide his or her publisher with a line of works that will make money for him. Nowhere is it written that they have to be quality literature; sometimes it's the trash that sells. Put yourself in the position of an editor for one of the publishing companies that were involved. The door open, Heinlein walks in and dumps the manuscript of, say, *The Cat Who Walks through Walls* on your desk. You read it and see that it lacks coherence in many ways. You have a conscience so you mention this fact to him. He frowns and tells you he's sorry you feel that way, and he wonders if your rival Bigbuck Books, just across the street, would think that.

That's when you explain very quickly that what you said didn't mean you didn't *like* his book; indeed you want it to lead your fall list and you'll talk money with his agent as soon as you can get him in the phone. Because, you see, there's no future for an editor in rejecting a book that needs work but will sell a lot of copies if the author can walk across the street and sell it as is. Not when his boss walks into your office with the latest *Publishers Weekly*, which is open to the Bigbuck ad for their edition of the Heinlein, and he's asking you, "How did we let this one get away?"

And After You've Gone...

For every writer, the ownership of what he has written stays with him as long as his copyright lives, except in cases where he has sold specific rights to others. This includes the right, if he wishes to exercise it, to make changes in the work or to sell it to others.

When Robert died of a combination of emphysema and heart failure in the spring of 1988, he left everything to his wife Ginny, who quickly assumed an active role in managing the estate, as she had every right to do. However, in a few cases I do think she made a decision that I wish she hadn't.

My publisher, Tor, had invited me to edit a series of volumes celebrating the authors to whom the Science Fiction and Fantasy Writers of America had awarded the title of Grand Master. The first to receive that honor was, quite properly, Robert A. Heinlein, and I immediately began to assemble examples of his work — a couple of short stories and essays, and extracts from a few of his most famous books, including *The Moon Is a Harsh Mistress*. I then assembled cuttings and sent them to Ginny, with a letter outlining payment plans and requesting permissions. When two weeks had passed with no response, I called her. She said, "Of course, Fred. Tom" — that's Tom Doherty, our publisher — "has been on the phone already, trying to hurry me up. I'll try to get back to you next week."

That's when my heart began to sink inside my chest. "I — uh — hope there isn't any problem, Ginny."

Silvery laugh. "Problem? No, no, nothing you could call a problem, just that this is a big thing for Robert's fans, and I'd like to be sure we're getting it just right."

Hesitant question from me: "Are there any of my selections that you'd rather I think over?"

"No, no, nothing like... Well, no, the fact is there is one." Hesitation. Then, "Well, it's that dialect piece from *The Moon Is a Harsh Mistress*."

Sound of me swallowing hard. "The opening chapter? The book did win his last Hugo, Ginny."

"I know, Fred, I know, but let me just think a bit more. And I'd like to talk to a few of my friends."

Swallowing harder than ever. "Of course, Ginny. I'll call you next week." And do you know what she said then? She said, "I'm truly sorry, Fred, but they just don't think that piece would be appropriate to celebrate Robert's life. They think it's a bit vulgar."

Then there's the case of *Grumbles from the Grave*. Robert had talked to me quite a few times about his intention to write a collection of the letters he *wanted* to write to various fans, editors, critics and others he didn't think it a good idea to tell what he really thought of them, and when I heard that a book with that title was actually coming out I made sure I got one of the first copies. But what a disappointment! Milquetoast for five-year-olds. Not a bit like the scalding comments Robert could produce when he got a good mad on. As I knew, because I had seen several such, including one or two directed to me (though — I hasten to add — the worst of them was over the *Farnham's Freehold* brouhaha, something his agent had given permission for, though without telling his client).

It seems clear to me that Ginny had done her best to turn Robert into a gentleman, even in his writings — which, of course, would have swiftly cost him a major share of his readers. Robert, of course, isn't the only writer whose wife tried to do him such a disservice. Mark Twain's beloved Olivia tried the same feat. And I am so glad neither of them quite succeeded. The view across the breakfast table, when the husband is not yet either shaven or fully articulate, is not the one best suited to revealing greatness of character.

Frederik Pohl (1919–2013) won most of the awards in the field of science fiction as writer, editor, and blogger. He received the SFW's Grand Master Award in 1993, and in 1998 was named to the Science Fiction Hall of Fame. This foreword was written in February 2013.

Preface
by Joe Sanders

Robert A. Heinlein was the dominant writer of American science fiction in the twentieth century, both in terms of his own popularity and of his influence on other writers. However, interpretations and judgments concerning specific works have varied disconcertingly. Criticism of his writing, ranging from chuckleheaded reverence to myopic disdain, has tended to flatten out nuances and outright contradictions too easily.

Observations about Heinlein himself have varied even more wildly:

According to Julius Schwartz, Heinlein coldly snubbed navy officer and fellow sf writer Malcolm Jameson at a party because Jameson was not an Annapolis graduate...

According to Theodore Sturgeon, Heinlein learned that he was suffering from writer's block and sent him a list of lovely story ideas along with a check to help him through the tough time...

He cultivated the image of a no-nonsense commercial writer who cared about satisfying paying customers and who paid no attention to literary criticism....

He protested at length (but absolutely in private) negative criticism of his writing and went ballistic at one insufficiently diffident young critic...

His fiction advocated complete sexual freedom...

He accepted Virginia Heinlein's insistence that the two never had fooled around before they were married...

He was a rude bully and a generous friend, a thick-skinned pro and a nervous artist, a disciple of Priapus and Mrs. Grundy. He expressed with absolute certainty whatever opinions he was voicing at the time, as if no reasonable person could disagree.

Turning from Heinlein's fascinating but ultimately unknowable personal secrets but accepting that reasonable people *can* disagree about what they read, this book simply tries to observe important aspects of Heinlein's writing. It offers a reading but doesn't pretend to be the only reading of Heinlein's fiction. It attempts to pay attention both to the continuity of Heinlein's work and its variety, assuming that a writer may test persistent concerns in different ways during his career and that grappling with contradictions may lead to the irritation and energy that can produce art. Late in life, Heinlein played with the notion of the multiverse, a vast network of alternative universes within which *all* of his science fiction and fantasy stories could find a home, "true" within some particular context. This book notes some of the connections Heinlein suggested between works that had been written as stand-alone pieces, but usually have concentrated on each by itself— stepping stones along the way to the multiverse.

A few words on how this book came to be written:

Thomas D. Clareson (1926–1993) was a pioneer American academic sf scholar, founder of the journal *Extrapolation* and of the Science Fiction Research Association (SFRA). Among other books, he wrote *A Reader's Guide to Frederik Pohl* for Starmont House, part of a series of compact surveys of major sf writers' work. He had begun a draft of a Starmont House book on Heinlein at the time of his death. After Starmont folded, the incomplete manuscript went to another small-press publisher. Several years later, when that publisher shut down, Tom's widow Alice asked if I would try to get it ready for publication.

That's taken some time. For one thing, I've had a long, uneasy relationship with Heinlein's writing. One of the very first sf stories I ever read was "The Black Pits of Luna," in one of my mother's *Saturday Evening Post*s. The Scribner's juveniles were among the few sf novels in my local library. I loved *The Puppet Masters* and Heinlein's other mid–'50s novels. Robert A. Heinlein was largely responsible for the fact that I began reading sf and developed a love of it. When I had finished my Ph.D. and saw what Heinlein was doing in the 1970s and later, though, I was appalled. Reading some of those late novels felt like touring a second-rate nursing home. I said as much in the sf classes I taught — until I was challenged by Stacie Hanes, an unusually mature, perceptive, and determined student. Eventually, after much discussion, Stacie accepted that there was more to Heinlein's early work than she'd appreciated, and I realized that perhaps it was unfair to read the later fiction as if it was unsuccessfully attempting to duplicate the earlier stories' success.

When I was ready to look at Heinlein's later novels *sui generis*, as individually unique accomplishments, I next discovered that Tom's manuscript was very uneven. On the one hand, it showed marvelous scholarly persistence as Tom tracked down the identity of Heinlein's first wife and unearthed details of Heinlein's work during World War II — material that I regretfully have left out because it does not contribute directly to understanding the fiction. Tom covered the earlier portion of Heinlein's writing career from his first publications to the end of the Scribner's juveniles, in what sometimes looked like a polished rough draft, sometimes a very preliminary version; I've revised and expanded this material. Everything else in this book, the discussion of *For Us, the Living* and of Heinlein's adult fiction in the '50s and later, is my responsibility.

Besides Alice and Stacie, I owe thanks to the attendees at the annual conferences of the SFRA and ICFA (International Conference on the Fantastic in the Arts) who listened to earlier versions of some of this material; thanks also to David Hartwell, Kevin Mahoney, and the rest of the staff of *The New York Review of Science Fiction*, where four of those conference papers were later published.

Heinlein probably would have disapproved of both Tom and me. We both were college professors, mere academic critics and scholars. I even occasionally taught a course in creative writing. Heinlein probably would also have been irritated at our presumption in claiming to explain what his fiction is really trying to say and in sometimes attempting to estimate how well it succeeds. That's unfortunate but irrelevant. To paraphrase Ben Jonson on Shakespeare, Tom and I both love the man this side of idolatry. Personally, as I concluded a 1990 fanzine article on Heinlein's juvenile fiction,

> I sometimes wonder how Heinlein felt, watching readers like me grow away from him, so that he was just one of the SF writers we read and listened to. Admiring him as I still do, I'd like to think he might have actually have been satisfied at having provoked thoughtful disagreement. In *Between Planets*, the colonists' rebellion against Earth is rooted in "a belief in the dignity and natural worth of free intelligence." In *The Rolling Stones*, the twins' father secretly is pleased that they don't passively accept his wishes: "Good boys! Thank heavens he hadn't been saddled

with a couple of obedient, well-behaved little nincompoops!" So I'd like to think that going beyond Heinlein's brand of storytelling and thinking was part of natural growth. I hope that my own growth has incorporated the best of what Heinlein taught by words and example. And that includes what he did in writing his juvenile novels. By taking the challenge of going outside the SF magazines, Heinlein recruited new readers, counseled adolescents, and extended the emotional and ideological range of science fiction. As a witness who was both new SF reader and adolescent, I can testify to what Heinlein accomplished. He made us pay attention to the world around us, and he helped us imagine building better worlds. He pulled and pushed us; he led us and prodded us; he entertained, stretched, encouraged, and challenged us. He helped us all grow up.

With luck, Heinlein also prepared his readers to look fairly and clearly at what he wrote.

A Note on Texts

Heinlein's final versions are the texts used here. He himself revised several early works for book publication, and others were edited (usually shortened) before their initial publication. Although a study of Heinlein's revisions would be valuable and although a case can be made for the authority of some edited versions, this book refers to the author's preferred texts. The only exception is *Podkayne of Mars*, since the Baen edition makes possible a comparison of the novel's multiple endings.

Since Heinlein's fiction is available very widely, page citations to a specific edition would be a bothersome affectation. Again there's an exception: *Grumbles from the Grave*, the posthumous volume of excerpts from Heinlein's correspondence. Critical works by other writers are cited by page.

Heinlein's letter in the last chapter is quoted from the Frederik Pohl Papers, Special Collections Research Collections Research Center, Syracuse University Library.

ABBREVIATIONS FOR WORKS CITED MOST FREQUENTLY

[Bleiler I]   Nicholls, Peter. "Robert A. Heinlein." In *Science Fiction Writers*. Ed. E. F. Bleiler. New York: Scribner's, 1982.

[*Classic*]   Slusher, George Edgar. *The Classic Years of Robert A. Heinlein*. San Bernardino, CA: Borgo, 1977.

["Frontiers"]   Samuelson, David N. "Frontiers of the Future: Heinlein's Future History Stories." In Olander and Greenberg.

[*HID*]   Panshin, Alexei. *Heinlein in Dimension: A Critical Analysis*. Chicago: Advent, 1968.

[RAH]   Franklin, H. Bruce. *Robert A. Heinlein: America as Science Fiction*. Oxford: Oxford University Press, 1980.

[*Reader's*]   Gifford, James. *Robert A. Heinlein: A Reader's Companion*. Sacramento: Nitrosyncretic Press, 2000.

[*RH*]   Stover, Leon. *Robert Heinlein*. Boston: Twayne, 1987.

["Youth"]   Williamson, Jack. "Youth against Space: Heinlein's Juveniles Revisited." In Olander and Greenberg.

1

A New Calling:
For Us, the Living

In the late 1930s, Robert A. Heinlein began seriously to consider writing fiction. Incongruously enough, later in the century, Heinlein's recurring hero Lazarus Long compares the activity to masturbation in his *Notebooks*, remarking that, "Writing is not necessarily something to be ashamed of— but do it in private and wash your hands afterwards." Appropriate as such disdain might be for the man Heinlein had aspired to be, committed to duty with his cohorts and dabbling in the arts only as an amateur for recreation, in fact Heinlein in the '30s was a young man who knew himself to be blessed with abundant talent but who hadn't found any stable, satisfying career since being invalided out of the navy. As an intelligent reader of sf, he realized much of the stuff in the magazines was trash; certainly it wouldn't be hard to write better than *that*. Moreover, if he could use fiction to communicate valuable ideas about social improvements, perhaps he could accomplish something praiseworthy.

For Us, the Living was the first product of Heinlein's determination to become a writer who was both popular and influential. He wrote the novel in 1938–39 and submitted it unsuccessfully to two publishers. Long suppressed as unworthy prentice work, a copy of the manuscript was located in 2002 and finally printed in 2004.

Rather than modeling his story on lightweight space adventures to be found in the pulp sf magazines, Heinlein followed the example of literary sf writers such as H. G. Wells, who had developed a straightforward, no-nonsense style into a powerful instrument for depicting extraordinary objects, beings, and ideas. Moreover, by this time, Wells had passed beyond the limits of mere sf. He had become a commercially successful mainstream novelist and had published his *An Outline of History* in 1920. He was an extremely attractive role model for a young writer. In particular, Wells's *When the Sleeper Wakes* (1899) appealed to Heinlein because it combined thoughtful social extrapolation and vivid action — the latter serving to whet readers' interest so they would be willing to pay attention to explanations of the former. It also seems likely that the situation of Wells's hero, ejected from his familiar world and trying to find a meaningful new role, appealed to Heinlein as the starting point for his hero because it reminded him of his own position.

But Heinlein could not use the underlying *attitude* of Wells's model. The central character of *When the Sleeper Wakes* is a victim. He arrives in the future due to his own emotional and physical failure, and through much of the novel he is (understandably) overwhelmed by an avalanche of strange events. He is tugged about by different factions in the new society, and when he does choose to endorse the workers' revolt against their bosses, his contribution almost certainly is too little and too late. He has learned to fly an "aeroplane" and finally uses it to attack the air fleet bringing troops to reinforce the Masters; however, the novel ends with his machine damaged and falling toward the Earth. Nor is it likely that a successful uprising by the workers would really matter. Earlier, the head of the Masters had sarcastically excused his and his cohorts' behavior: "'And you would emancipate the silly brainless workers that we have enslaved and try to make their lives easy and pleasant again.... Suppose — which is impossible — that these swarming yelping fools in blue get the upper hand of us, what then? They will only fall to other masters. So long as there are sheep, Nature will insist on beasts of prey.'" Nothing in the novel disproves this statement. In fact, Wells's first novel, *The Time Machine* (1895), shows how this natural process eventually will lead to the extinction of humanity. The narrator of that novel comments that "the growing pile of civilization [may be] only a foolish heaping that must inevitably fall back upon and destroy its makers in the end." The only encouragement that Wells's narrator can offer is not to think about the subject: "If that is so, it remains for us to live as though it were not so."

By the time Heinlein wrote his first novel, Wells had suppressed this negative attitude and had written determinedly optimistic (and longer-winded) utopian novels. This was the positive attitude Heinlein applied to the basic situation of Wells's earlier, bleaker story. Naturally enough, he refused to believe that an enterprising young man was doomed to remain adrift in strange circumstances or that humans would be unable to choose a healthy direction for their shared lives.

For Us, the Living begins almost exactly where *When the Sleeper Wakes* ends, with its hero falling toward certain death. Readers who have spent the novel in the company of Wells's protagonist can appreciate the valedictory sharpness of his sensations as he approaches the ground; they can notice that he is finally engaged with the world around him and (perhaps) give him credit for having at last fully committed himself to improving it. Time also slows down as Heinlein's Perry Nelson plummets downward after his car goes over a cliff, but the opening stresses how vividly aware he is of "a blonde girl in a green bathing suit" gracefully catching a beach ball a hundred and thirty feet below him, of the rocks by the beach, of one particular "handsome rock, flat on one side and brilliant white in the sunshine" that is rapidly nearing his eyes. Although not yet acquainted with Perry, readers still can feel disappointment that this clearheaded observer is about to be snuffed out. The world seems so full of interesting objects that it seems a shame that Perry won't get a chance to explore it.

He regains consciousness in a snowstorm. Naturally disoriented, he imagines that the girl from the beach has transformed into a fur-clad young woman who helps him to his feet and steers him inside before he passes out. When he awakens, he becomes aware that he is in an oddly but comfortably furnished house. He also notices that he is naked. When Diana, his rescuer, peels off her furs, she is blithely naked too, a fact that startles and fascinates the young twentieth-century man "for she was young, nubile, and in every way desirable." This scene establishes that Perry is a truly unfamiliar place, where not only the physical surroundings but also basic social attitudes are different from what he is used to. After Diana initiates a brief conversation during which she is puzzled by the notion of a bathing suit and can't understand how Perry was in a vehicle that could go out of control, she realizes that something is amiss and discovers that he believes the year is 1939. Actually it is 2086. The question of how Perry got to the future is never fully answered, but that seems much less important than the question of what to do now that he obviously *is* here. Fortunately, Diana is both kind-hearted and influential, as a famous dancer/singer/actress, and she does everything she can to help Perry adjust by talking with him herself and by bringing in friendly experts to educate him on the background and opportunities of his new world.

Besides many aspects of *For Us, the Living*'s world that show up in Heinlein's later fiction, from specific names to technical and social predictions, readers will notice how Perry's education proceeds by methods that Heinlein used throughout his career.

One technique used through the novel but first in its opening pages looks like a friendly conversation, very informal though circling around serious ideas. As Diana asks Perry about marriage in the twentieth century, she is increasingly disturbed by the concept of a permanent, monogamous union, especially when she realizes that Perry is just repeating what other people have told him since he never has been married himself. In particular, she can't understand why one person would want to possess (or be possessed by) another for the sake of sex:

> "Didn't you ever see a woman you wanted to enjoy physically?"
> "Of course. Many of them."
> "Then why didn't you marry?"
> "Oh, I don't know. I guess I didn't want to be tied down."
> "If a man didn't have children to support and a wife to support would he be tied down by marriage?"
> "Why yes, in a way. She would expect him to do everything with her and would raise Cain if he stepped out with other women and would expect him to entertain her sisters and her cousins and her aunts, and would be sore if he had to work on their anniversary."
> "Good Lord! What a picture you paint. I don't understand all of your expressions but it sounds unbearable."

Unknowingly, Diana is practicing a Socratic dialogue, an extremely effective teaching strategy by which a questioner lets a student respond in order to demonstrate how much (although appallingly disorganized and haphazardly considered) information the student already has. Also, as the student struggles to verbalize adequate answers to the questions or to form useful questions of his own, the dialogue demonstrates how much more clearly an ordinary person *can* learn to see and interpret. Diana indicates that she accepts her role in this process early on, as she exclaims, "Good Heavens, Perry, what a lot there is to teach you. I don't know where to start. However, I'll just plunge in and try to answer your questions."

This kind of teaching by dialogue is quite different from education by lecture, in which the teacher delivers a mass of information and interpretations to students who may ask questions only to clarify their understanding of what they've heard. A lecture is to be preferred when a considerable amount of information needs to be transmitted rapidly and when the teacher's authority is unquestionable — in a sermon, for example. The disadvantage is that students' attention tends to wander at inopportune moments and that a lecturer's assumed superiority can feel oppressive. A Socratic dialogue feels like a discussion between equals when the questioner shares authority with the answerer, each having power to focus on different aspects of an issue. Thus the dialogue is less immediately efficient as a teaching technique than a lecture because it tends to meander through the subject matter under discussion. When it succeeds, however, it engages an individual in clarifying previously unexamined preconceptions, as when Perry admits, "Why yes, in a way." It also encourages him to recognize that he needs to do more such rethinking, as when he remarks, "Oh, I don't know. I guess."

Most fiction, even when consciously didactic, allies itself with the Socratic dialogue.

Although the author can be thought of as the authority behind the story, most writers choose not to stress that role. Instead, they try to engage readers in an active exchange of perceptions. Perry's initial reaction to Diana's nakedness is divided between pleasure at seeing a beautiful girl's body and shock at seeing an apparently nice girl casually expose herself before a stranger. The physical description never becomes very detailed in the novel. It's the *idea* that is attractive and disturbing. Heinlein assumes that readers would have a similar mixed, semi-hypocritical response. But Diana "replies" to this reaction by her innocently unembarrassed, generous behavior toward Perry. Perry may wonder what is wrong with Diana even as he perceives that nothing can be wrong, but this exchange of perceptions actually focuses readers' attention on the unhealthy inconsistencies in Perry's thinking — and in their own. Heinlein rather neatly encourages readers to question themselves and then to make up their own minds regardless of how they've been accustomed to thinking.

Heinlein frequently was accused, especially in his later novels, of lecturing his readers, and "lecture" generally is used negatively in discussions of fiction to indicate that an author is stopping the story in order to deliver a lump of ideas that he can't think of any way to introduce subtly within the characters' experience. It must be admitted that some students thrive on lectures because they don't want to waste their time in unstructured discussions, just as there are some lecturers who are such skillful fact-packers and entertaining performers that they can hold an audience efficiently. And so there are readers who find this aspect of Heinlein's fiction especially enjoyable and who truly love the later novels for the places where Heinlein appears to be lecturing them. As a beginning writer in *For Us, the Living*, however, he had not figured out how to balance action and ideas, how to keep readers' attention when the dialogue becomes contrived and leaden and when meetings become mercilessly one-sided presentations.

Most of the novel consists of Perry receiving explanations and demonstrations of the better life available to twenty-first-century Americans. Readers of Heinlein's later fiction will be struck by echoes of technical extrapolations such as the moving sidewalks that were mentioned in Wells's *When the Sleeper Wakes* but are presented in more practical detail in *For Us, the Living* and later form the basis of the famous short story "The Roads Must Roll." They also will be interested to see how, at this stage of his political/social thinking, Heinlein believed that a national government could improve the lives of its citizens by giving them a guaranteed income that would allow them freedom to develop their personal interests. As Davis, one of Perry's lecturers, says,

> The urge to work exists in more than ninety per cent of the population. Free him from drudgery and he putters in the garden, in a workshop, learns to draw, tries to write poetry, studies, goes into politics, invents, sings, devises salad dressings, climbs mountains, explores the ocean depths, and tries to fly to the Moon. Few are those who sit in the sun and whittle.

Readers who come to the novel without the preparation of reading Heinlein's other fiction will probably be less interested in enduring page after page of economic theorizing. Still, *For Us, the Living* never quite lets its readers go because Heinlein does have a story to tell. He is genuinely interested in seeing how his protagonist can succeed. Having miraculously been saved from death, Perry still has to come to terms with the realities of his new life. He is a practical man, an engineer, who doesn't try to argue with facts. Nevertheless, he has trouble accepting the new society's customs. He and Diana, not surprisingly, become lovers, and she helps him get used to social nudity and even to the fact that she performs her dances in the nude. However, when Bernard, one of Diana's "tall, well muscled and beautifully made" dance partners, practices a routine with her—moving with her, kissing her, touching her naked body with his—Perry can't stand it. He punches the young man, who reports him for committing "a major atavism ... involving an antisocial violence." The novel's American twenty-first-century society realizes that punishing such misbehavior after the fact is useless, but Perry obviously must be prevented from repeating his attack. He must be cured of possessive sexual jealousy. This is accomplished by more talk, chiefly between Perry and Master Hedrick, chief psychiatrist at the State Correctional Hospital at Tahoe. Perry also becomes friends with Olga, a staff physician who is quite unlike the artistic, athletic Diana physically ("She had the hips and breasts for childbearing and the calm eyes of the natural mother"), but who is equally realistic and generous. When Perry realizes that there is nothing wrong with wanting to make love with Olga while he still loves Diana, he does so. He wakes up the next morning snuggled between the two women, who seem content to share the couch and him. By accepting twenty-first-century thinking, he demonstrates that he no longer suffers from sexual selfishness: He is cured.

As yet another lecturer reminds Perry, this society is not Utopia. Its calm tolerance does, however, make possible the best arrangement yet devised for humans as they are. People aren't required to believe the same thing or to live by one set of rules; they can do whatever they feel they need to as long as it doesn't interfere with someone else. So the second part of Perry's salvation depends on his discovering what *he* needs to do. Otherwise, beset by twentieth-century compulsions, he tells Diana that he will feel like a "gigolo." She does not understand the concept and cries when he explains it to her, but evidently his "urge to work" cannot be satisfied by simply loving and being loved. Actually, Perry indicates where his interests lie when he picks the most extreme hypothetical activity out of Davis's list: "Say, are they really trying to reach the Moon?" The speaker sloughs off the question, for most people evidently aren't especially curious about space travel. When, for example, Perry and Olga visit the Moon Rocket Experiment Grounds they find it "almost deserted." Moreover, artistically oriented Diana seems uninterested in rockets, while motherly, protective Olga dislikes the experimental moon rocket because it could be dangerous. But Perry seizes the idea. He agrees with Joe, a young man working at the test site, who answers Olga's objections by saying "'You can't make a man permanently contented in a nice, pretty, upholstered civilization. We've got to [go out into space], that's all. There's something out there to be seen, and we're gonna have a look,' Perry nodded. Olga held her peace." Since Perry has the necessary engineering talent and skills—and since this will satisfy his need to work usefully while also living up to the values practiced by his lovers and the rest of twenty-first-century America—he becomes a rocket pilot. At the novel's end, he is about to pilot the first spaceship to orbit the Moon. Before he leaves, he demonstrates how far he has come by taking the role of teacher in a clarifying dialogue with Diana and Olga. The conversation becomes a lecture as Perry's emotions seize him when Olga plaintively asks whether such foolhardiness is why humans labored to make the world safer and saner. He replies,

> This *is* what men have striven for. Economic systems are nothing, codes of customs are nothing, unless they are the means whereby man can follow his urge to fulfill himself, to search for the meaning of things, to create beauty, to seek out love.... After me someday will come a man in a better ship, who will land and walk on the Moon, and come back to tell about it. Then in the next few years and centuries the human race will spread through the planets like bees swarming in the spring time—finding new homes, new ways to live, new and more beautiful things to do. I won't live to see it, but, by God, I can live long enough to show them the way.

This passionate commitment is echoed in many of Heinlein's mature works, such as the climax of *The Rolling Stones*. Humanity's instinctive outward urge may be temporarily embodied in specific economic systems or codes of conduct, but such constructions are never absolute. They can survive only as long as they don't get in the way of further development. Humans *will* find a way to get to where they need to go. That is what Perry has finally discovered, the message that Heinlein found worth preserving and reiterating throughout his career.

It must have irked him that his novel did not attract a publisher after he had devoted so much time not just to its writing but to the thinking behind the action. He could have shrugged off the whole experience and gone on to some other activity. Instead, he continued writing.

Later in his career, Heinlein described his first steps as a writer rather differently. How he wrote his initial story, "Life-Line," in response to the announcement of a contest in *Thrilling Wonder Stories* but then submitted the manuscript to John W. Campbell at *Astounding Science Fiction*, which paid him a penny a word for it—$70 instead of the $50 "Grand Prize" offered by *Thrilling Wonder*—all this has become an established anecdote. As he recounted events years later, the story was dashed off as a fluke, for money, and its sale meant that "there was never a chance that I would ever again look for honest work." Actually, besides the fact that the anecdote's specifics aren't accurate, as James Gifford has shown in *Robert A. Heinlein: A Reader's Companion*, the manifest seriousness of *For Us, the Living* demonstrates that Heinlein did not take writing casually. Certainly, like Dr. Johnson, he believed that a writer should receive money for his work, but he also believed that a man needed to *earn* the money he received. Perhaps the best proof of this is that over the next few years he committed himself to learning the craft of commercial short story writing. That serious dedication didn't altogether fit the personal legend he was constructing, and the legend in turn would lead to difficulties in responding to serious analyses of his writing. At the time, however, he did whatever it took to become a successful as well as a thoughtful writer of magazine sf.

2

Early Professional Writing

"Future History"

The beginning of Heinlein's career as a professional writer shows several of his continuing concerns.

One was money. From the first, Heinlein was much concerned with the income his writing brought in. At that time, the label "professional science fiction writer" was virtually an oxymoron. Having an sf story published once, in some pulp magazine, was the most anyone could hope for. Professional writers like Will F. Jenkins (aka Murray Leinster) or L. Ron Hubbard wrote many varieties of pulp fiction to make a living, and publication in book form was only a dream. Very conscious of his own worth, Heinlein did what he could to change this situation.

More than money, Heinlein was concerned with the effect of the stories he was beginning to tell. Heinlein's earliest published stories can be faulted for matters of style and narrative technique, as critics Alexei Panshin and David Samuelson have observed. Nevertheless, from his first published fiction in 1939 Heinlein was an accomplished storyteller. He knew and could adapt familiar sf conventions to his own ends — in keeping with his subsequent remarks about wanting to expand the parameters of the field and to escape from pulp formulae.

His first published story, "Life-Line" (*Astounding Science Fiction* [*ASF*], August 1939), presents a genius whose invention opens up a new field and thereby brings him into conflict with the scientific establishment. In this case, Doctor Hugo Pinero develops a "chronovitameter"— a grandiose name echoing back through the sf magazines to the Craig Kennedy scientific detective stories — enabling Pinero to predict the exact moment of a person's death. The narrative opens with a scene in which members of the Academy of Science denounce Pinero as a charlatan; such a confrontation between establishment and genius/rebel became seminal to Heinlein's fiction. Before Pinero is manhandled from the stage, he voices one of Heinlein's recurrent themes: "Your kind have blocked the recognition of every great discovery since time began."

To the newspapermen who surround him, he remarks that a human is a "space-time event" and denies that life is simply "electrical in nature"— the first murmur of Heinlein's lifelong attack against the concept of determinism — but he makes no attempt to explain the workings of his device. He tries to silence the disbelief among the newsmen by predicting the imminent death of a reporter who is killed in an accident twenty minutes later. Within months his accuracy — backed by his bond — causes such havoc in the business community that the Amalgamated Insurance Company and its lawyer gain a temporary restraining order against him. The narrative shifts to a courtroom scene where the injunction is canceled.

Pinero voices another theme essential to Heinlein's fiction when he declares: "There are but two ways of forming an opinion in science. One is the scientific method; the other, the scholastic. One can judge from experiment, or one can blindly accept authority." The judge also reprimands the plaintiff for the assumption that government and the courts will assure the continuing profit of reigning corporations to the detriment of innovation.

Abruptly — conveniently — the story ends with the murder of Dr. Pinero and the destruction of his machine: a timeworn convention in early sf to assure the irrevocable loss of the secret. Here, however, the catastrophe does not result from the scientist's hubris versus implacable nature but is the outcome of a struggle between entrenched power and the free individual. Shortly before Pinero's murder, a brief scene shows Amalgamated's lawyer beginning to discuss a "proposition" with a suspicious character — inferentially, the assassin. In Heinlein's first depiction of the struggle between entrenched power and the free individual, the powers-that-be triumph.

The second of Heinlein's stories, "Misfit" (*ASF*, November 1939) — the first of his narratives to focus on a juvenile protagonist — celebrates the mathematical genius of Andrew Jackson Libby, a member of a paramilitary unit, the Cosmic Conservation Corps, made up of youths who could not adjust to the changing conditions within the governing Federation on Earth. (The reader should notice that although their commanding officer calls them misfits, he understands that many of them had their job training nullified by new inventions, while others could not handle "modern leisure.") Now, however, these boys "are going out as pioneers to fix up the solar system so that human beings can make better use of it." Not only is this an early mention of terraforming, but it is the first occasion when Heinlein uses the term "pioneer," a concept that was to become a mainstay of his fiction as well as much of the criticism of his work. Specifically, Libby's group is to transform an asteroid into a space station by moving its orbit between Earth and Mars so that it will be one of three stations available to Earth-Mars voyagers.

The narrative has something of the economy marking Heinlein's best work, for it blends together an account of the trip out to the asteroids and the preparation of planetoid HS 5388 for its new role as E-M3. Libby's discovery of miscalculations which would hinder/destroy the project lead to his assignment to a ballistic calculator — "three tons of thinking metal ... he loved"; when the computer fails, Libby must make the calculations fixing the planetoid in an exact orbit. This story is routine except for two facts. First, the reader learns that not until after the death of Libby's father did his family accept the so-called Covenant, that code of law under which the Federation has ruled the world and which shows up in Heinlein's later stories; secondly, Libby becomes one of the major figures in "Methuselah's Children" (1941) in that he is the member of the Howard families who invents the space drive needed to achieve interstellar flight. Such cross-references are the first allusions to that part of Heinlein's early fiction making up the "Future History" cycle.

The close relationship between Heinlein and John W. Campbell, Jr., during the early years of the 1940s has long been general knowledge, and is verified by the excerpts from their letters included in *Grumbles from the Grave* (1989). As a beginning writer, Heinlein sometimes defers to Campbell, editor of the most prestigious and best-paying sf magazine. When he sent "Life-Line" to Campbell, he offered it either to *Astounding* or to its companion fantasy magazine *Unknown* because he was uncertain "which policy it fits the better," that is, whether Campbell would read it as science fiction or fantasy. Relatively soon, though, Heinlein was scolding Campbell for writing blurbs that telegraphed the point of a story. For the most part, the two viewed each other as respected, ambitious equals. Campbell refers to other writers as Heinlein's protégés; Heinlein insists that he does not want to be identified as a pulp writer and does not want to give more emphasis to "action-adventure"; they give much attention to his rate of pay, settling on a cent and a half a word so long as this rate is the highest paid anyone. It still remains unclear, however, which man recognized that the connected references now evident in Heinlein's early stories could be the basis for a coherent "Future History." The idea is first mentioned publicly in an *Astounding* editorial (March 1941) in which Campbell mentions a "common background of a proposed future history of the world and the United States" intended as a backdrop for Heinlein's fiction. An editorial two months later presents a chart apparently prepared by Heinlein that outlines the highlights between the present (1941) and 2125. The reprint of that chart in the short story collection *The Green Hills of Earth* (1951) gives insight into some of the complex tensions shaping Heinlein's imagination from the beginning of his career. It measures both his hopes for the future and his dissatisfaction with the present. Although he dismissed the third quarter of the twentieth century as "THE CRAZY YEARS," remarking on "a gradual deterioration of mores, orientation and social institutions, terminating in mass psychoses in the sixth decade (the 1950s)," he predicted immediate technical advances leading to space flight and exploration/colonization of the solar system, particularly the Moon and Venus. For example, according to the chart, the first rocket to the Moon flew in 1978, while Luna City was founded shortly afterwards. This expansion was part of a brief "PERIOD OF IMPERIAL EXPLOITATION, 1970–2020," which was ended by revolutions in Antarctica and the U.S. and on Venus. Two intriguing but unexplained notes add conflicting dimensions to this period. First, reference is made to an "American-Australasian anschluss"; secondly, after a reference to "the Voorhis [sic] financial proposals" that brought about temporary financial stability and a "chance for re-orientation," the so-called "Interregnum ... was ended by the opening of new frontiers and a return to nineteenth-century economy." Such action did not bring a solution; instead a "New Crusade" gave rise to a religious dictatorship which dominated American life through most of the twenty-first century. That idea was not original with Heinlein. He shared with many of his contemporaries the fear that a new Puritanism would bring an end to scientific research and technological advances, as described, for example, in Isaac Asimov's "Trends" (1939) and Leigh Brackett's *The Long Tomorrow* (1955).

In speaking of Heinlein's "Future History," one must remember that fully two-thirds of the stories were set in the period between 1975 and 2000; moreover, while all of them were published during the 1940s, at least half of them were written after World War II. Once this is said, however, one must infer that the basic scheme for that future had developed early, for three of his first seven narratives deal with the world beyond 2050. The cornerstone—the point of departure—for his vision of the more distant future, is his first serial/short novel, "If This Goes On—" (*ASF* February–March 1940; revised version in *Revolt in 2100* [1953]), which concerns the overthrow of a theocracy that has ruled the U.S. for three generations. In passing, the reader learns that a Federation came into existence sometime after the Johannesburg Treaty ended World War III. Again, like his contemporaries Heinlein accepted the prospect of a nuclear war as a given, but no historical detail is offered. The Federation, in turn, gave way to a religious dictatorship.

The action of "If This Goes On—" is presented as a first-person account by John Lyle, a recent graduate of West Point serving in the Angels of the Lord (the personal guard of the Prophet Incarnate). Particularly in the novel's early chapters, the narrative reads like a court intrigue, for the initial sequence deals with Lyle's infatuation with Sister Judith, one of the Order of Virgins that actually provides the "brides" ministering to the sexual appetite of the reigning Prophet as he follows the Lord's commandment to be fruitful. In successfully rescuing Judith, Lyle becomes a member of the underground Cabal, a group which wishes to restore a government concerned with the "ideals of freedom and human dignity." Since this is a tale of initiation, political as well as sexual, at times the narrative becomes talky. For Lyle must be instructed in order to overcome his previous conditioning which makes him either consider something the will of God or dismiss it as sinful; then he must be given the opportunity to voice what he has learned. During that early period when he is still hidden in the palace, old friends whom he never imagined as members of the Cabal explain its doctrines. Such names as Tom Paine, Patrick Henry, and Thomas Jefferson are invoked. At one point Lyle declares, "Revolution is Big Business," and certainly revolution serves as Heinlein's favorite story line when he is not dealing with the inventive and heroic exploits of an individual. Thus Lyle reflects that "you can't conquer a free man; the most you can do is kill him."

The action of the novel — perhaps in part a result of the original serialization — is episodic. After his acceptance into the Cabal, Lyle assumes the identity of a traveling salesman in order to carry messages to the Cabal's general headquarters; this leads to near capture and a cross-country chase ending in Phoenix. At headquarters he listens to more doctrine and hears the plans for the coming revolt. The leaders of the Cabal plan to bring the nation to disorder by disrupting the celebration of the Miracle of Incarnation, the annual occasion when the first Prophet — Nehemiah Scudder, who led the New Crusade three generations earlier — seems to take over the consciousness of the reigning Prophet in order to reaffirm his authority and extol the virtues of the theocratic power structure. Lyle is one of those who watch TV as the Cabal takes over the ceremony, denouncing the regime and calling for Armageddon. The ensuing riots and civil turmoil give the Cabal uneasy control of the country, so that its leader, Huxley, declares himself military-governor, although in a final chapter a task force preceded by bombers and led by battle wagons and heavy cruisers must storm New Jerusalem. All of this is dealt with summarily by Lyle, who describes himself as Huxley's "flunky" but flies him to the scene of battle. Essentially an observer, Lyle takes command momentarily when Huxley is wounded and battle plans must be put into action immediately. Yet Heinlein achieved neither drama nor panorama in this final scene. Only two things about the assault have possible significance in sf terms: The so-called "psychoperators"/"sensitives" who coordinate the action may represent an early treatment of cyborgs, while the implication that chosen shock troops have received information hypnotically anticipates later descriptions of military units.

Interestingly, although Lyle's infatuation with Sister Judith is downplayed almost to the point of exclusion in the original magazine serial, that romantic impulse, as noted, does set in motion the action of the expanded novel. Yet once they are separated and she has been hidden in Mexico, she writes that she has married a Mr. Mendoza but will always think of Lyle "fondly" and regard him as a "strong and wise older brother." To this, his closest friend replies, "I could have told you, Judith is a very female sort of woman, all gonads and no brain." Although this may be regarded as one the earliest of Heinlein's controversial judgments of women, in the novel Judith's flightiness releases Lyle from a dilemma. Indeed, the fact that Lyle needs to be freed from Judith shows how little she represents all women, for Lyle already has found someone better to love. Repeatedly, as his early correspondence with Campbell shows, Heinlein expressed the wish to emphasize character study more than the action-adventure associated with the pulps and the tradition of the space opera. In "If This Goes On —," his most successful effort occurs when he explores the relationship between Lyle and another of the palace virgins, Sister Magdalene, who easily accepts her new role as Staff Sergeant Maggie Andrews in the Cabal. Not only does she excite him, but her behavior and opinions trouble him as he struggles with the sexual inhibitions ingrained in him by his societal training. Because he has never seen a woman smoke, he tries to ignore Maggie when she does, although he also notices that as she "squatted tailor-fashion" on a bed, she showed "a rather immodest amount of limb." Essentially Heinlein concentrates on a single episode that emphasizes Lyle's youthful inexperience when he and Maggie and another couple go swimming. He quietly protests against the idea of mixed bathing and blushes when the other young woman tells him not to peek as she undresses behind a nearby rock; he burns with shame but cannot stop looking at her when she goes nude into the water. As Maggie emerges from the water, however, he sees her as an "unclothed ... Mother Eve." When he worries because the other couple remains away for some time, Maggie reprimands him by first telling him it is none of his business and then reminding him that they are there of their own free will. After Maggie tells him that she has no romantic interest in the other man, she and Lyle kiss; although she returns the kiss, she hastily retreats, telling him that Judith is a lucky girl. If all of this seems very juvenile, it is in keeping with Lyle's naïveté. But the sequence also marks Lyle's awakening; indeed, the first-person voice falters so that it seems to be Heinlein asking, in the midst of Lyle's dilemma, "What is it about the body of a human woman that makes it the most terribly beautiful sight on earth?"

All in all, besides embodying the principle of Femaleness, Maggie is a grownup, realistic woman. A little later when Lyle proposes marriage, Maggie agrees to be his housekeeper but refuses marriage because as a cast-off "bride" of the Prophet, she has had a number of sexual encounters. The loveless sex from which innocent Judith had to be saved — the traditional "fate worse than death" — is part of the varied experience Maggie has had to survive and learn from. She has a lot to teach Lyle if he can get past his social immaturity, including his romantic infatuation with Judith. Yet everything does work out, for Judith's letter frees Lyle, and he and Maggie marry on the eve of the assault on New Jerusalem.

Despite its importance as one of the foundations of the "Future History" cycle and as a demonstration of Heinlein's early interest in character exploration, "If This Goes On—" remains such an uneven work that its value lies in its introduction of ideas that recur throughout Heinlein's fiction. There is frequent mention of semantics, while both the Cabal and the Prophet's regime are much concerned with psychological control of the populace. Politically, the first-person voice wears thin as Lyle reflects, "I think perhaps of all the things a police state can do to its citizens, distorting history is possibly the most pernicious," a view that anticipates/echoes George Orwell's *Nineteen Eighty-Four* (1948). Yet Lyle insists, "No people was ever held in subjection long except through their own consent." Almost as soon as the Cabal has gained power and Huxley has declared himself military governor, even as a "provisional constitutional convention" reinstates the old Constitution and Bill of Rights, Heinlein intrudes into the narrative of the novel a figure not unlike "an angry Mark Twain," who denounces the Cabal as just another authoritarian government. He insists, "Free men aren't 'conditioned!' Free men are free because they are ornery and cussed and prefer to arrive at their own prejudices in their own way.... We haven't fought, our brethren haven't bled and died, just to change bosses, no matter how sweet their motives.... The American people are not children." One sees this "Winters, from Vermont" as Heinlein's effort to replace Lyle momentarily with a credible voice able to criticize the Cabal; that he exists only in the novel and not the serial may well have some significance. That he has no other function suggests itself because as soon as he has spoken he drops dead.

Besides politics, though commentators and critics have given so much attention to this aspect of "If This Goes On—," the novel shows other aspects of Heinlein's world/cosmic view. A number of times in "If This Goes On—," Lyle refers to "the Great Architect" who has shaped the universe—a pale echo of eighteenth-century deism. At least once, he shows something of the disenchantment troubling the twentieth century when he declares that the Architect "isn't even watching." Perhaps something of that modernity is most vividly shown in the assertion "Each man is his own prisoner, in solitary confinement for life," a remark which calls to mind Silverberg's view that each human being is a prisoner within his/her skull.

Heinlein's characters frequently are challenged to discover how their limitations set boundaries on future society. The "Future History" chart in *The Man Who Sold the Moon* indicates that in 2075 after the overthrow of the theocracy "THE FIRST HUMAN CIVILIZATION" was founded, relying upon "The Covenant" to guarantee civil liberty to every citizen. Three generations later, the protagonist of "Coventry" (*ASF*, July 1940), David McKinnon, rejects that society. This is the tale of the initiation of another of Heinlein's juveniles. (How old he actually is remains a matter of conjecture, for throughout the narrative he is referred to as "kid," "lad," and "boy," while he shows at least a casual interest in fifteen-year-old Persephone.) Initially, at least, he is also the most rebellious of Heinlein's early youths. In the opening courtroom scene, although he acknowledges that his grandfathers fought in the Second Revolution, he denounces the present society where "Nobody is ever hungry, nobody ever gets hurt." Having broken the Covenant by striking a fellow citizen, he refuses to undergo therapy at a psychodynamics laboratory to rid him of his hostility. Instead he chooses to be exiled beyond the barrier that appears to separate the United States from the western lands of the continent. After David has railed against the system, the judge reminds him that the Covenant tolerates any action by an individual "as long as your action did not damage another" and points out that he "is not free to expose us to the violence of your nature," an attitude bringing to mind John Stuart Mill more than any other passage in Heinlein's early published fiction.

Before this, David seems to have evaded really looking at society. The guard escorting the young man to the "Gate" in the barrier labels him a "rugged individualist," and as he enters Coventry, he thinks of Robinson Crusoe and Jack London, for he has long been under "the romantic influence of the classic literature of a bygone day"; he later explains that he has read "all the classics: Zane Grey and Emerson Hough." Indeed, he is the only one of Heinlein's young men who has devoted himself to the study of any type of literature, although he begins to speculate that perhaps instead he should have gone in for science or engineering.

David's hope for "an anarchistic utopia" vanishes as soon as customs inspectors beyond the barrier stop him, arrest him when he resists, impound his goods, and throw him in jail. In short, he quickly learns that there is no "place where a man can live quietly by himself without all this insufferable interference." In jail he meets Fader McGee, who becomes his role model and who, in their first conversation, calls McKinnon "mother's little man." McGee informs him that the Outside is split into three political entities—New America, where he has been jailed; the Free State, an absolute dictatorship whose political theory derives from "the old functionalist doctrines"; and the area occupied by the Angels, that remnant of the populace still believing in the Prophet. After this first encounter in jail, the narrative gives itself over to action-adventure that initially takes the form of escape and pursuit and then of refuge among a secret group, a guild of thieves who demand David's allegiance. When he learns that New America and the Free State have resolved their differences and made an alliance in order to attack the Covenant, McKinnon — like Fader before him — attempts to cross the Barrier to give warning. Taken first to the infirmary, McKinnon is transferred to corps area headquarters, where he finds McGee in the uniform of a United States Army captain, a member of the secret service. When McKinnon offers to undergo psychological treatment for his maladjustment, the commanding general informs him that he has cured himself and thus has regained his status as free citizen. The story closes with his vow to give up the study of classical literature and his wish to join the secret service. Thus McKinnon becomes the only one of Heinlein's young rebels to return to the fold of the society that he once despised. Ostensibly, according to David Samuelson, MacKinnon has learned "to appreciate the net of civil interdependence" necessary in any society, although that lesson seems lost in the youth's enthusiasm for the role of spy that he has projected for himself ("Frontiers" 40). Yet earlier, as the customs guards accosted him, he did voice what one may infer to be Heinlein's basic concept of the ideal government — at least at this early date: "honest, conscientious, reasonably efficient, and invariably careful of a citizen's rights and liberties."

Of the narratives dealing with this period of Heinlein's "Future History," the most important remains *Methuselah's Children* (*ASF*, July–September 1941; revised 1957), not only because it introduces the concept of the Howard families, but also because of the appearance of Lazarus Long, who grew into a truly mythic figure in Heinlein's lengthy novels of the 1970s and '80s. Long had a special place in Heinlein's thinking as early as the serial, for he is the only character whose lifeline extends throughout the whole period. (Incidentally, the lack of a consistent chronology of the stories reveals itself in their internal dating. For example, because MacKinnon's grandfathers fought in the Second Revolution of 2075, then the action of "Coventry" must take place sometime after 2125. Heinlein himself states that the action of *Methuselah's Children* begins eleven years after the last meeting of the Howard families in 2125 — that is, 2136. Lazarus Long contributes to the chronological problem early in the narrative when he insists that he is 213 years old in 2136, an age that ignores the eleven years between 2125 and 2136 since his birth date is given as 1912. The eleven years vanish. No mention of the Howards occurs in "Coventry.")

Methuselah's Children is based on events long before the "Future History." By 1874, Ira Howard, a man fearful of death, had established a Foundation — "an openly chartered non-profit corporation"— which bred for longevity. Only those whose ancestors had proved long-lived need apply; participants agreed to marry only individuals registered with the administering law firm. Since "its avowed purpose of encouraging births among persons of sound American stock was consonant with the customs of that century," it gained no special attention, although its members experienced increasing difficulty counterfeiting new identities to cover the discrepancies between even public (let alone actual) age and personal appearance. So difficult did this policy of Masquerading, as the families called it, become that at their last general meeting in 2125, a half century after the Covenant had brought a new enlightenment, the families agreed that individuals could voluntarily reveal themselves. This was a misjudgment. At the meeting called in 2136, their "psychometrician" tells them that an accelerating mob-hysteria against them has been building during the past several years because the 9,285 who disclosed how they differed "from the balance of the human race" had told the short-lived humans that the Howard's supposed secret of longevity "could never be theirs."

The narrative opens with that meeting, which becomes another of Heinlein's expository dialogues. Because Lazarus Long is the oldest Howard present, he takes the chair from Mary

Sperling after he interrupts the speakers. After allowing the discussion to muddle through several hours, he calls a recess after emphasizing the courses of action they may choose to take. But the next morning, in the company of Mary Sperling, he learns that it is too late for rational decision by the Howards.

By an Action-in-Council the previous evening, the nation's highest governing body has instructed the Federation Administrator, Slayton Ford, to employ any methods necessary to apprehend and question every known member of the group, for by withholding "the secret of eternal youth" from the general public, they have committed "*treason*— treason against the whole human race." Within the day the Covenant is suspended; all too soon the hundred thousand Howards are confined in a "reservation" in Oklahoma near "the ruins of the Okla-Orleans road city."

Essentially such action takes place offstage, for Heinlein's expository dialogues continue. At a meeting of the Howards before their subterranean headquarters falls, one of them, Bertram Hardy, declares:

> The so-called human race has split in two.... On the one side *Homo vivens*, ourselves ... on the other— *Homo morturus!* With the great lizards ... their day is done. We would no more mix our living blood with theirs than we would attempt to breed with apes. I say temporize with them ... gain time, so that when these two naturally antagonistic races join battle, as they inevitably must, the victory will be ours.

Thus does he enunciate the theme of evolutionary conflict echoing back through such a novel as Olaf Stapledon's *Odd John* to writers in the nineteenth century. To Heinlein's credit he does not follow the timeworn path, for Lazarus Long is the first to think of a starship and emigration from Earth.

But Long is not the only one to reach this solution. When H. Bruce Franklin condemns government official Slayton Ford, focusing on a single statement (*RAH* 40), he ignores the context of the dialogue between Ford and the Senior Trustee of the Howards, Zaccur Barlow. Weary and frustrated, restricted by a Council Order with which he does not agree, Ford asks Barlow to help him find a solution and immediately accepts the idea that the Howards do not possess some special secret. The crisis in public morality occurs, he points out, because "now Death plays favorites," and even if the Howard men were to impregnate as many women as possible in order to spread the longevity, the result "would be psychic death for all other men." He suggests that the Howards must be quarantined somewhere other than Earth; only when he realizes that no Administration can stop space travel and that the issue would thus only be postponed does he voice the opinion Franklin damns him for: "The only point left undecided in his mind was whether to liquidate them all, or simply to sterilize them. Either would be a final solution and there was no third solution. But which was more humane?"

Ford knows that either procedure will end his career, perhaps exiling him to Coventry, so he immediately agrees when Barstow suggests a third answer: Allow the Howards to leave the solar system itself. The starship *New Frontiers* is being readied in orbit around the Earth for its maiden voyage. Lazarus Long's capture of the ship and the boarding of it by the Howards are summarily narrated. After a crucial modification by Long, Andrew Jackson Libby develops offstage a space drive achieving the speed of light. Driven from office, Ford joins the Howards, and Long nominates him to be Civil Administrator during the voyage. Thus, at the end of the first part of the novel, the Howards plunge into the depths of space aboard *New Frontiers*.

Although the voyage itself lasts seventy-four Earth-years, so quickly are events dealt with that is seems to end before it is well started. The narrative concerns itself primarily with the Howards' landings on two planets inhabited by intelligent aliens. Both encounters test Campbell's assertion that fictional aliens should never equal humanity, and they give credence to the view that Heinlein's most sympathetic treatment of aliens occurs in his juveniles.

Although Lazarus does not initially like the Jockaira, the humanoid inhabitants of the first planet, they try so hard to please the humans that he moderates his view. They give the Howards one of their cities, warn them not to enter their temples, and virtually take over the task of farming for the humans. The Jockaira, however, cannot understand the human desire for privacy. That may give more of a clue to their nature than one first supposes. Another clue appears when one of the Jockaira, Kreel Sarloo, tells Lazarus that before the coming of the gods, his ancestors understood space flight until the gods bade them not to. Also, from the approach of the Howards' ship when the Jockaira communicated telepathically with Hans Weatheral, a semi-moron with neuro-muscular deficiencies, they lavish attention on the telepathic defective among the families (some five percent of the Howards display some defect because of the inbreeding); yet when Jockaira nurses attend the defective, everyone more intelligent than Weatheral develops "spontaneous and extreme psychoses." The final crisis occurs when Kreel Sarloo announces that the time has come for the humans to choose surnames and temples. Slayton Ford as "responsible executive" feels it his duty to be the first to enter a temple; he emerges, weeping and speechless, to cling to Lazarus. Sarloo says he should be taken away, that what has happened in the temple is a "very bad thing." Lazarus immediately declares that the aliens whom they have considered human are really "*domestic animals*" and that the dominant people on the planet are the creatures inside the temples — that is, the so-called gods. Sarloo soon informs them that the gods have decreed that the humans must leave the planet because they can never be civilized. After Lazarus consults with Libby, the Howards are teleported back to their ship, and the *New Frontiers*— its controls dead as it travels away from the Jockairas' planet — is launched toward a world the gods have chosen.

When Libby suggests that the Howards could have learned "a lot of wonderful things" from the Jockairas' masters, Lazarus asserts that "it's not a man's place to be property." When asked what man's place is, Lazarus replies, "It's a man's business to be what he is ... and be it in style." He briefly resumes a book-long discussion of the nature of life with Mary Sperling, who is afraid of death. To his assertion that "I'm not planning on dying," Mary asks, "But what is the purpose of our long lives?" He admits that he does not know — but he intends to go on playing because "it's the only game in town."

The second planet is an idyllic pastoral world inhabited by Little People who can "masterfully" manipulate life-forms. One provides Lazarus with trees that taste like mashed potatoes and gravy, brown bread and butter, or charcoal-broiled steak. But the Little People are not individuals; instead a "telepathic rapport group" could be made up of from thirty to ninety or more bodies and brains.

Troubled by many things, including this paradisiacal "Never Never Land," Lazarus isolates himself so that he may take "out his soul and examine it." He concludes that such a world as this is not to his taste: "No philosophy that he had ever heard or read gave any reasonable purpose for man's existence, nor any rational clue to his proper conduct. Basking in the sunshine might be as good a thing to do with one's life as any other — but it was not for him, and he knew it, even if he could not define how he knew it." He even regards the flight of the Howards from Earth as a mistake because they escaped their problem rather than solving it; he feels "unbearable humiliation" because superior beings could flick *New Frontiers* "across the deeps of space as casually as a man might restore a baby bird to its nest." No man could compete with a telepathic group of Little People, yet to form some group identity would be to give up "whatever it was that made them men.... He admitted that he was prejudiced in favor of men. He *was* a man."

When he returns to learn that Mary Sperling has submerged herself into one of the groups so that one of the Little People he encounters professes to be her and to belong to this planet, Lazarus weeps. Further shocked and troubled by the sight of a three-week-old baby who has been manipulated — "improved on" so that it looks inhuman, though it may in fact be some kind of superman — the Howards decide to go back to Earth. When they arrive home, they learn that once again they have been restored to the Covenant because during their absence scientists have discovered the means of prolonging life; yet they remain suspicious of a trap until the delegate who comes to board the ship proves that he has worked with Ford. Instead of a neat resolution, however, Lazarus begins the conclusion with his questions and speculations during a conversation with Libby:

> The last two and a half centuries have just been my adolescence, so to speak. Long as I've hung around, I don't know any more about the final answers, the *important* answers, than Peggy Weatheral does. Men — *our* kind of men — Earth men — never have had enough time to tackle the important questions. Lots of capacity and not time enough to use it properly. When it came to the important questions we might as well have still been monkeys.

When Libby remarks that there may not be reasons, Lazarus replies, "Yes, maybe it's just one colossal big joke, with no point to it ... whatever the answers are, here's one monkey that's going to keep on climbing, and looking around him to see what he can see, as long as the tree holds out."

One wonders why Heinlein did not return to Lazarus Long until the 1970s. For that matter, the final portion of *Methuselah's Children* could have been lengthened in order to develop the story line fully, more dramatically; as it is, the character and the subject matter seem not so much finished as set aside. Nevertheless, the novel did provide Lazarus Long with a vehicle to enunciate a complex question which persisted throughout Heinlein's fiction. At times more pragmatic social and political questions may have taken Heinlein's primary attention, but in various ways he kept returning to the same question that has haunted modern letters: What does it mean to be human? — or, to phrase it as does Heinlein's favorite, Mark Twain, "What is Man"?

Although two stories of the distant future were not republished in the omnibus collection *The Past through Tomorrow*, both "Universe" (*ASF*, May 1941) and "Common Sense" (*ASF*, October 1941; combined version as *Orphans of the Sky*, 1963) are included as the last entries in the "Future History" chart. The final date given in *The Past through Tomorrow* is 2100; in the collection *The Man Who Sold the Moon*, however, both stories are placed at 2600. With "Universe" Heinlein, created the image of the multigenerational starship to serve as the backdrop for the narrative, a setting that immediately became a popular convention with sf writers at mid-century, Leigh Brackett, Brian W. Aldiss, Samuel R. Delany, and Alexei Panshin among them. The basic assumption is that humanity will seek the stars, even if it must do so in huge slower-than-light ships that will take literally centuries to reach their destinations. That premise allows writers to study/dramatize the changes in a society existing in a closed environment, and the majority of such narratives have followed

Heinlein's lead in "Universe" by imagining a society that has fallen into decadence and consequently has garbled the original plans and records of the mission. "Universe" remains one of Heinlein's finest stories.

A brief prefatory statement announces that in 2119 the Jordan Foundation sent out the initial Proxima Centauri Expedition: "whatever its unhappy fate we can only conjecture." Considering that Heinlein did attempt to tie so many of his early stories into his "Future History," commentators and critics have said that those explorers must have used a prototype of the *New Frontiers,* considering that the ship the Howards pirated in 2136 was being prepared for the Second Centauri Expedition.

Except for the prefatory statement, however, "Universe" is timeless. The narrative is the tale of Hugh Hoyland's initiation, growing from childlike trust in the rules and beliefs of "normal" society into knowledge of a larger, threatening reality—and acceptance of personal responsibility to act on that knowledge. As readers soon realize, the society Hugh takes for normal is an artificial construction, though its context is not immediately comprehensible. Hugh knows no other way of life. His teacher, a "witness" who wants to prepare Hugh for the priesthood, reads to him from a poem that resembles the book of Genesis as it relates how the god-like Jordan made both a plan and regulations governing the Crew and the Captain, whom he created; but "accursed Huff ... stirred rebellion" so that darkness fell upon the ship and "sin prevailed." The poem remains Heinlein's most skillful and innovative means of introducing the exposition necessary to explain how members of a society, having forgotten the past through fear, have both reverted to and garbled traditional ritual in order to establish an authority that they hope will ensure their survival. Hugh's teacher also demonstrates how completely people aboard the ship have lost their knowledge of science when he declares that their forefathers were "incurable romantics" and explains the Law of Gravitation as "the poetical way the old ones had of expressing the rule of propinquity which governs the emotion of love." A man designated only as "the scientist" tells Hugh that he is far more talented than the common run of people—even at birth his head was "too large" so that he was almost destroyed because of this deviation from the physical norm—and is destined to be a leader, a scientist, "one of the custodians" (crucial word), not one of the peasants.

Against this background, almost the only activity described of the crew/peasants who live on the levels at the core of the ship is a continuing guerrilla warfare against the "muties," descendants of the mutineers, many of whom are also physical mutants because they live in the ship's outer levels and are exposed to extra radiation. Readers, absorbing Heinlein's skillfully planted clues, are putting this situation together more easily than the characters can, but when Hugh is left for dead after a skirmish and taken prisoner by the muties, "Universe" begins his initiation too. After denying that there can be anything larger than the ship, Hugh is taken to the Main Control Room by the two-headed chief of a mutant gang, Joe-Jim, who argues that the ship itself moves. At first Hugh denies that possibility, then, from the "captain's veranda," he sees the stars; "he knew, subconsciously, that, having seen the stars, he would never be happy again." Hugh's intellectual initiation to reality is complete. Because he wants to revive the original plan to reach Proxima Centauri, he returns to the core of the ship; his former friends disbelieve him; they intend to try him for heresy; but Joe-Jim, the gang, and two friends—Alan Mahoney and Bill Ertz—rescue him. For a few pages plot action overwhelms idea, but in the final scene Hugh insists that their real goal must be to convince the crew of the truth. Stating this as a simple, matter-of-fact reminder, he says, "We've got to do it, you know."

Actually, there are fewer things rarer than common sense. "Common Sense" (*ASF*, October 1941) continues Hugh's efforts "to overthrow an entire culture." Unfortunately the narrative gives so much attention to the struggle for power that it does not have the impact of "Universe." Because Hugh first buries himself in the Control Room and then must pore over the old books in order to bring the ship into orbit around a nearby star, much of the focus moves to Phineas Narby, who gains popular support while he appears to agree with Hugh and Joe-Jim. Keeping the new information secret for security reasons, he consolidates his power until he can condemn the Control Room as "an enormous hoax." Narby always rationalizes his actions by an appeal to common sense, declaring that "when an apparent fact runs contrary to logic and common sense, it's obvious that you have failed to interpret the fact correctly. The most obvious fact of nature is the reality of the ship itself, solid, immutable, complete." He reveals his intellectual limitations when he declares that "it wasn't necessary" to verify physically that the stars he has seen from the Captain's veranda were actually the "trick lights" that he has called them. Thus "Common Sense" becomes one of Heinlein's harshest and most effective indictments of that frame of mind which resists new knowledge and change.

As the drama moves toward the confrontation with Narby, Heinlein uses an effective expository device to help the reader understand what has happened aboard the ship. Hugh's group discovers the log of the starship *Vanguard*, beginning 2 June 2172 at the time of the mutiny. They learn that every pilot officer and every engineering officer was killed so that no qualified person remained to operate the starship; as a result a "Storekeeper Ordinary" became captain and hoped to "restore some semblance of order." Because the anti-radiation shield no longer existed, mutations had already begun.

Even a bit earlier, the most controversial element of the novel had been introduced. A variety of commentators have questioned Heinlein's treatment of women in the story. Intrusively, as though Heinlein abruptly realized its necessity because of the turn the plot was taking — at a moment when such concepts as "*deep* space: and "*metrical* time" both frighten and bewilder Hugh — Heinlein allows him to take some "time sorting over the women available." He selects two wives: one a widow whom he allowed "to retain her former name of Chloe"; the other, "a maiden, untrained and wild as a mutie ... [who] made him feel funny." She had bitten him "while he was inspecting her; he had slapped her, naturally ... [and] had not got around to naming her."

When Narby informs Hugh, Joe-Jim, and their companions that he intends to destroy the Control Room and seal its door as well as annihilate the muties, he precipitates a final running flight. When Hugh, Alan, and Ertz realize that the entire ship is against them, Hugh decides that they must flee in the one ship's boat that escaping mutineers had left — one which he conveniently had stocked with bare survival necessities. Thus as Narby's "Universe" continues to drift like so much flotsam, the three men and their wives abandon ship in the landing craft. Hugh's younger wife "bore a fresh swelling on her lip, as if someone had persuaded her with a heavy hand."

Heinlein emphasizes the "ridiculous improbability" of Hugh's luck — for which Panshin reprimands him (*HD* 26) — but the small craft lands by autopilot on the Moon of a planet larger than Jupiter. The scene is not dramatized, and Heinlein reminds the reader that Hugh's "unnamed" wife "kept out of his sight after losing a tooth, quite suddenly," apparently not as a result of any trouble during the landing. Heinlein thus opens the action for a possible — apparently never written — third tale by employing a quaint variation of the familiar Adam and Eve motif at little cost to Hugh's intellectual initiation and the action/adventure.

Although the reader learns that for "uncounted generations," the *Vanguard* has drifted like space debris, neither "Common Sense" nor "Universe" is specifically dated. No date is assigned them in the chart of "Future History" in *The Past through Tomorrow*; they are the last titles entered on the chart, but they are not included in that collection, the most probable reason being that they saw separate publication in *Orphans of the Sky* (1963). On the chart in *The Man Who Sold the Moon*, they are placed at 2600, almost five hundred years after *Methuselah's Children*. Apparently no stories were planned for that interval. One is struck by another characteristic of these stories dealing with the far future: In none of them does Heinlein portray a utopian society. Although most critics make much of the Covenant, pointing out that after the fall of the theocracy in "If This Goes On—" that "THE FIRST HUMAN CIVILIZATION" came into being, but the government under the Covenant persecuted the Howard families. Moreover, those same critics ignore the last entry in Heinlein's sketch of his "Future History." On all the charts, originally opposite the date 2600, almost like an after-thought undeveloped in any story—"Civil disorder, followed by the end of human adolescence, and beginning of first mature culture." Nowhere in Heinlein's early published fiction—certainly nowhere before the lengthy novels of the 1970s and 1980s returning to Lazarus Long—does such a mature culture on a societal level show itself.

Whatever the vicissitudes of the distant future, the brief decades centered around the year 2000 are distinguished by technological breakthrough. Whether written before or after World War II, seventeen stories included in *The Past through Tomorrow* cluster in these years. In them Heinlein dramatized the achievements of individuals who make possible, each in his own way, humanity's escape from Earth into the vastness of the solar system, the first essential step toward the stars. Perhaps only Arthur C. Clarke matched Heinlein's enthusiasm as they celebrated what was for them the imminent and inevitable conquest of space. Despite the importance of the relationship between the individual and the state, certainly such a triumph became Heinlein's central theme during the 1940s, and these were his most influential early stories.

One might well argue that a principal motive of sf writers has been to escape the gadgetry and emphasize character. In a letter to Campbell dated 6 September 1941, Heinlein spoke to that issue when he explained that he intended to stretch the field by creating stories with more subtle themes and more realistic psychological motivations (*GG* 13). His most successful early effort occurred in "Requiem" (*ASF*, January 1940), his third published story, as it deals with the final episode in the life of D.D. Harriman, who fulfills a lifelong dream by flying to the Moon. Ironically, as the subsequent "The Man Who Sold the Moon" (1950) chronicles, Harriman is the individual who created the Company responsible for spaceflight, but he himself has always been prevented from making the journey. The title "Requiem"— taken from Robert Louis Stevenson's 1887 poem—sets the tone for the earlier story. Knowing that the flight will undoubtedly kill him, he nevertheless provides a ship for two former space pilots, Charlie and Mac, whom he meets as they barnstorm county fairs. Heinlein's own depth of feeling shows itself in that Harriman meets the two at the Bates County Fair and buys them dinner at the best hotel in Butler, Missouri, the territory of Heinlein's boyhood. After Harriman loses consciousness because of a heart spasm, something of Heinlein's politics shows through, for when Charlie protests that the two ought not help Harriman kill himself by taking him to the Moon, Mac replies, "Why not? It's neither your business, nor the business of this damn paternalistic government, to tell a man not to risk his life doing something he really wants to do." Harriman is, of course, ecstatic during the flight though he dies as the ship touches down on the Moon.

"The Roads Must Roll" (*ASF*, June 1940), which the members of SFWA voted into the Science Fiction Hall of Fame in 1965, reveals even more of Heinlein's early political stance. Its premise grows out of one of his continuing concerns, the relationship between an individual and general society. Because of the shameful waste of oil and coal resources during the first half of the twentieth century and because by 1955 the number of automobiles mushroomed until there was one for every two persons in the U.S., the National Defense Act of 1957 declared all oil, above and below ground, "an essential and limited material of war," giving the military first priority in its use and rationing civilians. Some major technological innovation became essential, because great cities like St. Louis and Chicago had extended themselves along the superhighways until they merged into a great megalopolis. Heinlein solved the problem through the use of mechanized roads, the first connecting Cleveland and Cincinnati in 1960. Because of his (and Campbell's) primary interest in the impact of technology on society, Heinlein remained vague about details of the roads' operation. Readers simply are told that the roads are powered by solar energy and that their elaborate underground mechanisms are supervised by a paramilitary class whose cadets graduated from the United States Academy of Transport. Looking back at the labor trouble of the 1930s, Heinlein bases his plotline on a strike by the workers of the Sacramento Sector of the Diego-Reno Roadtown, culminating in the military action of the cadets against the strikers. To say this, however, ignores that manner in which action is downplayed in favor of a series of scenes between Larry Gaines, the Chief Engineer of this roadway, and Shorty Van Kleeck, Gaines's Chief Deputy, who incited the Sacramento incident. When Heinlein remarked in the 6 September 1941 letter that he had "completely abandoned the hero-and-villain formula" (*GG* 13), he obviously forgot "The Roads Must Roll," for Gaines is one of Heinlein's unflappable heroes, while in their last personal confrontation, Van Kleeck ends up a weeping hysteric, "blubbering like a frustrated child." However, the conflict between Gaines and Van Kleek exemplifies a larger power struggle between an ultra-competent representative of stability and an unstable weakling who hopes to seize nationwide control for the "New Order" through a "functionalist revolution." Heinlein intrudes a comment denouncing Paul Decker's *Concerning Function: A Treatise on the Natural Order in Society* (1930), whose "glib mechanistic pseudo-psychology" fails "to note that human beings are neither dogs, nor chickens." Important as this early statement about society and the individual is, another statement about Gaines points to an issue which was to cause Heinlein more difficulty than any of his political views. Gaines "was aware that, from a standpoint of strict logic, no reasonable case could be made out for the continued existence of the human race, still less for the human values he served." If one asks, in other words, *why* the roads must roll, the answer is to keep 'em rolling. No one in the story stops to ponder this issue, and readers might never question it either if Heinlein himself had not pointed it out. Close consideration of this subject could lead either to a retreat into the isolated self or to the creation of a group to replace humanity.

Although "Blowups Happen" (*ASF*, September 1940) also contains a Chief Engineer whose sense of social responsibility makes him a sympathetic character, the narrative does not focus on a single character but on all those atomic engineers who maintain and supervise the atomic breeder plant isolated in the desert of the Arizona plateau. Heinlein creates a background of continuing stress affecting those men responsible for "the most dangerous machine in the world." No one, not even the engineers themselves, could know whether or not a mass explosion of the pile would destroy the human race. Yet while on duty at the pile each man became responsible for whatever happened; consequently, "Insanity was an occupational disease." Against this backdrop the plotline develops two interdependent threads. An atomic fuel capable of escape velocity is developed so that the Arizona pile may be placed in orbit around the Earth; there, some fifteen thousand miles from Earth outside the satellite ship itself, the pile will be an artificial star, "shining in the vacuum of space." The story's other concern is how the discovery will be used, so its most significant scene focuses on the confrontation between the Board of the Company developing the reactor and the atomic engineers; even in the face of a public relations campaign that its members regard as blackmail, the Board resists all changes until one engineer declares that "you are none of you atomic physicists; you are not entitled to hold opinions in this matter." Again, this time in terms of knowledge, Heinlein relies upon an elite.

"Blowups Happen" is quite lively despite its heavy subject matter. Surprisingly, in a brief scene buried amid expository material, Heinlein slips in a young woman of nineteen or twenty—"very seductive in an evening gown that appeared to have been sprayed on her lush figure"—who offers her companionship to several engineers in deLancey's Sans Souci Bar; should they change their minds she suggests, when dismissed, that they "ask for Edith." Perhaps Heinlein assumed that such a tidbit would increase his audience. Perhaps it did. "Blowups Happen" was included in Groff Conklin's pioneer anthology, *The Best of Science Fiction* (1946), the first of Heinlein's stories to be published in hardback. In a 1979 "Afterword" to the story when he included it in *Expanded Universe*, Heinlein asserts that he "had some doubt about republishing this because of the current ignorant fear of fission power, recently enhanced by the harmless flap at Three Mile Island." In view of the threat of impending doom throughout the narrative, one wonders at his change in tone.

Sprightly in itself, "—We Also Walk Dogs" (*ASF*, July 1941) nevertheless remains the most negligible tale in the Future History cycle. Indeed, it was the only story in the cycle originally published under his pseudonym Anson MacDonald. It is also the most humorous of Heinlein's prewar narratives. Although General Services does not think well of many of its customers, it described itself as "the latter day equivalent of the old servant class.... We walk dogs for people who are too busy to walk 'em themselves." In this case, however, so that an interplanetary conference of all the intelligent species within the solar system may convene on Earth, GS's people are asked to adjust the environment so that everyone will be comfortable, a task involving the nullification of gravity. An eccentric genius accomplishes the task, but only after they provide him with a replication of a Ming vase, "The Flower of Forgetfulness," the original of which remains in the British Museum. The GS workers are overwhelmed by its beauty, suggesting that they keep it instead of completing the task; their consolation is that they hope to visit the scientist in order to contemplate the bowl.

These early "Future History" stories cluster between 1975 and 2000. Two allusions to the Prophet Nehemiah Scudder link the last of the stories from this early period, "Logic of Empire" (*ASF*, March 1941), with "If This Goes On—." Although H. Bruce Franklin calls it "the most radically 'left' of [Heinlein's] career" (*RAH* 24), "Logic of Empire" is less than fully effective because of problems in its narrative structure. Despite its publication date, one imagines it to be one of Heinlein's earliest stories. Once its subject matter—slavery on Venus—is announced in a brief exchange between Humphrey Wingate and Sam Houston Jones, the first third of the narrative devotes itself to Wingate's being shanghaied to Venus, where he is sold on the auction block to a plantation owner. Throughout, what happens to him is essentially a translation of the experience of a black American slave, even to the threat of being sold "South" to great factory-like plantations. When he escapes into the unmapped jungle interior, he is surprised that "fugitive slaves" have been able to "develop an integrated society," but no detailed picture of that society is given. Conveniently, at that point, Sam Houston Jones turns up to return Wingate to Earth.

Through a former professor of economics and philosophy who is now enslaved, as well as through Wingate's proposed book, a single theme is advanced: Although colonial slavery is economically unsound, it is "the inevitable result of imperial expansion, the automatic result of an antiquated financial structure." The occurrence of this theme is amusing in a sense because throughout 1940 and 1941 in his letters to Campbell, Heinlein insisted that he felt obligated to turn away from fiction long enough to write a book on monetary theory. "Logic of Empire" names the problem but offers no solution. The story's other noteworthy idea surfaces just once when Heinlein declares that "the ceaseless fight of life against life which is the dominant characteristic of life anywhere proceeds with special intensity" on Venus, thereby providing subsequent critics with early ammunition for their attack on him as a social Darwinist.

This, then, was the first group of stories that made up Heinlein's "Future History." Although diverse writers from utopian romancers to such individuals as Ray Cummings, E. E. "Doc" Smith, and Olaf Stapledon had dealt with the history of the future, none of them had provided a complex, systematic cosmology which subsequent writers could supplement or adapt as they chose. Certainly no one will disagree with Peter Nicholl's judgment that "ever since Heinlein, the idea of presenting a history of the near future that focuses not on new technology per se, but on the interplay between this technology and the social development of mankind, has been basic to genre science fiction, a thematic norm to which it keeps returning" (Bleiler I 186). With the advent of technologies concerned with atomic power and space flight, one may argue that the time had come when such a cosmology was acceptable, particularly within the closely knit community of American science fiction. Between 1939 and 1942, all but one of the narratives Heinlein published in *Astounding* under his own name fitted within the history cycle. More importantly, as noted by Panshin (*HD* 123), from "Logic of Empire" (set in 2010) to "Universe"/"Common Sense" (2600), the seven stories sketching the distant future from the imperialistic exploitation of Venus to the journey of the *Vanguard* had been published by October 1941. Otherwise Heinlein gave his attention to the problems of atomic power and the triumphs of space flight.

Yet, as Heinlein's commentators have agreed, Heinlein never gave the stories dealing with the late twentieth century a recognizable sequence; they do not form a structural whole. He was never deliberate about the ties he included in each one; the most frequent linkage between them seems to be casual references to the road-cities. In addition to revising, sometimes he simply changed his mind. For example, "Let There Be Light" (*Super Science Stories*, May 1940, under the pseudonym Lyle Monroe) was included in the cycle as late as 1950, probably because it dealt with the development of cold light and solar energy, but was omitted from *The Past through Tomorrow* (1967). On the other hand, "We Also Walk Dogs" was excluded from the list until it was printed in that volume.

However much impetus Heinlein — always promoted by Campbell — gave any formalization of the concept of a future history, Isaac Asimov provided the idea of a complex narrative framework in his novellas and novelettes written between 1942 and 1949 for *Astounding* and collected in *Foundation* (1951), *Foundation and Empire* (1952), and *Second Foundation* (1953) — the famous Foundation Trilogy, several times voted the most popular and influential series in sf. Essential to that trilogy is the principle of the cyclic movement of history. Between them — and one must always keep in mind that Heinlein and Asimov became friends and wrote for Campbell during the so-called Golden Age of Science Fiction — they created a pattern of rise and fall, unity and isolation, which both writers and readers could share. In short, they provided a context that the field could explore. Whatever the tone of an individual work or a single writer, at the heart of that narrative framework lay the vision of humanity and its technology spreading through the galaxy.

Outside the "Future History"

Between 1940 and 1942, fully half of Heinlein's fiction fell outside the "Future History" cycle. With three exceptions, he published all of it under pseudonyms: Anson MacDonald, Lyle Monroe, Caleb Saunders, and John Riverside. Because he wrote almost exclusively for Campbell, Anson MacDonald was Heinlein's most frequently used pen name, appearing in both *Astounding* and its fantasy companion *Unknown*. Much has been said about the use of pseudonyms when Heinlein had more than one story in a single issue of *Astounding* particularly, but one also assumes that Campbell decided to associate the name Heinlein only with those works within the history cycle. The name Lyle Monroe served for the four stories not published in a magazine edited by Campbell; the other two were used once each. Three of the short stories proved so slight that they have seldom or never been reprinted: "Beyond Doubt," Heinlein's only collaboration — with Elma Wentz (*Astonishing*, April 1941) — links the Easter Island monoliths with Lemuria; "Pied Piper" (*Astonishing*, March 1942) not only allows an elderly scientist to kidnap the children of an enemy country but lets him dispose of a dictator in another dimension; "My Object All Sublime" (*Future*, February 1942) — under his own name — must be regarded as an attempt at slapstick humor, for an inventor uses an invisibility device to shield him while he sprays synthetic skunk juice on truck drivers who bother him.

As noted, the earliest of the Monroe stories, the first story not published by Campbell, "Let There Be Light" (*SSS*, May 1940) was not included in the history cycle until 1950. It combines a love story involving two scientists — one a brilliant young woman who is a blonde bombshell and consequently is treated in a flippantly sexist manner — and their successful development of both cold light and solar power. The result is one of Heinlein's favorite situations: the confrontation between inventive genius and those corporations wishing to suppress any innovation disturbing their profits. The young woman breaks the stalemate by telling her husband-to-be to reveal the secret to the public.

"— And He Built a Crooked House—" (*ASF*, February 1941) presents a light-hearted account of a young architect who designs an eight-room house in the form of a developed tesseract; when a California earthquake collapses it into a single room, there are problems with the fourth dimension.

The lightweight "—We Also Walk Dogs" is discussed above as a "Future History" story.

The next Anson MacDonald story, "Solution Unsatisfactory" (*ASF*, May 1941), returns to the problem of atomic weaponry. Although its first-person narrator, a long-time friend of the protagonist Colonel Clyde C. Manning, wishes to set the record right by giving a sympathetic view of the world dictator, characterization fades away into what becomes more of an essay than a dramatic study of character. Be that as it may, instead of finding a bomb capable of "a single explosion that would flatten out an entire industrial center," American researchers discover a radioactive dust which irradiates everyone and everything it touches.

It is the ultimate weapon, "a loaded gun held to the head of every man, woman, and child on the globe." Even before the U.S. supplies Britain with enough dust to reduce Berlin to a "dead city" and bring about the capitulation of the Third Reich within a week, its leaders revive the concept of *Pax Americana* to end all war. Yet when the suggestion is made that "a worldwide democratic commonwealth" be formed, Manning objects because there are hundreds of millions of people "*who have no experience in, nor love for, democracy*" and predicts that sharing the secret of the dust will initiate "*a vicious circle*" of warfare ending only when most people are dead and the world reduced to a "peasant-and-village" culture. Nor is the American tradition of isolationism an answer, for scientists of other countries will discover the dust. In response to a Peace Proclamation outlawing war, the only resistance comes from the Eurasian Union (i.e., the U.S.S.R.), whose scientists also have developed the dust; a first strike precipitates a Four-Day War (a variation on the nuclear holocaust that Heinlein and his contemporaries saw as inevitable after Hiroshima). Manning becomes the first commissioner of the Commission for World Safety and envisions "a corps of world policemen, an aristocracy which, through selection and indoctrination, could be trusted with unlimited power." (International, interplanetary, interstellar—here again is the old sf convention of an elite, a paramilitary class, who will guide and protect the citizenry of their society against all evil, cosmic or localized; Jack Williamson's Legions of Space and Time and "Doc" Smith's Lensmen afford other sf examples.) Inevitably, responsible for the whole of humanity, Manning becomes "the undisputed military dictator of the world," but as the narrator acknowledges, he is thoroughly hated, a detail that most analyses of the story fail to mention. Nor would Manning justify his status since neither he nor the narrator can be "happy in a world where any man, or group of men, has the power of death over you and me, our neighbors, every human, every animal, every living thing." Heinlein would have his readers believe that such authority—the whole of this *Pax Americana*—has been thrust on Manning, who rules altruistically to keep the awful power from evil men and nations.

Heinlein did not reprint "Solution Unsatisfactory" until 1979 in *Expanded Universe*, at which time he noted that "the solution is still unsatisfactory and the dangers are greater than ever." After half a century the story/essay does not sit well with many readers, not only because of Heinlein's pervasive pessimism, but also because it voices a naïve idealism which has echoed variously through the corridors of American foreign policy as late as the occupation of Iraq. To say, as some have done, that Heinlein has found his solutions in the status quo or in the past may seem irrelevant here, but one should keep in mind that after the fall of the Reich a provisional government restored the old German monarchy with a cousin of Kaiser Wilhelm as ruler.

The last of the Anson MacDonald stories concerned with inventions, "Waldo" (*ASF* August 1942) may serve as a transition to the speculative, dissatisfied side of Heinlein. Its protagonist Waldo F. Jones has become an overweight, eccentric, inventive genius who lives in "Freehold," his gravity-free home in a satellite circling the Earth; he has not been on the surface of the planet in seventeen years. From birth he has suffered from myasthenia gravis, a muscular weakness which so handicapped him that as a child he could not lift a spoon in one hand—until at the age of ten he invented a device which held and lighted a book, even turning its pages. (Heinlein describes the wide variety of mechanical hands with which Jones manipulates objects, and scientists were inspired by the story to develop such "waldoes" with which they actually do such tasks as handling radioactive materials.) In his isolation, Waldo has come to think of people as "his servants, his *hands*, present or potential," for he never thinks of himself as "a crippled human being, but as something higher than human"; he has no regard for the "nameless swarms of Earth crawlers." Yet the story shows him becoming something more than the "caricature" that Franklin labels him (*RAH* 52).

The twofold problem bringing Waldo back to Earth stems from the use of radiant energy as the chief source of power for at least the American society. On the one hand, the DeKalb power receptors used by the North American Power-Air monopoly have begun to fail sporadically; should such failures spread to the cities, the society would break down. On the other hand, the ever-increasing amount of background radiation has begun to deteriorate "the performance of the human animal" to such an extent that in twenty years, according to Waldo's extrapolation, no human will have "strength enough to work in heavy industries." No solution offers itself until Waldo listens to Grandfather Schneider, a Pennsylvania Dutch oldster, who insists that whether repairing a DeKalb receptor or curing Waldo of his weakness, one must reach into "the Other World" to draw on the power there to effect the change. Schneider declares that what happens depends on how one thinks, for "the mind — not the brain, but the mind — is in the Other World and reaches this world through the body." The receptors can be fixed to use power "never before in this world" so that, as in "Let There Be Light," an inexhaustible supply of free power becomes available. Thus the monopoly enjoyed by North American Power-Air will be broken, while Waldo himself can gain strength so that he can participate in/enjoy life as he never has before.

Philosophically, although Waldo dislikes the idea that thought can control physical phenomena, he recognizes that Schneider has introduced phenomena beyond his previous experience. He does not deny his own experience but develops new ideas "contrary to the whole materialistic philosophy in which he had grown up" as he studies "the arcane arts as aborted sciences abandoned before they had been clarified." Consequently he is able to solve both problems: the defective receptors and the debilitating radiation. In contrast, Dr. Rambeau, head of research for North American Power-Air, believes in "an inexorably ordered cosmos, ruled by unvarying law"; terrified, he goes mad and actually disappears from human kin, for he believes that "Nothing is certain.... Chaos is King, and Magic is loose in the World." Among Heinlein's earliest critics, only Bruce Franklin emphasizes the relationship of "Waldo" to the persistent strain of Berkeleian idealism throughout Heinlein's fiction, but he does not name this line of thought as a means by which Heinlein attempts to escape another restriction that increasingly bothers him.

Although most of the narrative concerns itself with the solution of the DeKalb and radiation problems, the final portion focuses on Waldo himself as he grows strong. He changes from an isolated misanthrope who is generally despised to a beloved and accomplished dancer (who is also a successful neurosurgeon). This transformation does not come as a surprise tacked on to the end of the narrative, for a framing scene at the beginning has introduced Waldo at the end of a performance as he thinks, "It was wonderful to dance, glorious to be applauded, to be *liked*, to be *wanted*." One is leery of suggesting that this somehow reflects Heinlein's feelings as he views his new success against the disappointments of the 1930s, but Waldo is the only one of his protagonists to react in this manner.

Heinlein had first introduced the concept of a working magic in "The Devil Makes the Law" (*Unknown*, September 1940), but as the title implies his interest was political instead of philosophical. In an America where magic is practiced as an accepted part of every phase of business, the main thrust of the narrative concerns the efforts of Ditworth to organize Magic, Inc. and seize monopolistic control of the field of magic. Much of the emphasis is on an involved legislative battle which allows Heinlein to damn lobbyists and politicians, although the climactic action involves an incursion into the "Half World" to find the demon that possesses Ditworth.

Although they differ, the opening rounds in Heinlein's attack on determinism occurred in two stories published under pseudonyms in 1941 during the height of his identification with the "Future History" cycle: "Elsewhen" (*ASF*, September 1941), the only story to appear under the unique pseudonym Caleb Saunders; and "Lost Legacy" (*Super Science Stories*, November 1941), the most noteworthy tale under the pseudonym Lyle Monroe. Both stories make reference to J.W. Dunne's *Experiment with Time* (1927), with its theory of serial universes. The slighter of the two, Heinlein's first time travel story, "Elsewhen"—later published as "Elsewhere"—opens at the home of Professor Arthur Frost during an evening meeting of his class in speculative metaphysics; he first refers to his own experience on several timelines and then offers his five students the chance to travel alternate tracks. Anticipating Heinlein's later explorations of the "multiverse," the professor explicitly tells one young woman that if one believes the philosophy of Bishop Berkeley, "the infinite possibilities of two-dimensional time offer proof that the mind creates its own world." Four of the students successfully project themselves to some track; Frost scolds the one who fails to do so, a young engineer whom he has already called a "Spencerian determinist," telling him that "engineers are as bad as metaphysicians—you believe in a mechanistic, deterministic universe, and ignore the facts of human consciousness, human will, and human freedom of choice—facts that you have directly experienced." From that point on, the tale devolves into all-too-familiar sf scenarios as action replaces idea. When the second young man returns to Frost's home briefly to pick up math books, a slide rule, and whatever else may be of aid to the people he has found and identified with as they fight a war against aliens, Frost suggests that perhaps "the Great Architect intended for him to cross over." Using Frost as a guide to help him make the journeys, the lovesick young engineer finds his beloved Estelle and then redeems himself by taking a "blaster ... sort of a disintegrating ray" across the worlds so that it can be the decisive weapon in the struggle against the aliens.

If the action of "Elsewhen" echoes a hundred old sf stories from the 1930s back through the Munsey magazines, so does the more ambitious novelette, "Lost Legacy." Ben Coburn, a brain surgeon; Philip Huxley, a psychologist; and Joan Freeman, a young woman who has given up the study of philosophy for psychology, all share an interest in parapsychology. Indicting his professional colleagues as "behaviorists," Huxley gathers data "on all sorts of phenomena that run contrary to orthodox psychological theory"—from telepathy and levitation to clairvoyance and fire walking—"on the chance that the mind can control the body and other material objects in some esoteric fashion." He believes that at some time in the past all of humanity was adept in "these strange powers," but his work has gotten him in trouble with academic authorities, such as the president of his university, who warns Huxley of difficulties with his contract and admonishes him for not undertaking "useful research along lines of proven worth." Told to take a vacation, Huxley and his two friends drive up to Mount Shasta, where Coburn breaks his leg accidentally. An old man simply calling himself Ambrose attends Coburn and escorts the three of them to a sanctuary within Mount Shasta itself—where, of course, Coburn's leg heals overnight.

Thus does Ambrose Bierce, who retired to Mount Shasta in 1914 in order to avoid oncoming world events he was powerless to stop, introduce the three to a group of some thirty mystics (telepaths), some of whom have dwelt at Shasta since the eighteenth century. Many details—the isolation, the founding of the haven in 1783 by a young friar at the instruction of Fra Junípero Serra, and the certainty that the group has regarding some new crisis threatening the world — remind one of James Hilton's *Lost Horizon* (1933).

The differences between the two stories may be explained in large part by the exigencies of writing for the action-packed pulps. For immediately Heinlein's three protagonists dream, each in a slightly different way, of the Twilight of the Gods and the subsequent loss of humanity's legacy due to conflict between benign and hostile superhumans. Huxley's nightmare is typical. He dreams that he shares the consciousness of one of the older rulers and witnesses the confrontation between Jove and the cabal he calls the Young Men, whose spokesman is Loki. The Young Men demand that the ancient knowledge (ESP) "be the reward of ability rather than the common birthright" and that the "greater should rule the lesser." Vulcan breaks in to insist the Young Men are "sick of this sheeplike existence. We are tired of this sham equality." The Elder Council, eager to move to another world, abdicates, and the rebels gain power through savage warfare. The empire of Mu and her jealous colony, Atlantis, rise to glorious heights, but again rebellion flourishes in warfare that kills two-thirds of the world's population and leaves the remainder with damaged germ plasm as a result of the terrible force unleashed. The isosatic balance of the Earth's crust is disturbed, and both Mu and Atlantis sink beneath the seas. In the morning, Coburn, Huxley, and Joan Freeman agree that their shared nightmares prove the theory about the degeneracy of the human race. (Influenced by the pessimism following World War I and by Toynbee's theory of the cyclic nature of history, this scenario of a fall from the golden heights of civilization to a fragmented barbarism because of terrible warfare in Mu and/or Atlantis became an accepted motif of sf/fantasy during the 1920s and 1930s, as illustrated by such a novel as Pierrepont B. Noyes's *The Pallid Giant* [1927]. Notice that the reference to damaged germ plasm suggests weapons as deadly as anything developed in the twentieth century.)

The group at Mount Shasta opposes taking any action against the malevolent cabal controlling humanity for fear of degrading the human spirit; the excesses of Mu and Atlantis must never occur again. Yet they sense the approach of a new crisis, one that began with the rise of Napoleon, one that espouses totalitarianism and reduces humanity to political and economic units without individual importance. Long a "refuge of freedom," America is now the target of "the forces that killed enlightenment in the rest of the world." They need recruits and ask the three young Americans to join them in their fight against evil. What began as one of Heinlein's stories of the confrontation between innovative spirits and a torpid establishment is transformed into the more simplistic tale of a struggle between absolute good and absolute evil.

After the three have received further training in the ancient knowledge, they return to Huxley's university, where he attempts to gain attention and support through a demonstration of levitation by Joan Freeman in his largest class. Instead he is dismissed by the president of the university, whose mind he finds to be a "matrix of pure evil." Arrested, they escape by levitating to Mount Shasta, where they decide the way to get around those forces which have infiltrated American society from the classroom to the legislatures is by teaching telepathy to Boy Scouts, boys who have not yet been corrupted by their parents and environment, but who have been trained "in the ideals of the ancients — human dignity, helpfulness, self-reliance, kindness." Two years later, a jamboree — Camp Mark Twain — is held at Mount Shasta for some five thousand chosen scouts. The final struggle with the forces of evil dissolves into sentimentality and a catalogue of the culprits' deaths — except for a single dramatized scene in which Joan Freeman and the leader of the adepts confront a faceless thing in a wheelchair and its chief lieutenants as they plan a revolution to seize control of the country before Camp Mark Twain completes its work. In a struggle of wills the thing is reduced to a "gory mess on the floor." So much for the bad guys. Huxley is chosen senior of the adepts, and a woman reminds Joan that the "human race was not meant to stay here forever." In a surprising final vignette, an idyllic, verdant Earth is sketched, but there are no humans, only a single great ape who climbs high on a mountain to rest uneasily on a flat stone — generations before one of his kind will "understand what was left there by those who had departed." It is a moment which perhaps calls to mind Arthur C. Clarke more than Robert A. Heinlein.

Such quasi-mystical hocus-pocus contrasts sharply with the tight logic of one Heinlein's most generally admired stories, "By His Bootstraps" (*ASF*, October 1941), an exploration of the motif of time travel that opens with a gentle irony in that the protagonist, Bob Wilson, is writing a Ph.D. thesis which denies the possibility of time travel. The story takes as its point of departure the simplest of time-travel paradoxes, the closed loop.

As Bob Wilson is blearily trying to finish his thesis at the last minute, he is interrupted by a battered-looking intruder. The stranger — who looks vaguely familiar — insists that Bob go through the Time Gate, "a great disk of nothing, of the color one sees when eyes are shut tight," that suddenly has appeared in the room. They are interrupted by a second agitated fellow who demands that Bob *not* go through the Gate. In the ensuing fight, Bob is tossed through the Gate, 30,000 years into the future, where an older man who calls himself Diktor persuades Bob to go back in time and entice a man to enter the Gate. Bob realizes that the man sitting at a desk is *himself,* that he himself is the fellow who interrupted his thesis writing. Although he tries to exercise "free will" by altering their conversation, a combination of drunkenness and stubbornness shapes their behavior into an exact replay of what happened earlier in the story. The man who interrupts the frustrating exchange is yet a later version of Bob, who has come to distrust Diktor's motives.... And so it goes.

As the protagonist encounters older manifestations of himself so that there are more and more of him on what he calls "this damn repetitious treadmill," the story also becomes one of Heinlein's most notable solipsistic fantasies in that Bob Wilson is the only consciousness developed in the narrative: Heinlein repeats each scene in which Wilson meets one of his older selves, but the perspective of each scene changes, for as durational time has passed the central consciousness has become/is that of the older character. The climax occurs when Wilson has been in the future setting for ten years; he has long sought Diktor, the ruler of this apparently Arcadian land — never pictured graphically — for he wishes "to come to grips with him, establish which was to be boss." Only after he brings the Time Gate to his boardinghouse in 1952 does he realize that *he* is Diktor, that he himself set into motion the whole cycle of events. The narrative itself comes full circle because it ends with the initial scene. But now the reader can appreciate the irony in Wilson/Diktor's remark to his younger self: "There is a great future in store for you and me, my boy — a great future." One agrees with George Slusser when he says that "By His Bootstraps" is "a ritual of damnation" because Wilson must reenact the action of this closed loop endlessly, "without surcease or hope" (*Classic* 16), but the eagerness with which his younger self accepts that empty future adds to the final sense of horror.

More recent critics have observed that the loop actually is not closed, since Wilson/Diktor lives through events in his life only once; it is the reader who feels the effect of looping through time and observes that the story's end fuses with its beginning. In other words, Bob Wilson exists as points on a timeline (in a Euclidean fourth dimension) and the line goes on with Diktor, who at the story's end is free to do whatever he wishes. The problem with this rather cheerful reinterpretation is that the future situation seems to offer no satisfying role for its central character. What will he live *for*? Who will he live *with*?

The story offers little encouragement. In accepting the kingdom of Norkaal as an Arcadian world, commentators on "By His Bootstraps" have overlooked an element of the narrative tying it to at least three other stories of the period and, more importantly, opening wide a backdrop of horror which contributes to the impact of those other stories. At some time in the past, beings called "The High Ones" came to the Earth with their Time Gate and dominated humanity. While the people remaining appear human physically, they differ sharply from Wilson's memory of twentieth-century Americans, for "the competitive spirit was gone, the will-to-power." These docile, childlike creatures call themselves "The Forsaken Ones" (and, though much less substantial, remind one of Wells's Eloi). Because Wilson wants to know more about "The High Ones," who have left no artifacts, Wilson searches for them with the Time Gate; when he sees one, he runs away, screaming. A sense of sadness, of "insupportable" grief, "of infinite weariness" had overwhelmed him. Terrified, he showed no further interest in them because he felt that he had learned all about The High Ones that a man could learn and still endure.

Two more things are worth noting about the story. For one, Heinlein deliberately leaves plot threads dangling: Early in his stay in the future, Wilson is delighted to find a notebook containing a vocabulary of the natives' language; he assumes that Diktor must have done the work — but if he is/will become Diktor, who filled the notebook in the first place? Second, to obtain the contents of a list Diktor gives him (books and other paraphernalia that Diktor hopes will help revive the spiritual vigor of the pallid humans of the far future), Wilson has no compunctions about writing bad checks since he is sure he won't be held liable because he'll have gone through the Time Gate. He callously seduces his girlfriend with the same certainty. Thus the story's beginning demonstrates that he is ready to become Diktor.

Like "By His Bootstraps," "They" (*Unknown*, April 1941) — the only story in that magazine to appear under Heinlein's name — concentrates on a single character. It has been labeled both a paranoid and a solipsistic fantasy. An unnamed man, apparently an inmate in an insane asylum, discusses his feelings of isolation and uniqueness with his doctor as they play chess. Although he sees everything and everyone, including his wife, as part of a plot to deceive him, he insists that "all this complex stage setting, all these swarms of actors, could not have been put here just to made idiot noises at each other." In short, his concern is with the lack of meaning he finds in the exterior world. He asserts that he is the center of the universe — the doctor reminds him that everyone feels himself to be "the center" — and complains of "emptiness and otherness" when he has tried to communicate. Nevertheless, he believes in the basic reliability of his sense perception, for "all philosophies that claimed the physical world around him did not exist except in his imagination were sheer nonsense." Yet because "the world as it had been shown to him was a piece of unreason, an idiot's dream," he returns to the idea that he is being consciously deceived. He rejects the idea that he must die, for he transcends "this little time axis," but both the common-sense view of the world and the "religio-mystic solution" remain unacceptable because the former is "utterly irrational" and the latter "a flight from reality of any sort." Though the unnamed man appears paranoid, Heinlein has put together the most complex discussion of those philosophical matters that have troubled him throughout these early years. The chess game with the patient's doctor ends in stalemate, while the conversation with his wife yields nothing reassuring. He remains in "the agony of his loneliness." Yet he refuses to surrender his certainty about the event that confirmed his tortured view that "reality" must be a sham: One day he observed that it was raining in front of his house while the sun was shining in back. Since the inmate's wife cannot convince him otherwise, she leaves him in his cell, hurries to join her colleagues "without stopping to change form," and tells them to "adjourn this sequence." Emphasizing that genuine reality is not what the inmate — or, moreover, the reader — had believed, the Glaroon, the alien being in charge of the conference, admonishes one companion for "failing to extend the rainfall all around him" and orders them all to "Bear in mind the Treaty." When both New York City and Harvard University are dismantled, while the inmate's wife suggests that the Taj Mahal be included in the next sequence, one thinks of those stories in which aliens either experiment on humans or keep a human specimen in a zoo.

To classify "They" as a variation on the encounter-with-superior-aliens motif gains credibility by the letters Heinlein sent Campbell in 1941 regarding "Goldfish Bowl" (*ASF*, March 1942), published under the pseudonym Anson MacDonald. Although Campbell had originally rejected the story sent to him as "Creation Took Eight Days," Heinlein defended the story as more than an alien-invasion-of-Earth yarn. He wanted to explore a "much more humiliating possibility — alien intelligences so superior to us and so indifferent to us as to be almost unaware of us. They do not even cover the surface of the planet where we live — they dwell in the stratosphere." Nor can we ever know their origin (*GG* 16). Instead of concentrating on a single character in order to strengthen the psychological impact of the narrative, "Goldfish Bowl" externalizes the action as two protagonists set out to investigate the so-called Pillars, twin stationary waterspouts; they intend to use a bathysphere to ascend the Kanaka spout (upward flow) and descend the Kahini spout (downward flow). After much talk about phenomena such as waterspouts and fireballs, the protagonists fall unconscious, only to awaken as prisoners. (This sacrifices Heinlein's concept of the complete indifference of the aliens, for the protagonists are fed, watered, and observed.) There ensues much talk about the nature of the aliens — ranging from "an intolerable menace to the whole human race" and talk of "our duty" to fight back and try to escape to wondering if "we are just — pets" to a final realization that "we're outclassed." Finally, one protagonist etches a message into his own skin so that humans will be warned when they retrieve his body. Unfortunately, by that time he is no longer quite sane, and in what Samuelson calls "a Kafkaesque conclusion" ("Frontiers" 45), the cryptic message in scar tissue, "BEWARE—CREATION TOOK EIGHT DAYS," goes uninterpreted and unheeded. But even if humans could understand the warning, what could they do about the situation? Humanity's inferiority is "hammered home," as every principal commentator has pointed out, by the presence of pet goldfish in the office of the men trying to solve the puzzle, although no one has noted that one fish continually tries to bite the finger of the sailor cleaning the bowl. Whether this is a touch of humor or Heinlein's warning to even superior aliens, one can only conjecture.

The only title published under the pseudonym John Riverside, the last of Heinlein's prewar stories, "The Unpleasant Profession of Jonathan Hoag" (*Unknown Worlds*, October 1942) reads like a detective story as a husband and wife team of private investigators, Ted and Cyn Randall, try to help Hoag remember what he does during the day, for he has forgotten his profession. Immediately, an organization called the Sons of the Bird assails the couple, and the novella becomes another of those struggles against powerful forces of pure evil. One senses that it needs a good editing, for the action is both diluted and confusing. Hoag finally explains that a young artist of a superhuman race created the universe under the guidance of a teacher; at first the Sons of the Bird were the dominant feature, but the teacher did not approve of them and suggested certain "improvements." For whatever reason, haste or carelessness, the artist did not remove them but painted over them. Thus the Sons of the Bird remained a potent evil power, lurking behind mirrors. Hoag reveals that he actually is an art critic who must judge the world in the person of a man. Because the world has certain pleasures — eating, sleeping, drinking, and not "ridiculous" sex, but the "tragedy of human love"— Hoag will spare the world, but he promises the couple that the Sons of the Bird and "all their works" will be dealt with. He sends the Randalls away, telling them not to lower their car window; when they do, instead of Chicago they see nothing "but a gray and formless mist" as the world is being cleansed of the evil/inappropriate elements. Bruce Franklin has given the final action a political interpretation in terms of "flight from the overwhelming, threatening, supposedly delusory reality of modern working-class urban America" (*RAH* 47); however, even though Hoag does not take kindly to workers or children the story will not support such readings. Leon Stover comes closer to grasping the story's stress on the loving partnership between Ted and Cyn (*RH* 64–65), especially when they learn that, just as Hoag didn't immediately realize his real nature, one of them also might be a critic — in which case, the merely imaginary person might fade away when his or her lover's hyperreal identity surfaced. They can't be certain if one or both of them *is* unreal, but they still need their love even if it could be based on illusion. At the story's end, they are literally inseparable because they are afraid that one of them could vanish at any moment. They even handcuff themselves together at night for fear of losing touch.

Important as these stories outside the "Future History" cycle are for giving the reader insight into some of the philosophical problems bothering Heinlein even in these early years, as a unit they show him trying his hand at highly familiar sf conventions and situations, often at less than inspired moments, as also occurs in his first full-length novel, *Sixth Column* (*ASF*, January–March 1941), the first of his works under the MacDonald pseudonym. In *Expanded Universe*, he carefully explains that novel was the only work of his "influenced to any marked degree" by Campbell. Apparently Campbell asked him to rework "All," an unpublished story that Campbell had written a number of years earlier; he told Heinlein the plot but did not show him the manuscript. Heinlein's development of the basic idea is characteristically colloquial and brisk. Campbell trudged through his plot in prose that emphasized the high, deadly seriousness of faith through repetitious cadences, inverted word order, and archaic diction. Here, for example, is a personal conversation between two of the American officers as they plan to set up their sham religion:

> "We want no converts of an alien race," said David Muir slowly. "How, John, do we turn them away?"
> "If my guess be more than guess, though he come in skin-dyed white as ours, with hair like golden grain and eyes blue as liquid air, set straight and true across his face, though we make him gladly welcome, still no convert shall slip through to spy and warn and reveal!" said John Reid. "We have a thousand thousand inventions yet to make, and a hundred days to make them."

Overall, Campbell's first try at telling the story is virtually unreadable, not a very promising template. Since Heinlein needed a car, however, he accepted the writing assignment. The slightest of his novels, *Sixth Column* looks back to the "Yellow Peril" thrillers so popular from the turn of the twentieth century through the 1930s. Unlike so many of its predecessors which gave detailed accounts of present-day campaigns fought with essentially conventional weapons, Heinlein's tale takes as its point of departure a trans-polar nuclear strike by

PanAsians which wipes out the American government and military and allows four hundred million PanAsians to occupy the U.S. and undertake "the planned elimination of the American culture as such." Instead of dwelling on the initial conquest of the West, the narrative focuses on activities at an underground Citadel in the mountains near Denver where a field officer, Major Whitey Ardmore, tells six surviving scientists that they must prosecute the war. The six are the only personnel who lived through an experiment that mysteriously killed all their companions, the so-called Ledbetter effect — named for the man who directed the experiment — and that thus provides them with an ultimate weapon: a controlled, directional atomic radiation which destroys the hemoglobin protein in the blood. Heinlein has explained that because he did not "believe the pseudo-scientific rationale of Campbell's three spectra," he worked hard to make "it sound realistic." Although the Ledbetter effect works by means of the natural wavelength/frequency of the individual person, Heinlein's scientists find that those frequencies group themselves according to race. The radiation can kill whites, but they set it for the Mongolian frequencies.

Commenting on the story in *Expanded Universe*, Heinlein declared that he had "to reslant it to remove racist aspects of the original story line," though all commentators have found it to be one of his most racist fictions. He very carefully explains that the PanAsians are neither Japanese nor Chinese — but while they are not "*bad*," they are "different," for behind "their arrogance is a racial inferiority complex." They are "simply human beings, who have been duped into the old fallacy of the State as a super entity"— successfully so, one might add, for they have "conquered and held half a world," including the "amalgamation" of India. Consequently, as every commentator has noted, as far as Heinlein's characters are concerned, the only good PanAsian is a dead PanAsian. The racist vilification goes on from there.

Because the PanAsians hold the American populace hostage and massacre any rebels with such a device as an "epileptogenic ray," the men at the Citadel realize that they cannot conduct the war until they have built up an effective underground. Ardmore thinks of that organization in terms of the fifth columns operating before "the final blackout of European civilization"— this premise becomes a given in much of Heinlein's fiction, perhaps owing something to L. Ron Hubbard's "Final Blackout" (*ASF*, April–June 1940) — but Ardmore envisions it as "a sixth column of patriots whose privilege it would be to destroy the morale of the invaders." The story line follows them as they found a new religion devoted to the worship of the various manifestations of the god Mota. Obviously the religion has a strong Oriental flavor. Fortunately the Ledbetter Projector — a kind of laser beam — not only cuts through walls and solid rock but also transmutes base metals into gold. The Americans confound the yellow horde and achieve a final, overwhelming victory, although Ardmore must first refuse the suggestion that the democratic process be replaced by "a truly scientific rule" and later, using the old French Republic as an example, warns his colleagues that no victory will "settle things 'once and for always.'" In short, paperboard heroes defeat paperboard villains. Published in book form by Gnome Press (1949), reissued as *The Day After Tomorrow* (1951), and still later republished with its original title, the novel has enjoyed "financial success," but Heinlein did not "consider it to be an artistic success."

While Franklin finds *Beyond This Horizon* (*ASF*, April–May 1942) to be Heinlein's only prewar attempt "to describe what he conceives to be a good society" (*RAH* 57), Samuelson suggests that it "could pass for the Future History's 'First Human Civilization'" ("Frontiers" 43). Originally published under the MacDonald pseudonym, *Beyond This Horizon* brings together Heinlein's chief prewar interests: economics, politics, genetics, social philosophy, and metaphysics. The society is, indeed, utopian; war, poverty (food is free), and disease have been abolished, while its citizens have *"more freedom than Man has ever enjoyed."* All of this is made possible in an ever-expanding economy because, in a rigidly structured capitalism, the government computes exactly "the amount of new credit necessary to make the production-consumption cycle come out even." To achieve this balance, an unspecified percentage of profit is included in cost, while a subsidy price ("dividend") is given each individual, always allowing for an undistributed surplus to be reinvested. By implication at least, this system represents the survival of the fittest—a theme frequently referred to in the narrative—because it has emerged after the Atomic War of 1970 and at least two genetic wars, one the result of reverting to "an obsolete form—totalitarianism" in the Empire of the Great Khans.

Samuelson calls the utopia a world-state, while Nicholls speaks of the initial appearance of Heinlein's "publicly acknowledged elite, openly ruling, to which entry is not gained through democratic means" (Bleiler I 187). Both assertions need modifications. While the society's power may well be worldwide, geographically it is confined to the two continents of the Western Hemisphere, for "the scattered tribes of Eurasia and Africa" were barbarians "fighting their way back up to civilization after the disasters of the Second War." The image of an elite ruling a helpless majority also misses Heinlein's focus. Besides the elite produced by a breeding program active for at least four generations, the only other members of society mentioned in the novel are "control naturals" and a single "experimental" woman. The former are those the geneticists need to check the normal development of humanity, while the woman—the beloved of a secondary protagonist—is the descendant of a dexter grandfather whose favorable mutation involved emotional stability. Moreover, when an attempted coup is put down, reference is made to the inferior genetic makeup of its participants. The problem, if you will, is a matter of numbers; implications suggest the population is relatively small, and there is no mention of persons within the state who are completely outside the system of genetic breeding. Thus the elite may constitute almost the entire population, as occurs in "Methuselah's Children."

Heinlein himself groped for a way to tell a story about people, one that didn't involve immense or external conflict. In a letter to Campbell dated 25 September 1941, Heinlein complained of the difficulty of finding "a theme, a major conflict" for an "adult" sf novel, particularly one involving "a world that is all peace-and-prosperity." While he was seemingly at a dead end, "a possibility occurred to me which, while not new, has been fuzed with rather than dealt with—the possibility of genetics, and in particular, What Are We Going to Make of the Human Race?" (*GG* 19, 20).

In October, beginning to write *Beyond This Horizon*, he found its idea "grand, wonderful," with "more interesting angles to it every day," although it seems increasingly impossible to work it out for pulp storytelling; again, he wants it to be "full of gore and action as a Greek tragedy, but tragedy in the Greek sense" (*GG* 22). By November, however, "the current struggle ... stinks." His chief problem was "to get enough illustrative action into the story and keep it from bogging down in endless talky-talk" (*GG* 23). And that remains the central difficulty of *Beyond This Horizon*, as it does in so much of Heinlein's fiction given his penchant for dialogue as a means of exposition. That problem may well explain why he gave so much attention to an unessential attempted coup d'état that at least stirs the characters to get up and move around.

The protagonist, Hamilton Felix, is discontented, bored with utopia. A successful "game tycoon" who represents "the careful knitting together of favorable [genetic] lines over four generations ... the star line." He recognizes his superiority and wants to be "an encyclopedic synthesis ... a leader, (one of) the philosopher-kings of whom the ancients had dreamed"; unfortunately, he does not have an eidetic memory, an essential quality of the synthesis, although he is told that his son *will* have. Almost petulantly he echoes (and anticipates) other Heinlein characters as he declares, "I know of no reason the human race *should* survive ... there's no sense to the whole bloody show. There's no point to being alive at all." Nor does he choose to have children to improve, or at least continue, the race. This reaction leads to an impasse, for Claude Mordan, the District Moderator of Genetics, explains to Hamilton—an important point in all of Heinlein's thinking—"We can advise but not coerce. The private life and free action of every individual must be scrupulously respected." Fortunately Longcourt Phyllis, the designated mother of Hamilton's children, makes an early appearance; although the two scuffle, they become infatuated at first sight. In short, except for Hamilton's metaphysical ponderings, the novel shapes up as a love story.

At that point, for comic relief Heinlein introduces J. Darlington Smith, whom he has already billed as the man from 1926 discovered in the Adirondack Stassis when it was opened. Not only does Darlington serve as the traditional visitor to utopia, providing Hamilton Felix with another chance to explain the financial workings of the society, but he scoffs at Monroe-Alpha's sentimental misconception of life in the 1920s as "the primitive, basic struggle with nature" when he assures him, "The simple life is all right for a few days' vacation, but day in and day out it's just so much back-breaking drudgery." (This appears to be the only time that Heinlein satirizes the frontier style of life with which Franklin and subsequent critics have identified him; it can perhaps be explained by his desire to undercut Monroe-Alpha's romanticizing of a period when "gadgeting was beginning to spoil the culture.") Darlington's clichéd defense of his own lifestyle and the values of the Coolidge administration, with its "plateau of permanent prosperity," echoes Sinclair Lewis. But he is abruptly laid aside amid Heinlein's talk of revolution.

Hamilton is recruited by the Survivors Club, ostensibly a drinking club but actually the front for a group of revolutionary malcontents who resemble the Young Men of "Lost Legacy." They see themselves as the "'natural' leaders of a 'scientific' state. As he waits for 'the Change' and undergoes instruction in the principles of the 'New Order,'" Hamilton learns that they believe "The Whole is greater than the parts." Their spokesman assures Hamilton that they will undertake genetic experimentation to adapt humans to live on other planets of the solar system. They are already mating experimentally with women, usually captured from the barbarians; when the Change occurs they will save some barbarians for experimentation and exterminate the others—as well as the control naturals. In short, in their arrogance they repeat all of the mistakes of the totalitarian empire of the Khans before the disastrous Second Genetic War. When Hamilton is instructed to assassinate Director Mordan as the coup begins, he joins with Mordan to defend the plasma bank, the longest sustained scene in the novel. Despite his apparent alienation, Hamilton has been roused to defend humanity's future.

Yet the rebels' excesses seem the natural outgrowth of a society which emphasizes survival of the fittest. From the outset Mordan lectures Hamilton that "Natural selection automatically preserves the survival values in a race." He explains that after the Atomic War of 1970 the geneticists made the mistake of trying "to breed the fighting spirit out of men ... without any conception of its biological usefulness." "Genetically speaking," he explains, "we are descended from wolves; not sheep.... The fighters survived. That's the final test. Natural selection goes on always." Yet "the fighting instinct should be dominated by cool self interest." The geneticists of the Great Khan made the same mistake that was made earlier thinking they could "monkey with the balance of human characteristics resulting from a billion years of natural selection." At least twice Hamilton "rebelled against the idea that a man was necessarily and irrevocably the gene pattern handed him by his genetic planners"; in fact, "a man is something more than his genes and his subsequent environment."

During their final encounter with the Survivors, when Hamilton protests that there should be no need to recruit a civilian militia to put down a revolt because there should be "enough" police, Mordan responds that "the police of a state should never be stronger or better armed than the citizenry. An armed citizenry, willing to fight, is the foundation of civil freedom." This is, of course, an unchanging principle of Heinlein's. The men of this utopian society are armed and indulge themselves in dueling whenever they feel affronted. Those who do not participate may wear a brassard that indicates they won't fight, but late in the novel when Hamilton says he has thought of wearing a brassard, Mordan himself tells him not to do that because "The brassard is an admission of defeat, an acknowledgment of inferiority." This forced independence does complicate personal relationships. When Longcourt Phyllis invades Hamilton's privacy, she wears a handgun, and Hamilton accuses her of being "one of those 'independent' women, anxious to claim all the privileges of men but none of the responsibilities." He imagines her "swaggering around town with damned little spit gun ... picking fights in the serene knowledge no brave will call your bluff." At the threat of a duel, he disarms her; they scuffle; she bites him, while he slaps her; then, sitting her on his knees, he kisses her and finally invites her to dinner. At that point, having established how this particular romantic union will operate, Heinlein refocuses the story on humor and revolution.

Once the coup d'état is crushed and the Survivors exterminated, the characters seem to have no further reason to *do* anything, Hamilton's original concern. As Mordan and Hamilton lie outside the plasma bank, uncertain of the outcome, Hamilton declares, "The one thing that could give us some real basis for our living is to know *for sure* whether or not anything happens after we die." In fact, the novel's conclusion does offer unavoidable clues pointing toward such certainty—which Hamilton manages to avoid. He is certain that his and Phyllis's infant daughter Justina does contain the reincarnated soul of someone who has lived before, a fact that answers his "main question: '*Do we get another chance?*'" He ignores strong indications that the baby contains the soul, still not asserting itself because it is suffering from "shock amnesia," of a specific individual, the just-deceased Madame Espartero Carvala, controlling member of the ultra-elite Board of Policy. In fact, Hamilton almost simultaneously takes satisfaction in the belief that his son Theobald will be able to understand more than he himself can, then thinks, "It was nice that Theobald seemed to have gotten over that ridiculous fixation identifying Justina with Old Carvala." The fact that Hamilton dismisses the idea as "ridiculous" means he certainly won't pursue it himself. Thus, in large part, he discards the concern that has obsessed him throughout the bulk of the novel. Even though he has found an understanding that satisfies him and lets him build a satisfying life, a reader leaves the novel with the uneasy suspicion that in some ultimate sense—the impulse that kept Lazarus Long trying to climb the tree—Hamilton has failed.

This acceptance of limitations echoes a passage earlier in the novel, as Hamilton emerges from gas-induced coma. He first thinks how pleasant it would be to die but realizes how lonely he would be, then thinks of the people he'd miss if he left this life, then realizes that his identity as Hamilton Felix is an arbitrary choice that he can change "next time," then settles back into that role as he regains consciousness. Panshin calls this the "Mystical Solution" that Heinlein unfortunately rejects (*SFiD* 159–61). In his introduction to the Gregg Press edition of the novel, Norman Spinrad sees the scene as an anticipation of Heinlein's much later development of a multiverse of equally valid futures and identities, when Hamilton momentarily awakens from his limited human consciousness into "an awareness of itself [sic] as the Godhead, the stripping away of the veil of Maya" before reattaching itself to normal identity (xii). Spinrad's observation may be a brilliant hunch anticipating Heinlein's last novels. However, Heinlein's letters to Campbell concerning the novel indicate much less deliberate control of the material than Spinrad assumes, even stating that some of the material that supports the notion of reincarnation was inserted at Campbell's suggestion.

Overall, then, Heinlein's first independently developed, full-scale novel is a perplexing performance. He says he wants to write a "high tragedy ... in the Greek sense," but part of Greek tragedy is the heroes' recognition that they do not control their actions, that they live at the (nonexistent) mercy of fate. However, Heinlein begins with the idea of developing more control over human life, since "the *possibility* [emphasis added] of genetics" lets us seriously ask "What Are We Going to Make of the Human Race?" One can see this disconnect as the result of a writer wanting to explore serious ideas in a commercial field that discourages anything beyond easy-to-read adventure — especially while writing for an editor who pays well but who strongly encourages stories that lead to calm, productive problem-solving rather than cathartic failure. That seems an oversimplification, though, since Heinlein's fiction has been pulled in different directions throughout his career. Following the hiatus of World War II, when he returned to writing in different markets, the same concerns appeared.

3

Transitions

In reflecting on the late 1940s, Heinlein wrote, *"After World War II I resumed writing with two objectives: first, to explain the meaning of atomic weapons through popular articles; second, to break out from the limitations and low rates of pulp science-fiction magazines into anything and everything."* For whatever reasons, his first aim never succeeded, perhaps in part because his increasingly strident attitudes led him to the "Heirs of Patrick Henry" episode of the late 1950s and beyond. Certainly there is no simple explanation for that failure. In the same 1979 passage, he contrasted the dangerous public ignorance of 1945 and 1979:

> *In 1945 we were smugly ignorant; in 1979, we have the Pollyannas, and the Ostriches, and the Jingoists who think we can "win" a nuclear war, and the group — a majority? — who regard World War III as of no importance compared with inflation, gasoline rationing, forced school-busing, or you name it. There is much excuse for the ignorance of 1945; the citizenry had been hit by ideas utterly new and strange. But there is no excuse for the ignorance of 1979. Ignorance today can only be charged to stupidity and laziness — both capital offenses.*

In this judgment one senses something of the disappointment in and anger with contemporary America which increasingly became a part of Heinlein's mind-set. Perhaps he came to see that public ignorance was just a superficial sign of Americans' more fundamental, unalterable lack of curiosity or energy — their clinging to "common sense."

Heinlein's second aim succeeded — perhaps beyond his wildest expectations. Although 1946 saw nothing new published, in 1947 he broke into *The Saturday Evening Post*. Immediately after the war, Lurton Blassingame had become Heinlein's agent and undoubtedly deserves much credit for placing his fiction into what was probably the best-known "slick" magazine. But Heinlein himself painstakingly, painfully learned to refit his vision to reach a wide, general audience. At the same time, these stories stealthily redirect his concern with dangerous public ignorance.

Much has been said about the manner in which Heinlein domesticated the future. None of his fiction, certainly to that date, shows that ability better than do the *Post* stories. Gone are the involved, often attenuated plots of the *Astounding* stories; from a well-chosen narrative perspective the brief *Post* stories concentrate on a single sequence of action, often on a single character. Most importantly, against the unfamiliar backdrop of the near future (he later clustered all of the *Post* stories between 1975 and the early twenty-first century) he presented plotlines which would be familiar to his new readers. That is to say, he adapted sf materials to the *Post* audience, beginning with "The Green Hills of Earth" (February 9, 1947).

In that story, an unidentified narrator informs his readers that while he is about to tell them "the story of Rhysling, the Blind Singer of the Spaceways," it will not be "the official version." Rhysling is a familiar culture hero whose songs they have sung in school, about whom they have heard many stories, but unless they are spacemen they do not know his ribald verses which cannot be quoted in "family magazines," and they must remember that the "traditional picture of Rhysling" is not "authentic" and was manufactured by his literary executor and publishers after his death. This tale will reveal the truth about the man whom the narrator's readers would not have wanted in their parlors. From the outset, then, the narrator captures that tone which characterizes those innumerable articles in popular magazines which disclose the intimate/confidential lives of famous men and women. *Post* readers would feel at home. Summary narration recounts Rhysling's accidental blinding aboard the first atomic-powered spaceship, the *Goshawk*, and his subsequent wanderings, like a drunken troubadour, through the inner solar system; a perhaps apocryphal, imaginary conversation introduces the final sequence when, now an old man, Rhysling dies in another nuclear accident as he seeks to return to Earth, perhaps to his native Ozarks. The story becomes an explication of the writing of his finest song, "The Green Hills of Earth." Undoubtedly some postmodernists and others will consider the tale overly sentimental, but it catches Heinlein at his lyrical heights; his verses have been set to music and have become part of the folklore of modern sf fandom.

In terms of *Post* reader familiarity, "Space Jockey" (April 26, 1947) can be described as an examination of the tensions between a wife and her husband because of his job. In this case, however, instead of being a medical doctor or detective, Jake Pemberton is one of the most skilled space pilots, whether on the run to Luna City or to Mars or Venus. Heinlein reveals something of his basic attitudes in an "affectionate ... superficial" letter Jake writes to his wife when he reminds her, "You've got a job, too. It's an old, old job that women have been doing a long time — crossing the plains in covered wagons, waiting for ships to come back from China, or waiting around a mine head after an explosion — kiss him goodbye with a smile, take care of him at home." He tears up that letter because his boss, Commodore Soames — aware of the problem between husband and wife — offers Pemberton a more stable position flying the regular Luna City run; when Jake phones his wife to ask if she will come to Luna City, she acquiesces so quickly that he wonders "why he had ever doubted her." The story's attitude toward marriage undoubtedly is dated. Although the body of the narrative deals with incidents showing how skilled and devoted a pilot Pemberton is, the high point of the narrative occurs in a scene when the control room is invaded by a thirteen-year-old boy who proclaims that he need not have anything explained to him because *he* is a Junior Rocketeer of America; he promptly fires the jets, thereby wasting fuel and giving the story its central problem to be solved. The incident also gives Heinlein the opportunity to confront the boy's stock-holding father and, implicitly at least, to celebrate the man of action at the expense of the ignorant intruder.

The story line of "It's Great to Be Back" (July 26, 1947) deals with a middle-aged couple eager to return to Earth after having worked at Luna City for an unspecified number of years since the beginning of that colony. Disheartened by conditions on Earth — especially the gravity, to say nothing of common colds and the attitudes of people who actually know little or nothing about the lunar project — they decide to return to the Moon, "*to go home.*" The narrative provides Heinlein with the opportunity to promote both space travel and lunar colonization.

Despite its ominous title, "The Black Pits of Luna" (January 10, 1948), deals with a most commonplace topic: a little boy lost during his family's vacation. Only this time the child is lost on the surface of the Moon and faces death because his oxygen will be exhausted in a few hours. Heinlein's work with juvenile characters, which attracted interest from the publisher Scribner's, shows itself throughout the story, especially in the choice of a young boy probably not yet in his teens as narrator. That choice gives the narrative both tone and movement, for the boy's expected derogatory remarks about his kid brother, Mother's "Baby Darling," give way to a real concern as he realizes that "the runt" may die like a fish out of water. He rescues his kid brother, of course, because as he explains it, he knows that little boy better than any of the adults and thus can predict his actions. More importantly, Heinlein voices a theme that resounds throughout the novels for Scribner's: the inadequacy of many adults on the new frontier of space. The narrator's father is cut from the same blustering mold as the father in "Space Jockey"; of his wife's willingness to "give in," he remarks, "I suppose women just don't have any force of character." If his father is obtuse, however, the narrator echoes this judgment of at least one woman when he says that he should not have relied on his mother to look out for "the runt": "She's the kind of person that would mislay her head if it wasn't knotted on tight — the ornamental sort. Mother's *good*, you understand, but she's not practical." His parents must be numbered among those earthbound adults of "It's Great to Be Back" who cannot comprehend or participate in humanity's movement to the stars. The story's climax underscores that point. Once "Baby Darling" is safe, their host/guide on the Moon asks as a favor that they not return to the Moon: "You don't belong here; you're not the pioneer type." But when the narrator tells the man that he will be back, the man shakes his hand and remarks, "I know you will, Shorty."

These are the four stories that Heinlein placed in *The Saturday Evening Post*. Although they differ from his other fiction of the period, they carry several of his central themes and images. Another "slick" story, "Ordeal in Space" (*Town and Country*, May 1948) resembles them by interweaving contemporary and future issues by focusing on a former spaceman's efforts to rescue a kitten from a ledge thirty-five floors above street level. That experience cures him of the acrophobia which had driven him from space after an incident in which he drifted away from the hull of the ship *Valkyrie* as he tried to replace an antenna. Two hours passed before a patrol ship from Deimos rescued him. Heinlein's description of the protagonist's fear of falling dominates one of his finest early characterizations as the man overcomes his disability.

Even if they didn't make it into the slick-paper magazines, other stories written during this period show Heinlein's efforts to reach a general audience with sf themes. One such is "Columbus Was a Dope" (*Startling Stories*, May 1947), a brief dialogue in a bar in Luna City that debates why anyone would undertake the initial voyage to Proxima Centauri aboard a "generation-ship." While one of the speakers suggests that there is no rational explanation, the idea of progress lies implicit; essential to Heinlein's thinking is the idea that such ventures are important because no one has yet undertaken them. It all ties in with unquestionable, unstoppable human curiosity.

Most of the other short stories of this postwar period are run-of-the-mill sf tales. Genetic engineering provides the point of departure for "Jerry Was a Man" (*Thrilling Wonder Stories*, October 1947), which ends in a courtroom sequence turning on the issue of whether or not Workers, Inc., may simply dispose of the anthropoids it has developed to do the "dirty work" of the world. The company has no use for those creatures when they can no longer work efficiently — that is, when they become "senile." The story's conclusion, in which the court reaches the humane decision that the anthropoid Jerry "was a man," does not blot out how Heinlein uses the narrative to attack the greed and whims of the very wealthy American aristocracy. Mr. and Mrs. Bronson van Vogel journey to the Phoenix

Breeding Ranch because van Vogel, a parasite living on his wife's money, is willing to pay two million dollars to the engineers if they will create a Pegasus large enough for him to fly to his club so that he can outdo a rival who has shown a six-legged dachshund. Meanwhile, his wife "simply must have" a "darling" statuette-sized elephant, one of "a limited edition of six"; at her persistent command, her husband writes a check for $350,000. In a sense, thus, Jerry is a side issue that Mrs. van Vogel takes up only after her husband "brutally" goads her by saying that the corporation will "liquidate" Jerry and the other "senile" anthropoids and sell their bodies as "dog food." This is not to say that the main issue is unimportant to the writer. At one point an executive from the Ranch suggests that "an animal is a machine, primarily a heat engine with a control system to operate valves and hydraulic systems"—a concept that bothers Heinlein when applied to human beings. He continues his emphasis on unattractive aliens when a Martian, the finest of genetic engineers, declares in court that it is "*not self-evident*" that men are more intelligent than anthropoids.

Argosy, latest incarnation of one of the pulp magazines which had prepared the market for science fiction by publishing the stories of such writers as Garrett Smith and Ray Cummings as early as World War I, contained two of Heinlein's post–World War II stories. Both are variations of the popular catastrophe motif. In "Water Is for Washing" (November 1947), untrained civilians try to escape from the Imperial Valley after an earthquake breaks the southern shield of mountains and allows the waters of the Gulf of Baja California to flood the valley. In its characters and action, "Water Is for Washing" is as close to social realism as Heinlein comes.

In the second *Argosy* story, "Gentlemen, Be Seated" (May 1948), a first-person narrator, a journalist, gives an account of how he and two engineers are trapped in an air lock of a tunnel being constructed on the Moon. Despite the anxiety of the narrator, Heinlein obviously tries for humor in that the narrator and a companion must sit on the hole through which their precious air is escaping. Both are exhausted and almost frozen, but they are fortuitously rescued by a search crew.

In contrast to these two, his first story in *Boy's Life*, "Nothing Ever Happens on the Moon" (May 1949), celebrates the actions of a young Eagle Scout, Bruce Hollifield, an emigrant from Denver who is blithely certain that he can quickly earn the badges necessary to qualify him as an Eagle Scout on both the Moon and Venus. Like so many of Heinlein's youthful protagonists, Bruce must learn humility. In a close detailing of the action, he does so as he saves himself and his companion during a two-person hike taking them into previously unknown territory. He proves that, despite his seemingly overconfident façade and the superlatives of the publicity preceding him, he really does have the ability to master circumstances.

Like the early twentieth-century *Argosy*, *Bluebook* magazine had prepared an audience for science fiction with the fiction of such writers as Edgar Rice Burroughs and William L. Chester. It published one of Heinlein's postwar stories, "Delilah and the Space-Rigger" (December 1949). G(loria) Brooks McNye proves to be one of the earliest of Heinlein's highly competent women, and he seems to anticipate the concern for gender which has become so much a part of recent fiction. The story centers on the furor that ensues when McNye becomes the first woman assigned to work on Space Station One as it is being built; moreover, she is to serve on the permanent staff as Chief Communications Officer. The supervisor of the project, "Tiny" Larsen, refuses to have a woman on the Station and wants to send her Earthside on the first available ship. Although the Fair Employment Commission is referred to and although "Miss Gloria" accuses Tiny of discrimination in that she has been "penned up" until she can be relieved, the overall narrative seems dated, not reading like recent treatments of such a story line. "Miss Gloria" remains shadowy even when she is onstage. The narrative is talky, relying mostly on the exchanges between Tiny and "Doc," the sympathetic first-person narrator who acts as observer/adviser. The story's only action depends on a large but faceless number of men who threaten to resign if "Brooksy" is relieved. Consequently, at Doc's suggestion, Tiny instructs the home office to send more "female help," but the story shows its age when Doc suggests that Tiny not forget married couples and "some older women" and reminds him to tell the home office to send a chaplain as soon as possible so that the couples who inevitably will form can be decently married. Yet "Delilah and the Space-Rigger" was the first sf story to deal with sexual discrimination in the workplace and stands unique in Heinlein's fiction.

In the same month, *The American Legion Magazine* published "The Long Watch" (December 1949), Heinlein's second unique story of the period. By the end of the 1950s he would be embroiled in a continuing debate about his alleged militarism, but the story stresses the dangers of military men acting on their own. "The Long Watch" focuses on Lt. Johnny Dahlquist, recently appointed to Moon Base. When the base's executive officer, Colonel Towers, declares that "control of the world" can no longer be left in "political hands" but "must be held by a scientifically selected group"—namely, "the Patrol" which mans Moon Base—and adds reassuringly that there will be no war, "just a psychological demonstration [destruction of], an unimportant town or two." Lieutenant Dahlquist enters the underground atom-bomb armory to defuse the weapons before Colonel Towers can launch them. At one point as he labors on, Dahlquist muses that "he wouldn't let his baby girl grow up in a dictatorship just to catch some sleep." He works until none of the bombs is usable. Although the coup fails when Colonel Towers shoots himself after a government ship has landed at the Base, that revelation is almost an afterthought, for the body of the narrative stays with the young hero. When the news comes, he has already died from a severe overdose of radiation. The story's framing narrative describes the cortège of ships which brings his body back to Earth for burial in a marble shrine in his hometown. Heinlein intends the account of the four-day absence of commercial programs from television and the ninety-eight hours of an "endless dirge" to remind readers of the burials of great leaders and heroes such as Lincoln. Perhaps the story is most important because it suggests something of the struggle going on even in 1949 in Heinlein's mind, as one idealistic military man violates orders in order to prevent another idealistic but misguided military man from violating orders. Although Heinlein believed that heroic men would keep the world free, he was unsure how their actions would square with the military chain of command.

These short stories were not all that Heinlein wrote during the late 1940s. To begin with, there was the occasional story outside the field of sf. Under the pseudonym Simon York, he published "They Do It with Mirrors" (*Popular Detective*, May 1947). He also used the transparent pseudonym "R. A. Heinlein" for two stories about a college-aged girl, Maureen (aka Puddin')—"Poor Daddy" (*Calling All Girls*, 1947) and "Cliff and the Calories" (*Senior Prom*, August 1950). At best, however, these seem incidental to the development of his main career. Scribner's had begun to publish his juvenile series with *Rocket Ship Galileo* (1947). Finally, he is one of three writers credited with scripting George Pal's film *Destination Moon* (1950). Except, perhaps, to the most ardent Heinlein fans, that film now has little more than historical interest. Described as being adapted from a Heinlein novel, the film shares nothing with *Rocket Ship Galileo* except the name of the chief protagonist, Dr. Caruthers, the scientist who instigates the mission. It is obviously dated. For example, private industry finances the undertaking because the government could not mount the effort to complete the project quickly. Yet the industrialists do not agree until a U.S. general voices what became one of Heinlein's continuing themes: whoever controls the Moon will dominate Earth because of the threat of atomic missile attacks. The most "amusing" touch remains the spaceship's radar-radio operator, Joe, who needs to have explained to him all the information that would be familiar to Heinlein's sf readers. The film still *looks* convincing and did gain an Oscar for its special effects, particularly notable for Chesley Bonestall's paintings of lunar landscapes. "Destination Moon," an associated short story (*Short Stories Magazine*, September 1950), covers the same plot but leaves uncertain whether the American space travelers succeed or not.

The science fiction short stories that Heinlein published during these years do have special importance. First—and in some ways foremost—although *Argosy* in particular had included sf stories by such writers as Murray Leinster and Arthur Leo Zagat as late as the autumn of 1939, Heinlein opened more magazines beyond the genre pulps to his colleagues and subsequent writers. This in itself brought significant economic changes to sf. *The Saturday Evening Post* bought only four stories from Heinlein and, like other "slick" magazines, did not long continue a strong emphasis on the field. Yet the publication of sf stories in magazines aimed at a wide, general audience—together with the publication of books, both hardback and paperback, often made up of stories and serials taken from/revised from the sf magazines, and the proliferation of magazines devoted to sf and fantasy, however oftentimes short-lived—all broadened the audience for science fiction. It was as though publishers and readers alike sought quick answers to what had happened at Hiroshima and afterwards. One must acknowledge that interest slackened in the mid–1950s, but by then sf paperbacks had created an audience the field had never had before. And it is safe to say that Robert A. Heinlein more than any other individual writer liberated sf from the isolation of the genre pulps.

Important as the economic effects were of Heinlein's cultivation of larger markets, his stories during this transitional period are also notable because they indicate the direction much of the field was to take. Heinlein was continuing to experiment in terms of both material and technique, carrying on things he had tried in his stories for John W. Campbell. It oversimplifies to say that Heinlein de-emphasized action in favor of characterization *per se*. He sought his own manner, his own voice, in order to escape the inflexible patterns of "space opera." At the same time, he concentrated on the effects of extrapolated future situations on his characters. Nothing shows the effect of the resultant differences more vividly than "Gulf" (*ASF*, November–December 1949), the last fiction he wrote specifically for John W. Campbell. That Heinlein and his wife Leslyn had stayed with the Campbells when they first came east in 1942 suggests that they remained friends well into the war; by the late 1940s, however, in addition to Heinlein's search for new markets, his concept of sf had come to differ sharply in practice from Campbell's. Indeed, "Gulf" differs radically from Heinlein's other fiction of the period. The story exists because an *ASF* reader had mailed in a letter "commenting" on the issue that would be published a year in the future; Campbell was amused enough to actually commission material to produce the issue as described.

"Gulf" begins with a splash of action and suspense. Hardly has the protagonist arrived on Earth from Moonbase before he changes disguises to avoid unidentified enemies. Afraid that he has only minutes to live, he mails three spools of microfilm before he temporarily eludes pursuit—only to fall victim to phony police officers who "chill" him with a ray-gun and imprison him in a cell with "Kettle Belly" Baldwin, "King of the Kopters," who already knows about the microfilm. Although the sequences differ in particulars, the encounter reminds one of the meeting in jail between David and Fader Magee in "Coventry," if only because the two men become friends and allies. Despite the untrustworthiness of appearances in the first section of the story, Baldwin demonstrates his innate humanity by sparing the life of a spider that lands on his hand. By contrast, when the protagonist confronts his captor, the elderly Mrs. Keithley, she offhandedly has an innocent girl tortured to death in front of him in the hope he will give up the microfilm to stop the victim's pain. But the protagonist knows that millions of lives are at risk and suppresses his sympathy for the individual, although he vows vengeance on Mrs. Keithley and the selfish brutality she represents.

After he and Kettle Belly escape from Mrs. Keithley's prison, the protagonist returns to the offices of the Federal Bureau of Security, where he learns from his boss that the films he was carrying contained the only existing plans of "the absolute weapon." Now they are missing, and he is accused of selling out. He must manhandle his boss as he again escapes so that he can flee across country to meet Kettle Belly, who first explains that the new weapon is "a means of destroying a planet and everything on it completely — by turning that planet into a nova." *He* has the plans, so by mutual agreement he and the protagonist destroy them; then Kettle Belly also reveals that he is "sort of the executive secretary of this branch of an organization of supermen," the New Men. Their chief enemy is old Mrs. Keithley, the "queen bee — or the black widow" of an American power group who pretends to support the present administration and is thus untouchable by any legal organization. With this explanation of the struggle between supermen and mere *Homo sapiens*, the action comes to a screaming halt. For some twenty pages thereafter, Kettle Belly expounds his philosophy, while the protagonist, now identified as Joe Greene, undergoes training that reveals that he himself is also a superman — a fact already indicated by his abnormal self-control and his willingness to see the plans for the ultimate weapon destroyed.

Peter Nicholls has denounced "Gulf" as a "notably unpleasant novella ... one of the most brutal political statements Heinlein has made," in which he shows "his contempt for democracy" as well as the common man (Bleiler I 188). Nicholls also noted that the chief weapon of the supermen is assassination. The story justifies this violence if humanity in *any* form is to survive. Kettle Belly identifies the supermen as "New Man, *homo novis*, who must displace *homo sapiens—is* displacing him — because he is better able to survive than is homo sap":

> "Supermen are superthinkers; anything else is a side issue.... Man is not a rational animal; he is a rationalizing animal ... homo novis was not even a separate breed until he became aware of himself, organized, and decided to hang on to what his genes had handed him.... It's the hour of the knife. Someone must be on guard if the race is to live; there is no one but us.... Most New Men are scientists, for obvious reasons.... For a hundred and fifty years or so, democracy, or something like it, could flourish safely. The issues were such as to be settled without disaster by the votes of the common men, befogged and ignorant as they were. But now, if the race is simply to stay alive, political decisions depend on real knowledge of such things as nuclear physics, planetary ecology, genetic theory, even system mechanics.

Early in the discussion, protagonist Joe Greene confesses "to a monkey prejudice in favor of democracy, human dignity, and freedom," but he voices no protests while his training proceeds in such areas as Speedtalk, "a symbolic structure invented instead of accepted without question, similar in structure to the real-world ... structured as much like the real world as the New Men could make it." Joe's ability to absorb this instruction and to use it to clarify his thinking confirm that he really is one of the New Men. Moreover, the situation Heinlein imagines is even more desperate than that of mid-twentieth-century America. The story is set after World War III and a communist interregnum, and Kettle Belly points out that even though New Men "helped" form a new republic and a new, liberal, workable constitution, the result was not good because "The evil, ethic of communism had corrupted, even after the form was gone." Joe can counter this position only feebly, out of vague hopes that normal humans *could* learn to do better if only New Men would become their teachers. But Kettle Belly answers Greene's final objections in a last speech, insisting that the

> common man *can't* learn to cope with modern problems.... We can give him personal liberty, we can give him autonomy in most things, we can give him a great measure of personal dignity—and we will, because we believe that individual freedom, at all levels, is the direction of evolution, of maximum survival value. But we can't let him fiddle with issues of racial life and death.

Thus meditates the spokesman for the genetic elite. A reader must be careful in assigning the view of any single character to the author; however, the recurrent chorus of the characters' voices should give insight into the chief concerns shaping Heinlein's fiction. These concerns are not resolved easily. Much has been written about the highly competent men, especially, in Heinlein's fiction; perhaps not enough has been said about worried men, perhaps even frightened men. Kettle Belly is not certain he's right, even though he is willing to kill for whatever he supposes and hopes will keep humanity from destroying itself—and the New Men. He is frightened of what he believes will happen if he hesitates too long or doesn't act at all. The story's conclusion validates Kettle Belly's interpretation by picturing a future in which the people he sends to their deaths are remembered as heroes, but that doesn't make his decisions less anguished. Like Joe watching the girl being mutilated according to Mrs. Keithley's orders, the leader of the New Men doesn't enjoy what's going on; he just can't see an alternative.

Once Kettle Belly concludes his lecture, the action resumes. Mrs. Keithley has caught them all "flat-footed" by finding another set of plans for the ultimate weapon. She has established a base on her home on the Moon from which she may turn Earth into a nova unless she can be world dictator. Earlier, Joe Greene has expressed the desire to kill Mrs. Keithley; now he is given the opportunity, for he and Gail, the young woman who not only instructs him in Speedtalk but also wishes to marry him, gain access to Mrs. Keithley's stronghold as domestic servants. They kill her and disarm the firing circuit—a complex action taking place essentially offstage and reported in fragmentary lines of dialogue. Unlike the familiar opening, this crucial sequence is not dramatized. Instead, the end of the story focuses on a telepathic dialogue in which, as Gail faces capture offstage, she and Joe recite the marriage vow. Both of them die, but a metal marker on the Moon salutes Mr. and Mrs. Joseph Greene, "WHO, NEAR THIS PORT, DIED FOR ALL THEIR FELLOW MEN." Thus readers know that their self-sacrifice was successful and that it benefited *all* of humanity, the old men as well as the New. Whatever else, during these years Heinlein apparently wished to celebrate heroes. Offhand, one does not recall a similar trumpets-blaring ending in *Astounding* during the decade of the "Golden Age."

Notable in the story is the amount of sexual suggestiveness Heinlein got past *Astounding*'s editorial scrutiny. In addition to Joe and Gail's rather suggestive banter through much of the narrative, Heinlein early on includes a stripteaser ("a remarkably shapely ectocyst") working down toward her last string of beads and a "very young waitress ... [whose] plastic costume covered without concealing"; she asks Joe if he is "lonely" and when he demurs, suggests a "redhead ... real cute." (The waitress is the girl later tortured to death by Mrs. Keithley's thugs.) A bellhop inquires if he needs "company" and turns on the stereo so that "a svelte blonde creature, backed by a chorus line" in the hotel's restaurant seems almost to leap into his lap. One wonders how assistant editor Kay Tarrant, with her reputation for censoring any sexual allusions, permitted such racy background detail, but after all the story *had* been directly solicited by the magazine's editor.

The degree to which "Gulf" differs from the rest of Heinlein's works of the late 1940s shows itself if one examines his essay "On Writing Speculative Fiction," contributed to Lloyd Arthur Eshbach's symposium volume, *Of Worlds Beyond* (1947). This brief article has particular importance in any analysis of Heinlein's theory of writing because it is the first formal presentation of his views, including the initial use of "speculative fiction," the term that became so popular in the 1960s when Judith Merrill and Samuel R. Delaney promoted its use as a substitute for "science fiction." Although, like them, Heinlein's first use of the label seems to refer to the entire genre, he later equates it with the "Just suppose—" or "What would happen if—" story.

After saying that he prefers to write about people instead of gadgets, he names the "three main plots for the human interest story": boy-meets-girl, with all its variations; "The Little Tailor" type, concerned with "the little guy who becomes a big shot, or vice versa"; and "the-man-who-learned-better," a category whose discovery he credits to L. Ron Hubbard, at least to the extent that Hubbard identified it for Heinlein. He declares his preference for the story in which the protagonist faces a problem that he must work with; when he copes with the problem, "the man is changed in some fashion inside himself." The completion of that change marks the climax of the story, although "external incidents may go on indefinitely." For him such a narrative "has more interest than the most overwhelming adventure story."

"In the speculative science fiction story," he writes, "accepted science and established facts are extrapolated to produce a new situation, a new framework for human action." The key phrase, of course, is "human action," for although he could enjoy reading a "gadget" story, he rejects that type as "a fictionalized framework, peopled by cardboard figures, on which is hung an essay about the Glorious Future of Technology," citing both Edward Bellamy's *Looking Backward* and his own "Solution Unsatisfactory" as examples of such an essay disguised as a story. He repeats his central thought that a science fiction story is produced by "human problems arising out of extrapolations of modern science." Whatever the quality of the results, the stories Heinlein sold to *The Saturday Evening Post* exemplify this pattern, whereas "Gulf" is antipodal to it — a combination of lecture and physical event, always granting that somehow Joseph Greene came to believe in the aims of *homo novis*. While Heinlein readily admits that in his own fiction he has broken every rule he lays down in this essay, at this time he has voiced a preference and set up a model that he would wish to achieve.

Beyond this central discussion he gives his readers certain practical suggestions. Chief among them are the admonitions never to allow a story to be "at variance with observed fact" and to undertake whatever preparation is necessary to make the fiction accurate. This also seems to be the origin of his insistence that one must write and finish what one begins, as well as keeping the story on the market until it sells. "On Writing Speculative Fiction" thus marks an important transition in Heinlein's career. However popular he may have been before the war, during this postwar period he emerges as a major spokesman for the sf establishment.

4

The Juveniles for Scribner's

It makes sense to discuss the book-per-year novels Heinlein wrote for Scribner's as a unit. Still, there are difficulties with separating them from his other work. Several of these novels were first serialized in magazines aimed at a grown-up audience, such as *ASF*, *Galaxy*, and *The Magazine of Fantasy and Science Fiction* [*F&SF*], and since their initial Scribner's editions they frequently have been republished without any indication they were intended for younger readers.

Also, the writing of Heinlein's first juvenile novels overlapped the production of several novels that many consider his best work. In fact, one could argue that besides Heinlein's obvious desires to write juveniles that would both broaden sf's audience and earn himself more money by entering a steady, lucrative market, he also wanted to put himself in a situation that would force him to write *novels*. He supplied most of the discipline himself, of course, though his skirmishes with Alice Dalgliesh, juvenile editor for Scribner's, at least helped him recognize the compromises that he could make and those that he couldn't. He began the period as a successful writer of short fiction in the sf pulps; he emerged as a skillful novelist for major publishers.

Moreover, Heinlein seems to have made little distinction between "adults" and "juveniles."

First of all, he didn't write down for younger readers. Consider, for a moment, one of the earliest fully developed juveniles, *Between Planets*. The novel begins with Don Harvey, its young hero, riding his horse through the New Mexico desert. There is no indication of the date, so a reader might assume that the story is set in the Old West — until Don shoots a rattlesnake and looks down to see the remains, "Its head lay by it, burned off. Don decided not to save the rattles; had he pinpointed the head he would have taken it in to show his marksmanship. As it was, he had been forced to slice sidewise with the beam before he got it." Heinlein trusts readers to figure out what kind of "gun" Don must be using and thus to realize the story is set in the future. (Because Heinlein worked future gadgets into his stories so matter-of-factly, some of his extrapolative clues elude contemporary readers, such as the fact that Don is summoned back to his boarding school by a call on his mobile phone — an sf device when the story was written.) What *kind* of future is indicated a few pages later, when Don mentions the title of a suppressed political tract and his headmaster quizzes him, "Don, have you been dealing with a *booklegger?*," enough clue to let a reader visualize a repressive worldwide intellectual Prohibition. Heinlein trusted young readers to catch what was going on — to observe and extrapolate elaborate situations from rather subtle hints.

In much the same way, he trusted young readers to stretch their own understanding of what was right and proper, especially in terms of religion or race. In *Rocket Ship Galileo*, for example, the name of one young character, Morrie Abrams, clearly indicates that he is Jewish, but that is never mentioned in the story. Just so, the names of several Patrol members in *Space Cadet* clearly indicate that they are non–WASP; moreover, when cadets are debating the limits of human–Venerian understanding, one remarks, "Matt hasn't any race prejudice and neither have I. Take Lieutenant Peters — did it make any difference to us that he's as black as the ace of spades?" This fact is news to readers, for dialogue and action haven't suggested Lt. Peters's race until now; evidently Heinlein wanted to show that it simply didn't matter practically. This is so skillfully done that it almost makes a reader today excuse Heinlein for not including explicitly *female* space cadets or academy staff.

Besides the favorable reactions of generations of readers, critics agree on the excellence of Heinlein's juvenile novels. From Jack Williamson to Lois Bujold a virtually unanimous opinion praises the twelve juvenile novels that Heinlein published with Scribner's, saying, in part, that they introduced at least a generation of readers to science fiction and made them enthusiastic readers, to say nothing of those who became professionals in the field. Virginia Heinlein lauds his achievement in breaking into the slicks, but immediately asserts that this "was soon eclipsed by the success of his juvenile novels." In the finest appraisal yet made of the series, Williamson finds them unified by the "inspiring theme of space conquest" and concludes, "Built on sound futurology, they still make a fine primer for the new reader. The best of them are splendid models of literary craftsmanship, with more discipline and finish than most of Heinlein's other work. Revealing significant conflicts and shifts of thought, they are relevant to any survey of his whole career" ("Youth" 30, 31).

For a number of reasons, the first volume, *Rocket Ship Galileo* (1947), was not one of the best of them. Peter Nicholls dismisses it in a single sentence: "*Rocket Ship Galileo* never recovers from the silliness of its first half" (Bleiler I 188), while even Williamson calls it "a sometimes fumbling experiment [that] does no more than suggest the bright appeal of the later titles" ("Youth" 17). Published before the appearance of *Grumbles from the Grave*, neither judgment had the advantage of information from Heinlein's letters; yet Williamson captured the reason for its flaws when he called it an "experiment."

On 27 September 1946 Heinlein was delighted to hear that Alice Dalgliesh, an editor at Scribner's, liked *Young Atomic Engineers*, and by 1 February 1947 he had signed a contract; the manuscript had been revised and was being typed (*GG* 44). By midsummer he had planned the second book of the series, although he did not undertake its writing until later in the year.

One must remember that despite the youngsters in his adult fiction of the late 1940s, Heinlein had never undertaken a novel aimed at the juvenile audience. Long an avid reader of the predecessors of modern science fiction, as all sources agree, he turned to what he knew. In a long letter to Lurton Blassingame dated 19 February 1946, he promises a "finished manuscript" by March 15 and explains that friends had "convinced me that my own propaganda purposes will be served best by writing a series of boys' books in addition to the adult items previously described." To prepare himself for this task, he analyzed several samples of popular series novels for boys (*GG* 41). While he does not name those titles, one assumes that they might include the adventures of Tom Swift; of Jack Darrow and Mark Simpson in the books issued under the pseudonym Roy Rockwood by Cupples and Leon; and of Alan Kane and Theodore Dolliver, the young heroes of Carl H. Claudy's "Adventures in the Unknown," originally in *The American Boy* — all of which were available as late as the 1940s. While Heinlein obviously knew their predecessors, the juvenile travelers of Jules Verne's *voyages extraordinaires*, these young Americans were the boy inventors that he must have had in mind since the working title of his first juvenile was *Young Atomic Engineers* and that he proposed to Blassingame three specific additional titles involving the further adventures of the youthful engineers as well as "at least" another two for which he had not yet come up with double titles (*GG* 43). There were problems with this approach. In particular, Heinlein's belief that the main character of a good science fiction is changed by coping with an exterior problem goes against the idea of a series of books dealing with the same, set characters. Even if the characters he was beginning to imagine were "atomic engineers," they would have to remain "young" ones.

During the first eight chapters of *Rocket Ship Galileo*, Heinlein simply updates his predecessors; all of the established conventions are, at most, simply modified. Although the three teenagers—Ross Jenkins, Art Mueller, and Morrie (Maurice) Abrams are going to college in the fall—"Tech"—during the summer they continue to experiment with rockets in a field belonging to Ross's parents. When, after developing more thrust than the boys have previously achieved, *Starstruck V* explodes, Art confidently remarks, "So we blew up another one. So what? We'll build another one." Then they discover that the man who has been watching them is none other than Art's "'Atomic Bomb' uncle," Dr. Donald Cargraves, who had been "mentioned for the Nobel Prize." He is impressed by the fact that, unlike most American boys who "build and take apart almost anything mechanical, from alarm clocks to hiked-up jalopies," they "understand the sort of controlled and recorded experimentation on which science is based"; although their equipment is crude and their facilities limited, Dr. Cargraves suggests that instead of competing for school prizes, they shoot for the senior prizes by going to the Moon with him. All of his life he has wanted to be a participant in the conquest of space and the exploration of the planets, and he recognizes that the boys are young colleagues who are not content with dreaming and reading, but instead want to be part of the action. With a degree in mechanical engineering and a doctorate in "atomic physics," he is the incarnation of Verne's learned adult who will plan and lead the voyage; the boys are merely an adaptation of Verne's uninformed youthful travelers, though more "scientific" than previous boy inventors.

Once the basic format has been laid out, in a chapter entitled "The Blood of Pioneers," the three must get the permission of their parents, each one getting a different response so that Heinlein may more easily introduce his own views. Earlier, the reader has learned that the boys have "the usual low opinion of the mental processes of adults," perhaps realizing subconsciously that they make up "a generation as a whole incapable of realizing that the world had changed completely a few years before, at Alamogordo, New Mexico, on July 16, 1945," with the first explosion of an atomic bomb. Now Dr. Cargraves reminds Art's widowed mother, a refugee from Nazi Germany, that Americans "have a tradition of freedom, personal freedom, scientific freedom. That freedom isn't kept alive by caution and unwillingness to take risks." He tells Mr. Jenkins that neither the American government nor American industry will undertake a space program, and while he has "nothing against" the Russians and would congratulate them if they reached the Moon first, he feels that "it would be a sour day for us if it turned out they could do something as big and as wonderful as this when we weren't even prepared to tackle it, under our set-up." When Mr. Jenkins insists that his son concentrate on getting his degree, Ross's mother enunciates Heinlein's central theme that "this country was not built by people who were afraid to go. Ross's great-great grandfather crossed the mountains in a Conestoga wagon and homesteaded this place.... I would hate to think I had let the blood run thin."

With their mentor, the boys go to an abandoned proving ground and set about building an atomic-powered spaceship. Despite an effort by unknown persons to sabotage their effort, they succeed and head "skyward, out and far."

The chapters involving the journey itself, surprisingly perhaps, are not highly graphic; most space is given to a discussion of "The Method of Science." The most intriguing sequence involves Dr. Cargraves himself. When the sabotage occurred, he had momentary doubts about continuing the project; now as he readies the rocket for a manual landing on the Moon, he realizes that he cannot do it: "He knew right then that he was not the stuff of heroes, that he was getting old and knew it." He first tells Morrie that he is going to take the ship back to Earth, but then tells the boy to land it because, he realizes, "he would never be a hot pilot — not by twenty years. These kids, with their casual ignorance, with their hot rod rigs, it was for them; piloting was their kind of a job." This may be one of *Rocket Ship Galileo*'s most effective bits of propaganda. Essentially Dr. Cargrave's discovery is the only change occurring within any of the characters, who remain stereotypes, very probably; static, most certainly — despite their experiences. Indeed, the boys become passive, almost a negligible factor as Dr. Cargraves routs a nest of surviving Nazis, who have bombs. The major part of that sequence is not given over to dramatic action but to a haranguing exchange between Cargraves and the Nazi officer he contemptuously calls "Joe Masterrace."

The novel fulfills one other long-established convention when they discover that the Moon was once inhabited and Morrie blurts out, "They [the dead Lunarians] did it themselves.... They had one atomic war too many." With admirable restraint — he has not yet realized that he can never be a pilot — Dr. Cargraves replies, "Could be."

One gains insight into Heinlein when he says that in this "period of extreme change" he sees "two major possibilities":

> either a disastrous atomic war which will destroy for a long time the present technological structure, followed by a renaissance, the nature of which I am unable to predict, or a period of peace in which technological progress will be so enormously accelerated that only short range predictions can hope to be reasonably accurate [*GG* 41–42].

As a novel, *Rocket Ship Galileo* may leave much to be desired, largely because it was Heinlein's first effort in the juvenile field and because he stuck to a preexisting formula while getting certain pet ideas across to his audience. Nevertheless, it was sufficiently popular to inaugurate a series of twelve novels, particularly because its readers would see themselves as the group who must undertake such a future project.

Unlike *Rocket Ship Galileo*, *Space Cadet* (1948) owes little or nothing to earlier boys' series books; instead it sketches the career of Matthew Brooks Dodson from the time he takes the entrance exams for the Interplanetary Patrol Academy in Colorado in order to become a member of the class of 2075 until he learns that he will gain his commission as a lieutenant within another year. General consensus agrees that Heinlein drew heavily on his own memories of and feeling for Annapolis. Essentially the book is a *Bildungsroman*, the characteristic form of most of Heinlein's juveniles for Scribner's. Matt Dodson is never offstage for long: Somehow he constantly gets behind in his studies; he debates resigning from the academy; during a flashback involving a brief leave, he realizes how much his training has divorced him from his family and friends in Des Moines — a fact, he is told by a young lieutenant, that every member of the Patrol discovers; and during a training cruise aboard the *Aes Triplex* he is appointed ship's "farmer" in charge of the hydroponic tanks, later being commended for introducing the growth of pansies into his crop to use for table decoration. Yet Heinlein scatters his attention among three additional cadets as the novel skims through a number of familiar situations: a homesick youth from Ganymede, who disappears from the narrative when he is allowed to go home on leave before going on his initial training flight; a young Texan who must provide all of the comic relief in the novel; and a colonist from Venus, whose main task is to communicate with the amphibious Venerian natives during the final sequence of action. Nor should one forget Girard Burke, the stereotypical young know-it-all who resigns from the academy to work for his father and who causes the trouble with the Venerian natives that precipitates the final sequence of action. This diluted focus keeps *Space Cadet* from realizing its full potential. In addition, the novel is episodic—unevenly so, for the first quarter deals with the period of initial exams and ends with the first muster, while, as in *Rocket Ship Galileo* that veers off course with the appearance of its Nazis, the final third of the novel is given over to a rescue mission on Venus.

However, the novel does have its strengths. As Jack Williamson has pointed out quite rightly, with *Space Cadet* aliens at least begin to come into their own—yet in sharp contrast to the minor roles given to aliens in Heinlein's stories aimed at an adult audience during the 1940s and 1950s. The reader learns in passing that Martians have a different concept of reality than do humans, and when the *Aes Triplex* finds the ship for which it searched in the asteroid belt, that ship—with its crew dead as a result of an accident—contains both fossil-bearing rock and "artifacts, items worked by intelligent hands"; an experiment to date the materials suggests the hypothesis that the plant "was disrupted by artificial nuclear explosion"—another variation of Heinlein's warning to his young readers against atomic warfare. On the other hand, although both of these examples are passed over quickly, the Venerians get more attention. Their alien culture remains shadowy overall, but the matriarchal nature of their society reveals itself through the conversations between the group's ruling "mother" and Oscar Jensen, who convinces her that he and his companions ("sisters") are "people" in that they, like all members of the Patrol, honor and observe the customs of local native cultures. Most importantly, the natives function as a *deus ex machina* when the situation seems desperate, with Matt and the other humans marooned in the equatorial forests of Venus. Although the Venerians help the humans salvage both their ship and Burke's, they find both totally inoperable; at this point, the matriarch gives them the ship *Astarts*, which the natives have preserved intact ("Venusized"), even though it has lain in the jungle since its arrival from Earth in 1971. Besides this boon, through a superior knowledge of chemistry the Venerians somehow produce the ethyl alcohol and liquid oxygen needed to fuel the ships. Before they depart, the cadets formally arrest Burke for crimes against the Colonial Code that protects aborigines.

Significant as are the changes in Heinlein's treatment of aliens, his most memorable accomplishment in *Space Cadet* remains his portrayal of the code uniting the Interplanetary Patrol and the manner in which he ties it to the Future History cycle. In the rotunda of Hayworth Hall Matt had seen the portrait of "Lieutenant Ezra Dalquist, Who Helped Create the Tradition of the Patrol—1969–1996." Dahlquist is the protagonist of Heinlein's "The Long Watch," the officer who thwarted the attempted coup, the so-called Revolt of the Colonels, by disarming Moon Base's atom bombs. At the first muster of the class of 2075, his is one of four names called for whom one of the new cadets answers; moreover, as the cadets are dismissed, they march away "to the strains of the Patrol's own air, 'The Long Watch.'" As the ceremony begins, the commandant tells the new class, "You are of various colors and creeds. Yet you must and shall become a band of brothers.... Each living, thinking creature in this system is your neighbor—and your responsibility." He ends his remarks by emphasizing that the Patrol has entrusted to it "such awful force as may compel, or destroy, all other force we know of":

and with this trust is laid on them the charge to keep the peace of the System and to protect the liberties of its peoples. They are soldiers of freedom.... The trustees of this awful power must each possess a meticulous sense of honor, self-discipline beyond all ambition, conceit, or avarice, respect for the liberties and dignity of all creatures, and an unyielding will to do justice and give mercy. He must be a true and gentle knight.

Later as Matt debates resigning from the academy and joining the marines, his tutor reminds him, "you wear a uniform. But your purpose is not to fight, but to prevent fighting, by every possible means. The Patrol is not a fighting organization; it is the repository of weapons too dangerous to entrust to military men." After Matt realizes how distant he now is from his family, as the *Aes Triplex* speeds toward the asteroids, he is reminded by another young officer, "We've given the human race a hundred years of peace, and now there is no one left who remembers war. They've come to accept peace and comfort as the normal way of life. But it isn't. The human animal has millions of years of danger and starving and death behind him; the past century is just a flicker of an eyelash in his history. But only the Patrol seems aware of it." The officer concludes that while the general public regards the Patrol as "a kind of expensive, useless prize pet — their property," in reality, of course, the Patrol guards the welfare of all beings, human or alien, throughout the planetary system. Jack Williamson has pointed out that Heinlein and H.G. Wells are alike in that they believe both "that common men must be guided and guarded by a competent elite" and that "we need social training to save us" ("Youth" 18). Certainly no one will disagree with this judgment of the two writers' overall views, yet *Space Cadet* seems a unique variation in Heinlein's handling of that central theme, for the Patrol is neither a genetically bred ruling class, a newly emergent breed of supermen (Matt's tutor tells him there is no such thing as a superman), nor a scientific/military group which has imposed its authority on the public. One should forget neither that the members of the Patrol are all officers nor that, like "priests and ministers, teachers, scientists, medical men, some artists and writers," the Patrol "is meant to be made up exclusively" of men having the "professional type" of motivation. "The idea," Matt is told, "is that such a man believes that he is devoting his life to some purpose more important than his individual self." Earlier, when Matt was in the doldrums because of difficulties with his studies, his tutor told him, "Your real job is to learn how to think.... This school is based on the idea that a man who can think correctly will automatically behave morally." One can surmise the reactions of many individuals in the twenty-first century to such idealism. To see a major source of Heinlein's idealism in his deep feeling for the naval academy and the career it had once promised him will undoubtedly draw negative reactions from those who, at least between Vietnam and the Iraq War, can see nothing good in anything that even smacks of the military. To understand an opposite reaction, however, one needs only to go back to those Americans raised on the brief interlude between the Spanish-American War and U.S. participation in World War I. In addition, the Patrol did not come into existence in Heinlein's future history until after the "Disorders in the cities" during the "Crazy Years" of the late twentieth century. One could do worse than seeing the idealizing of the Patrol as an early expression of Heinlein's hope, of which he spoke often, as in the "Pandora's Box" introduction to *The Worlds of Robert Heinlein* (1966).

Space Cadet inspired the TV series, *Tom Corbett, Space Cadet*. Amusingly, in a letter to Blassingame dated 5 January 1951, Heinlein remarked that he did not want any "air credit," although he appreciated the royalty checks. This may have reflected not just Heinlein's disdain of TV generally but the fact that one of the show's supporting characters, the smart-mouthed sharpie Roger Manning, was more interesting than the straight-arrow lead.

From his tentatively inexperienced *Rocket Ship Galileo* and his high seriousness in *Space Cadet*, Heinlein turned to *Red Planet* (1949), relying once again on the motifs of an encounter with aliens and a boy's schooling. Yet this novel does not resemble a *Bildungsroman*. On one level it may be read as the story of a boy and his pet; on another, as the confrontation between a ruthless Company and pioneering settlers; yet unlike some of Heinlein's loosely episodic novels, *Red Planet* meshes together into a smoothly unified narrative.

Early in the narrative, Doctor MacRae, a commentator anticipating such later worthies as Jubal Harshaw, reminds the Marlowe family that Mars is "a frontier community" which should not be troubled by the "pantywaist nincompoops who rule it." His pronouncement occurs when the Marlowes wonder if they should obtain a handgun license for their young teenage daughter, Phyllis, so that she can obtain her own handgun. Their son Jim, several years older than Phyllis, already goes armed as a sign that he is a "responsible, trusted adult." Somewhat later, Jim quotes Doc as saying that "the right to bear arms [is] guaranteed ... it's the basis of all freedom." Doc has also voiced that ever more familiar dictum of Heinlein's that "Trouble is the normal condition for the human race."

Doc and the Marlowes are among the first generation of colonists on Mars. Only the pilot plant of the project to restore oxygen to the atmosphere from the iron oxides in the sands of Mars has just begun to operate. The severity of Martian winters makes it mandatory that South Colony migrates between the polar areas, although the Company governs from the city at Syrtis Minor. Much of the planet remains unpopulated and only superficially explored. Humans have been on Mars so short a time that, as Doc remarks, they do not have full knowledge of its flora and fauna. In particular, they do not yet realize that Jim's little companion and pet, Willis, a creature they call a "Bouncer," represents the first stage in the development of a twelve-foot-tall, intelligent Martian. Not only can the ball-like Willis exactly mimic all sounds and voices that he hears, but he can repeat verbatim all conversations he hears. While this mimicry moves much of the plot, equally important is Jim's repeated declaration that Willis is not "property" but an "individual," a "friend." The two have become inseparable.

On the way to school when Jim and Willis encounter a Martian, the alien attempts to separate them, but its voice "was filled with such warmth and sympathy and friendliness" that Jim is not frightened. When Willis insists on accompanying Jim, the Martians do not object. However, at Lowell Academy in Syrtis Minor a harsh new headmaster, Mr. Howe, orders all of the boys to surrender their personal guns and stop keeping pets in the dormitory rooms. This precipitates a crisis, for Howe and Jim quarrel over Willis. Jim reiterates that Willis is not a pet but a friend. Insisting that Jim has given up all claim to Willis, Howe takes the rare Martian bouncer into personal custody, suggests that Willis may be the "property" of the school and in a conversation with a visitor speculates about selling this interesting scientific specimen to the London Zoo. Willis surprises Jim and his roommate by escaping from confinement and repeating conversations he has overheard in Howe's office, in one of which the local boss of the company that runs the colony reveals his plot to deny the colonists their legal right to migrate away from the harsh Martian winter. The three flee into the increasingly wintry countryside only to be hunted as criminals. The Martians rescue them, delivering them to South Colony. The remainder of the book focuses on the confrontation between the colonists and the bureaucracy of the Company. The question of whether Mars should continue as a colony of Earth or prepare a Declaration of Autonomy is briefly mentioned, as is the fact that a frontier society must fight for its rights. At the crucial moment, Willis and the Martians bring victory to the beleaguered colonists. So much for the action of the novel.

Besides being a success itself, *Red Planet* brought up some ideas that Heinlein was to explore later in more depth. During the initial contact with the Martians, Jim witnesses their trance-like "growing together" ceremony, and the Martian Gekko shares water with him. Later, taking up the passing reference in *Space Cadet*, he is introduced to "the Other World," where an ancient Martian explains that Jim and Willis "have grown together until neither one of you is complete without the other." Because of that friendship, the Martians do not exterminate all human colonists, as they do Howe and the company boss who had stolen their "little one" and planned to sell him to a zoo. Jim and Willis's bonding has importance beyond this narrative as well, for Virginia Heinlein suggests that it was during a brainstorming session sometime during this period that she and Robert came up with the idea for "The Man from Mars," the initial concept for *Stranger in a Strange Land* (*GG* 52). In *Red Planet*'s emphasis on "growing together" and sharing water, one sees an early treatment of two ideas important to the later novel.

Amusingly, *Red Planet* also gives insight into the mind of the mid-twentieth-century publishing industry, for Alice Dalgliesh required Heinlein to censor the narrative before Scribner's would publish it. She objected to what she saw as the sexual suggestiveness of Willis and deplored the boys' use of handguns. Although Willis proved to be a "she" who laid eggs, Dalgliesh's concerns neutered her; in similar fashion, Phyllis's interest in guns and Jim's reaction to Mr. Howe's taking Willis from his room ("I should have burned him.... I should have burned him down where he stood") had to be eliminated. For more than a month Heinlein objected, saying that she had a "dirty mind," that "good Freudians" would always find symbols, and that they should be able to tolerate disagreement about "socially useful regulations" regarding guns. He even suggested to Blassingame that Dalgliesh be named as co-author. In the end he complied "with *all* her instructions and suggestions," although he remarked to Blassingame that "I expect this to be my last venture in this field; 'tain't worth the grief" (*GG* 45–58). This was far from the last time he would say so. Heinlein's continued chafing under Dalgliesh's editorship may simply show different philosophies at work. Miss Dalgliesh appeared to believe that she was producing books for parents and librarians who wanted juvenile readers to be entertained and ultimately reassured, not disturbed. Heinlein, on the other hand, believed that his audience of young adults *should* be disturbed — shaken out of their simple trust in authority and their confidence that problems would work themselves out without serious changes in the readers' thinking. In this, he may have anticipated the publisher's discovery that "Young Adult" could be a viable category of fiction.

At the end of *Red Planet*, after Doc refers again to the need for Martian autonomy and to the men who fought "for their liberties" in the past, he alludes to the "food and population problem" on Earth. That continuing crisis serves as the point of departure for *Farmer in the Sky* (1950), a loosely episodic novel concerning the colonization of Ganymede. Serialized as "Satellite Scout" in *Boy's Life* (August–November 1950), the narrative gives the impression that ideas once again were more important to Heinlein than the people involved, despite his use of Bill Lermer, Eagle Scout, as the first-person narrator. Perhaps at least some of the difficulties with the concluding installment arose because his time was taken by the shooting of *Destination Moon* in the fall of 1949, so that he was having difficulty cutting the manuscript for *Boy's Life* (*GG* 58–59). Although Bill's character does grow enough that the novel can be read as another *Bildungsroman*, it is not especially effective because Bill's decisions and insights come too quickly, too easily. With one major exception he seems too much the observer. That exception occurs when the ship he is riding to Ganymede — the

Mayflower — is holed by a meteorite during its flight; Bill stuffs his scout uniform into the fist-sized opening and thus saves the lives of the twenty boys housed in the compartment, quick thinking for which he receives a commendation.

The basic problem with *Farmer in the Sky* may be something that has always dogged Heinlein: summarized narration instead of graphic, dramatized scenes. Or it may be that this novel seems to combine disparate actions with intermittent lectures, as occurs during a session of school when a young ship's officer begins with a tour of the ship, describes the spaceship development, and concludes with a discussion of the possibility of faster-than-light speeds. In terms of action, for example, Bill and his chum Hank call a meeting aboard the *Mayflower* to organize a Scout troop, but Hank is the one who gives the inspirational "little speech": "He said that the Scouting tradition was the tradition of the explorer and pioneer and there could be no more fitting place and time for it than in the settlement of a new planet. In fact the spirit of Daniel Boone demanded that we continue as Scouts."

Bill is chosen troop leader, and when a four-year-old kid turns up missing, they find him in twenty minutes, but once they land on Ganymede and learn that a troop already exists and considers the newcomers tenderfeet, Scouting quickly disappears from the action except for a casual mention that Bill has not gained the two merit badges he needs to become an Eagle Scout on Ganymede. Again, during a later expedition to select sites for new settlements, Bill and Hank find artifacts left some time in the past by an unknown "other people"; Hank declares that this discovery makes "Columbus ... a piker." Perhaps the most obviously important alien artifact is a "perfect machine" for traveling overland in rough country. When Bill's appendix bursts, his group uses the ancient device to rescue him while he plays "games with the Pearly Gates" all during the "considerable excitement over what we had found." Finding the artifacts in the cave in which they were cached, incidentally, is delayed by a lecture beginning with the idea that "Life is all through the universe.... Life is persistent" and ending with "a short dissertation on population dynamics" intended to prove that colonizing the planets will never lessen the problems of hunger and overpopulation on Earth; sometime within the next forty to seventy years, the speaker speculates, a nuclear war will be inevitable, although the colonies need not be affected. Thus Heinlein embeds his familiar warning about a future war in a lecture about its probable causes.

Once the *Mayflower* lands, Bill gives most of his attention to descriptions of how Ganymede is being terraformed so that it can support human life and so that it can be farmed ("homesteaded"). The initial project, already completed after some fifty years, created a "heat trap" — "a green house effect" — to make the weather more viable. The current, seemingly unending task involves creating soil which will grow crops. Every would-be farmer must begin with blasting the bare rock of Ganymede and then taking a turn with the single rock crusher available to prepare his five acres, but each farmer actually cultivates much smaller areas because he needs specially prepared "pay dirt" from Earth containing bacteria, fungi, and other organisms necessary to create arable earth. Bill's best neighbor, a Mr. Schultz, is a successful farmer who has grown the only tree on Ganymede, thereby gaining the nickname Johnny Appleseed; not only does Schultz give Bill a much-needed load of garbage, but he also provides him with eight apple seeds so that he will have eight trees. In true frontier spirit, a troop of Scouts erects Bill's house for him. Bill himself interrupts this sequence to give a lecture on ecology.

Catastrophe strikes in the form of an earthquake which disrupts the powerhouse so that the heat trap is destroyed; the resultant blizzard kills two-thirds of the thirty-seven thousand colonists. The Schultz family, however, survives because they have kept warm by burning all of the wood of their single tree. Once again the reader feels that Bill exists as an observer or as a handy audience whenever Heinlein decides to deliver a mass of facts and opinions. Other examples could be cited, but even while observing Heinlein's method in this narrative, one must make a significant reservation. One gains the impression that Heinlein wanted to introduce his readers to as much scientific knowledge as he could, while whetting their appetites with as wide a selection of sf materials as possible so that they would become fans of the field. The testimony of many persons, especially young people who read these works at the time of their publication, suggests that he succeeded admirably.

As in *Red Planet*, the politics of the novel seems to focus on a confrontation between the Colonial Commission (and its bureaucracy running the world) and the new colonists (some six thousand of them, the largest group ever to land on Ganymede at one time). Rather than deliberate treachery, however, the basic problem is misrepresentation, misunderstanding. Almost all of the emigrants from Earth, like Bill's family, have been attracted by the "promise of free land and a chance to grow [their] own food." However, although there is ample unoccupied acreage, not only is the land unready for settlers, but Ganymede's society does not have the capacity to help them. It could absorb five hundred immigrants a year, not the inundation of six thousand arriving aboard the larger ship. It doesn't have enough machinery. Three tractor trucks provide transportation. The colony needed manufacturing, not farmers. As Bill himself remarks, the new arrivals realize that they had been "swindled" but understand that "there was no help for it." The competent ones among them set to work; the survivors survive.

Thus *Farmer in the Sky* assumes special importance because, instead of a conflict with a faceless corporation, Heinlein turns on that group of persons who most anger/disgust him. On Ganymede this is personified by Mr. Saunders, the would-be farmer who knows his rights and insists that he will never be a "share cropper" working for another farmer while he waits for his own land. When he is asked how he will feed himself and his family during the indeterminate interval, he proposes that "the government will just have to feed us until the government can come through on its end of the deal." Later he suggests that the government should bring out trained crews from Earth to do the initial blasting as part of the contract with new colonists, but his prize idea involves the government's shipping millions of tons of "good, black, rich soil" from the Mississippi Delta to Ganymede for the colonists' use, a layer at least two feet deep. Asked if he can imagine the cost, Saunders replies, "That's not the point; the point is, that's what we've got to have. The government wants us to settle here, doesn't it? Well, then, if we all stick together and insist on it, we'll get it." He has his moment on the stage before Bill's father sends him packing. Such parasites Heinlein loathes — not only because they are incompetent but also because they count on someone else taking responsibility for their maintenance.

After the Earthquake destroys the farm Bill has grubbed out, he and his father plan to return to Earth. However, when Bill reads the list of the names of those giving up — the cowards, the weaklings, the ne'er-do-wells — he changes his mind because he does not want to be classed with such persons. Finally, after a time lapse, he is told that he should return to Earth to gain a degree and he recalls that he has experienced the quake and reconstruction. He grasps the real situation. Taking a phrase from Rhysling or perhaps Kipling, he concludes, "I have lived and worked with men." With that realization he quickly decides to forego any formal education on Earth and to remain on Ganymede, which has become his home — although he already imagines going to the new frontier on Callisto once the atmospheric project there is completed.

While Bill's reference to Rhysling and his repeated playing of "The Green Hills of Earth" on his accordion provide the only tie between *Farmer in the Sky* and Heinlein's Future History cycle, *Between Planets* (1951) plunges the reader into the breakdown of the period of interplanetary imperialism on the eve of a Venurian revolt against the hated Federation, the setting and mood of which suggests "Logic of Empire." First serialized in *Blue Book* as "Planets in Combat" (October–November 1951), *Between Planets* does seem to hark back to the Future History stories in the prewar *Astounding*. The presence of a schoolboy protagonist scarcely changes the basic line of action. A partial explanation for this similarity may lie in Heinlein's return to those earlier works as he revised them for publication in book form during the late 1940s.

Called home from school by his parents with instructions to join them on Mars, Don Harvey unwittingly becomes the courier of a message destined to change the politics of the solar system. From the time he is sent a cheap plastic ring by his parents and then leaves Earth from Gary Station, New Chicago, Don runs afoul of agents of the Federation. After detaining him and threatening physical violence, they release him, ordering him not to miss his rocket for Mars. They are among the first to question Don's loyalty because he is not native to any planet. He was born in space; moreover, his mother was a Venurian colonist, while his father was a citizen of Earth. Both are famous scientists. On the way to Circum Terra, a strategic space station from which all interplanetary flights originate, Don befriends Dr. Isaac Newton, an intelligent Venurian dragon, who seems initially to be just a comic character. Once on Circum Terra, Don watches a small task force from the Venurian Republic seize the station. Although its commander reminds the cities of Earth that he could destroy them all with the nuclear arsenal kept on station, he advises his audience that the Republic wishes only to escape the "tyranny" in which the Terran Empire has held its "victims" for more than a century. Only the base itself is blown up; as Don watches the aftermath, Heinlein — as narrator — recalls "the many terrible times" a mushroom cloud from an atomic explosion had hovered over the Earth.

Because no one is certain of Don's loyalty or his citizenship, Sir Isaac has had to use his considerable influence to keep the boy from being returned to Earth and get him aboard the rocket for Venus. Although the action seems to slow once he arrives, many people try to obtain the ring. Don gives most attention to his financial difficulties — his Federation currency is no longer good — but he does solve the problem of the ring by entrusting it to Isobel Costello, a teenage girl who has helped him. When the Federation Peace Forces invade and torch the capital city, Don is again detained and tortured slightly (his little finger is bent "sharply"), but he escapes into the countryside before sodium pentothal can be administered. He enlists with the guerrillas, but after he has become a combat veteran and just before he can go off on a night raid, Sir Isaac again uses his influence to bring Don into his home.

The subsequent, extended scene of confrontation and revelation at first seems overdone because Heinlein wants it to accomplish too much. Essentially expository and therefore "talky," it must reveal the contents of the message Don has been entrusted with and see that it gets into the right hands, while also at least preparing the stage for the climactic action. Besides, after briefly hinting at his hero's military experience, Heinlein attempts to demonstrate the desired change in Don's character all at once, for the usually passive youth violently resists when he is commanded once more to surrender the ring.

One reason this is such an important but confusing scene is that it emphasizes one of the novel's main themes: choosing someone or some ideal to trust. Don's experience shows that trustworthiness can't be determined by appearance, superficial behavior, or rhetoric. Young Don finds himself actually liking the first security officer who interrogates him on Earth; even though he threatens Don, he seems friendly, and Don shakes his hand in parting. It's only after the officer tells him that Dr. Franklin, his parents' friend who was detained at the same time, died of "a heart attack" during questioning that Don stares at his hand and vows to "wash it as quickly as he could." On the contrary, the initial spokesman for the adult group demanding the ring at the novel's conclusion — the domineering Montgomery Phipps — makes the worst possible first impression. He begins their meeting by reminding Don that some years ago when he last saw him as a young boy he "spanked [him] properly ... for biting my thumb." Phipps is first seen as an obnoxious, condescending bully, even if he does claim to represent Don's parents. But even if this is true, does it mean that the movement Phipps represents is benign? Don is particularly upset when Phipps admits that the adults do not intend "precisely" to help the soldiers of the Republic oust the Terran invaders. If it is hard to judge the trustworthiness of individuals, it is even more difficult to evaluate the claims of a cause that demands personal commitment. People get no help from either side's official propaganda, as reported in the novel, which obviously employs rhetoric to conceal rather than reveal the facts about situations; the rebel side seems to be telling the truth more often than Earth's government, but one would have to know that *before* deciphering the news.

It is in this uncertain situation that the confrontation between Don and Phipps comes to a boil. Showing little regard for Sir Isaac personally or for the amenities of the Venerian culture, Phipps continues to treat Don as a child who should obey without question, telling him not to "quibble" about whether or not a secret message is implanted in the ring. When Don reveals that he gave the ring to Isobel Costello for safekeeping, Phipps is overjoyed, for Isobel and her father conveniently have been in Sir Isaac's home since the invasion. However, Isobel also refuses to give the ring to Phipps. Although his reaction to Phipps is interrupted by Isobel's affectionate entrance, Don continues to defy the overbearing adult and even reprimands Sir Isaac for calling him "dear boy," explaining that "I'm a grown man now" and must "know the real facts." Sir Isaac and Isobel's father are little help, being able to tell him only the message involves "how space is put together — and how to manipulate it." And so Don is pressured to make an immediate choice, not knowing whom he can trust but also knowing that he must not make a mistake. Instinctively, he goes to the person who is naturally incapable of lying, even though that means trusting someone who isn't even human. He gives the ring to Sir Isaac, saying, "I'm sorry. I had to think." With the message's secrets, the conspirators (including an apologetic Phipps) undertake building the ship and the weapons that will enable them to defeat the Federation.

Don's decision is as visceral as the choice made by Old Charlie, Don's Chinese boss back in the Venus town of New London, to defend his property even at the expense of his life. One may see Old Charlie's heroism as a necessary catalyst in Don's own choice to join the rebels, to commit himself to a dangerous, uncertain cause. And one may see *that* as a response to a remark from his roommate back on Earth, as Don is about to leave the planet while his allegiance is unsure. The boy asks whether Don is going "to sign up" when he reaches Venus, then adds, "it wouldn't make any difference between us. My old man says that when it's time to be counted, the important thing is to be man enough to stand up."

Finally making that choice after the Federation invades Venus, Don learns to trust and be trusted by his comrades, the other men he can count on. He also, quite likely, has had to kill enemies, so his threatening Phipps is not a bluff. This is clearly hinted at in the novel, when Don is summoned by his company commander and packs up his hammock: "it weighed only four ounces and had cost the Federation a nice piece of change on cost-plus contract. Don was very careful of it; its former owner had not been careful and now had no further need of it."

This implied background makes the emotional tone of the scene in which Don decides what to do with the ring somewhat more plausible. Probably, in view of his Scribner's editor's squeamishness, it was as far as Heinlein could go to suggest that Don has become a responsible, dangerous adult. *Starship Troopers* lay years in the future.

Besides the novel's development of character under pressure, *Between Planets* contains a political layer important both in developing the storyline and in giving insight into Heinlein's state of mind at mid-century. As soon as he touches down at Gary Station, amid "the noisy swarming mass" of its populace, Don "felt the loss of dignity that comes from men behaving like ants," and when he first meets the man who gave him the ring, he is reminded that "the first system empire" was governed from "the noblest planet of them all," which was somehow broken up and transformed into the rubble of the asteroid belt. Early in their meeting, Phipps informs him that there exists "an organization—a cabal, a conspiracy, a secret lodge.... We just call it 'The Organization.'" This group is made up "mostly of scientists" who share "a belief in the dignity and natural worth of free intelligence." On Mars, making use of "certain mystifying records of the First Empire," some of their members—Don's parents among them—have sought to unravel ancient secrets giving them undreamed-of power—ranging from the ability to move planets and develop atomic-powered ships and weapons to consolidating the solar system politically. Phipps echoes the reaction of Heinlein and his contemporary sf writers when he admits, "All I know is that we are about to turn loose into the world forces the outcome of which I cannot guess.... We are resetting the clock, but we don't know what time it will be." By implication at least he has already indicated the aims of the Organization by telling Don, "In many different ways we have fought—and fought unsuccessfully, I should add—against the historical imperative of the last two centuries, the withering away of individual freedom under larger and even more pervasive organizations, both governmental and quasi-governmental." In case a reader misses the point, Don himself spells it out when he tells Phipps, "I don't much care how they run it—except, well, there ought to be a sort of looseness about it. You know—a man ought to be able to do what he wants to, if he can, and not be pushed around." Phipps agrees: "Any government that gets to be too big and too successful gets to be a nuisance. The Federation got that way." The Organization, then, is another of Heinlein's elite groups. It could have been lifted from a number of his earlier works. More importantly, as Williamson has pointed out, it voices Heinlein's growing dissatisfaction with both urbanization and the centralization of political power taking place in mid-century America and the other industrial nations.

Although Heinlein relies more on talk than onstage action, the final sequence of *Between Planets* looks back through his prewar serials in *Astounding* toward the space opera so popular in the pulps between the world wars. The Federation has sent a task force of rocket ships to Mars "to liquidate" the scientists and their research project, but the journey will take the better part of a year; consequently, members of the Organization on Venus have time to convert a "superstratospheric shuttle" into an atomic-powered ship, christened *Little David*, that is capable of accelerating at twenty gravities so that it can speed through a "discontinuity" of space and intercept the Federation's armada. Initially, because among the specialists "there was nothing he could do to help," Don grows restive, wanting to return to active duty with the rebel army—until he gains a place on the nine-man crew of *Little David*. He is in charge of the dead-man switch, the one trusted to destroy the ship if they are about to be captured. This is a job for a man, not a boy, showing that Don has made his point. In the actual battle, super-metals and super-weapons abound; combat is disposed of in little more than a paragraph as, without the aid of its deadliest weapons, *Little David* annihilates the task force. Even before that brilliant victory Don muses about being chosen for "the Long Trip ... out to the stars" aboard the *Pathfinder*, obviously a generation ship though no explanation is given. That its crew must be made up of married couples does not trouble him, for he has understood for some time — perhaps when Isobel grabbed him by the ears, kissed him, and ran just before he departed for Mars — that he would marry her, and she "was the whither-thou-goest sort [who] wouldn't hold him back."

When Heinlein turned from the shopworn melodrama of *Between Planets* to the delightful humor of *The Rolling Stones* (1952), he complained to Blassingame that he found domestic comedy "harder to write" than bloody action (*GG* 62). Still, having "ruled out ... space warfare and intrigue," he was having trouble with the plot because he wanted the characters to do "something important" (*GG* 62–63). The result proved to be a loosely episodic novel in which each character — with the exception of an eighteen-year-old daughter — had a turn at center stage. First serialized as "Tramp Space Ship" in *Boy's Life* (September–December 1952), it became the odyssey of the Stone family of Luna City, with stops on Mars and in the asteroid belt.

Ostensibly the protagonists are the fifteen-year-old twins, Castor and Pollux, boy inventors and entrepreneurs, whose business ventures shape much of the story line. They provide the catalyst, for the narrative opens with their efforts to buy a second-hand spaceship to use as a merchant vessel. Not quite in the background is their four-year-old brother, Lowell/"Buster"—who consistently beats his grandmother at chess (perhaps because he might be a telepath and is reading her mind)—but who has the spotlight at a crucial moment when his reaction to free-fall or to his medication threatens to end the journey. Another supporting character is the twins' mother, referred to as Dr. Stone more often than she is called Edith, who insists on transferring from their ship to the space liner *War God* in order to treat an epidemic aboard the larger vessel and who later ministers to various prospectors in the Asteroids. Almost all of her medical work remains offstage, although she is much talked about. Usually quiet and inconspicuous, she nevertheless voices opinions that determine the actions of the family.

More crucially, the twins share center stage with their father, Roger Stone, and his mother, their ninety-five-year-old Grandma Hazel. The novel plays the two off against one another throughout in order to develop both theme and plot. With the twins, especially, their father can act the stern authority figure, as when he makes them completely redo their work when they use old gaskets instead of waiting for the replacements he has ordered; he tells them that they must learn "that orders are meant to be carried out," adding, "You need a taste of strict ship's discipline a durn sight more than you need to go to school." Although Grandma Hazel sometimes mediates between them and often advises the boys, she does not allow them to criticize their father; that is a privilege reserved for her. Between Roger and his mother there is a give-and-take banter which can occasionally become sharp. At times Hazel voices opinions that one may identify with Heinlein, as when she briefly remarks that the "so-called normal man is a figment of the imagination." With the two characters as his mouthpieces, Heinlein does not have to intrude his own often irrelevant asides — except for a diatribe denouncing the inefficiency of the automobile during a discussion of the three developmental stages of technology.

He achieves his most effective satire when Mr. Stone and his mother work together. An ex-engineer and former mayor of Luna City, Roger Stone wagered that he could produce "better stuff" than was being channeled up by TV from Earth; as a result for two years he has been trapped into writing a "marathon adventure serial, 'The Scourge of the Spaceways.'" When Heinlein says of Stone that he "had gotten himself caught in a quicksand of fat checks and options" and Stone himself adds, "I can't afford to quit," one wonders to what extent Heinlein is speaking of his own situation.

Be that as it may, although Hazel tells him that he should break the contract because he has won his bet, when he is pressed to meet a deadline, she dictates the needed episode overnight, introducing into it a "Galactic OverLord," and suggests that as a result the show's ratings will go up. He protests the inclusion of such a clichéd villain. She declares a willingness to write the next seven episodes that will bring the serial to the end of the present option period. Her plan is to kill off all of the characters, though Roger would deny her "the fun" of killing his hero, for he has hated "that mealy-mouthed Galahad ever since I thought him up" and wants to write that death scene himself.

Like Heinlein, Stone has tried to keep his plots as scientifically accurate as possible. Grandma Hazel has no such concern. After Stone learns that she has taken a new option because the network offered her more money than she could resist, she admits that she gets her "best ideas from Lowell, he's just the mental age of my average audience." She also points out that her episodes have attracted three new sponsors, indicating that her low opinion of the viewers is correct. She gives synopses of the two newest episodes, which parody space opera as it appeared in the pulps, in the comics, and on television. Although Heinlein directs his barbs at contemporary TV specifically, one cannot be certain whether or not he is thinking of such programs as *Tom Corbett, Space Cadet*, which he had damned in a letter to Blassingame in 1951, or is attacking the kind of clichéd magazine fiction that he so disliked, as his early letters to Campbell indicate. Throughout the first decades of his career he spoke repeatedly about enlarging the parameters of the genre, with special attention to characterization. In view of the way he played with the conventions — the "furniture" — of the genre from *Glory Road* (1963) on, "The Scourge of the Spaceways" ("The Scum of the Waste Spaces," Roger Stone calls it) has importance as his first deliberate parody of the field.

For whatever reasons, he de-emphasizes that satire as *The Rolling Stones* plunges toward Mars. The space odyssey of the Stone family provides the backdrop for an examination of the twins' business efforts, the core of the story line. Castor and Pollux are cocky, neither of them having "much confidence in the skill and knowledge of their elders." When their father will not let them use any of the money he holds in trust for them as a result of royalties from an earlier invention, they remind him, "We weren't too young to earn it." He opposes their desire to obtain a secondhand ship to use as a freighter, warning them that "the sharp traders running around the system" would skin them, but he talks about getting a ship for "an occasional pleasure trip." Manipulated by Hazel, however, he buys a ship and announces that he is "going on a picnic, a *wanderjahr*"; anyone in the family who wishes may join him, but he refuses to let the twins "run the show."

He relents enough to allow Castor and Pollux to take a cargo of used bicycles to Mars, but the bureaucracy of Mars, with its bonds that all terrestrials must post, its customs duties, and its profits tax, takes all of their money except for a few coins, two-thirds of which must go to Grandma Hazel, who demanded a fee after she successfully defended them in what must be one of Heinlein's funniest court scenes. Despite their apparent failure, however, the twins' abilities as entrepreneurs do not go unrewarded. While they were casing the bicycle market, in one of those rare moments when they thought of someone else, they bought a "flat cat" for Lowell, who wanted to see "a real Martian." Fuzzy Britches, as they name Lowell's new pet, is a "furry heap ... a pie-shaped mass of sleek red fur [without] discernible features" except when it looks at one with its three "trusting" eyes. An "affectionate little" creature, a flat cat "just purrs and snuggles up to you." The shopkeeper also tells them that it is a great favorite among the lonely prospectors in the Asteroids. Not only does this fact provide Heinlein with a link between major episodes of the novel, but it also leads to the solution of the twins' business problems.

Tired of Mars, all the Stones want to leave. When their father suggests Venus, the boys counter with the Asteroids because a new strike of core metals and uranium has occurred in the so-called Hallelujah Node and because the bodies in the solar system are in the best position for travel when between Mars and the Asteroid Belt. The family chooses the Asteroids since they have never been there. Hazel advises Castor and Pollux not to be miners but, like the people who got rich during the Gold Rush of 1849, to provide something the miners must buy. The boys purchase lots of groceries, especially luxury foods, although they include such goods as antibiotics, surgical drugs, vitamins, song and story projectors, and a "supply of pretty girl pictures," censored by the adults. Complications develop en route. Early in the voyage Fuzzy Britches has eight golden kittens; in sixty-four days each of her kittens has eight golden kittens, and in sixty-four days each of their kittens reproduces — eating so much of the groceries and taking up so much room that the Stones have to conduct "Operation Roundup," shooing the flat cats into the unheated hold where they hibernate. In the Asteroids once the twins trade a cat to a prospector they have befriended, they realize that in "Rock City" they have an "unexploited market"; enthusiastically they broadcast a "music & chatter show" (another media satire) as a means of advertising flat cats while they milk their audience "for all the traffic would bear."

The flat cats caused another bout of "'sex' trouble" between Heinlein and Alice Dalgliesh, for she thought them "a trifle too Freudian in their pulsing love habits"— that is, apparently, in their purring and snuggling. In a letter to Blassingame dated 8 March 1952, Heinlein defended his conscious intention "to write wholesome stories for boys and meant to leave out entirely the sophisticated matters which appear in my writings for adults." Early in the letter he had (again) suggested that *The Rolling Stones* might be his last juvenile or he would offer the next to someone other than Miss Dalgliesh (*GG* 63–65). Defending his treatment of the flat cats, he asked her, "*What* love habits? ... I most carefully desexed the creatures completely ... the circumstances make it clear that the first one, and by implication, all the others, reproduced by parthenogenesis.... Do you object to the fact that they liked being petted?" Most importantly, he attacked Freud, who "was not a scientist; he was simply a brilliant charlatan. He did not use the scientific method, and his theories are largely unsubstantiated and are nowadays extremely suspect.... I grant you that Freudian doctrine has had an aura of scientific respectability for the past generation, but that aura was unearned and more and more psychiatrists are turning away from Freud" (*GG* 65–66).

In fact, that disavowal has continued, and until recently Freud's most ardent contemporary supporters have been members of the literary community, both critics and writers, who have used his theories in their analyses and characterization. One must realize that in denouncing Freud and Freudian theory Heinlein turned his back on speculations that Western intellectuals had espoused from the turn of the twentieth century, after nineteenth-century materialists/naturalists had undermined religious tradition and reduced humanity to mindless, soulless creatures, the victims of forces they could not control. To phrase it another way, the naturalists pictured each human being as an isolated individual estranged from an apparently meaningless universe. One thinks of Émile Zola, as early as *Le Roman experimental* (1884), searching his fictional worlds for the great laws of heredity and sociology upon which to base a just ethic. The American literary naturalists from Dreiser and Norris through Steinbeck and Dos Passos examined the external social/political/economic world to find the forces determining human behavior. As opposed to this, Freud delved into the recesses of the human mind. Grappling with forces that sometimes were difficult to conceptualize because they could not be studied directly but only at secondhand through their effects — and that sometimes energetically resisted being brought into the open — Freud gave his readers a different explanation of human nature than the naturalists. Amusingly — perhaps because they were both responses to the same dilemma of individual passion versus impersonal constraint — both Freudian theory and literary naturalism seized upon human sexuality as perhaps the dominant factor determining human behavior.

At the same time he was rejecting Freud in his letter to Alice Dalgliesh, Heinlein repeatedly attacked the position of the materialists/naturalists in his fiction. In *The Rolling Stones*, for example, Roger Stone remarks, "I'm not a determinist and you can't get my goat. I believe in free will." After Pollux calls it "another very shaky theory" and his father replies, "Make up your minds.... You can't have it both ways," Hazel asks, "Why not? ... Free will is a golden thread running through the frozen matrix of fixed events." The twins dismiss the concept as "not mathematical ... just poetry." In *Red Planet*, when Jim asks Doc MacRae to explain how he saw everything that Willis remembered of their relationship in a very short time, Doc speaks of memory. When Frank suggests that Jim was hallucinating, Doc says that they both may be right. Only then does he declare that "the most wildly impossible philosophy of all is materialism," and he soon tells their returning parents, "We were having a go at solipsism." In short, by the 1950s at the latest, Heinlein had consciously divorced himself from the two driving forces which had shaped modern American letters. This self-inflicted exile made it increasingly imperative that he find a philosophical stance that would give his literary output more substance than a mere adventure story. His task was all the more difficult because his training and interests led him to admire inherited values but also because in his emphasis on science and the scientific method he found an affirmation — an optimism — at a time when the literary community was becoming increasingly anti-scientific and pessimistic. That pessimism would culminate in the often stoic existentialist confrontation with a meaningless universe, to say nothing of the dystopian mood and concern for "inner space" which troubled/shaped science fiction especially in the 1950s and 1960s.

Despite his philosophical unrest and despite the success of the twins as entrepreneurs, Heinlein appropriately gives the climactic sequence of *The Rolling Stones* to Grandma Hazel. Throughout the novel, from remembering that she was one of the first colonists on the Moon and wrote free speech into the lunar charter, through writing the episodes of the endless adventure serial and making certain that her son obtains the ship that makes their odyssey possible, to defending the twins in court, Hazel has resolved every difficulty faced by the males of the family. In one quick moment, she explains her approach to intimidating problems and gives the readers a glimpse of things to come on the American scene when she explains that she quit engineering because she "saw three big, hairy, male men promoted over my head and not one of them could do a partial integration without a pencil. Presently I figured out that the Atomic Energy Commission had a bias on the subject of women no matter what the civil service rules said. So I took a job dealing blackjack." As the twins are forced to do repeatedly in the novel, Hazel does not waste time feeling sorry for herself by blaming society (naturalism: I'm a victim) or dithering (Freudianism: I'm a mess). She just shrugs and moves on.

By chance she uses a small ship, a so-called scooter, which the twins have not finished repairing to take Dr. Stone to the home of a patient unable to travel. On the way back with Lowell, she is lost when the gyros controlling the flight path fail. Repeatedly she radios for help, and when Lowell's oxygen bottle is empty, she gives him hers. She loses consciousness. Of course the twins find her, and as their father prepares them for her death by telling them that at her age people do not have much "comeback," she awakens. When Roger speaks of returning to Luna City after their two-year odyssey, Hazel announces that *she* is going out to Titan. Asked why she wants to go, she replies: "Why did the bear go round the mountain? To see what he could see. I've never seen the rings.... The race has been doing it for all time. The dull ones stay home — and the bright ones stir around and try to see what trouble they can dig up. It's the human pattern." Even though she may never come back because she *likes* free fall, the family votes unanimously to accompany her. She smiles and wonders what destination will follow Titan, as Heinlein creates a final image while the ship blasts off: "In her train followed hundreds and thousands and hundreds of thousands of thousands of restless rolling stones ... to Saturn ... to Uranus, to Pluto"; momentarily he captures his own dream of humanity's "rolling on out to the stars ... outward bound to the ends of the Universe."

Jack Williamson acknowledges that the characters in *The Rolling Stones*, which he calls "a delightful romp through space ... a dream of personal freedom," are all variations "on the brilliantly competent man" ("Youth" 22, 23), a term for Heinlein's protagonists first used by Alexei Panshin (*HD* 12). But in saying this Williamson traps himself in a sense, for he is hard pressed to find individuals who fulfill Heinlein's essential criterion that a character must change/grow. So talented is each of the Stones that no major change needs to occur in anyone during their *wanderjahr*. They simply carry out the roles Heinlein initially gave them. However, acknowledging that the "self-centered twins change only slightly," Williamson suggests that "they do gain some sense of obligation toward a wider humanity" ("Youth" 23), specifically shown in additional commitment to the welfare of the people around them. For example, before they rescue Grandma Hazel and Lowell, their father scolds them for not reporting that the space scooter needed repairs and confined them to their room under arrest; after the rescue he tells them that they are "two very intelligent men — when you take the trouble," though he again scolds them about the faulty gyros.

The same issue shows up in Heinlein's next novel for Scribner's, *Starman Jones* (1953): How can someone whose talents make him superior to the people around him develop a sense of responsibility to others? Especially in a system less personal and benign than the Stone family, how can one move from grudging acceptance of the letter of external law to genuine commitment to law-abiding self discipline?

As Bruce Franklin has pointed out, Max Jones, the protagonist of *Starman Jones*, calls to mind Andrew Jackson Libby of "Misfit," for they are both Ozark farm boys and mathematical geniuses. The opening sequence of the novel also brings to mind a typical pattern of nineteenth-century fiction — perhaps Dickens — because fatherless Max's "Maw" returns home with a new husband who announces that they have sold the farm. Almost immediately the new family head begins to paw through the books Max's uncle, a member of the Astrogator's Guild, had given the boy before his own death. His new "father" wonders how much they can be sold for; when Max objects, the man threatens to beat him, but Max flees into the night. Deciding that his father's admonition to take care of his mother no longer applies,

Max gathers together a few belongings—the books among them—and runs away from home. Along the road he meets a hobo called Sam who feeds him but steals his books. This opening carefully sets up a variation of the orphan-runaway, one who dreams of being an astrogator. *Starman Jones* becomes a futuristic Horatio Alger success story.

Initially Max has only his dream of being an astrogator. When he goes to the Guild Hall of the Mother Chapter of Astrogators in Earthport, the officials tell him that the dream is impossible because his uncle never officially nominated him; as an act of charity toward one of "its own" the High Secretary of the Guild offers to sponsor him as an apprentice in any "respectable trade" that is not "hereditary." Max refuses the offer. On the street again, he encounters Sam, who immediately takes the boy under his wing and proposes that they use forged papers to secure places as crewmen aboard the starship *Asgard*. Although he knows such action is illegal, Max has no other choice if he wishes to get into space, and thus he ends up Steward's Mate Third Class. During his second conversation with Sam, the reader learns that his "funny memory" allows him to repeat verbatim the mathematics in the astrogators' books.

The first five chapters demonstrate how skillfully Heinlein could domesticate the future. Everyone agrees that he did this by mixing the familiar and the unfamiliar. He chose a hill boy who has never been to the city and who prefers reading math books to watching "slobbering stereovision serials" as his protagonist. As often as possible, Max watches the train that passes by the farm; as he runs away he sneaks across a fence into the enclosed truck stop near "the freight highway" and in the restaurant befriends a driver who gives him a ride. To these familiar actions Heinlein fuses descriptive detail placing the machines, the setting, in the future. The train, for example, is not a coal or diesel engine pulling a string of rail cars but a cylinder relayed through the air between electromagnetic rings at supersonic speeds. In Earthport, instead of extended graphic description, Heinlein suggests glimpses of what would most impress a boy: The crowds, the buildings, the "slidewalks" are taken for granted as part of the natural setting, overlooked as soon as Max sees his first alien and, on the vast field, the starship *Asgard*. In the same way, the dialogues between Max and Sam not only advance the action but also provide the exposition, revealing that on Earth there is no chance, no place, for either the boy or his roguish companion. In an America (perhaps) ravaged by nuclear war, where a Food Conservation Act keeps farmers on their land amid other implications of drastic shortages, even teenagers like Max must carry a Citizen's Identification Card. At the top of the social hierarchy are the wealthy and the hereditary guilds; then come the service trades, ranging from metalworker to chef or tailor, organized into guilds to which anyone may become an apprentice. The stratification of society reinforces the idea of an authoritarian government, for Earth rules an empire spreading far beyond the solar system. While the government apparently encourages emigration to the multitude of habitable planets, few can afford the fee required to emigrate, although the government ships convicts and paupers to the colonies. Franklin identifies these unfortunates as "a semi-slave proletariat" (*RAH* 83) perhaps because at one point Sam declares that the "whole planet is one big jail." Such a judgment may oversimplify, however, for when Sam suggests that the only alternative to fleeing the Earth is to "Sign up with one of the labor companies," he does not imply that all of the work is extraterrestrial. Yet the world of *Starman Jones* does seem the most dystopian Earth that Heinlein sketches in his juvenile novels.

Aboard the *Asgard*, Sam points out that when their records are turned in after the voyage, their deception may well be discovered so that they could be arrested; therefore, he urges Max to jump ship with him on Nova Terra. Although Max senses the trap they are in, he can't bear to escape, for he "liked it aboard ship, he had no intention of ever doing anything else." He remains strangely passive. Granted his "menial position" gives him little power, he does not *do* things; things happen to him. As he cares for one of the pets brought on by the passengers, an extraterrestrial spider puppy named Mr. Chips, its young female owner Eldreth Coburn appears; momentarily they bicker, but since the spidery puppy likes Max — conveniently it can speak — the two young people become friends. She visits Max daily, first with a stewardess as a chaperone and then alone because he is regarded as "a perfect little gentleman." When she inquires about the three-dimensional chess set he has, he gallantly shows her how to play the game. Not only does he tell her about his uncle, but Heinlein uses the interlude as a means of having Max explain the phenomenon of Horst anomalies which allow a starship to break the Einstein Wall and make jumps light-years in length through space's folded congruencies. She says that she does not understand, and soon explains that her father had sent her to Terra to learn to be a lady, but she had "created a reign of terror" at three schools, each of which had expelled her. Now she is on her way home. Sam kids Max about marrying the boss's daughter, and he becomes angry, learning only then that Eldreth Coburn is the only daughter of His Supreme Excellency, General Sir John FitzGerald Coburn, O.B.E., K.B., O.S.U., Imperial Ambassador to Hespera and Resident Commissioner Plenipotentiary. How many earlier, popular British and American novels does *that* revelation call to mind? Hardly has the reader learned of Eldreth's elevated position before she asks Max if his uncle was Chester Jones. The next day he is summoned to the Captain's cabin; according to his false record, he once tried out for "chartsman" while on another ship, so he is asked if he would like to try again. The Astrogator, Dr. Hendrix, informs Max that he studied under his uncle.

His change of status to apprentice chartsman introduces the strongest section of the novel as Heinlein skillfully reveals the workings and the personal politics of the control room. Inadvertently Max reveals his eidetic memory and knowledge of the astrogators' tables; Dr. Hendrix tests him but warns him not to use his ability during an actual maneuver unless he thinks a mistake has been made. The only fly in the ointment is Mr. Simes, the Assistant Astrogator, a young man who finds fault with everyone and strongly dislikes Max, disdainfully calling him "a smart boy." After Max impresses the Captain with what Dr. Hendrix calls his "vaudeville act," Hendrix has him figure out the transition through an anomaly. At this point, he is told that he should try for an astrogator — but only after he has confessed to Hendrix that his personnel record is completely phony. Obviously Heinlein wants his readers to understand that Max gets this new opportunity only because of his moral strength. He is made an officer of the watch, and Ellie continues chasing him (she kisses him on both cheeks) and warns him against a flirtatious young matron until he decides that "Marrying Ellie wasn't such an impossible idea now that he was an officer — if he ever decided to marry."

Once again the action has reached a plateau. As they approach the next transition, Dr. Hendrix dies of a heart attack, and Mr. Simes becomes Astrogator. When the Captain takes command of the transition and changes standard procedure by introducing a rash innovation—"a wrinkle that takes the strain out of astrogating"—Max soon warns him he has made an error but is told to step down. Between them, the Captain and Simes compound the error so that the *Asgard* emerges lost in unknown space. As the Captain sinks into depression and Simes quarrels with the members of the control room gang, revealing his personal inadequacy, the ship prepares to land on an unknown planet that they name Charity.

It appears that they are hopelessly lost and must settle there. However, the First Officer announces that the ship will not be decommissioned, meaning that the crew will not be allowed to become colonists. Max picks up on a suggestion by one of the passengers that the Captain marry him and Eldreth, although he is crew and "not eligible to colonize." He asks the First Officer to allow him to return to his original appointment as steward's mate so that he can become a colonist like the Chief Steward. His request is refused, but the First Officer gives him permission to marry anyway.

At this point, it appears that Max's career problems have been solved. Cut off from the oppressive society and the makeshift hierarchy of discipline on the ship, he will be able to make his way as a hardy settler. A worthy mate is handy too. As he and Ellie go walking out from Charityville, she tells him of "Putzie," the man on Hespera who caused her father to ship her to Earth; however, she adds that she might keep Max "in reserve if you weren't so jumpy." But before they can share more secrets, they are captured by centaurlike creatures who apparently are the dominant species on the planet, for the two see "grotesque humans" who obviously are mere slaves. Captivity gives Max and Ellie a chance to get to know each other better, sometimes with startling results. When they play three-dimensional chess and she plays him to a draw, he compliments her condescendingly; only then does she retort that "the world being what it is, ... women sometimes prefer not to appear too bright." In fact, she was junior chess champion on Hespera.

They are rescued by Sam, who has been led to them by Ellie's pet spider puppy. Sam tells them that both the Captain and Mr. Simes are dead; the Captain died by an overdose of sleeping pills, and Sam broke Simes's neck when he obviously needed killing. The humans must leave the planet now that they realize that the centaurs have established a "symbiotic enslavement" of all creatures there. Sam dies heroically fighting the centaurs; his monument identifies him as a sergeant late of the Imperial Marines. Since Max is the only one with the talents and skills to save them by guiding the ship back to known space, the ship's officers declare him captain. Reluctantly, he accepts. He also, albeit reluctantly, takes their advice that he can't be accepted as captain unless he looks and acts like a captain — unless, in short, he fits into the system *as it is* in order to do what is necessary.

Of course, Max does take the *Asgard* successfully back through the congruency to familiar skies. Just before that success he explains to the first officer that he no longer tries to justify himself but is fully willing to pay whatever debt he must for having come aboard ship with false records. The first officer tells him that "no code is perfect. A man must conform with judgment and common sense, not with blind obedience." He thinks the experience has "matured" Max. A final decision must be made: Should the ship play it safe by creeping to the nearest safe landing or boldly continue to its next scheduled destination, Nova Terra? Told that a captain does not ask passengers and crew to take a vote, Max sets course for Nova Terra, relying, of course, on his memory of the "neat columns of figures." Maximilian Jones proves to be one of Heinlein's competent men. One way of looking at him would say that while he may have learned what it means to be captain, he does not change throughout the novel. His extraordinary talent was there from the beginning. He simply had to have the opportunity to show his potential. If the novel is seen from a slightly different angle, however, Max's attitude changes considerably, creating a context in which he can use his talent for more than private satisfaction.

At the novel's end, Max accepts financial punishment for violating guild rules but is allowed to continue as an astrogator. He can't return to the *Asgard* in a subordinate role, but he is pleased to hear that the new ship he has been assigned to is "taut." Although he remembers that he was treated unfairly, he resolves to correct the system by working within it: "The guilds were set up wrong; the rules ought to give everybody a chance. Some day he'd be senior enough to do a little politicking on that point." In short, he has made peace with his situation. He knows what he loves most about his life, and it isn't Eldreth Coburn, Heinlein's most competent (and complicated) female character to date. Perhaps that is why Heinlein thought the short, three-page final chapter was an appropriate way to end the novel, showing Max back on the farm, again watching the C. S. & E. *Tomahawk* plunge by through the air. A letter from Ellie has announced her marriage to Putzie, though she sends both Mr. Chips's and her own love. Max realizes that life might have been satisfying in a different way if they all stayed on Charity.... But "an astrogator ought not to get married."

Just as *Starman Jones* reminds one of "Misfit," so *The Star Beast* (as "Star Lummox," *F&SF*, May–July 1954) brings to mind *Red Planet* because once again the basis of all the action is the close relationship between a youth and a pet: John Thomas Stuart XI and the eight-legged Lummox. Four generations of Stuart boys have cared for the affectionate extraterrestrial since John Thomas VIII sneaked it aboard the *Trail Blazer* in his jump bag when that first starship touched down briefly on a planet 900 light-years from Earth. By opening the narrative from the point of view of Lummox, Heinlein provides an essential clue that some on first reading will dismiss as so much unnecessary anthropomorphism but that actually validates an outsider's bemused inspection of familiar objects. The novel's humor comes from this jamming together of the ordinary and the alien — and from its demonstration that they eventually can coexist in jittery harmony. Bored, hungry, and lonely on a day that John Thomas spends with his girlfriend Betty Sorenson, Lummox — who gobbles anything from hay and mastiffs to lumber and iron — gives in to the impulse to go through a massive grating in order to eat the roses in a neighbor's garden just beyond the ten-foot concrete wall surrounding the Stuarts' property. The six-ton, triceratops-like Lummox is as frightened as the humans when he is chased by a woman with a broom and shot at by a man with an anti-tank gun — "a relic of the Fourth World War." Fleeing into the village of Westville, Lummox innocently causes havoc as the police try to corner him. (Because of Heinlein's tone and narrative perspective, the sequence becomes a parody of those films from *King Kong* to [choose your Japanese film], in which a crazed monster destroys London, Washington, or Tokyo.) When John Thomas is brought to the rescue, he scolds the docile monster; in his "baby-girl voice," Lummox explains, "I didn't *mean* to," while Johnny wonders how much iron he has eaten, for "since the mishap of the digested Buick," Lummox's metal-induced growth spurt had increased his size more than he had grown "in the preceding generation."

The Westville Chief of Safety — representing the mob of citizens who "don't hold with animals talking" — informs Johnny that he and Lummox are under arrest. Meanwhile, at Federation Capital, His Excellency the Right Honorable Henry Gladstone Kiku, M.A. (Oxon) Litt.D. *honora causa* (Capetown), O.B.E., Permanent Under Secretary of Spatial Affairs, learns of the incident because the extraterrestrial cannot be classified and, consequently, his staff has no precedent to guide any action in this specific case. Kiku sends Sergei Greenberg to represent DepSpace by presiding at the court hearing that is enlivened by Betty, whom Franklin calls "cool, audacious, and supremely competent" (*RAH* 85). Although she has no legal training, Betty insists that she will defend Johnny and Lummox because everyone else — including Johnny's mother — is prejudiced against Lummox and wants him destroyed. Because she is part owner of Lummox, Greenberg allows her to sit inside the rail; she is momentarily satisfied, "just as long as I can have my say." Betty's criticism contributes to the satire of the society of Westville and also to Heinlein's continuing critique of the American legal system.

At stake is Lummox's life. The owner of the roses wants him destroyed, as does the state executive secretary of the Keep Earth Human League. The spokesman for one of the insurance companies "expected to levy against the beast itself; he will bring a good price in the proper market." Trying to find a reasonable and humane solution, Greenberg several times expresses his belief that such a unique specimen should not be destroyed. Initially he suggests that DepSpace withdraw from the case because, despite Lummox's ability to speak, his other limitations — perhaps especially the absence of hands with which to manipulate things — would keep his breed "from rising to a level where we could accept it as civilized." Thus Lummox would be classified as an animal. Yet in his verdict, after dismissing criminal charges because no intent can be found, Greenberg asserts that this court cannot make a final decision whether Lummox is an animal or "a sentient being within the meaning of the Customs of Civilizations." While the Court starts proceedings on its own motion, local authorities must be responsible for both public safety and that of Lummox. Unfortunately, while this is going on in the courtroom, in the steel pen outside where Lummox has supposedly been confined during the hearing, he decides that it is time to find John Thomas and go home. His superhuman hearing also lets him hear voices being "mean" to Johnny, so he chews his way through the pen and breaks into the courtroom. Because Greenberg told John Thomas that if "that beast gets loose again" it will go hard with him, he has no alternative but to order Lummox's destruction. Back at Federation Capital, Greenberg and Kiku debate this decision intermittently while coping with more pressing concerns, and the two eventually decide that Lummox should not be destroyed until "a complete scientific analysis of this creature has been made" — knowing that this is a task xenobiologists would never complete. However, this new message never arrives in Westville, and Lummox's fate is left in the hands of the short-sighted, bumbling local authorities such as the nervous chief of police who already has attempted unsuccessfully to drown Lummox in the city reservoir.

Johnny and Lummox (and Betty) can't depend on protection from *any* level of official authority. The hostility between mother and son, present in *Starman Jones*, is even more obvious in *The Star Beast*. Having already supported those who would destroy Lummox, Mrs. Stuart arranges an appointment between John Thomas and a representative of the Exotic Life Laboratory of the Museum of Natural History, which wants to purchase Lummox. Johnny twice refuses, but when the agent agrees to pay $20,000 net, Mrs. Stuart accepts the offer. She even refuses to let Johnny think of accepting a job with the Museum so that he can be near his friend; he ends up signing a bill of sale, though he protests he will take no money. (To be fair, one should note that both fathers have told their sons to take care of their mothers, and both women are left without financial security; still, Johnny's mother spends money only selfishly when she has a chance later in the novel.) The agent leaves mother and son to settle their differences. She tells him that Lummox's days at home were numbered anyway. She had always planned that on the day he went to college — she insists on this — the house would somehow cease to be a zoo. Morose, John Thomas talks briefly with Lummox and retreats to his attic hideaway, where he rereads the notebooks of his great-grandfather. He is jolted into action when Betty calls him to inform him that the Chief has received authorization to kill Lummox, then breaks the connection when he tells her about the Museum deal. So John Thomas runs away from home with Lummox, into the wilderness leading up to the Continental Divide. Betty soon joins him as the police search for them and while Lummox sprouts a pair of workable arms. In a sense, Heinlein seems to have painted himself into a corner, trapped into a series of narrow escapes on the trail. But the pursuit and eventual capture of Johnny and Lummox occur well before the novel concludes. The "action" may be over, but the real story is just getting going.

Alexei Panshin suggests that the novel is "about a diplomatic incident, not about unusual animals from outer space" (*HD* 69), while Williamson declares that the "actual protagonists are not young John Thomas Stuart and his girl, Betty Sorenson, but rather Mr. Kiku ... and Lummox" ("Youth" 25). Williamson goes on to suggest that "this wildly delightful comedy [has] grown from Heinlein's continued concern with the able individual in conflict with incompetent pretenders." All of these judgments note the shift in emphasis occurring halfway through the novel, but all make their points by distorting what happens in the entire narrative. Certainly Henry Gladstone Kiku and his negotiations at DepSpace dominate center stage in the latter half of the novel, just as John Thomas and Lummox did earlier. However, Heinlein frequently moves back and forth between those realms since the initial chapters, inviting readers to make a connection — after all, if Johnny and Lummox aren't related to Mr. Kiku's much larger concerns, why are those parts of the story printed next to each other? When the connection *is* discovered, it reveals the huge importance of an apparently insignificant boy and his pet animal as well as validating Mr. Kiku's larger perspective. The sometimes broad physical comedy of the novel's earlier portion is replaced by a sharper satire. At the same time, the issues involved become more serious as the threats change, from a bombastic small-town police chief trying incompetently to kill the invulnerable Lummox, to a warship full of bombastic aliens threatening to destroy Earth.

Before John Thomas's flight, even as Greenberg and Mr. Kiku believe they have cancelled the order to destroy Lummox, they learn that a warship crewed by the Hroshii, a previously unknown alien race, is circling the Earth. Through a go-between, Dr. Ftaeml, a Rargyllian who describes his own people as the "gossips" of the universe, these new aliens inform DepSpace that the Hroshii have come to rescue "one of their own," demanding that *she* be surrendered. Dr. Ftaeml obviously stands in awe of the Hroshii and intimates that, although they are not at all warlike, their one ship could destroy Earth and that they plan a "display of force to convince" authorities that their Hroshia must be given up. Quickly, Mr. Kiku determines that the Hroshia is indeed Lummox. Since John Thomas and his pet are in custody by then, it should be simple to resolve the dispute. The confrontation between humans and Hroshii occurs when Lummox refuses to leave Earth without *her* pet, for "she has been raising 'John Thomases' for a long time"; if her commander does not "recover her pet at once," she will "remain here and continue raising 'John Thomases.'" The alien commander issues an ultimatum demanding that John Thomas be surrendered immediately; determined to defend the individual's rights Mr. Kiku rejects the ultimatum "with contempt."

At this point, Mr. Kiku indeed is shoved to the center of the stage — unwillingly, since he prefers to work behind the scenes. His ensuing diplomacy remains one of the high points of Heinlein's satire, as he manipulates the involved parties. Readers can appreciate Mr. Kiku's shrewdness versus the oblivious boorishness of those he nudges in the proper direction. Moreover, he is justified in manipulating others because serious issues need to be settled despite the reluctance of small, selfish people. Interestingly, Heinlein gives initial, lengthy attention to the confrontation between the Under Secretary and his official superior, the vacuous political appointee Space Secretary MacClure, who makes a dangerous fool of himself. After he has received a full account of the crisis, MacClure favors "a simple emergency police action"; even after further discussion he is "not sure but what that attack is still the thing to do." By contrast, Mr. Kiku stands alone among Heinlein's governmental authorities largely because he tells Dr. Ftaeml, "I do not like weapons, Doctor; they are the last resort of faulty diplomacy." One can hear Heinlein making Mr. Kiku's reply to MacClure: "We should bargain ... but bargain as men." When MacClure leaks information to the papers — the headlines scream, "ALIEN INVADERS THREATEN WAR!!!"— Mr. Kiku and a newly introduced press associate force the Secretary's resignation as Mr. Kiku reflects how fortunate it is that the Hroshii do not read Terran newspapers. Then, in perhaps the novel's angriest sequence, Mr. Kiku faces down Johnny's mother, reminding her both that she has "no moral right to keep him an infant" and that the courts "have long taken a dim view of the arbitrary use of parental authority."

The ship from the planet Hroshii has landed at the spaceport near Federation Capital and is surrounded first by barricades and police and then troops. (How many sf films does that scene conjure up?) Mr. Kiku arranges for a conference at the Spatial Affairs building in order to sign a treaty and open full diplomatic relations. The tough-minded Mr. Kiku — everyone seems to describe him that way — sticks to that agenda, while at every point the Hroshii commander simply insists that John Thomas be produced and turned over. When Mr. Kiku demands that they understand Johnny will go as a "free being, not a slave, not a pet," the Hroshii march out of the meeting. (Given the tensions of the 1950s one cannot completely escape the inference that Heinlein wrote this sequence with petulant Cold War conferences in mind. Significantly, on several occasions Secretary MacClure speaks of the "Hoorussians.")

Besides acting out contemporary international tensions, however, this section of the novel — and Mr. Kiku's behavior generally — demonstrates Heinlein's continuing concerns with responsible versus irresponsible authority, self-restrained versus selfish liberty. While understanding Franklin's reaction to Mr. Kiku's "authoritarian, anti-democratic" speech in which he declares that the government of the Federation is "jury-rigged" and not "democratic," one must fit it with Kiku's many other remarks about the bureaucracy becoming paternalistic. Perhaps one gains more insight into both Heinlein and Kiku by emphasizing that portion which echoes the speech in which a similar image is used: "We find ourselves oftener like pilots of a ship in a life-and-death emergency. Is it the pilot's duty to hold powwows with passengers? Or is it his job to use his skill and experience to try to bring them home safely?" This image of the pilot occurs just after Mr. Kiku has declared that "I conceive it to be our duty to hold this society together while it adjusts to a strange and terrifying world." The word "duty" is crucial, for it sets Kiku apart from most of the officials Heinlein portrays within established governments. Usually an absentee ruler — often a corporation — ruling through a corrupt bureaucracy incites a revolution. *The Star Beast* marks a notable exception to this pattern, for Mr. Kiku is a shrewd, highly competent idealist within the establishment who must not only struggle against outsiders but must overcome incompetents within the government. This technique breeds satire instead of melodrama. When the protagonists are among the rebels, Heinlein recreates the frontier/colonial experience, often relying on the town meeting to allow the speakers to voice his themes (though the speaker on those occasions is seldom a strong woman). Within the juveniles *The Star Beast* provides a notable exception to that predominant pattern of bumbling, remote administration that must be overthrown because it has become too unwieldy. Indeed, as part of the satire, Mr. Kiku reminds MacClure that the government which they represent involves not just the Earth but all the sovereignties of the Federation. Although he is a member of

Heinlein's elite, he speaks in a manner befitting a civil servant and an officer of that vast government.

Heinlein does appreciate the virtues of efficient, humane government, though he questions the possibility that government at any level can remain both efficient and humane. As Mr. Kiku tries to explain to Johnny's mother, "the commonest weakness of our race is our ability to rationalize our most selfish purposes.... You have no right to force him into your mold." When she protests that she does have that right because she's Johnny's mother, he attempts one last time to make her see: "Is 'parent' the same thing as 'owner'? No matter, we are poles apart; you are trying to thwart him, I am helping him to do what he wants to do." This is the best any kind of government can do, and that is why Mr. Kiku is an exception to Heinlein's typical bureaucrats. By and large, as *The Star Beast* reiterates, responsible freedom cannot be passed down by a superior authority. It must be seized. Johnny demonstrates that he is ready to make his own decisions when he flees with Lummox. Even if that isn't an especially well-planned or eventually successful action, at least he tries to do something, and Betty respects his instincts even though she adds that he has "less brains than a door knob." Betty herself, in a passage that outraged some contemporary reviewers recommending wholesome library books for young people, explains how she divorced her parents because they were unfit to guide her, then implies that Johnny should consider doing the same: "So be yourself, Knothead, and have the courage to make your own mess of your life. Don't imitate somebody else's mess."

Superior to run-of-the-mill administrators as Mr. Kiku is, Heinlein uses three things to keep him from being obnoxiously perfect. For one thing, he is not omnipotent, as illustrated by the fact that a new clerk at DepSpace sends the message intended to spare Lummox's life not to Westville but to Pluto. Secondly, even Mr. Kiku has to struggle with his unthinking xenophobic revulsion against the Medusa-like appearance of Mr. Ftaeml; he succeeds, but he obviously is not as open-minded as he ideally should be for his job. And finally, the master manipulator can be out-manipulated — as will be seen in his final conference with Betty.

Obviously, events in the novel work out well because of Mr. Kiku's interference. The best that can be said for government is that it permits the intervention of someone who sees more than most of the people around him but who also recognizes his limitations. Mr. Kiku tells Johnnie's mother that the "potential' of the relationship between humans and Hroshii lies in the friendship of her son and Lummox, and however he may manipulate the persons involved, the success of his venture lies outside his own hands. After the commandant leads the Hroshii from the conference, the situation at the spaceport is "an armed truce, tense on both sides" until John Thomas introduces Mr. Kiku to Lummox so that through the go-between he may ask the Hroshia if her commander has reported the outcome of the conference to her. Through Dr. Ftaeml, the reader learns that, outraged, Lummox scolds her commander and declares that "so long as the Galaxy shall last the friends of Johnnie are her friends." The commander grovels before her. After that, only the final arrangements are left to be made. Crucial to the conclusion — and to the benign satire — is the meeting between Mr. Kiku and Betty, for she is the only one who can stand toe-to-toe with him. He is happy to hear that she has intended to marry John Thomas, though she hasn't proposed to him yet; that means there will be more John Thomases for Lummox to raise. However, when he would dismiss her, she insists that since John Thomas is indispensable his importance should be recognized. She wants her almost-fiancé named as ambassador to the Hroshii. She settles for a "nominal" rank but equal pay and promises get everything arranged with

John Thomas within twenty minutes. Having been thoroughly out-negotiated, Mr. Kiku asks, "wonderingly," why *she* did not ask to be ambassador. The narrative ends as "Her Imperial Highness, the Infanta of that Race, 213th of her line," aka Lummox, contentedly takes her two pets aboard her imperial yacht. The broad humor encloses the ultimately good-natured satire in a closely knit narrative which may well be Heinlein's most successfully sustained novel.

Both Panshin and Williamson make much of *The Star Beast* being serialized in the prestigious *The Magazine of Fantasy and Science Fiction*. Panshin mentions that it was published both as "an adult novel" and then "as a juvenile novel marketed in a juvenile package" (*HID* 68); Williamson notes its appearance in "the most literate of the category magazines ("Youth" 25). This may be seen as a mark of Heinlein's progress as a novelist. His first juvenile novel rather timidly clung to the model of boys' series fiction, but only a few books later he was writing novels that stretched and elevated the standards of young adult fiction. At the same time, for at least two generations critics in general have declared that a large part of any science fiction magazine audience was made up of teenage males. In a letter to Blassingame dated 8 October 1954, in which Heinlein says that "I am finding the nonsense connected with juveniles increasingly irksome" (*GG* 69), he concludes by stating that even though he is pleased by the warm response to the Scribner's books, he is tempted "to drop them and concentrate on adult novels, where I can say what I think and treat any subject I please without being harassed by captious chaperones" (*GG* 72–73). One may infer that what began as just another boy's series book ended up as a novel aimed at a much more sophisticated audience. If *The Star Beast* started as broad comedy, it turned toward potentially ugly melodrama with a confrontation between humans and the alien Hroshii. One recalls the letter to John W. Campbell concerning "Goldfish Bowl," in which Heinlein wrote of "alien intelligences so superior to us and so indifferent to us as to be almost unaware of us" (*GG* 16). In the novel, however, Heinlein maintained a light touch.

Two elements of the novel deserve at least passing attention. For one, as critics have noted, when the Secretary General makes a brief appearance at the conference it actually is a double playing his part; this anticipates the role of the protagonist of *Double Star* (1956), Heinlein's next novel written for an adult audience. Another thing worth noting, considering Heinlein's struggles with Scribner's' editor Alice Dalgliesh's tendency to find hints of violence or sex everywhere is Heinlein's choice of the name "John Thomas"—British slang for "penis"—for *The Star Beast*'s protagonist. If Ms. Dalgliesh was disturbed by the ambiguous sexuality of the Martians in *Red Planet*, one can only imagine her reaction if she had noticed how amused the characters become at the thought of the female Lummox happily spending generations "raising John Thomases." It is difficult to imagine that this element of the novel was included accidentally. One may suspect that the contentious issue of children divorcing their parents was included at least partially as a decoy, to draw Ms. Dalgliesh's attention away from "John Thomas"; one also may note that Heinlein had been severely provoked by repeated demands to remove accidental transgressions, novel after novel.

Throughout the writing of his next juvenile — working title "Schoolhouse in the Sky"— Heinlein remained upset about the bickering that had risen with *The Star Beast* concerning children having the right to divorce their parents. When he sent the finished manuscript of *Tunnel in the Sky* (1955) to Ms. Dalgliesh, he told Blassingame that "It is not exactly a juvenile although I've kept it cleaned up so that it can pass as a juvenile" (*GG* 74). It is a study in human survival. In particular, it is an examination of the mixture of romanticism and realism required for individuals to survive as *human* beings. It also studies the varieties of authority that human beings might develop for themselves if they *didn't* have a system ready-made and waiting to be imposed on them. The novel daringly extends the themes in Heinlein's most recent juvenile novels — though in doing so it strays into some of the uncertain territory of his other fiction.

For an overpopulated Earth sometime after World War III, during which "hydrogen, germ, and nerve gas horrors ... were not truly political" but rather a matter "of beggars fighting over a crust of bread," the Ramsbotham Gates provide the only relief from the unrelenting problem of overpopulation, for the Gates allow instantaneous access to thousands of earthlike planets that may be colonized. These Outland worlds must exist indefinitely on their own because hard-pressed Earth has little to export; indeed, "food and fissionable metals were almost the only permissible imports." Therefore, all people who leave Earth must be self-reliant, and in America that means that anyone who wants a career off Earth must pass a course in Advanced Survival by the time he or she finishes college. Heinlein's protagonist Rod Walker is taking the course while a high school senior. As the novel begins, his class has been notified that their "final examination in Solo Survival" is scheduled for tomorrow. Each student can still back out; the class members who choose to take the test will be sent through a gate to scattered points on an alien world, to survive or not for several days until the gate reappears. Rod's teacher is "Deacon" Matson, one-eyed survivor of several off-world expeditions. In a private conversation, he advises Rod *not* to take the test because he is "way too emotional, too sentimental to be a real survivor type." As he explains,

> this is a very romantic age, so there is no room in it for romantics; it calls for practical men. A hundred years ago you would have made a banker or lawyer or professor and you could have worked out your romanticism by reading fanciful tales and dreaming about what you might have been if you hadn't had the misfortune to be born into a humdrum period. But this happens to be a period when adventure and romance are a part of daily existence. Naturally it takes very practical people to cope with it.

On the way home from school, in what looks at the time like a gratuitous scene, Rod observes two groups of emigrants leaving for the Outlands. A commentator explains that the Australasian Republic's government has use of gate five for forty-eight hours in order to "move in excess of two million people ... predominantly South Chinese" from an encampment in the Australian desert to a previously uncolonized planet. The commentator has explained that the target future for all emigration for the year is "only seventy million." The description of "this mob being herded like brutes into a slaughter-house" by brutal Mongol cops almost justifies Franklin's calling the scene an example of Heinlein's racism (*RAH* 86), though it actually illustrates the cruelty of an authoritarian government — and perhaps also an extreme form of *un*sentimental practicality. The scene is different at another gate. In contrast to the "poverty-stricken band of [Oriental] refugees" a well-equipped Conestoga wagon train sets out for "the premium planet," New Canaan, described as "the rose without thorns"; well-mounted cowboys drive a herd of prime Hereford steers after them. Each immigrant to New Canaan has paid $16,400 to the Terran Corporation for the privilege.

Rod yearns to be like the stalwart captain of the wagon train, but in any event he wants to get out "where things were going on." And so Rod Walker takes the test, stepping through the gate into Africa-like bush country.

Matson had warned his students that the most dangerous animal they will encounter in the wilderness is "the two-legged brute," and Rod soon learns this is true. One of the first things he discovers is the corpse of a fellow student whom someone has murdered for his rifle. After surviving a frightening night in a tree, aware of the half-seen but very audible creatures around him, Rod himself is beginning to practice his skills as a hunter when he is knocked unconscious and wakes up to find that all his equipment — from his rations and antibiotics to his matches and hammock — has been stolen, leaving him only his shorts and a single knife that he had concealed under a bandage.

Rod survives the next few days alone, though he spends part of the time delirious after being clawed by a predator and thus is worried that he may have missed the signal at the end of the test, summoning students to a rescue gate. He makes an ally of a student from another school when he overpowers the individual, who is stalking a buck Rod already has wounded. His new-found companion, giving the name of Jack Daudet, suggests first that they team up and then that they try to locate more people. Jack confirms Rod's fear that there never was a recall at the end of the prescribed test period. Their rescue never happened, and there's no telling when or if it will. While Franklin is the only critic to suggest that Heinlein has created a bourgeois fantasy going back at least to *Robinson Crusoe*, "the individual overcoming a strange natural environment" (*RAH* 86–87), he is one of many who contrast William Golding's *Lord of the Flies* and *Tunnel in the Sky*. Still, to say, as Williamson does, that Golding's British schoolboys revert to savagery while Heinlein's youth — both boys and girls — establish the beginnings of a "vigorous new civilization" ("Youth" 26) seems to oversimplify. Selfish individualism clearly is a dead end, as seen when Jack reports finding Rod's stolen knife on the mangled corpse of the same boy who also had murdered a fellow student to steal his rifle; hunting alone, the thief trusted his weapons too much. To survive and to remain human, Heinlein's young people must find a way to live together and support each other. When Williamson writes that the theme of *Tunnel in the Sky* seems "blurred," he may be reacting to a shift in emphasis from the survival of the individual to the evolution of a newly organized social group. Throughout Heinlein's fiction, tension exists between the rights of the individual and the necessary demands of a sophisticated society; increasingly that issue lies at the heart of his dramatic conflicts.

Once again this novel falls in two parts, and it certainly is much easier to identify with Rod earlier in the story while he is being unfairly denigrated by his teacher and parents, and even later when he is forced to survive on his own without even the basic aids he selected. The tone changes when Rod achieves a bit of security and begins making a life of his own. Without losing reader sympathy, Rod does demonstrate repeatedly that Matson wasn't wrong in labeling him "way too emotional, too sentimental to be a real survivor type." The question is whether he can control his tendency to indulge in romantic fantasies well enough to survive. The first addition to Rod and Jack's group is Jimmy Throxton, a classmate of Rod's who is injured and feverish but not too far gone to notice that "Jack" is really a girl, upsetting Rod's elaborate but foolish reluctance to include females on his team. So long as their smoke signals bring in a few persons who will strengthen the team, Rod remains the unquestioned leader; unconsciously he simply takes charge, as he did when he and Jack teamed up. But the group mushrooms. After an older newcomer challenges him and he is knocked to the ground, Jack and Caroline Mshiyeni — the "big Zulu girl" who was once Rod's schoolmate and whom he chose as his hunting partner once she reappeared — must rescue him by shooting his opponent and covering him and his cronies with a dart gun. In the aftermath of this confrontation, Rod is approached by Grant Cowper, a college student majoring in the theory of colonial administration. He tells Rod that he got into trouble because he did not have proper authority from the group; therefore, elections should be held at once. At the equivalent of a town meeting, for everyone is there, Cowper makes an eloquent though vague speech that panders to the crowd's romantic fantasies of founding a new nation, forming a government, drawing up a constitution, and building a wonderful future for their children. *He* is elected leader by an overwhelming margin.

Rod is shoved to the side, baffled, during Heinlein's satire of direct democracy. Cowper begins by appointing committees for every aspect of their lives. Each evening he calls a town meeting which begins with the reports of committees — from artifacts and inventory to conservation of the arts and sciences to city planning, though all the committees produce only "endless talk." Rod is too fair-minded to play politics. In a week, a motion to recall Cowper in favor of Rod fails only because Rod insists any leader needs more time to get things done, then calls for adjournment. The next morning Cowper asks him to be his police chief; although Rod believes Cowper to be "all talk and no results," he eventually does agree to supervise the day-to-day activities of the village. Instead of the expected personal rivalry, the central issue for much of the remainder of the narrative becomes more impersonal. However reluctantly, the man of ideas and the man of action must work together if the colony is to survive, so Rod becomes even less central in directing the village. For example, Rod encouraged building a stone wall between the cliff and the river to protect/defend the group against attack. However, he wasn't able to articulate this long-term policy clearly enough to overcome the popular desire for immediate gratification. Not only is the wall never completed, but Cowper uses much of the stone to build small shelters for the several newly married couples. Also, Rod continues to insist that they should not keep building homes where they first came together, because the site is indefensible. He and a companion go downriver to find a new location, preferably a cave. On the shore of a sea they find "millions on heaping millions of whitened bones" but no animal carcasses; on their way back to camp they discover "terrace on terrace" of empty cliff dwellings that had never been inhabited by humans. Both discoveries exemplify the imaginative, rich promise texture of background for which Heinlein is famous, but both are simply throwaways mentioned only in passing. The entire episode of the search downriver serves only to remove Rod from the camp while changes take place. The camp has become more and more like a permanent settlement by the time he returns. The wall has been replaced by a thornbush barricade, while such improvements as a city hall have been added. Cowper talks of iron and coal, explaining to Rod that "we have taken root." In view of the time and effort the colonists have expended, he dismisses Rod's reminder that the camp is exposed and dangerous. That exchange simply underscores the reader's certainty that disaster will strike. It comes in the form of a seemingly berserk migration of animals. In particular, the camp is almost overwhelmed by swarms of small, vicious carnivores in a bloody fight that lasts all night — during which the community's first baby, a girl, is born. In self-defense, Rod and his companions burn everything flammable in the camp while sending the younger boys and the women up to Rod and Jack's original cave. Hardly has Cowper admitted his error in not having the group go to the caves Rod discovered before he dies during a fight with the small carnivores. Wounded, Rod wakens to find that his companions have unanimously elected him mayor. They assume that the trek to a safer location will take place as soon as possible, but Rod does a turnabout, declaring, "We're *men* ... and men don't *have* to be driven out, not by the likes of those." Besides, Grant Cowper "paid for this land," so Rod chooses to stay "and keep it for him." Thus he becomes the second mayor of Cowpersville.

At this point, the novel's focus changes again. Comparing what happens to Rod to the progress made by the protagonists of earlier Heinlein juveniles, one must agree with Williamson that the final chapters of the novel "seem oddly flat and hollow" ("Youth" 26).

Taking on the responsibilities of a community executive, Rod now must figure out how to subdue romanticism to realism for the sake of others; he is no longer free to go exploring. For example, one wonders whether the bleached bones by the sea are those of animals from previous migrations who, like lemmings, have repeatedly fled to their deaths. That's no longer one of Rod's concerns. However, as he finds himself stuck with the responsibility of more-or-less-gently herding the villagers toward a frontier civilization, he continues to display both the admirable drive and the distressingly superficial thinking that he has shown since the novel's beginning. He has trouble recognizing what's right in front of him, and he also has difficulty putting evidence together when making plans. Readers remember his failure to remember that "Jack" was really Jacqueline. At the same time, besides foolishly opining to his supposedly male companion that females wouldn't be desirable members of their survival group, Rod also argues that the test must have been a fraud and that they actually were dumped somewhere in Africa — an error that Jacqueline easily demonstrates. As the group grows, Rod misjudges one cluster of troublemakers and has to be rescued by Jacqueline and Caroline. After all this cautionary experience, as mayor, he again underestimates one of the earlier bullies, the brother of the man who defeated him earlier; believing that his role demands that he fight the man hand-to-hand, he is badly beaten and regains consciousness to discover that several of his companions have "worked over" the thug for "trying to shove the Mayor around." In short, Rod doesn't fully understand how to use authority. Heinlein's attitude toward the young man is constantly sympathetic but frequently ironic, sometimes almost mocking.

That mixture of attitudes is especially clear in the novel's conclusion. After Rod has established order in the rebuilt village, everyone talks about this world being "home" and about not wanting to return to Earth. At this point, of course, the Gate is reestablished. The energy from a nova had caused a great space-time distortion that disrupted the system, but now everything is back to normal as far as the adults are concerned. This renders everything that has happened in the novel officially irrelevant. Officials from the Terran Corporation and swarms of predatory media personnel make no effort to understand what the young people have accomplished. For them, the colonists are "kids" who must stay out of the way while the grownups tidy up the mess, though they know the young people "are anxious to get out of [their] predicament as quickly as possible." Rod is told not to take himself "too seriously." What people back on Earth can imagine are romantic fantasies of children helplessly reverting to savagery — spiced with some violence and nudity. As one media team briskly informs Rod, a woman writer, "the highest paid emotional writer in the system," will make readers "cry over you and want to comfort you" by picturing them as "cultured boys and girls slipping back to illiteracy, back to the stone age, the veneer slowly slipping away." This distortion angers Rod. He is also is angry to see that Cowperstown can't compete with the luxuries of Earth's society once the gate is open. A few of his closest friends say goodbye to him, but most of the colonists just scurry back to Earth as quickly as possible. He sits alone in his domain until his military-officer sister and her new husband — his former teacher in the seminar — persuade him to return and accept social restrictions long enough to get an official license to leave.

Rod Walker remains the most eccentric of Heinlein's youthful protagonists. Unsure from the first of his ability to pass the final test, he shows himself highly competent in the jungle, searching for a new location downriver and fighting the animals. He is less at ease with people, particularly young women. Leaving aside his obtuseness around "Jack," it is noteworthy that his hands-off attitude toward the "Zulu" girl Caroline is not dictated by the color of her skin; no one in the novel indicates that race is a concern, and some even suggest that Rod might have romantic feelings for her. He never imagines any such thing. (Gifford proposes — and reports Virginia Heinlein's agreement — that Rod himself is African American [*Reader's* 201]. If so, this is not simply another instance of Heinlein unexpectedly revealing a character's racial or ethnic identity to broaden his readers' sympathy; it is a trick intended merely to satisfy the writer's sense of superiority.) Not only does Caroline hunt with him and save his life, but repeatedly she asks when he will have sense enough to call her when he is in trouble. As mayor, however, he rationalizes that he can't play favorites. He never pays "marked attention to any female" and never asks the same girl to dance twice with him at the square dance. Although he likes to dance with Caroline, "he was careful not to spend much social time with her because she was his right arm, his alter ego" since she was his Chief of Government. Franklin remarks that he "embodies the extreme form of the outward-bound man ... as fundamentally celibate as Starman Jones. He is oblivious to the advances made by all girls" (*RAH* 87). While Williamson suggests that Rod "avoids sex relationships in a hardly normal way," he points out that "his behavior may have been only Heinlein's concession to his juvenile editors" ("Youth" 26–27). Certainly Rod's celibacy is not the norm in the novel; Heinlein leaves the interval between (civil) marriage ceremonies and births deliberately vague. There are, it seems, types of human relationships that Rod never even guesses he should try to understand, let alone experience. Fortunately for his self-esteem, the novel doesn't force him to learn. Competent in all his contacts with nature, Rod remains the same throughout the book, another individual who is thrust into challenging situations by circumstances outside his control but must learn to master by controlling himself.

At the novel's conclusion, in one of Heinlein's nicest touches, the reader last sees Captain Walker as a stalwart trail master leading a party of Conestoga wagons through a Gate to the Outlands. He takes full advantage of the event's dramatic possibilities: "He was dressed in fringed buckskin, in imitation of a very old style; he wore a Bill Cody beard and rather long hair." Thus Rod has achieved his earlier, boyish dream. Heinlein does not suggest that Rod has not truly earned his position by surviving the ultra-rigorous test on the other side of the Gate as well as by putting up with the obtuse adults back home. At the same time, Heinlein is too mature not to recognize what a juvenile dream it is. The image of an ideal hero is what kept Rod focused during his ordeals. Yet, the description at the end is a bit disquieting, suggesting that Rod is like Buffalo Bill in being both a hero and a fraud, a man of genuine accomplishments and a showbiz performer. As things have worked out, he is genuinely admirable and heroic; yet it is difficult not to note that he also bears a slight resemblance to Wile E. Coyote.

Working from a single sf premise, the Ramsbotham Gates, *Tunnel in the Sky* confines itself so much to its primitive world that it seems the least science-fictional of Heinlein's juveniles, largely a character study of Rod Walker. In contrast, *Time for the Stars* (1956) combines the idea that telepathy occurs instantaneously, whatever the physical distance involved, with a swarm of huge starships dispersing on another quest for habitable planets. In addition to elegantly worked out sf extrapolation, Heinlein also produces, through the novel's first-person narrator, Thomas Paine Leonardo da Vinci Bartlett, his most effective *Bildungsroman*, for Tom does undergo a change.

Despite a century of space travel during which humanity has spread throughout the solar system, the crucial problem remains overpopulation. In early expository passages, Heinlein echoes *Tunnel in the Sky* when one speaker refers to an Earth "crowded to the point of marginal starvation more than a century ago" with a population only half its present five billion. *Time for the Stars*, however, ignores *Tunnel in the Sky*'s warning that spaceships cannot move colonists to other planets fast enough to compensate for humanity's uncontrollable breeding. In fact, the need to find habitable planets is reinforced when Tom's Uncle Steve suggests that "the root cause of war is always population pressure no matter what other factors enter in." To find more "living room," the Long Range Foundation undertakes Project Lebensraum to send a dozen starships traveling just under the speed of light to various parts of the galaxy. However, communication is handicapped by the limits of physics — as far as currently understood. The ship the Foundation launched toward Proxima Centauri six years ago, the *Avante Garde*, has not been heard from because any radio messages it generated could not reach the Earth before the ship's return. To overcome that difficulty, the Foundation hopes to use telepaths as interstellar communicators. Because research has shown identical twins are potentially the best telepaths, an agency affiliated with the Foundation brings together many sets of twins for testing. Tom and his brother Patrick Henry Michelangelo Bartlett (Pat) are among those selected. One of them will remain on Earth, while the other will go aboard the *Lewis and Clark* to the stars. The boys learn early that the journey may last for a century, but Uncle Steve, who will serve on the *L.C.* ("*Elsie*") as commander of the ship's guard — that is, the landing parties — tells them that "nobody at the top" expects the ships to return; the ships and crews are expendable, but the information they gather is not: "we've *got* to locate those earth-type planets; the human race needs them." The telepaths must "report back. Then it won't matter." It is breezy, self-assertive Pat who goes to Switzerland for the necessary training, but almost at the last moment he is brought home "on a shutter," paralyzed from the waist down after a skiing accident. Tom fulfills their contract by shipping on the *Elsie*, while Pat remains at home, marries the girl they both were attracted to (for a time they date as a trio), and gets rich by using both their wages from the Foundation to finance a business.

The relationship between the twins lies at the heart of Heinlein's psychological study of Tom. From the outset he seems uncertain of himself, always questioning. During the initial testing, for example, before he commits himself he asks what Pat is doing or saying. Although Pat first realizes that they are telepathic, when Tom wonders why they did not read each other's minds earlier, Pat replies, "There's never anything much going on in your mind, so why should I notice?" Again, when Tom suggests they have been hypnotized, Pat acknowledges that he might be hypnotized but Tom could not be: "Nothing there to hypnotize." This sounds like mere teenage sibling ragging, but it is consistent with the way Pat always dominates their activities and plans. He is the one who makes things happen even when the boys work together. When, for example, their uncle warns them to keep quiet and not to "try your usual loathsome tactics" if they want their parents to accept a contract with the Foundation, Tom insists that "We would not take that sort of talk from most people. Anybody else and Pat would have given me the signal and he'd have hit him high while I hit him low." In an offhand manner, Pat constantly takes charge, instructing Tom — treating him, at best, like a kid brother. Early on, Tom accepts that Pat will be the one to travel through space, declaring, "I knew he was determined to go and I knew I would lose"; after the fact, once Pat has left for Switzerland, he complains that he was "swindled." Maude, the girl they both date, emerges from the background as an independent character to scold him, commenting, "You liked having him push you around. You've got a 'will to fail.'" He protests, but readers recognize that she is right: For the most part Tom has expected Pat to succeed, which means that he himself will fail.

Heinlein's challenge here is twofold. First, since Tom is the narrator, he *cannot* notice how willingly he accepts a subordinate, nonresponsible role; the diagnosis has to be presented through the observations of other people (though the fact that Tom can hear and remember their words does suggest that he has not withdrawn from reality altogether). Also, Heinlein must be careful not to exaggerate Tom's "will to fail" to the point that he becomes an unsympathetic whiner. In other words, Tom's problem must be obvious enough for Tom's companions (and readers) to notice, yet it must not disable him so thoroughly that he can't solve it. His personal crisis begins a week after the *Elsie* has begun her flight, when surgeons operate on Pat. Tom remains in telepathic contact, and he reacts violently to the experience, giving "a perfect clinical picture of a patient terminating in surgical shock." His trauma even produces two stigmata on his back matching the incisions of the operation. Vaguely acknowledging resentment and guilt before and after Pat's accident, Tom admits that he remains unhappy after his brother's recovery while Pat gets use of his legs back. At the same time, the loss of a sister ship, the *Vasco da Gama*, to which they have a telepathic connection, apparently contributes to his emotional withdrawal, a reminder that the *Elsie* probably will never return home. Tom feels isolated, miserably hopeless, and confused about what is really bothering him. Uncle Steve notices his gloom, and the next day the ship's psychologist, Dr. Devereaux, chats with him.

Their exchange makes up one of the few scenes in Heinlein's fiction in which psychology is not dismissed or ridiculed. Although Devereaux calls the field "a wonderful racket," his therapy works. He does not use Freudian labels, but he does explain everything in terms of the struggle between Tom's conscious and unconscious mind. Consciously, Tom loved his brother and wanted to be the one selected for the voyage. Unconsciously, he resented being pushed around, and he was pleased that Pat was going to be exiled from the family while *he* could stay safe at home. Tom resists both realizations, but Devereaux points out that Tom has every right to dislike his brother: "He has bossed you and bullied you and grabbed what he wanted." Tom demurs. Devereaux next contends that *neither* twin wanted to go on the voyage. As evidence he introduces medical records showing that the operation found no damage whatsoever to Pat's spinal cord. He agrees that Pat did not fake his paralysis deliberately—that could have been detected—but declares that Pat felt the same struggle between conscious and unconscious desires that is agonizing Tom. He suggests that Tom's main problem is that he wants to go home but can't. So that Tom may effect his own cure, Devereaux recommends that he write a kind of private autobiography "as if you didn't know anything about yourself and had to explain everything." Just as telepathic messages must be put into words and sentences before they can be transmitted, so that fully verbalized and complete thoughts make up what reads like a conversation, in the same way Tom must begin to bring his genuine feelings into the open. It is this therapeutic exercise, continued as a journal, that makes up the novel.

The very existence of the novel—and the fact that Tom can not only report the troubling remarks by Maude, Uncle Steve, and Dr. Devereaux but also share them with readers—shows that Tom has healed himself. As he says, "I found out, after I admitted that I despised and resented Pat, that I no longer did either one. I cured him of bothering me unnecessarily by bothering him unnecessarily." To further show Tom's emergence from the isolation into which he had withdrawn, Heinlein includes a brief, seemingly irrelevant account of Tom's adolescent infatuation with Prudence Mathews, a telepathic shipmate whose twin Patience is back on Earth. It goes well until Tom tries to kiss her; when he asks what is wrong, Pru tells him, "My sister is angry.... My sister doesn't like you." Much later, when he tells a friend what happened, the young man remarks that "her sister is going to ruin her life." So far as Tom is concerned the episode did not anger him, but after that he "enjoyed" the company of all the young women on board. He does not report any realization that his life could have been ruined too if he had remained under Pat's thumb, but neither does he let himself be crushed by this rejection. He just takes things in his stride. Likewise, in a throwaway line, Tom reports frequently playing dominoes with Uncle Steve, but most importantly, after long silence he reestablishes telepathic contact with Sugar Pie McNeil, the Earth-bound great-niece of a telepathist (Uncle Alfred) aboard the *Elsie*. In all, the latter portion of the novel is livelier than the first, as Tom interacts more with the people around him and discovers that he can enjoy it.

Heinlein has been praised as an excellent storyteller and damned as someone who stops the story to lecture his readers on topics ranging from sex and politics to scientific data. Nowhere does he show his narrative skill more effectively than in *Time for the Stars* when he combines his presentation of Tom's psychological conflicts and an account of the concepts of relativity and simultaneity which are so important to various elements in the book from ships traveling faster than light to the differences between ship-time and Earth-time.

Heinlein gives so much attention to Tom's inner conflicts that the external physical actions conventional to an interstellar journey are dealt with only in the final third of the narrative. Once again Heinlein's skill with narrative makes itself apparent, for while he gives as much attention to the reactions of the crews to outside events, he allows Tom to summarize much of what takes place, implying that he is continuing the diary writing he began at the suggestion of Dr. Devereaux. With few exceptions there is no sense of immediacy, but compressing the discoveries made by the searching ship strengthens the illusion of the passage of time, whether it be a matter of months aboard the *Elsie* or a matter of generations on Earth. Due to the time dilation effect as the ships approach the speed of light, events seem to speed up back on Earth. It is startling but believable to get news of developments in Tom's family. By the arrival at the Tau Ceti system (eleven light-years from Earth) Pat and Maude have daughters; by the end of the journey Tom has a great-grandniece.

In the Tau Ceti system, the *Elsie* discovers an earthlike planet, Constance, which provides an idyllic interlude, including stargazing at a familiar sky. Yet Connie, as Tom calls the planet, starts their trouble, for thirty-two crew members die of a plague. In the Beta Hydri system they must land at a frozen world they call Inferno to refuel with liquid ammonia. "'Whistle Stop' [a small sun] wasn't worth a stop," so the *Elsie* undertakes her fourth jump to Beta Ceti, sixty-three light-years from Earth. After Beta Hydri Tom communicates through his great-niece Kathleen; by the jump to Beta Ceti he has begun to communicate with his great-grandniece, Vicky. While four years have passed aboard the ship, seventy-odd years Greenwich have passed on Earth.

Dwarfed by the vast universe and the ceaseless flow of time, the *Elsie* sails on. Knowing that by now in Earth-time Connie must already be settled, they land near an island as big as Madagascar on the watery world Elysia, which seems to be as idyllic as Constance according to all tests. However, Tom introduces his account with the remark, "We are a sorry mess. I don't know what we can do now." In a detailed sequence that captures dramatic urgency Tom watches as great whale-like creatures capsize the three landing boats and drown the crew members and then sees the behemoths destroy the copter that tries to save eight survivors from a hilltop. Williamson refers to "space aliens as mysterious and implacable as the physical universe itself" ("Youth" 27), and one must agree with his assessment that "the whole story is bleak in tone" ("Youth" 28). *Time for the Stars* remains unique among Heinlein's juveniles, if not his entire body of fiction up the mid–1950s, at least, in that it portrays a journey to the stars that ends in disaster. The only story of human-alien contact that it resembles is the early "Goldfish Bowl," but that tale has less impact because in it the aliens, at worst, are indifferent to humanity. In *Time for the Stars*, on the other hand, the *Elsie*'s new captain strongly implies that there inevitably will be further confrontation because he advises that an additional report be made to Earth — "of the hazard encountered today in order that the first colonial party be prepared to defend itself."

The remainder of the novel continues developing highly serious themes. Only four of the original 12 ships remain active, but although the massacre has decimated the *Elsie*'s crew, the new captain, Urqhardt, proposes to set/shape a course for Alpha Phoenicis, the fifth of their originally planned six stops. When members of the crew propose a single jump to Earth, he declares that "we are here on an assigned mission." The only concession that he is willing to make occurs after Tom points out that although they are in touch with Earth, the jump to Alpha Phoenicis will take approximately 30 Greenwich years, and the three communicators left may have no telepartners left. Sugar Pie McNeil is now as old as her great-granduncle, while Vicki at nineteen has no children and will be near 50 when they come out with "no chance of kids before we peak." Urqhardt *does* suggest that "we will consult authorities Earth-side." There is talk of mutiny among a number of the crew members, and the Captain places Tom under arrest in his room because he has talked with several of the agitators. He receives an anonymous note which suggests mutiny to him: "The ugliest word in space." Yet, under the circumstances, wouldn't the surviving crew be justified in disobeying the Captain? Doesn't a more realistic understanding of the situation make them right?

Tom has to make up his mind alone. Franklin asserts that "we get a heavy lecture on the sanctity of authority and the dangers of democracy" (*RAH* 88), summed up in the motto "The captain is right even when he is wrong." This was a remark of Uncle Steve "way back when we [Tom and Pat] were kids." While Franklin may be right in principle, he does miss the anguish with which Tom reaches his decision: "It wasn't nearly enough to be right." Tom is not simply regressing to childish dependency by accepting a superior authority; he realizes that *someone* must be able to make vital decisions, and he assumes that anyone who accepts that responsibility will try to exercise it carefully. Events prove this to be correct. The Captain drops charges against Tom in the morning. Moreover, checking with Earth brings new orders for the *Elsie*. They are to wait at Ceti Beta for a rendezvous with an "*irrelevant ship*," one that can travel faster than light. Their heroic expedition is over. An unimpressive bureaucrat, Mr. Whipple from the irrelevant ship *Sarah*, boards the *Elsie* with the news that Project Lebensraum is finished and that the *Elsie* will be scrapped when she returns home. The new line of ships can do the mission much better. The irrelevant ship *Zero* alone, for example, has located seven Earth-type planets in a month.

Thus, even when Heinlein takes Tom and the survivors of the crew off the hook, so to speak, the conclusion is still bleak. It is not unlike Rod Walker's realization that the community he has helped build was a sham. True, the new ships can ignore the limitations of light speed because research with telepaths like Tom and Pat demonstrated that distance could be irrelevant when approached from a different angle. True also that Tom tries to encourage a glum Captain Urquardt, all of whose training and experience are irrelevant for service on the new ships, by talking about job retraining, and so forth. The fact remains that all their efforts and all the deaths of their shipmates and of the crews on the lost ships turn out to be unnecessary — irrelevant. This is fairly grim stuff for younger readers to absorb.

In view of the difficulties he had previously with Alice Dalgliesh, another factor makes one wonder at the state of Heinlein's mind in the mid–1950s. One characteristic of young Pat is that he remarks about every pretty girl he sees. There is the matter of kissing and not kissing Maude — which can be explained perhaps as showing the rivalry between Tom and Pat. During the brief interlude with Pru, Tom comments on how well chaperoned they are: "But it was always just enough and not too much. Nobody objected to a kiss or two if somebody wanted to check on taste; on the other hand we never had any of the scandals that pop up every now and then in almost any community." That exercise of authority is so obviously reasonable that Tom barely mentions it, never questions it. On the other hand, young-in-ship-time but mature Tom must assert his own will at the novel's conclusion — though rather equivocally as it turns out. When he arrives home Tom has a final confrontation with his aged brother in which he announces that he is his own man; more importantly, after a courtship lasting twenty seconds initiated by Vicky, his nineteen-year-old great-grandniece, she announces that they are going downtown to be married. She promises to go back to Babcock Bay on Constance, if he wishes. Pat is "eyeing" the couple as the novel ends, while Tom says if he is bossed it will be by her. In the novel itself, the only contact between Tom and Vicky is telepathic. Yet it seems clear in retrospect that Heinlein was leaving the juvenile market.

On 8 February 1957, Heinlein delivered a lecture on science fiction as part of a series at University College, the University of Chicago. Later included in the collection *The Science Fiction Novel: Imagination and Social Criticism*, Heinlein's contribution was "Science Fiction: Its Nature, Faults and Virtues," and he used the opportunity to survey the condition and potential of sf — which he would prefer to call "speculative fiction" — just emerging from the disreputable pulps but certainly not considered as respectable as serious mainstream fiction.

In fact, Heinlein regards sf as more valuable than highbrow literature because it applies the scientific method to imagining change in the real world, recognizing that "The future is all that we can change — and thank Heaven we can! — for the present has obvious shortcomings." He disavows the notion that the purpose of sf is to predict specific gadgets and admits that most of it is not well written. Nevertheless, "It is the most important, the most useful, and the most comprehensive fiction being published today. It is the only fictional medium capable of interpreting the changing, head-long rush of modern life. Speculative fiction is the main stream of fiction — not, as most critics assume, the historical novel and the contemporary-scene novel." In fact, looking at the whining little victims who populate what others call "mainstream" fiction, Heinlein asserts that science fiction "is alive when most of our current literature is sick and dying." Young people in particular need to recognize how fast the world is changing around them and to learn how to speculate reasonably about the nature and desirability of those changes. Reading science fiction can help them.

Thus Heinlein justifies his own practice in writing and presciently rejects the approach of New Wave sf that frequently is concerned less with exploring the choices that can lead humanity to escape into outer space than with understanding the hangups that can leave us huddled back on Earth, trapped in our "inner space."

As early as *Heinlein in Dimension*, Alexei Panshin referred to *Citizen of the Galaxy* (1957) as "another of Heinlein's adult juveniles" (*HD* 80). A letter to Blassingame dated 11 December 1956 confirms that Heinlein was moving away from the tone and content of his earliest books for Scribner's by the mid–1950s: "As usual it is an ambivalent story, actually adult in nature but concerning a boy and with no sex in it that even Great Aunt Agatha could object to" (*GG* 78). Serialized in *Astounding* (August–December 1957), the last of his work to appear in Campbell's magazine, *Citizen of the Galaxy* remains one of Heinlein's most highly regarded novels and also one of the most difficult to pigeonhole as either juvenile or adult. Williamson has called it "a sort of epilogue to the whole Scribner's series [which was] an epic story of the expansion of mankind across the planets of our own Sun and the stars beyond" ("Youth" 28). Critics in general have agreed that the novel emphasizes education and growing self-awareness as Thorby searches for an identity that will give him roots in a society somewhere. Because he has been alone, an orphan, as long as he can remember, in moments of depression he suffers "an old, old nightmare": that he is "nothing and nobody." This is true of the grownup character and of the boy; it's hardly an exclusively juvenile concern even if chronologically adult people have learned not to show their anxiety in the matter.

One first sees Thorby—nothing more than a bruised and scrawny animal—on the auction block being sold as a slave in Sargon, capitol of the Nine Worlds. Heinlein's first description of him shows his despair; even in the slave ship "the boy had been someone, a recognized member of a group." Now, unwanted by the crowd, he is just an object, merchandise to be sold. The jest of a nobleman and the compassion of a cripple combine so that he is sold for a pittance to Baslim the Beggar. During the years they remain together not only does Baslim act as Thorby's teacher—from math to the art of begging in the Plaza—but he registers a manumission so that Thorby is officially free. At one point, concerned about Thorby's future as a free man, Baslim voices one of Heinlein's most frequently repeated ideas as he plots to "get the lad to any frontier world, where a sharp brain and willingness to work were all a man needed."

Thorby soon learns that "Pop," as he has been told to call the beggar, is involved in something that necessitates his disappearance on "little business trips." He knows, too, that Pop is interested in learning anything he can involving the slave trade. Thorby sometimes delivers clandestine messages within the city, aiding Baslim's information-gathering activities, and he promises, when Pop is dead, to take a message to a man and to do as the man instructs him. He learns the message by rote in three languages so that he can deliver it to any one of five captains of tramp freighters; he must give it to the first who calls at Sargon's spaceport. Sometime later, Pop puts him under light hypnosis so that he can memorize yet another, more complex message; he will know when to deliver it. The next day when Thorby finds police searching for him and the beggar, he learns that Baslim is dead—probably by his own hand to avoid breaking under torture—and gives the first message to Captain Krausa of the *Sisu*, one of ships of the society of Free Traders.

Captain Krausa accepts the task put on him by Baslim—to deliver Thorby to the commander of any vessel of the Hegemonic Guard—with the assertion that "Debts are always paid." Smuggled aboard the *Sisu*, Thorby gains a place in the patrilocal matriarchy when Krausa adopts him. During his years with the ship's Family, because of his knowledge of mathematics, Thorby is assigned to the starboard fire control computer and becomes in time an expert firecontrolman—a gunner—who destroys a pirate raider seeking to capture the *Sisu*. At the Great Gathering of eight hundred Free Trader ships he learns that Baslim was a hero among the Free Traders because he once saved the Family of the *Hansea*. Because of his heritage and his own talents, Thorby is accepted among the Free Traders. He *is* somebody.

But even as he thinks of marrying, Thorby is uprooted by Krausa, who fulfills his duty to Baslim, despite his personal feelings for the young man, by delivering him to Colonel Brisby, commander of the Hegemony Guard cruiser *Hydra*. Thorby gives Baslim's report, the second memorized message, to the Colonel. It contains important information about the space pirates/slave traders. Thorby learns at once that "Pop" was Colonel Richard Baslim, a legendary and revered agent of the Exotic (X) Corps, who went underground in Sargon in order to have a crack at slavers; he had rescued the *Hansea* Family from slavers at physical cost to himself — an eye and a leg — but he turned those handicaps to his advantage since they made it easier for him to play the part of a maimed beggar. From the first Baslim had guessed that Thorby came from "unmutated Earth ancestry" and for that reason he believed that the boy's identity lay somewhere in the Hegemony, whose center was the mythic Earth.

Although Thorby enlists in the Guard and again wins acceptance there, Brisby carries out Baslim's request to trace the young man's identity and finds that Thorby is in fact Thor Bradley Rudbek, sole heir to one of the richest and most powerful families on Earth. Thorby is again uprooted and sent "home." Heinlein returns to his fascination with legal infighting as shown in his earlier fiction, in that the action on Earth centers on a battle to gain control of the business, ending in a stockholders' meeting in which Thorby is elected chairman of the board.

Although he has found what looks like a secure identity and a place at the top of society, Thorby's work is not finished. Instead, knowing that the Rudbek industrial empire has supplied ships, repairs, and fuel to the slavers, the new Rudbek of Rudbek dedicates himself to helping the Guard in its fight against slavery.

The one recurrent criticism of *Citizen of the Galaxy* is that it is "clearly disunified" (*HD* 82); Williamson, for example, suggests that the "jumps from one setting to another break it almost into a series of novelettes, each ... with a new cluster of characters" ("Youth" 29). Granted that the transitions between settings are abrupt, but compensation lies in Heinlein's rich sketches of the four cultures, particularly that of the Free Traders, perhaps not surpassed in any of his fiction. He accomplishes scene setting by skillful suggestions, with a minimum of specific details. In the initial scene, for example, it is not mere atmosphere or heavy irony to explain that "the slave market lies on the spaceport side of the famous Plaza of Liberty, facing the hill crowned by the still more famous Praesidium of the Sargon" (note the Latin form of (presidio"). References to "Sargon Augustus of imperial memory," the "larger circus" that he decreed and that was interrupted by "the Second Cetan War," and to the labyrinth in which Baslim lives beneath the ruined amphitheater — all these give the reader clues that suggest a city and a culture like that of ancient Rome. When Heinlein adds the name "Jubbulpore, capital of Jubbul and of the Nine Worlds" and mentions the "three thousand licensed beggars," the scene shifts from Rome to the Near East and perhaps India itself— anyplace where power and decadence lie side by side, as in the very first pairing of the Praesidium and the slave market. To emphasize the ironic tension, the Plaza of Liberty is mentioned more frequently than any other site.

In the case of the Free Traders, Heinlein masterfully controls the narrative by presenting the details that an unsophisticated, apparently insignificant newcomer would be exposed to. No overall description of the spaceship is necessary, but only of such rituals as the initiation/adoption of Thorby into the Family. The declaration that "debts must be paid," like some medieval oath, as well as knowledge that each ship speaks its own language from ancient Earth (the family on *Sisu* speaks Finnish) identify them as descendants of Earth and set them apart as much as any hereditary guild. Other customs have been developed because of their present situation. They are an elite people, for although they can muster some eight hundred ships, the Free Traders, spread through a quarter of the galaxy, number only one hundred thousand. That their daughters must be exchanged with women from other ships to preserve exogamous marriage does not surprise but does emphasize their concern for inbreeding and mutation as well as their separation from all others. To preserve themselves, each ship has become a rigid caste system with senior officers serving for life. In terms of their societal organization, perhaps the nicest touch sets up the Captain's mother as Chief Officer, a position that passes on to his wife.

The Hegemony Guard exudes a far more romantic aura than does even the Space Patrol of *Space Cadet*. The Guard might seem the most familiar milieu for an experienced sf reader. Still, Heinlein uses all his skill to imagine "ordinary" routine that will make Thorby's experiences feel convincing and fresh. This organization's tradition of steadfast duty dominates the action. After Thorby delivers Baslim's coded message and enlists — because of his experience aboard the *Sisu*, he finds his place as an acting ordnanceman 3/c (cybernetics) — Colonel Brisby explains to him that the Guard has prevented major wars for two centuries; its crucial real task is "the impossible job of maintaining order on the frontier." Between Colonel Brisby's manner and Jubbulpore's atmosphere, the image of the British Bengal Lancers of the nineteenth century comes to mind more strongly than in any other of Heinlein's treatment of the military. This impression is intensified in these two chapters by the ever-present memory of Colonel Richard Baslim — the "most brilliant mind that [Brisby's Executive Officer] ever met." Brisby explicitly suggests that Baslim provides the Guard with an "example"; when "something unpleasant" turns up, "the Baslim conditioned-reflex will hit you." Details of Baslim's acts are omitted to enhance his aura as a legendary hero, while Thorby plays the initiate.

Earth's society combines something of the decadence, hard-headed commercialism, and reverence with tradition that Thorby has seen in the other cultures, with some flourishes of its own. Despite Thorby's success as Baslim's courier and then as "the most brilliant tracker" the *Sisu* has ever had, his role as observer makes itself most apparent once he returns to Terra. This is not to say that he is passive. His desire to perform his duties and his suspicions of the men who run the Rudbeck industrial empire in the absence of his parents precipitate the legal battle for control of the corporation. But essentially he must trust the experts as Heinlein once again does battle with evil, selfish corporate managers. Thorby doesn't understand this new milieu as well as his cousin Leda does, nor does he have the legal expertise of his attorney James J. Garech. All this goes without saying, especially after Thorby has been depicted as a fish out of water in three other distinct cultures earlier in the book. The tapestry of the novel's four cultures thus provides Heinlein with one of his most colorful backgrounds for the action. Thorby's experience within the different cultures also provides raw data as Heinlein probes his central theme. In addition to Thorby's individual quest for identity, *Citizen of the Galaxy* should be read as four complementary studies of the nature and elusiveness of freedom.

In Jubbulpore, at the "backbone of the slave trade," the auction of Thorby — the opening scene in the narrative — demonstrates the horror of the trade; Baslim's registering the manumission (offstage) provides the symbolic act of freeing the slave. However, Thorby must escape the Nine Worlds, then be nudged from one role blending freedom and subordination to the next until he winds up extremely powerful but also extremely conscious of being bound by obligations. It is repeatedly demonstrated for Thorby — and readers — that personal "choice" describes how one responds to external limitations, not the absence of limitations. Aboard the ship of the Free Traders, Dr. Mader, an anthropologist from Earth whose studies resemble Margaret Meade's, tells Thorby that if the ship were not a matriarchy and *men* were in control, "girl-swapping [among the ships] would be slavery; as it is, it's a girl's big chance." As Dr. Mader prepares to leave the *Sisu*, she reminds Thorby that the People, physically free to roam the stars as no culture ever has been, have paid for that collective freedom by surrendering individual freedom; they have codified their behavior; they "live by rules more stringent than any prison." The People are the slaves of their ship, their sovereign state. Because "Freedom is a hard habit to break," Dr. Mader advises Thorby that if he can't stand this new variety of slavery he should desert "at a planet that is democratic, and free and human."

True as her observations are, she touches on a paradox that makes itself most apparent in the Hegemony Guard. Earlier Heinlein himself had suggested, in authorial intrusion, that "With rank goeth privileges — so it ever shall be. But also with it go responsibility and obligation." When Thorby enlists in the Guard as a "raw recruit," Heinlein further comments that "he was no more handicapped than any recruit in a military outfit having proud esprit de corps." In talking to Thorby, Colonel Brisby speaks of slavery as "the most vicious habit human beings fall into and the hardest to break." With humanity's spread through the galaxy getting ever wider, no one can adequately police inhabited space, so it is a job "that can never be finished." While Heinlein cannot bring himself to say so, its sense of responsibility and obligation to try to keep order on the frontier bind the Guard as rigidly, though perhaps on a more idealistic level, as the People's family obligations.

To Colonel Baslim, fighting the slave trade was a passion that drove his life. Back on Earth — away from the frontier, finally — Thorby observes how people rationalize their actions in terms of slavery, as when Rudbeck corporate executive Weemsby, who has told Thorby to call him "Uncle Jack," says that "Nobody owns a business, the business owns him. You're a slave to it." It is grotesque for a man who has never experienced slavery himself to excuse his business dealings as a helpless response to economic pressures; Uncle Jack can justify *anything* his company does as long as it makes a profit, even supplying the slave traders' spaceships — and even, quite possibly, arranging the raiders' attack that killed Thorby's obstructive parents, thus leaving the child a slave and Uncle Jack in charge of the business. Feeling that way, he sees Thorby's squeamishness as an unjustifiable interruption in a smoothly functioning system.

Even more contemptible than Uncle Jack, however, are people who choose not to admit their ignorance about slavery, let alone recognize their participation in tolerating it. Thorby's dreamily authoritarian grandfather, long a teacher of history, declares that no slavery exists in the Sargony, at least "not chattel slavery." Instead, what Thorby imagined was slavery is actually serfdom that "derives from the ancient Hindo gild [sic] or 'caste' system — a stabilized order with mutual obligations, up and down." When Thorby protests that he was *sold*, his grandmother tells him not to contradict his grandfather. As further proof of their fanatical denial of reality, the grandparents believe in pacifism: "Nothing is ever gained by violence." If attacked, they believe, "then you surrender; that defeats his [the attacker's] purpose ... as the immortal Gandhi proved." Or so the theory goes. Thorby, who *has* been attacked, wouldn't wait for the attacker's moral defeat; he would burn a raider ship before waiting to see if it intended to "take slaves" or not. In fact, he did. One who lives in abstractions rather than the active scene cannot share Thorby's point of view based on experience in the real brutal world; neither person can convince the other.

All these examples of slavery and freedom are presented vividly, and each speaker justifies his or her behavior as convincingly as possible (though Thorby's grandfather is exceptionally naïve and rigid even for a college professor). But Thorby *must* fight slavery. Thorby tells Leda of the scars on his back and his dreams of Uncle Jack and Judge Bruder whipping him. He knows how cruel slavers can be and is haunted by his experience. The fact that Heinlein never uses Thorby's legal, "real" name after Colonel Brisby discovers it suggests that his identity is not so much his family inheritance as it is the accumulation of his personal experience. This is true of everyone. Thorby's grandfather, Uncle Jack, Colonel Brisby, Captain Krausa, even Pop — all rationalize their behaviors as they act out their compulsions. Thorby, however, has had enough experience with different styles of rationalizations to be aware of what he is doing as he commits his life to fighting slavery. Genuine slaves act unwillingly and without understanding of their actions' purpose. Others may claim more understanding but still picture themselves as "slaves" because they want to excuse their actions' consequences. Still others may deny knowledge that any variety of slavery exists because they want to deny responsibility for taking action. But some people who are lucky enough to be "free" have enough understanding of their position to act responsibly. The fact that the characters have been conditioned by their environments and their individual experience does not mean that they have no choice of how to act. At the end of the novel, Thorby remembers what Colonel Brisby once said about Pop's choice: "It means being so devoted to freedom that you are willing to give up your own ... be a beggar ... or a slave ... or die — that freedom may live."

This idea of rational, self-sacrificial bondage is a fairly complicated idea, built like so many important human realizations are out of paradoxes and finely sliced shades of meaning. But, despite Franklin's reservations about Heinlein's readiness to sacrifice individual freedom to larger authority, it is not nonsense.

Part of the rational aspect of Thorby's dedication is his realization of practical limits. Even before the case is settled, Thorby wants to join the Exotic Corps although the leader, Wing Marshal Smith, explains that the difference between what "the Guard *could* do and is *allowed* to do is very frustrating." Thorby won't see slavery abolished in his lifetime; it could happen, perhaps in two centuries — by which time it will break out in planets not yet discovered. However, he ends up dealing with the slave trade by looking for honest men to appoint as planetary managers for the family company so that they may "be taught how the slave trade operated and what to look for." Even though he might never have the opportunity to join Pop's Corps, he realizes that what he is doing must be continued for "a person can't run out on responsibility.... A captain can't, a chief officer can't." Thorby will try to do what he has to, although he is not innocently confident of his course's price. He has become what the novel's title promises: a *citizen* of the galaxy.

Although Heinlein identifies very much with Thorby's struggle and approves of his final realization, he maintains enough distance to remind readers that this is still a young man, still naïve when it comes to personal relationships. Authorial asides and the timely commentary of Dr. Mader show how little Thorby understands of what is happening around him; the degree to which he does come to understand shows his superior abilities and willingness to learn. This is especially true of Thorby's initial insensitivity to the fact that a female shipmate aboard the *Sisu* finds him attractive. This union is forbidden by the Family's marriage customs, but Thorby does realize that he has become marriage-bait by the time he is passed on to the Guard. At the end of the book, however, there is no hint of romance with Leda even though he thinks in passing how nice it is of her to help him so much and how much fun it is to spend time with her. She is just a really great pal. For once, the juvenile fiction ban on sex actually helps Heinlein's point.

Heinlein began his juvenile novels with an experimental rocket journey to the Moon, described the exploration and colonization of the solar system along with its attendant social tensions, and went on to consider different versions of humanity's inevitable spread to other solar systems. If *Citizen of the Galaxy* provides the epilogue to an epic of humanity's conquest of space, *Have Space Suit—Will Travel* (1958), serialized in *F&SF* (August–October 1958), recalls the earliest of Heinlein's juveniles for Scribner's. In an effort to justify an outrageously unlikely space opera coincidence—a young man, wearing a working, fully stocked space suit while out for a walk at night on Earth, innocently radios a landing signal to a spaceship and finds himself in the middle of conflict between alien space pirates and alien space cops—Heinlein presents the novel's protagonist Kip as a Young Engineer par excellence. His behavior is at once immediately silly but ultimately admirable. In almost every juvenile, Heinlein promoted a high school education emphasizing science and math (with a special plug for the slide rule), but *Have Space Suit—Will Travel* opens with his most extended tirade against contemporary public education. Kip already has decided that he wants to go to the Moon; after his father convinces him how worthless his school is, the boy starts using his brain and developing practical technical ability. With that motivation and skill-level established, the first sequence of action concerns Kip's entering a contest to win a trip to the Moon. His soap-advertisement slogan is a winner (perhaps thanks in part to his high school "applied English" course that focused on slogan writing), but he winds up with one of the consolation prizes, a surplus/obsolete space suit. Kip understands that the suit is useless and that he should sell it to help pay for his college tuition, but he is fascinated by the fact that the suit has been in space and by the technical challenges it provides. It is believable, then, that he devotes time and money to making it fully operable.

After Kip has refurbished the suit and is out for a walk one night while pretending he is on Venus and must stay in touch with base, he sends out a radio message that is answered by a spaceship that lands almost on top of him. In the confusion, a second spaceship lands near him, and Kip is zapped unconscious. He awakens to find himself a prisoner along with Peewee Reisfeld, an eleven-year-old self-announced genius who always carries a rag doll, Madame Pompadour. Peewee had piloted the spaceship Kip had contacted. Now they are aboard a flying saucer going back to the lunar base from which she had tried to escape. Their captor, Wormface, is the most unpleasant alien in Heinlein's juveniles, a cilla-sprouting alien who detests mere humans. When he interrogates Kip, he asks the Terran about the size of Earth's population as well as the tonnage of protein produced each year. Peewee thinks that he eats meat, and his two human stooges confirm, just before they displease him and disappear permanently, that the aliens enjoy human flesh. A horde of wormfaced monsters is preparing to invade Earth. Heinlein's loathing of the aliens recalls *The Puppet Masters* (1951), while the name "Wormface" anticipates his use of Black Hats in *The Number of the Beast* (1980). Opposing Wormface and his fellows is the so-called Mother Thing, a benevolent creature from Vega, who has allied herself with Peewee. A kind of galactic cop, she keeps tabs on the aliens. If Wormface personifies evil, then the Mother Thing epitomizes goodness. Her "talent," the "talent" of all her people the Vegans, is to understand someone else: "Call it empathy." Franklin calls her "the ultimate embodiment of maternal protection" (*RAH* 92), while Panshin likens her to "the ultimate security blanket" (*HD* 85). Kip says of her, "Around her you felt happy and safe and warm.... We had her with us so everything was going to be all right."

After justifying the outrageously unlikely coincidences that begin the novel, Heinlein shows his awareness of the clichés of heroic fiction, not taking them altogether seriously but not laughing at them either. On the Moon Kip tells himself, "But I had to take care of [Peewee] ... or die trying"; again, after trying to encourage her, he reflects, "This was propaganda, but why worry her? *Sans peur et sans reproche*— maiden rescuing done cheaply, special rates for parties." He has just dreamed "the wildest space opera I had ever seen, loaded with dragons and Arcturian maidens and knights in shining space armor and shuttling between King Arthur's Court and the Dead Sea Bottoms of Barsoom.... Will Beowulf conquer the Dragon? Will Tristan return to Iseult? Will Peewee find her dolly? Tune in this channel tomorrow night." Williamson acknowledges that the novel is "a melodramatic space adventure [with] a good deal of routine space opera in the plot action" ("Youth" 29), but Heinlein's tone differs radically from his previous fiction, anticipating what he does in a novel such as the *Number of the Beast*. Unlike such delightful comic novels as *The Rolling Stones* and *The Star Beast*, he seems here to mock good-naturedly the conventions of both romantic narrative and space opera. Panshin declares, "For frosting, the story turns a number of science fictional clichés conventions this way and that, as though to show there is a lot of delightful mileage left in them.... I like to look at the story as the ultimate in fairy tales: the knight errant rides forth to save the fair maiden from the all-time champion dragon— and so what if the damsel is only eleven?" (*HD* 85). At one point during their trek across the Moonscape, however, when Kip "wanted to be a hero," Peewee tells him, "Oh quit being big and male and gallantly stupid." At another point when Kip is rescuing Peewee, he says of one of his ideas, "A real knight-errant plan, I thought. I didn't waste two seconds discarding it." None of Heinlein's protagonists will sound so ironically self-aware until "Oscar" Gordon in *Glory Road* (1963).

In truth, many of Kip and Peewee's attempts at heroism are futile. On the Moon, the team of good guys (Kip, Peewee, and the Mother Thing) escape and hike over at least forty miles of lunarscape to the Federation outpost at Tombaugh Point—with Kip improvising a way to refill Peewee's air bottles and eventually carrying her—only to be recaptured by Wormface's minions. Whisked to Pluto, Kip tries to figure out a way to escape from his cell but must admit that the wormfaces have out-thought him. He persists anyway. Studded as it is with quotes from Shakespeare, *Have Space Suit—Will Travel* demonstrates the truth of one passage unquoted, Hamlet's recognition that "the readiness is all." Or, as Peewee's father explains to Kip at the end of the novel, their eventual success was the result of persistent, purposeful effort: "'good luck' follows careful preparation." In other words, if you prepare yourself to act and are *ready* to act, you may accomplish something when the chance comes. The Mother Thing demonstrates as much in the alien base on Pluto. She ingratiates herself with Wormface and his lab technicians so that she has the opportunity to build two explosive devices and a beacon to summon her own people from Vega V. The bombs destroy the wormfaces' base, but the Mother Thing is frozen to death outside before she can set up the beacon. Kip succeeds in the task, but his arms and legs are badly frozen. As their death from suffocation approaches, with Peewee asking, "Kip? It's been fun mostly. Hasn't it?," the Vegans arrive to whisk them to Lanador, their home planet, where the Mother Thing is thawed and restored to life and where Kip's limbs are regenerated. At this point, the tone changes abruptly; the relatively straightforward conflict of good versus evil is over as a much more ambivalent debate appears.

In terms of story line, the final sequence dealing with the intergalactic tribunal is certainly not an organic part of the whole. The Vegans have rescued the three principals, and the base on Pluto from which the wormfaces could launch their attack on Earth has been destroyed. The Mother Thing has returned from the dead, and Kip has been restored to health. That the Mother Thing is a cop does not mean the trial of the wormfaces must be staged. Yet Kip and Peewee are summoned to the hall of the tribunal just as that trial takes place, and they realize that it is not just the group of individual criminals but the *race* of wormfaces that is being judged. A spokesman for the wormfaces, in a voice full of "bone-chilling yet highly intelligent viciousness," denounces the "Three Galaxies" federation as lacking jurisdiction over the Only People and dismisses the Earth as a "useful but empty planet" containing nothing but animals. All living creatures other than the Only People are mere animals and will be eaten or exterminated. After this declaration, the court asks whether anyone in the vast hall, representing the myriad civilized races of three galaxies, can speak in the defendants' favor. No one does. The verdict is that their planet be "rotated" so that it is no longer a part of space-time continuum of the Three Galaxies. Kip thinks that the wormfaces have simply been confined in a kind of Coventry until he is told that their sun does not go with the planet; the race will be exterminated. Moreover, the judgment was carried out immediately.

The wormfaces condemned themselves not merely by justifying their action in Earth's solar system but by showing that they always would behave that way. The Only People, like the Edorrans in E. E. Smith's Lensmen series, were incapable of accepting kinship with any other race. That made them an irredeemable threat that had to be eliminated before it became actively dangerous to civilized peoples. That question settled, the tribunal now can take up the question whether humanity also might be such a threat. Samples have been taken at what should have been reasonable intervals — a caveman, a Roman soldier, and now Kip and Peewee — but obviously humans are changing very rapidly. They are too unpredictable for comfort. For safety's sake, it might be better to rotate Earth too.

The trial of humanity begins. The Neanderthal is dismissed from consideration because he is only a cousin to humanity. Iunio, the Roman Legionary, reviles the assembly, telling them "what he thought of vermin who were not citizens, not even *barbarians*." There is, somehow, a difference between the way the absolutely intolerant wormfaces vilified the assembly and the way the crusty human defies it to do its worst. As Franklin in particular has noted, Kip admires the "tough old sergeant" for his "courage, human dignity, and a basic gallantry"; even if he is "a scoundrel," he is Kip's "kind of scoundrel." One senses that the narrator's first-person mask — much as occurs in Mark Twain's *The Adventures of Huckleberry Finn* during the Colonel Sherburne episode — slips at this point. After hearing humanity called "a savage and brutal people, given to all manner of atrocities" and listening as the machine voice of the multi-consciousness magistrate proclaims that this is not a court of justice but instead something like a Security Council which has "simply formed police districts for mutual protection," Kip responds to the assertion that the idea that anyone can predict the future of the human race: "We have no limits. There's no telling what our future will be." The mask may well slip completely off as Kip exclaims, "All right, take away our star — You will if you can and I guess you can. Go ahead! We'll *make* a star! Then, someday, we'll come back and hunt you down — *all of you!*" To himself he reflects: "Oh, I didn't mean we could *do* it. Not yet. But we'd *try*. 'Die trying' is the proudest human thing."

When the voice asks if anyone will speak for humanity, the Mother Thing is the first. She admits that humanity is capable of violence but asks, "Can any race survive without a willingness to fight?" When accused of being sentimental she retorts, "Toward evil we have no mercy. But the mistakes of a child we treat with loving forbearance." Another race, represented by a large green monkey, emphasizes that humanity is young but asks that it be given its chance. The verdict places humanity on probation with the Guardian Mother (the Mother Thing) as "the cop on the beat, who will report at once any ominous change." Kip describes her as "more of a juvenile welfare officer" than a police officer.

That is an appropriate authority figure for this novel. Peewee and Kip are returned to Earth just a few days after they left, with alien artifacts that verify their story and with hints that will nudge human mathematicians in productive directions. That appears to be all humanity needs — some good tips and a bit of benevolent guidance. Neither Kip nor Peewee undergoes significant personal change during a story line covering the shortest period of time since that of *Rocket Ship Galileo*. For all the distance they have traveled and all they have accomplished, very little has changed back home. Kip naturally will go to a top college; Peewee's father calls "Oppie" at M.I.T. and arranges a scholarship, telling him also that Peewee is "fond" of him and reminding him that his father — the greatest mathematical psychologist of his time — married *his* star pupil. Such sugar coating is pleasant but not necessary to the story line. At the end of the book, Kip solves the problem of the loudmouthed oaf who has scoffed at his aspirations to go into space. He does so without surrendering or resorting to a hurtful physical attack. A small-scale conflict is settled in an appropriately small-scale way. Kip is a healthy adolescent, like the human race as a whole, and he's growing up in a healthy, thoughtful but determined manner.

How Heinlein's own thinking was going beyond this can be seen in his 1961 Guest of Honor speech at the World Science Fiction Convention in Seattle. There he sees a ninety percent probability of war or slavery in his listeners' future. That may account for his writing *Starship Troopers* as the next Scribner's juvenile, to jar young readers out of their wishful thinking. Another motive may have been at work also. As long as Scribner's accepted each of Heinlein's manuscripts, he was contractually obligated to submit the next to them. The only way to get free was to have a manuscript rejected. It is very difficult — considering Heinlein's struggles with his Scribner's editor over minor hints of violence, unconventional family arrangements, etc. — to imagine that he expected *Starship Troopers* to be easily accepted. This is not to say that he is insincere in the outrage expressed in his letter to Lurton Blassingame concerning Scribner's rejection of the novel. It may simply be that, as with many of us, a writer's left hand is not always aware of what the right hand is doing.

In any event, *Starship Troopers* will be discussed in the next chapter, as an adult novel.

5

The "Classic" Period

During the 1950s, as he wrote the juvenile/YA novels for Scribner's, Heinlein concentrated primarily on longer fiction. The novels he wrote in this period are extremely polished, relatively compact, and ingeniously structured crowd pleasers. Even readers who are wary of the later, longer, apparently looser novels cherish these works. The short stories of this decade are of lesser importance, though they include the superb "All You Zombies —."

In many of these stories, Heinlein continues playing with the theme of solipsism, the idea that only one's personal consciousness certainly exists. Philosophically, solipsism can be seen as an extension of Descartes' first premise, the one truth that *must* be true: "I think; therefore, I am"—with emphasis on the first-person, singular pronoun, since the existence of other individuals is less immediately self-evident. Practically, solipsism may simply be a response to recognition that one is the smartest person in a conversation, a group, or a neighborhood. If those other people don't deserve respect for their ability to process information or to act effectively, why bother about them at all? As one of Heinlein's long-term concerns, this issue is mulled over in the fiction he wrote during this period when he was consolidating his mastery of the tools of his trade.

"The Man Who Sold the Moon" (1950) was one of the last "Future History" stories to be written. In addition to filling a gap in the sequence by setting up the background of D. D. Harriman before he became the lead character of "Requiem," the novella was the linchpin of a collection of Heinlein's stories from Shasta Publishers, one of the ambitious semi-professional companies that flourished briefly as major publishers like Doubleday were just realizing that sf could be a profitable genre. Besides its use in literary marketing, the story also illustrates Heinlein's awareness that he was writing for a larger, more difficult audience. The first readers of "Requiem" in *Astounding Science Fiction* would have assumed that a trip to the Moon was self-evidently desirable. After World War II, it was obvious that space travel was possible; German rocket scientist Wernher von Braun had famously commented that the Nazi V-2 weapon was a working spaceship that unfortunately had landed on the wrong planet. However, it also was obvious that building a spaceship would take more than the resources of some brilliant scientist working in his secret laboratory, and the general public wasn't quite ready for that commitment—yet. People needed to be "sold" on the idea.

The story explores the idea of big-scale marketing, satirizing how the process works and showing what it does to its participants. As readers of "Requiem" remember, Harriman succeeded in creating a space program that got people to the Moon, established a base there, and built momentum for further space exploration. Still, at the end of "The Man Who Sold the Moon," he is trapped by his success, denied the chance to go into space himself because his business partners consider him necessary to keep the marketing program going back on Earth.

"You've got to be a believer!" Harriman exclaims in the story's first line. For some time, as Harriman expertly maneuvers his fellow tycoons toward backing construction of a spaceship headed to the Moon, it's unclear what Harriman himself believes. Certainly he is a ruthless opportunist, willing to exploit charity for publicity or buy judges as needed. When one crony remarks that he is "crookeder than a dog's hind leg," Harriman takes that as a compliment from one unscrupulous businessman to another. Naturally, he tries to sell this group on going to the Moon in terms of "experimentation, exploration — and exploitation." Underlying this, as readers notice even if Harriman's peers can't, is a personal need to escape the confinement of his present circumstances; when a discussion turns to who'll be aboard the first moonship, Harriman explodes, "Call it chicanery, call it anything you want to. *I'm going to the Moon!* If I have to manipulate a million people to accomplish it, I'll do it."

Nor is this merely a selfish desire. Harriman sincerely believes that the human race *needs* to climb up and out — to the Moon, the planets, the stars — and that this justifies the flim-flam he uses to further that purpose. He reveals another passionate concern when he is with people whom he can trust not to dismiss his aspirations rudely: He wants to meet aliens, whom he calls "people." He admits that they can't expect to find such people on the Moon, but

> I was speaking of the other planets — Mars and Venus and the satellites of Jupiter. Maybe out at the stars themselves. Suppose we do find people. Think what it will mean to us. We've been alone, all alone, the only intelligent race in the only world we know. We haven't even been able to talk with dogs or apes. Any answers we got we had to think up by ourselves, like deserted orphans. But suppose we find *people*, intelligent people, who have done some thinking in their own way. *We wouldn't be alone any more!* We could look up at the stars and never be afraid again.

Naturally, after this revealing speech Harriman appears "a little tired and even a little ashamed of his outburst, like a man surprised in a private act." Also naturally, his cohorts don't truly grasp what they've heard; they recognize only that the message could be an effective part of their advertising if they can find a real actor to punch the lines. And so it goes. Selling the Moon means cannily exploiting the self-interest of diamond merchants, stamp collectors, media moguls, etc. Even children, who could perhaps be attracted to the ideal of space travel, become paying customers once Harriman's sales campaign figures how to enroll them as Junior Spacemen with the proper dues.

Most of the story consists of negotiations or brainstorming along these lines, interspersed with chunks of news stories/advertisements that are part of the sales campaign. The major dramatized scene is the launch of the lunar ship, as Harriman can't stand to remain inside the viewing post with the crowd of superficial observers and so rushes outside, where he is buffeted by the tumultuous takeoff. That is as much direct contact with vital reality as he permits himself. He is too exhausted later to hear that the ship has landed safely.

Eventually, in the long run, the birth of space travel will be good for humanity. In the short run, selling a space program to the unimaginative, self-centered mass of people means that the program's real significance must be disguised. In "Requiem," Harriman dies but only after following his dream to the Moon; in "The Man Who Sold the Moon," his success means personal failure.

Heinlein's first novel for an adult audience since *Beyond This Horizon* was written for the new, upscale sf magazine *Galaxy* (September–November 1951). Much to Heinlein's displeasure, editor H. L. Gold began editing "The Puppet Masters" heavily; that mangled version has never been reprinted, but the first book publication also was considerably different from Heinlein's manuscript; eventual publication of the preferred text in 1990, in Gifford's opinion, was "significant enough to turn the work from one of Heinlein's borderline failures to one of his best works" (*Reader's* 155).

At first glance, it is surprising how well *The Puppet Masters* still works, considering that it is tied to a situation rapidly receding into history. The novel is so full of Cold War passion that some critics have seen it as a mere political allegory. Leon Stover, for example, mentions the novel only as one of Heinlein's valiant efforts "to defend the Terran frontiers of human freedom against ... Soviet expansionism" (*RH* 47–48); on the other hand, speaking as a Marxist, H. Bruce Franklin deplores its "exaltation of 'ferocity,' and the fear, loathing, rage, and hate directed against an alien life form" (*RAH* 100). And yet *The Puppet Masters* must be more than a timely tract, since it has triumphantly survived the Soviet threat. Somehow the novel succeeds.

A brief plot summary first: The story is narrated by "Sam," agent for an ultra-secret U.S. security organization. Sam's boss, the Old Man, teams him with Mary, a female agent, so that the three of them can investigate a flying saucer landing, a supposed hoax, in Iowa. They discover that an alien spaceship did land but that the people at the site have been taken over by "slugs," parasites that totally control a human once they attach to their host's nervous system. The slugs clearly intend to conquer the whole planet, but Sam, Mary, and the Old Man escape back to free territory. The rest of the book describes Sam and his allies trying to (a) get enough information to (b) convince the authorities to respond and (c) destroy the slugs and free their slaves. Each of these steps must be repeated, as the slugs demonstrate how difficult they are to detect, understand, and outwit.

The first thing to note about *The Puppet Masters* is how well it *does* fit the time in which it was written. The Cold War years themselves were borderline fantastic. Americans were frightened and angry: denied relaxation after winning a moral world war — suddenly threatened by alien subversion — unable to trust anyone. Consider the bizarre titles of two popular dramas about patriotic Americans who pretended to be disloyal so they could inform on traitors: *I Was a Communist for the FBI* (film and radio) and *I Led Three Lives* (TV). Any "fact" was uncertain. Even if people noticed that the number of "card-carrying communists" in the State Department varied each time Senator Joe McCarthy checked his list, somehow that didn't matter; by a kind of quantum politics, any number (or *all* of them) might be true. The only thing Americans could be sure of was that communists hated everything natural, that they were absolutely unscrupulous in subverting good, and that they could disguise themselves perfectly as normal human beings — a description that fits anyone in *The Puppet Masters* possessed by a slug. Moreover, Sam explicitly compares the reign of the slugs to Soviet life:

> I wondered why the titans [the slugs] had not attacked Russia first; Stalinism seemed tailormade for them. On second thought, I wondered if they had. On third thought I wondered what difference it would make; the people behind the Curtain had had their minds enslaved and parasites riding them for three generations. There might not be two kopeks difference between a commissar with a slug and a commissar without a slug.

Besides satisfying the passions of his Cold War audience, however, Heinlein involves readers in another, larger political/personal conflict. In fact, since the collapse of the political system *The Puppet Masters* attacks, readers can pay more attention to the system the novel claims to defend: American democracy. One repeated theory about the slugs is that they are essentially *one* organism — splitting like an amoeba when more human hosts become available and limited in communication when its parts are physically separated, but never developing separate personalities. If the slugs are bad because they deny individuality, it follows that expressing one's individuality is good and so is a system that permits a practical maximum of independence. If this is so, the slug-human struggle should demonstrate democracy's superiority to any collective philosophy.

The problem with this optimistic interpretation is that the slugs almost win. How close they come to victory shows democracy's weakness; Americans are victorious in spite of, not because of, the way they govern themselves. Most of the government people whom Sam, Mary, and the Old Man have to work with are politicians. They got into office in the first place because voters wanted to give away their civic responsibility. Now the officials represent the worst of that irresponsible attitude, being too self-centered, complacent, and stubborn to respond effectively to the slugs' subversion. Sam is in awe of American institutions — incredibly so for a grown man who's been working as a secret agent; however, he soon is disillusioned by the short-sighted foolishness of the U.S. government's behavior. Fortunately, he can rely on someone who's capable of seeing a situation whole and then acting decisively and unselfishly — the Old Man, whose relationship to his family of agents and to the American ideal Sam describes very early in the novel:

> If I had had any sense, I'd have quit [spying] and taken a working job.
> The only trouble with that would be that I wouldn't have been working for the Old Man any longer. That made the difference.
> Not that he was a soft boss. He was quite capable of saying, "Boys, we need to fertilize this oak tree. Just jump in that hole at its base and I'll cover you up."
> We'd have done it. Any of us would.
> And the Old Man would bury us alive, too, if he thought that there was as much as a 53 percent probability that it was the Tree of Liberty he was nourishing.

The novel is in favor of keeping liberty alive, of course, and it expects readers to accept the Old Man's tactics to that end; also, as a whole, the novel instructs readers in what Sam should already know: In the real world, problems appear in a fragmentary, confused mess. Whatever theories underlie a government, the most efficient way to protect citizens is for one person to make a decision rapidly and see that it's implemented. Any system that can't cope with new challenges won't survive, and the novel makes clear that the U.S. government would collapse without the Old Man's goading.

Heinlein's thinking on this point is almost, if not quite, self-contradictory. *The Puppet Masters* shows deep tension between reverence for the free individual's potential and disappointment at how most people actually behave. The novel has almost as much trouble deciding how to treat free humans as those who are slug-ridden. On the one hand, looking out at the city from a tall building, Sam imagines the "alive and individual" people who live there and reminds himself that it is "the Old Man's business — and mine — to keep those people down there safe." On the other hand, he disapproves of how government treats those little people *as* little people by not telling them anything that "the all-wise statesmen and bureaucrats decide we are not big enough boys and girls to know, a Mother-Knows-Best-Dear policy." The novel shows that people do need to be looked after, but it can't accept a system that would restrict individuals to an infantile, dependent role. Slugs and communists demonstrate the efficiency but ultimate brittleness of that approach. Heinlein's preferred solution — trusting one competent, informed decision maker — is more attractive but reminds some readers of fascism. Actually, dogmatic as Heinlein's characters sound, their stories are hard to fit to one dogma, and, besides, he denies that social or personal roles are fixed forever.

At this point, we're no longer talking only about politics, if we ever were, as we consider the relation between superior and inferior, one who leads and one who is led. A recurring theme in Heinlein's fiction is solipsism, a person's sense that he is the only real and significant part of the universe, surrounded by mere makeshift illusions and faint echoes of himself. The slugs are the ultimate solipsists, expressing total denial of other individuals. They call themselves "The people.... The only people." There is only one slug consciousness, dictator and mob simultaneously. Rather than cooperating or competing with independent intelligences they meet, the slugs absorb or kill them. To fight slugs, since resistance to dehumanization requires belief in human potential, one must believe that at least some people can and will improve if they have a chance.

If *The Puppet Masters*'s dated anticommunism is a cover for Heinlein's struggle with his persistent tendency toward solipsism, the struggle is carried out within individual people, and here again the novel moves into a deeper human concern. How do independent humans negotiate changing degrees of submission and control? By definition, slugs cannot become anything different than they are now. In the same way, communist or fascist tyrants will resist change because it threatens their self-image and their power. The American political system resists change too because of the inertia of a multitude of squabbling "leaders." Heinlein's novel, however, shows another kind of growth taking place at the personal level in the changing roles of Sam, Mary, and the Old Man. The question turns out not to be how a person can *believe* in someone else but how people can *love* each other, for love rather than logic is how Heinlein's characters escape solipsism.

Describing his career, Sam speaks of the utter, unquestioning trust the "boys" in the agency feel for the Old Man. It is startling to discover that Sam literally *is* the Old Man's boy: They are father and son. The fact that Sam is a grown man taking absolute orders from his dad is not the most incongruous thing about him. Consider: Sam supposedly is a tough secret agent who can describe feeling "warm and relaxed, as if I had just killed man or had a woman," yet this ersatz sophistication evaporates when he is attracted to Mary: "I got all tingly and felt like a fifteen-year-old. Second childhood, I guess." Sam can play adult roles, following the Old Man's orders, but emotionally he is barely a teenager. Mary's diagnosis, which Sam dutifully reports, is that while he was growing up he was criticized so much by his "arrogantly brilliant father" that he lost his self-confidence. This is quite reasonable, since the Old Man believes in pushing people to their limits — their real limits, well past the comfortable positions they want to settle into. With his son, apparently, he went too far. The coming of the slugs challenges Sam to use all his abilities for humanity in general and Mary in particular. In short, he has another chance to grow up: "whether ... the Old Man liked it or not. I was tired of being treated like a cross between a prince consort and an unwelcome child." The Old Man sets up this new father-son confrontation by remarking that perhaps he has been underestimating Sam; shortly after Sam has asserted his will, the Old Man acknowledges his son's independence by calling him by his given name for the first time: Elihu. In the Bible, after Job and his three friends have debated, Elihu angrily interrupts:

> I am young in years, and you are aged; therefore I was timid and afraid to declare my opinion to you.
> I said, "Let days speak, and many years teach wisdom."
> But truly it is the spirit in a mortal, the breath of the Almighty, that makes for understanding.
> It is not the old that are wise, nor the aged that understand what is right.
> Therefore I say, "Listen to me: let me also declare my opinion" [Job, 32: 6–10].

This doesn't sound like someone who is ready to jump in a hole and be buried alive. And so the Old Man declares that Sam has replaced him as boss, since by definition "A boss is the man who does the bossing." And Sam is ready. After being treated like a child throughout the novel, he evaluates the success of his first public performance as boss by saying, "I felt like a new man."

Sam discovers himself as an adult by commitment to another human being, Mary. The point of the angry intervention that marks him as the new boss is to keep the Old Man from rummaging through Mary's memories without her permission. "*Ask her,*" Sam insists. When she is asked, Mary does turn out to know the secret of killing the slugs, but Sam didn't realize that. He just wanted her personal importance to be recognized. And Mary recognizes Sam's needs by tactfully deferring to him because of the battering his youthful psyche endured. They grow by mutually giving and taking support.

The Old Man's position is more difficult. He doesn't seem to need emotional support, and it's difficult for someone like him to give it. Being genuinely superior to the people around him, the Old Man would seem especially tempted by solipsism. Somehow, he must recognize that other, weaker people need his help; then, in full possession of his skills, he must hand over power to an inferior. Growing up is, unfortunately, just preparation for growing old. At least, the Old Man can take some comfort at having dictated his own terms of surrender. The novel suggests that the Old Man is responsible for much of Sam's development, though he never diminishes Sam's accomplishment by telling him so. Sam states several times that his father is a master manipulator and even compares him to the slugs as "a puppet master." In particular, the Old Man remarks how much Mary reminds him of Sam's mother, and it's more than likely that he made sure the two got together, anticipating their marriage. For that matter, if Sam's given name shows youth refusing to submit to the authority of old men, readers should remember who gave him that name.

But the Old Man does not seem to have plotted Sam's life in order to replicate himself. He seems to have recognized that his time to step aside would come sooner or later, and he accepts it when it does come. An unwillingness to be replaced may appear only once, late in the novel, when the Old Man is taken over by one of the few surviving slugs and kidnaps Sam so that his son can be possessed and subordinated too. Right after that, however, when both are injured but free of alien control, Sam sobs "Dad ... don't die — I can't get along without you," but his father replies "Yes you can, son."

In context, the Old Man is simultaneously expressing faith in humanity, respect for the individual, and love for his son. It is Heinlein's genius to create a context in which so many levels of thinking and feeling can coexist, reinforcing each other. This is true of other aspects of the novel too. We all are distracted by current events, gripped by personal concerns to the point of obsession, and startled by finding ourselves close to other people. Heinlein sometimes manages to create a working model of that living complexity in his fiction, so that a story such as *The Puppet Masters* feels not just entertaining but *real*.

In important ways, "The Year of the Jackpot" (*Galaxy*, March 1952) is Heinlein's most atypical piece of fiction, a literal "end-of-the-world" story.

It's not uncommon for sf writers to wipe most of the people off the Earth as a handy way of freeing survivors from the corruption and complications of contemporary society so that they can build a simpler, healthier life. It's not even uncommon to threaten to exterminate the whole human race. It's rare, however, for an sf story to fulfill that threat, ending all of humanity's aspirations and potential.

As Heinlein's story opens, two people meet and begin their doomed love affair as society slides toward chaos. Meade Barstow is a wholesome young woman who suddenly feels compelled to take off her clothes on a busy street. Potiphar Breen, her rescuer, is a statistician who is charting the accelerating looniness of humanity and has concluded that people are like lemmings: Their supposed personal free will can't prevent them from acting irrationally in naturally reoccurring cycles. The two eventually flee Los Angeles during a flood and earthquake that somehow are associated with the outbreak of World War III. They settle safely and happily in a mountain refuge until Potiphar deciphers an ominous prediction in a scholarly journal, looks up at a misshapen sun, and realizes that the Earth is about to be destroyed by a nova.

Before that last development, Potiphar and Meade are obviously better off for the destruction of civilization. As Potiphar walks back to their cabin, which he has defended against Russian parachutists, he reflects, "Aside from mathematics, just two things worth doing — kill a man and love a woman. He had done both; he was rich." Being burdened with social restraint would have made both achievements more difficult.

The mood is more mixed at the story's conclusion. Since sf plays with the idea that humans are or will be able to understand and control the physical world, heroes of end-of-the-world stories usually find what satisfaction they can in at least *understanding* the catastrophe. In H. G. Wells's "The Star" (1897), for example, a character labeled "the master mathematician" calculates a wandering star's course through the solar system and concludes that Earth is doomed. He does not despair: "He looked at it [the star] as one might look into the eyes of a brave enemy. 'You may kill me,' he said after a silence. But I can hold you — and all the universe for that matter — in the grasp of this little brain. I would not change. Even now." Potiphar shares something of this satisfaction as he sums up his situation a few paragraphs before the story's end: "What good was the race of man? Monkeys, he thought, monkeys with a spot of poetry in them, cluttering and wasting a second-string planet near a third-string star. But somehow they finish in style." Still, he feels "an unexpected and overpowering burst of sorrow" as he clutches Meade's hand and realizes that everything is over — for them and all humanity.

It's very unusual for Heinlein to end a story with the characters hopelessly defeated. One can see "The Year of the Jackpot" as part of his continuing effort to warn readers to get off this planet, stop huddling here and spread humanity to the stars. Or it may simply be another "What if ..." story, developing a disturbing premise as convincingly as possible. Or, considering the date of its first publication, it may simply be a straight-faced April Fools joke.

"Project Nightmare," published in *Amazing Stories*'s April–May 1953 issue, returns to the theme of weaponized ESP. The story begins with Dr. Reynolds demonstrating a variety of ESP powers to military officers and bureaucrats, then segues into a demonstration that telekinesis can enhance the power of an atomic bomb. Meanwhile, however, Russia has been smuggling A-bombs into the U.S. and hiding them in major cities; they will be detonated unless America immediately surrenders to communism. Reynolds sets his scrappy little band of adepts — and as many more as can be gathered quickly — to locating the bombs and keeping them from going off. The gamble succeeds. Cleveland is the only city lost, when a political outsider distracts one of Reynolds's crew. At the story's end, the President asks them to locate the A-bombs back in Russia so that they can be detonated telekinetically.

The story generates tension as the diverse ESP characters — sweet little old lady, slick gambler, cute twins, etc. — struggle to stay awake and save the country. The conclusion, promising the imminent destruction of Russia, is emotionally justified by the fact that *they* tried to do it to us first. Serves 'em right!

"Sky Lift" is a minor story that was first published in a minor magazine, *Imagination Stories of Science and Fantasy*, in November 1953. Its basic premise is that a supply of blood must be rushed to a research station on Pluto that has been hit by a plague, and the only way to make the delivery on time is to send a manned ship at excessive acceleration. Most of the story is told through the viewpoint of Joe Appleby, the ship's co-pilot, who must take over after the pilot dies under the strain. Joe suffers severe physical pain and mental disorientation but completes the mission. The ordeal, however, leaves him physically enfeebled and prematurely senile, so the last scene shows a brief interview of Joe by the Commodore and the attending surgeon; then the story ends with a conversation between the two officers after Joe has been removed to the geriatric institute at Luna City. Both men agree that saving the 270 scientists was worth the sacrifice, but both recognize what a sacrifice it was.

On a similar theme, Tom Godwin's "The Cold Equations," which appeared the following year in *ASF* and was selected by the Science Fiction Writers of America for inclusion in *The Science Fiction Hall of Fame*, shows a young woman stowaway ejected from a ship on a mission of mercy; it's a terrible thing to do, but that's the only way that the mission — the greater good — can be accomplished. Heinlein's story stresses the weight of command, the Commodore's responsibility for sending men to their destruction. Slightly undercutting this is the fact that the Commodore is momentarily confused at the conclusion. When the surgeon remarks that the Commodore's decision "expended one man, but ... saved two hundred and seventy," the Commodore thinks of the dead pilot as the one who was "expended" until he is reminded of Joe's terrible condition. Not as immediately affecting as Godwin's story, "Sky Lift" does stick in the reader's memory because the person who has made a necessary, voluntary self-sacrifice is *not* dead and gone but lives on in baffled anguish.

Satisfying as it is within that novel, the conclusion of *The Puppet Masters* doesn't remain intact in Heinlein's next adult novel. Instead, *Double Star* (February–April 1956) focuses on related questions: Who *are* those little people that they deserve protecting? And what *is* this interactive society that deserves such ferocious defense? Displaying impressive legerdemain, the Hugo-winning novel operates by folding separate characters into one identity.

Double Star doesn't fuse character by revealing that they literally the same person, as in Heinlein's "By His Bootstraps." Initially, actor Lawrence Smith merely agrees to stand in for interplanetary statesman John Joseph Bonforte until the latter can be located after a political kidnapping — then until Bonforte recovers from the mind-numbing drug administered by the kidnappers — then until the politician can recover from a stroke — and then, finally, for the rest of his life after Bonforte dies. However, this job soon goes beyond mere impersonation. To fill Bonforte's place, Smith must do more than look and sound like Bonforte: he must *think* like him, and one mark of success is his discovery that even at press conferences "most questions I could answer without stopping to think." By the end of the book, in a kind of epilogue that lets him review what he has done with the last 25 years of his life, Bonforte/Smith states:

> I find I can "remember" Bonforte's early life better than I remember my actual life as that rather pathetic person, Lawrence Smith, or — as he liked to style himself—"The Great Lorenzo." Does that make me insane? Schizophrenic, perhaps? If so, it is a necessary insanity for the role I have had to play, for in order to let Bonforte live again, that seedy actor had to be suppressed — completely.

In addition to the merging of these two characters, the people around Bonforte turn out to be less than independent individuals too. As Bonforte's chief political adviser argues while trying to keep Smith from giving up the role after Bonforte's death, "A political personality is not one man; it's a team — it's a team bound together by common purposes and common beliefs." Initially, of course, one chooses to join a team: then, however, the individual inevitably is influenced by the will of the group so that Bonforte's team closes ranks around its "Chief." The testimony of one team member is especially revealing. As he becomes familiar with Bonforte's entourage, Smith realizes that personal secretary Penny Russell is hopelessly in love with her boss, so much so that she detests Smith's replacing him even temporarily. Yet at the book's end, Bonforte/Smith reports that his "wife Penelope claims that she remembers him [Smith] better than I do — and that she never loved anyone else." Penny may be innocently misremembering to flatter her husband, but she also could be saying that the only man she's ever loved is the Chief — whoever that happens to be at the moment. In any case, the ease with which Penny apparently has made the transfer of identities shows that Smith and Bonforte have fused as seamlessly for her as for the rest of the team that itself has coalesced into one political personality.

As in "By His Bootstraps," characters in *Double Star* surrender some rather important aspects of their personalities — their individual goals and loves — in accepting that they are parts of a larger identity. Unlike the shorter work of fiction, Heinlein's novel leaves its characters technically autonomous. Still, they can't be said to act or think independently. They may not see themselves as components within a larger self, but they're unable to make decisions apart from it. So it appears that time travel is not the only device Heinlein can use to fold characters together. Acting and politics also can do the job of combining identities. But if this is *what* Heinlein does, it also may be worth considering *how* he does it in this particular work.

In fact, studying that "how" is not an inconsiderable task. The notion of submerging oneself in someone else's identity is not naturally attractive; in fact, the back cover of one paperback edition speaks of the danger that Smith might be "*trapped* in his new role forever" [emphasis added]. To fit Smith into his life-role without him (and the reader) feeling it is an unjust "trap," Heinlein must be very careful about what he includes and what he leaves out, what he emphasizes and what he understates.

He must show, for example, that Smith's existence before Bonforte is unsatisfactory. What a reader initially notices about Smith is how clever he is but how little his cleverness benefits him. He can analyze the behavior of people around him so that he can use bits of business — clothing, gestures, etc. — in his acting. But Smith is unsuccessful in his profession, reduced to scrounging drinks in a spaceport bar. Not that this lack of employment reduces his self-esteem; he hands his engraved card to a newly arrived, rather furtive spaceman: "A little smugly perhaps. There is only one Lorenzo Smythe, the One-Man Stock Company. Yes, I'm 'The Great Lorenzo'— stereo, canned opera, legit —'Pantomimist and Mimicry Artist Extraordinary.'" He is unhappy, though, when the spaceman pockets the card: Those things cost money. To paraphrase Smith's favorite playwright, the pipsqueak doth protest too much, methinks.

Moreover, Smith's finely honed perception doesn't help him much in day-to-day relationships. As far as the book shows, he has no connection with any living person. In fact, his cleverness probably works against people liking him. Readers certainly observe that the spaceman Smith is talking to in the bar is nervous because he doesn't want his identity revealed; even Smith perceives as much. However, the actor simply prattles along to show off his powers of observation. He cares only about satisfying himself: "my vocal cords lived their own life, wild and free."

Besides his mixture of egotism and misdirected talent, Heinlein shows that Smith's thinking outside his field of expertise is warped. He hates Martians. While not prejudiced where humans are concerned, he views Martians as mere "*things.*" Consequently, he thinks of them as racists always characterize their targets: Martians are pushy, they're disgusting to look at, and they even smell bad.

While convincing readers that Smith's original condition is undesirable, Heinlein must also establish a theoretical justification for suppressing any person's individual goals. This is accomplished very early in the book as Smith rejects the idea of merely "doubling" for a public figure because that would not be creative art. Bonforte's associate first offers more money, then, when that is rejected, muses "Would you do it for other reasons? If you felt it had to be done and you were the only one who could do it successfully?" When Smith answers, "I concede the possibility; I cannot imagine the circumstances," Heinlein has established his premise. Now all he has to do is help readers imagine the circumstances of a task so important that it has to be done, in a situation constructed that only one person can do it successfully.

The task is the success of the Expansionist Party, led by Bonforte. As opposed to the Humanity Party, whose sentiments echo Smith's initial racism, the Expansionists want common citizenship for all intelligent beings who will accept it, along with less government control and more individual freedom. The Expansionists' long-range goal, moreover, is not simply expansion of citizenship but extension of humanity farther into space. As part of that expansion, humans must enlarge their sympathies. Smith parrots Bonforte to that effect when he is just beginning to settle into the role: "Our own race is spreading out to the stars.... The stars will never be won by little minds; we must be as big as space itself."

Growth seems to be both the cause and effect of winning the stars. For Heinlein, striving toward some goal is an innate, unquestionable part of human nature, so *Double Star* never discusses a moral basis for this effort. The novel does, however, try to demonstrate that the struggle is accompanied by increased understanding and competence, and thus presumably by greater capacity for moral action. In short, as people grow up, they understand better what needs to be done and what they can contribute to getting it done.

In the case of Lawrence Smith, growing up does produce a better — i.e., more likeable and useful — person. Early in the book, Heinlein demonstrates Smith's immaturity; most of the plot directs our attention not at an actor becoming another man but at an overgrown child becoming an adult. Significantly, the word Smith uses to describe his training in Bonforte's character is "education." It also is significant that Smith's first crucial performance is to take Bonforte's place at a Martian ceremony that makes him a full member of a Martian hive, with "a speech not unlike that, in spirit, with which an orthodox Jewish boy assumes the responsibility of manhood."

Probably the most important force pushing Smith toward manhood, though, is how much the content of this new education resembles what Smith learned from his father. Smith's father also was a dedicated actor. To help his son succeed in the theater, he taught the boy to be realistic, to concentrate on practical skills. He also insisted that his son respect social standards, such as avoiding inappropriate language. And above all, he preached that the show must go on. Smith discovers that Bonforte and his team practice the same values: politics as the art of the possible, deliberately chosen language, and continuity at all costs.

Yet what happens to Smith goes beyond "education." In particular, the way Smith comes to regard Bonforte is uncannily like his relationship to his father. Smith refuses to see the disabled Bonforte because it would distract him from his image of the man; he made a similar mistake when he went to his father's funeral and thereafter almost lost "the true image of him — the virile, dominant man who had reared me with a firm hand and taught me my trade." When he hears that Bonforte has suffered a stroke, Smith feels "a ghost of the lost feeling I had when my father died." When he sees the man himself for the first time, he is "almost startled out of character" because "He looked like my father!"; and he reacts to Bonforte's death especially strongly because "I had seen 'myself' die, I had again seen my father die." Therefore, carrying on the role of Bonforte means that the politician and Smith's father aren't dead; they live anew in Bonforte/Smith. Thus, at *Double Star*'s conclusion, Bonforte/Smith not only reassures himself that he has tried to do what Bonforte would have done but also takes comfort in believing that his father would applaud his performance. At least, he has lived up to the teachings of the two virile, dominant men who reared him firmly and showed him his calling.

Readers may be less satisfied with this conclusion if they notice the methods by which Bonforte/Smith's mentors made him what he is. His father made him "get off [his] lazy duff and learn the business" by beating him with a belt and reinforced his rules on proper language with a backhand to the mouth. Smith also comments that "Father could have given Professor Pavlov pointers in reflex conditioning." Happy with the results, Smith admires these techniques.

In the same way, Bonforte's team makes Smith over so that he can take Bonforte's place. The most serious obstacle is Smith's irrational hatred of Martians, which must be overcome before he can be adopted into the hive. So Dr. Capek, Bonforte's "personal therapist," offers to help Smith by hypnotizing him. The doctor promises not to alter Smith's "personal integration," whatever that is, but when Smith regains consciousness he discovers that he genuinely likes Martians. They even smell wonderful — like Penny's perfume "Jungle Lust." Smith doesn't object to this conditioning either. How can he? He is delighted. When he learns that Capek has used Penny's perfume to condition a positive response to Martian scent, Smith is momentarily confused, then blurts out, "I like it." "You can't help liking it," Capek replies.

This scene is exceptionally interesting because — working close up, like a skillful magician — Heinlein is showing a character who has been conditioned until he can't make an independent choice, who understands what has been done to him, and who accepts it so wholeheartedly that readers also see the treatment as necessary and proper. Following the exchange just quoted, Capek stops showing Smith pictures of Martians so that he can "get you [Smith] into something more useful." While he waits alone, Smith loses the scent of Jungle Lust and is "forced to admit to myself that it was all in the head. But, as an actor, I was intellectually aware of that truth anyhow." However, "When Penny came back a few minutes later, she had a fragrance exactly like a Martian." Later in the novel, Penny is the last person Smith talks with, several times, before he continues in the Bonforte role, suggesting that she is the "something more useful" that Capek has in mind. But, again, readers don't object. Smith already was attracted to Penny, and she is a decent, dedicated, and beautiful girl. And Bonforte/Smith do wind up doing what the novel labels the right thing, so Capek (as part of Bonforte's team) must be doing the right thing. Like Smith's father, the people who surround him now are simply helping him, preparing him to make the right choice when he must.

Readers who look carefully at the action, in fact, may wonder how many choices Smith ever makes. He is conditioned by his father and by Bonforte's team, submerged in Bonforte's personality and values, and fed incomplete information by the team. Consequently, Smith does exactly what others decide he must; he follows the part written for him. This could have disturbing consequences for the novel's conclusion. As children grow up, they separate themselves from their parents, more or less defiantly; then they are free to return to parental values, as many (like Sam in *The Puppet Masters*) do. But this process of rejection and return is unlike what Smith does, climbing directly into the identity of his parent.

Heinlein wants readers to be satisfied that Smith accepts Bonforte's policies as useful expansions of the best values he holds initially. Still, it is troubling to watch Smith make each decision in the role of Bonforte on the basis of "What would Bonforte do?" Almost all the official decisions described in the novel consist of Smith simply signing whatever is placed in front of him. It stands to reason that he must make some decisions in the 35 years after Bonforte's death — but Heinlein deftly skims through that in the summary. The one major policy decision readers actually see Smith making before Bonforte's death is whether to let one of his "team," Bill Corpsman, take a safe seat in the legislature. Smith doesn't like Corpsman, who has always treated him like a flunky, probably because Corpsman himself feels like an outsider, not fully part of the team. Other members of the team feel that official status would soothe Corpsman's ego, but Smith/Bonforte resists. He finally discovers a rationale: Bonforte didn't elevate Corpsman; therefore, he won't either.

The issue of choice becomes more uncomfortable in *Double Star* the more one thinks about it. The overall goal of Bonforte's Expansionist Party, remember, is individual growth, the calm acceptance of change that will lead to an increased ability to make significant decisions. But *Double Star* leaves unanswered the question of whether its central character *can* grow. Holding steadfastly to ideas is one thing; nailing oneself to existing policies is another. Since Smith compares Bonforte to Abraham Lincoln, readers might wonder whether an imposter taking Lincoln's place at the beginning of the Civil War would have realized the eventual necessity of the Emancipation Proclamation. Looking back, we can see a line of thought evolving through Lincoln's actions; it would have been harder at the time, hearing the man's sometimes contradictory statements. Closer to the present, who would have expected the vocally racist Harry S Truman to desegregate the U.S. Armed Forces after World War II? Real people grow sometimes by recognizing that they must find new ways to apply their principles. Apparently, Bonforte never has made a mistake, and the novel gives no indication that Smith falters either once he accepts the Bonforte role and the protection of the team that forms that role's political personality.

But considering how Bonforte's team protects him raises new questions. Real-life politicians are in danger from insiders as much as outsiders. Surrounded by a clique, they may hear only the advice they want to hear. However, Heinlein justifies Smith's secluding himself because being around non-team people who knew the real Bonforte would make the imposture difficult: "A man is not a single complexity; he is a *different* complexity to every person who knows him." Considering this fact could lead to recognition that these other people might be able to throw in divergent but useful ideas, or it even could suggest that although Smith is mastering Bonforte's public persona, the private man remains finally out of reach. But Heinlein does not encourage such uneasiness. As usual, he simply slides past this concern as Bonforte/Smith continues to ask "What would Bonforte do?" rather than "What should I do after absorbing Bonforte's principles?" No disturbing questions are allowed to come up. Father knows best. Early in the novel's action, Penny objects that the imposture is "dishonest" and "*indecent*"; Smith agrees but adds that it is both possible and "necessary"— it can and *should* be done. At the time, Smith is impressed by the loyalty that Bonforte's team of good people show their boss. Later he accepts that the rightness of his actions in the role of Bonforte is verified because the team approves, because it is what Bonforte would have done — and because it works. As Smith says of his father's beatings, "the results justified the method." And so *Double Star*'s action really ends when Smith "decides" to continue being Bonforte. The conclusion Bonforte/Smith writes 25 years later reaffirms that he made the right decision because of what he has accomplished, because his father would approve, and also because "there is a solemn satisfaction in doing the best you can for eight billion people." He adds, "Perhaps their lives have no cosmic significance, but they have feelings. They can hurt."

This concern for the individual does resemble the sentiments expressed in *The Puppet Masters*, but it is spoken by someone who has watched with minimal qualms while his own wild and free self was suppressed. It might follow that any one of those other eight billion people could be sacrificed too, despite momentary hurt feelings. And if any one could, any number could too.

To be sure, readers are not supposed to imagine that the people described with approval in the novel could act with such amoral ruthlessness. They may threaten torture and murder, but they would not actually carry out the threats — or at least Smith prefers not to think they might. But even if they did, after all, they would be right to defend themselves; they are doing only what they must for the good of the cause: expansionism. If they faltered, humanity might not be able to expand. And if it didn't expand, it would be unable to do what it must in order to expand.

Using the conclusion itself as an assumed premise leading to the conclusion is characteristic of a circular argument, and Heinlein's work contains a lot of such circular thinking. In *Double Star*, it is the characters who form a circle, as the elder Smith replicates himself by conditioning his son, etc., all enclosed by and/or enclosing Bonforte's team, in a plot that shows not so much a sequence of cause and effect as an effect that produces its own cause.

However, even if the characters are trapped in a loop, they don't let themselves be frozen in place. To quote Bonforte, "Take sides! Always take sides! You will sometimes be wrong — but the man who refuses to take sides must always be wrong!" Even though it is difficult to "take sides" in a circle, where one "side" curves into another, Heinlein's characters somehow manage. *Why*, in "The Roads Must Roll," must the roads roll? The only person who really considers long-term social consequences is Shorty Van Kleeck, whom the story dismisses as an insecure second-rater. Heinlein's hero, Chief Engineer Gaines, is simply concerned with keeping them rolling, so that in the story's conclusion he realizes that personnel can be conditioned to the unquestionably necessary task until they are "as dependable as machines." On the other hand, "Universe" asserts that individuals must question the narrow formulations of those in power; not being conditioned by surroundings is vital in a world hurtling directionless, out of control. So *Double Star* is not unique in revealing authorial attitudes pointing in different directions. The central character of "By His Bootstraps" tries to reinvigorate the listless people in the far future by studying the works of such masters of group manipulation as Machiavelli, Hitler, and James Farley, FDR's political coordinator; however, *Double Star* cites Farley approvingly as a practical manager of information.

Obviously, Heinlein is capable of seeing opposing positions, putting them together in the same work, and somehow getting away with endorsing neither or both. That barely disguised uneasiness is, in fact, the source of such stories' lasting power. Thus, Bonforte/Smith admits that he may be insane but calls it a necessary madness in the cause of better mental health for humanity as a whole. Heinlein appears convinced that by superimposing these extremes he somehow has reconciled them. Heinlein's ideal is the United States as described in "By His Bootstraps," in which healthy conflict between individuals forces the group onward. At the same time, he must recognize that many people actually find themselves trudging in circles. He *needs* to make those visions fit together somehow. The merging of personalities in *Double Star* may therefore not be an expression of solipsism but an affirmation that free will and determinism do fit together. By combining different identities, Heinlein makes a sleight-of-hand demonstration that different viewpoints can merge harmoniously. In that way, a person can make choices that are both determined and free; he can be aware intellectually that he has been directed toward a goal yet be sincerely devoted to the cause. He can be both a professional entertainer and a sage.

For that was Heinlein's own chosen role. With all his skill as a writer, Heinlein directs readers' attention away from loose ends and evasions, creating stories that are unified artistically if not philosophically. Inconsistencies certainly abound for anyone who looks at all closely. How many are deliberate? When, at this novel's conclusion, Bonforte/Smith regrets that the false death information planted to explain Smith's disappearance stressed that he was unemployed, is he revealing that his immature ego has survived — which might qualify Bonforte's triumph? Does Dr. Capek's name refer to the Czech writer best known for originating the concept of the robot — and what does that do to the notion of free will? Such questions are unanswerable. What the loose ends suggest is that Heinlein's texts are richer in ambiguities than sometimes supposed, left there by a man who perhaps could recognize discrepancies in his ideas but genuinely believed that he could force the extremes together, creating his own kind of "United States." The tension this effort produced, coming from the uncertainty Heinlein resolutely denied, probably accounts for both the divided interpretations his work has received, along with much of its continuing interest. As Bonforte/Smith comments, probably stepping out of character at the novel's conclusion, "I have tried, I suppose to create the perfect work of art. Perhaps I have not fully succeeded — but I think my father would rate it as a 'good performance.'"

"The Menace from Earth" (*F&SF*, August 1957) was one of Heinlein's attempts to write in the persona of a teenage girl. In this case, her name is Holly Jones and she is a cute 15-year-old inhabitant of the Lunar colony. Consciously, she wants to be a spaceship designer; actually, she wants a domestic relationship with her design buddy Jeff. Their bond is disrupted briefly by a glamorous tourist from Earth who dazzles Jeff until Holly is injured while saving her presumed rival during a meticulously described solo winged flight inside the colony's huge air storage tank. Jeff rushes to Holly's side, as the "menace" tells her later in the hospital. She already has confided to Holly that "we can't let men think they own us.... They do own us, of course. But we shouldn't let them know it." Holly takes this consolation to heart.

In the same year as *Double Star*, Heinlein published another novel in which the central character winds up locked in a circular pattern. In *The Door into Summer* (*F&SF*, October–December 1956, book 1957), he considers the same issues and offers what he considers a solution, a way out of such a circular trap. The novel begins by comparing the narrator, Daniel Boone Davis, and his cat, Petronius the Arbiter — Pete, for short. During winter, Pete used to prowl around and around inside the house they shared, looking for one door that would open into a better situation, the door into summer. Dan recognizes how futile the effort is, but he admires Pete's persistence, especially when his own personal situation becomes unbearable and he needs a way to escape.

How did Dan become trapped? His needs are simple: (1) a satisfying job, (2) enough money to get by, and (3) "love." He already has found the perfect job. A gifted inventor, he can be happy working on engineering projects that lead endlessly on into more projects. Money follows naturally, when Dan and his partner Miles found a company to build the home-care robots Dan creates. And Dan thinks he has found love with Belle, the curvaceous secretary who soon has him panting after her and who accepts a chunk of company stock as an engagement present. He is satisfied with Belle's excuse for not consummating their relationship physically: She doesn't want to burden him with a wife and kids until he becomes the great man she knows he can be. Essentially, Dan is content with life as it is; he is doing what he wants, cradled and flattered by the people around him.

When Belle and Miles turn on Dan and steal the company from him, he finds himself excluded from their companionship and, more importantly, legally prohibited for years from working at his beloved profession. After some initial floundering, he decides to put himself in cold sleep, suspended animation, for thirty years so that he can work again and also jeer at Belle's physical decline. He even arranges to take Pete along, so that his only regret is that he must leave behind Ricky, Miles's preteen daughter who has an innocent crush on him. Generally, though, Dan believes he has found a good solution to his dilemma and goes off to taunt Belle and Miles, whistling a tune because he has been working out new gadgets in his head. This all sounds suspiciously like Dan's earlier condition of blissful ignorance, and so it proves to be. In the confrontation with Belle and Miles, Dan guesses so many of their secrets that a shaken Belle reacts. As Dan foolishly turns his back on her, she injects him with an hypnotic drug. As he collapses, he feels "utter astonishment that Belle would do such a thing to me."

At this point in the action, Dan clearly is going in circles. And this reveals, perhaps more clearly than Heinlein himself observed, the real basis of his stories' recurring vision of a circular trap. More than the intricacies of time travel, political slogans, or the technological gimmicks of *Door*'s extrapolated 1970, lazy human nature is responsible for our winding up confined and frustrated. Letting ourselves fall into comfortable patterns can lead to repeating past mistakes. It also evidently is difficult to learn from our experience. Dan's failure shows as much. The question is whether he truly can see what is going on and then take steps that will set him free — for someone might not choose to struggle for freedom if the trap is comfortable and flatters his or her conceit.

Dan gets a second chance at freedom when Belle and Miles decide that rather than kill him they can keep him quiet by depositing him in his thirty-year cold sleep, though they stash him with an inferior company and thus disrupt his plan to take Pete along. As Dan awakens, his mind produces a montage showing some things he will need to recognize and use later — as well as things readers may interpret differently. For one thing, Dan blends memories of Pete trying to defend him from Belle and Miles with an imagined picture of Ricky doing the same: "Pete sat on my chest and wailed.... I did fall asleep while little Ricky wailed and begged me not to." He also imagines himself bearing a burden up an icy mountain that becomes a gigantic breast: "It was all white and beautifully rounded and if I could just climb to the rosy tip they would let me sleep, which was what I needed."

The story itself races along with little reflection on Dan's unconscious desires. When Dan awakens in Great Los Angeles in the year 2000, he is relieved of his old troubles and free to begin a new life — if he is able. In fact, the list Dan makes shortly after his awakening shows the same needs in a slightly different order than before his sleep. First, he needs an income to survive independently. Next, after enduring a pointless, unskilled job to make some money, he manages to regain a position in *real* engineering. Finding Ricky is, in fact, very high on Dan's list, even though he worries whether her husband will approve of a strange man contacting his wife; Dan never doubts that someone as nice as Ricky will have a family, but it follows that her husband will decide what's best for his wife. Dan also wants revenge on Belle and Miles for leaving Pete to die back in 1970. In addition, he needs a peer to share ideas with. He has been struck by admiration for some devices that look like ones he was thinking of before being thrown into cold sleep, and he wants to meet the inventor so they can be pals.

Personal relationships turn out to be the most important priority of all, for even with money and projects to play with, Dan is "bitterly lonely.... There were times ... when I would gladly have swapped it all for one beat-up tomcat, or for a chance to spend an afternoon taking little Ricky to the zoo ... or for the comradeship Miles and I had shared when all we had was hard work and hope." He still needs a pet, a child, and a friend.

Tying up these personal loose ends becomes Dan's primary concern. Miles, he discovers, is long dead. And any revenge against Belle would be superfluous, considering what time and laziness have done to her. Instead of Dan having to track her down, she pursues him, having genuinely forgotten how she betrayed him and thus being sure she still can seduce whatever she wants out of him:

> She was fat and shrill and kittenish. It was evident that she still considered her body her principal asset, for she was dressed in a Stick-tite negligee which, while showing much too much of her, also showed that she was female, mammalian, overfed, and underexercised.
>
> She was not aware of it. That once-keen brain was fuzzy; all that was left was her conceit and her overpowering confidence in herself.

Dan recognizes that she is hopelessly trapped in a loop and disengages himself as soon as he gets the only thing he really wants from her — information about Ricky. When he finds himself yearning to be with Ricky, he is realistic enough to wonder whether, like Belle, he is "living in a fantasy of the past." But he goes on searching, both for Ricky and for the master inventor.

He encounters major shocks in both pursuits. First, he discovers that the patents for the market-dominating gadgets were recorded in his own name in 1970; then he sees a newspaper notice of Ricky having been awakened from cold sleep, but he also discovers that she was met by a man whom she immediately married. When he sees the groom's name, he dashes off to Denver, where a semi-mad scientist has developed a time machine that transports people unpredictably into the past or future. Dan has the good luck to travel into the past, just early enough in 1970 to patent the ideas that will make him rich, rescue Pete outside Belle and Miles's house, discuss Ricky's future with her so that she will go into cold sleep from her twentieth birthday until he reawakens too, and put himself and Pete into cold sleep as he originally planned — to wake up again in the year 2000 and set up married life with Ricky.

Dan has escaped the trap. He has found the door into summer.

Mainly, of course, Dan has rediscovered Ricky. Earlier, it had appeared that he simply wanted to protect a helpless child, but it becomes clear to readers and eventually even to Dan that it is Ricky herself he needs. And this raises the question of what Dan is looking for in a female companion. What does he mean by "love"? His initial views of women seem straightforward enough: We chase them because they're the ones with big breasts, the ones who can give us the comfort we need as we reach for the nipple and drop our adult concerns.

Beyond that, early in the novel, Dan feels that Pete actually is his superior because he can forget a female easily: "He was the natural-born bachelor type." Later, he plans his household gadgets without worrying about a sensible scientific house; all women wanted was "a better-upholstered cave." And still later, after his reawakening, he listens without objection when a drinking buddy in Great Los Angeles explains his "theory that women were closely related to machinery, both utterly unpredictable by logic." Dan's experience with Belle, of course, at least partially accounts for this negative attitude. But Ricky is different. The fact that she is prepubescent, for one thing, means that she does not see herself as a powerful object of desire. Planning his cold sleep, despite Belle having soured him on women, Dan decides he can trust Ricky to look after the company stock he still has because "I had known Ricky half her life and if there ever was a human being honest as a Jo block, Ricky was she ... and Pete thought so too."

Readers don't get to observe what Ricky is, herself, as a person. Early in the novel, Dan mentions her only in passing, preoccupied with the adult fun and games around him. Theirs seems to be a comfortable but limited relationship. They get along because he doesn't talk down to her but instead treats her with the same respect he does Pete — remember how Pete and Ricky merged in Dan's reverie. She is not exactly a pet, of course, but she is not as complex as a grownup person either. Nevertheless, after Dan's sleep, he realizes that now Ricky will have had ten more years of experience than he and vows to marry her if he can: "I needed somebody older to look out for me and tell me no — and Ricky was just the girl who could do it. She had run Miles and Miles' house with serious little-girl efficiency when she was less than ten; at forty she would be just the same, only mellowed."

When he drifts off to sleep after that, Dan produces a remarkably revealing image: "I dreamed that Ricky was holding me on her lap and saying, 'It's all right, Danny. I found Pete and now we're both here to stay. Isn't that so, Pete?'" And Pete says he agrees. It is not exactly that Dan has reverted to childhood; instead, he had merged with Pete, to be cuddled and cared for by the child who also merges with Pete in Dan's thinking. Dan is simultaneously adult, child, and pet — and the same could be said of the others in this cluster. And it is this condition of undifferentiated identity that Dan fundamentally desires. Nor is this all. Remember that Belle is described as "kittenish"; earlier, Dan had commented on her sly persistence: "She had a lot of cat in her ... which may have been why I couldn't resist her." If Belle is included in the loop along with Pete and Ricky, it must be as an ultra-mammalian mother (or stepmother) figure. As parent, she briefly takes Ricky's place as an organizer and arbiter in Dan's and Miles's life, but as predator she enjoys manipulating, toying with, and ultimately smothering her progeny/prey; that's why Dan refers to Miles as her "cat's-paw." But including Belle in the circle certainly complicates a reader's understanding of Dan as a mature, loving adult. Time travel is not the only circular pattern in *The Door into Summer*, for the main characters form a circle of emotional dependence and/or domination.

This circular movement can be visualized in two ways: (1) With Dan in the center of the circle, all the others revolving around him while he reaches out for what he needs, or (2) with Dan as part of the circle, seeking to satisfy his need for childish dependence and sexual stimulation in Belle but discovering that Ricky can do it in a more friendly way, but that Pete is even better at companionship and gives the satisfaction of exercising parental authority too, etc.— in short discovering that one craving leads to another and so he must stretch just a little beyond what each individual can give...

Dan never notices such complications of personal relationships. For him, it is enough that he has broken out of the loop of circumstances that denied him satisfaction. He certainly has no further need to circle through time, for he looks forward to cruising ahead into the future, savoring each day. He can't imagine that laziness still may have him trapped in an immature, undifferentiated condition. After all, he *is* happy.

As Dan sees it, he has used his engineer's craft to grasp the elements of an unappealing situation and rearrange them in a more satisfactory pattern. He must admit that it was useful to know how his plans would work out because he had seen the results. He could be certain that the time machine would transport him into the past, for example, because he had seen his name on the patents and in the bridal registry. In other word, Dan knows what he must do because he knows he *did* do it. Dan discusses this mixture of choice and determinism most thoroughly near the book's conclusion: "'There's a divinity that shapes our ends, rough-hew them how we will.' Free will and predestination in one sentence and both true." Shortly later, Dan scorns the idea of "paradoxes" because whatever happens can happen "because the Builder designed the universe that way. He gave us eyes, two hands, a brain; anything we do with them *can't* be a paradox." Visualizing God as an engineer — i.e., himself writ large — Dan simply accepts that things worked out as they were supposed to and/or as he was able to shape them.

Readers may be less convinced. Dan's interview with ten-year-old Ricky is an especially perplexing scene. Dan is careful not to behave like a grownup ordering a child what to do. *She* is the one who asks whether, if she goes into cold sleep as soon as she is twenty, Dan will marry her when she wakes up. Dan describes this as an overwhelmingly emotional moment for himself. In fact, however, he already knows what she will do because he has seen their signatures in the bridal registry thirty years in the future. It is true that Dan is leaving Ricky with ten years to change her mind, to develop new relationships that she might not want to give up, but he trusts her — and anyway he already has seen the proof that she will do what they are planning.

Once again, it's necessary to consider the relationship between people of different sexes. Heinlein must be very delicate about this. When Dan goes to see Ricky at Girl Scout camp, he notes approvingly that the woman in charge is cautious, for "strange men who want to be allowed to visit little girls just turning into big girls should always be suspected." To avoid Dan looking like a pedophile, Heinlein never mentions the shape of Ricky's adult figure; readers must extrapolate from the fact that little Ricky "was a matchstick sketch of the woman she would become." Apparently, the mature results are at least adequate. But Dan stresses that he does not even touch Ricky during their crucial conversation. That's not necessary: "Our original relationship, back when she was six, had been founded on mutual decent respect for the other's individualism and personal dignity."

Again, though, what does this "respect" mean? How does it relate to "love"? We've noted Dan's somewhat dismissive comments about women, suggesting that they essentially are good for providing physical comfort and encouragement. The story as a whole supports this idea. The wife of Dan's next, honest partner is presented as a good, trustworthy woman — but limited. Jenny is "a very uncomplicated person"; her husband simply tells her what he decides she needs to know. Furthermore, at the novel's end, Dan is frustrated when he tries to lay out the pattern of events for his wife, Ricky. All she cares about is the comfortable results, and Dan shrugs, "I should never have tried to explain." Ricky is valued at the end as she was at the beginning, for innocence, enthusiasm, and the way she fits Dan's will. The one incident in which she appears to show some independence actually reinforces these qualities. Dan has told her when to schedule her awakening from cold sleep;

he even wrote out the directions for her. But when he goes to collect her, he finds that she has not left instructions to be awakened on that day. Dan is momentarily "disappointed and hurt," until the attendant explains that Ricky didn't want to be wakened on a set date, just whenever Dan came to get her. Without imagining that marriage should be built on perpetual confrontation, readers do observe that Ricky displays her individualism by being even more delightfully submissive than Dan expects.

To convince readers that this is a satisfactory ending, Heinlein must evade some issues the novel has raised. For one thing, how does Dan know how Ricky's figure will develop when all he has ever seen of her grownup looks is a snapshot of her face — unless he's been thinking about the subject more than he can consciously acknowledge? In addition, the comment about women and machines being equally illogical is a strange thing for one engineer to say and another to let stand. Does that suggest that what appears to be a smoothly functioning machine may be quirkily unpredictable — or the reverse, that what appears to be a personal choice may be a mechanical pattern? And what does it mean that by the novel's end Dan's need for the companionship of an intellectual peer has been scaled down to "an old machinist who thinks I'm crazy but follows my drawings to exact tolerance"? As usual with Heinlein, such loose ends may be due to carelessness — or to complications that he can see but more or less consciously has decided to evade.

Heinlein's skill as a writer and his natural talent for evasion are such, however, that readers are inclined to accept Dan's assurance that *The Door into Summer* ends happily. After all, Dan has enough money to do what he wants, a satisfying profession, and such "love" as he can envision and share. It is a little like the cat heaven he envisions for the aging Pete, "where catnip fields abound and tabbies are complacent, and robot opponents are programmed to fight fiercely — but always lose — and people have friendly laps and legs to strop against, but never a foot that kicks." The novel succeeds on its own terms. A reader's uneasiness with the way it works out may be due partly to a feeling that those terms are limited and that the opponents have been programmed too obviously. The novel itself, perhaps innocently, refers to such a situation when a doctor tells Dan that amnesia is the product of "the patient's own subconscious wish. He forgets a sequence of events, or rearranges them, because the facts are unbearable to him." Dan also makes a suggestive comment about advertisers: "These people who deal in fancification to fool the public think nobody can read and write but themselves."

Heinlein's hero falls between these extremes. Unlike an amnesiac, Dan can interact with his surroundings; unlike an advertiser, he rearranges circumstances without being fully aware of what he is doing. But Dan still may be fooling himself. If his mind is not as obviously fuzzy as Belle's, it still is unwilling to push past superficial human relationships. He has used the possibilities available to him so that he can loop through time in order to engineer a satisfying existence for himself and secure a wife and a pet so that he won't be lonely. At the end, though, Dan appears to be surrounded by reflections of himself, still going in circles.

"The Man Who Traveled in Elephants" was written in 1948 but resurrected for its first public appearance in *Saturn, the Magazine of Science Fiction* (October 1958). According to Spider Robinson, it was one of Heinlein's personal favorites among his short stories.

The surface action is very simple. John Watts, a fat old man, is riding a bus on his way to the Fair. He is by himself, his wife having died some time ago, but they had devoted themselves to traveling around the United States, soaking up the delights of fairs, expositions, all manner of public celebrations, so he continues the activity partly as a way of preserving her memory. The bus has a crash, in which — readers may later surmise — Watts is killed, though he notices only that he can't see very well because his glasses are broken, and so simply continues on his journey. When he arrives at his destination, he discovers that the Fair contains the best of every festival in the country, every glorious spectacle he's ever seen at its most intense. He encounters a dog that *is* the very dog he and his wife once loved, then reunites with his wife herself. He is recognized as the king of the Fair's endless parade, and the couple rides on together.

This wisp of a plot is brought to life by Heinlein's love of all things that are individual, regional, particular, eccentric. There is no ranting here about the degeneration of mass culture. This story has the sweet nostalgia of Ray Bradbury, as schmaltzy but sincere as a piece dictated by Jubal Harshaw.

Heinlein intended "Tenderfoot in Space" (*Boy's Life*, May–July 1958) to be part of a collection of Boy Scout stories, along with "Nothing Ever Happens on the Moon" and a third novella that he never wrote when the project ran out of steam.

The story itself is pleasant but predictable. Charlie Vaughn really, *really* loves his dog Nixie, so much so that his father relents and lets the little mutt accompany the family on their emigration to Venus. While his parents are busy with their readjustment to the new world, Charlie turns to a Boy Scout troop for companionship and for help in learning to cope with the planet's hostile environment — packed with flora and fauna avidly competing for space, food, and soft warm places to lay eggs. Readers expect that a catastrophe will occur, that Charlie will be heroic, but that Nixie will be the real savior. Sure enough, that's what happens.

Heinlein's depiction of Nixie's limited consciousness is charming, comparable to *The Star Beast*, and his picture of the ferocious Venusian jungle is effective too. The story's main weakness is lack of inspiration; it feels limp and tired, as if writing the juvenile novels for Scribner's hadn't shown Heinlein that he was better off abandoning or subverting clichés so that he could be free to develop something more original.

"All You Zombies —" (*F&SF*, March 1959) is effectively Heinlein's last short story. It may be his best, utilizing all his considerable skills to pursue one of his abiding concerns.

For a rather short story, it has an extremely complicated plot. It begins in 1970. The narrator is a bar owner who strikes up a conversation with one of his customers, the Unmarried Mother, so labeled because he writes schlock for confession magazines. As he gets the man drunk, the narrator draws out his story: He *was* an unmarried mother himself; being an unusually homely orphan girl, he was dazzled and seduced but then deserted by a stranger; after she gave birth to their child, whom she named Jane, the unmarried mother was informed that the surgeons had discovered she possessed both male and female sex organs but that they had been able to save only the male set so that she was now a man; to make things even worse, the baby Jane was stolen from the hospital. The Unmarried Mother would like to confront the man who wrecked her/his life. The narrator tricks him into a time machine and transports them both to

1963, when the narrator hands the other man enough money to impress a lonely girl, then leaves him and jumps to

1964, when the narrator steals baby Jane from the hospital and leaves her at an orphanage before jumping back to

1963, when he reunites with the morally-shaken male Unmarried Mother who has just had sex with the lonely girl — the narrator comments that this proves "you can't resist seducing yourself"— and the two jump to

1985, when the narrator leaves the Unmarried Mother in a futuristic military base to think over the offer of a meaningful career, "the best job a man ever held," as he himself jumps back to

1970, to get rid of the bar and jump to

1993, when he finally can relax, having completed his job as a recruiter for the Circle of Ouroboros time patrol. As he glances at the Caesarian scar on his belly from the birth of his baby girl, he thinks of the people he's encountered but who've been peripheral to the main action and finally addresses readers directly:

> Then I glanced at the ring on my finger.
> The Snake That Eats Its Own Tail, Forever and Ever ... I know where *I* came from — but *where did all you zombies come from.*
> I felt a headache coming on, but a headache powder is one thing I do not take. I did once — and you all went away.
> So I crawled into bed and whistled out the light.
> You aren't really there at all. There isn't anybody but me — Jane — here alone in the dark.
> I miss you dreadfully!

"By His Bootstraps" is a marvelously constructed story, twisting back on itself with the revelation that the main character has been reencountering himself at different ages, with different levels of understanding. "All You Zombies—" offers some of the same devious satisfaction but at less length and with the added complication of sexual reassignment. It packs more emotional punch too. At the end of a first reading, after readers realize that the narrator was the baby who grew up to be the girl who was seduced by the man who fled her but who went on to become — in short, when it becomes clear that they're all the same person, readers can look back and catch significant bits of the story that slid by unnoticed at the time. When, for example, the Unmarried Mother describes his female form as "horse-faced and buck-toothed, flat-chested and straight-haired," the narrator replies consolingly/revealingly, "You don't look any worse than I do." Because the story is so short, readers can flip pages back easily to review such clues. Heinlein uses all his skill in suggesting not just the high-tech future of the Circle of Ouroboros but also a web of connections and identifications that none of the characters except the narrator can grasp by themselves.

Nor is this dropping of hints merely clever. A large part of the fun of reading the story is figuring out what's going on. As readers absorb the complexity of its few pages, they become involved in the activity of connecting clues, figuring out a puzzle. In doing so, they observe how the narrator keeps one step ahead as he jumps from one year and situation to another — until the end, where the ultra-competent narrator crashes headlong into a puzzle he can't solve. The reassurance that human problems can be solved suddenly evaporates.

For some readers, "All You Zombies—" provided an "aha!" moment that revealed Heinlein's unacknowledged fundamental solipsism. As a matter of fact, Heinlein's possible titles for the piece include "The Solipsist," and the story may be taken as simply a superior example of "What if?" Other readers have observed that not everyone in the story is part of the uni-identity character loop. Still later, of course, other novels made clear that the Circle of Ouroboros is a going concern, protecting the integrity of the multiverse, so that the narrator of "Zombies" does have fellow agents to check for confirmation that he is not alone.

Still, that does not diminish the anguish the speaker feels at the story's end. Although the Circle may be a worthwhile organization, the narrator still feels a need for *someone else* to believe in. Those other people around him may be real individuals — or maybe not:

Wouldn't anyone who had looked casually at him, the Unmarried Mother, the young woman, and the baby have supposed that they were separate and distinct people too? Everything fits together too neatly for comfort. The narrator knows that his younger self will accept the offer of a place in the Circle and do well in the job; after all, *he* did. Once again, discovery of "the best job a man ever held" turns out to be just part of an endless circular process.

One can question the validity of the narrator's painful loneliness and doubt but not their reality. The story continues to be unresolvably troubling and brilliantly alive.

Although submitted to Scribner's as another juvenile, *Starship Troopers* was published in a magazine for grownups (*F&SF*, October–November 1959) and never has been marketed as anything but a novel for adults. Despite the controversy it roused among readers and other writers and despite the Hugo Award it won in 1960, there's really little to say about the novel—partly because it says exactly what Heinlein intended so that there's little need for additional commentary, but also partly because its effectiveness as a polemic makes it less resonant as a novel. The Israeli writer Amos Oz once said that when he already had an idea clearly in mind he wrote an essay but when he wanted to clarify his thinking he wrote fiction. In other words, readers go to an essay expecting to be told the conclusions a thoughtful writer has found; a novel, on the other hand, offers a presentation of people grappling with life's complexities in hopes of finding some coherent organizing principle. In *Starship Troopers*, Heinlein uses his skills as a writer of fiction to deliver an essay on duty and responsibility as exemplified in military service.

The novel's first chapter shows narrator Johnnie Rico taking part in a raid on another planet designed to intimidate the planet's natives, the humanoid "skinnies"; then in the last chapter Johnnie is the commander of a unit about to go into combat against a planetful of giant, intelligent bugs. Between those events is a chronological narrative describing his incremental growth from boy to man.

Initially, as he graduates from high school, Johnnie simply accepts the values handed to him by his society and family. Although only veterans can vote, most people disdainfully ignore the idea of service, and in particular Johnnie's father treats the notion as just "a predictable stage in a boy's growing up." Mr. Rico is a successful businessman who is used to doing his son's thinking for him: "Listen, and let *me* tell *you* what you are going to do—because you *want* to." In school, when the instructor in Johnnie's mandatory History and Moral Philosophy course (a military veteran, naturally) taunts him with the question "What is the moral difference, if any, between the soldier and the civilian?," all the boy can do is parrot the words of his textbook: "The difference ... lies in the field of civic virtue. The soldier accepts personal responsibility for the safety of the body politic of which he is a member, defending it, if need be, with his life. The civilian does not." The rest of the novel describes how Johnnie comes to understand and embody that statement.

Johnnie's first step, the first real choice he ever has made, is to enlist in the military. Much later in the novel, it's mentioned that Johnnie was "space happy" as a child, and the prodding of his H&MP teacher may have disturbed his teen-jock complacency; his most immediate motivation, though, is the examples set by two classmates, one of them a cute girl in front of whom he doesn't want to look weak.

But the result of enlisting is that Johnnie begins to discover who he really is. First, the army separates a recruit from the birth family he's been depending on for an identity. Basic training begins with sergeants insulting the boys as "drooling refugees from apron strings ... momma's spoiled little darlings," and the boys themselves joke that that their sergeants "don't have mothers." Johnnie's own mother unwittingly helps in this process of separation by writing a letter saturated with sentimental condescension. She calls him "my darling baby" and continues, "Whatever you are, whatever you choose to do, you are always my little boy who bangs his knee and comes running to my lap for comfort.... Little boys never get over needing their mother's laps — do they, darling?" No self-respecting young man could be comfortable in this degrading relationship.

The service doesn't want to eliminate the men's feeling that they are part of a family — quite the contrary. "Family" gives its individual members a sense of purpose in their lives, encouraging support while they go about their activities, an emotional place of rest: home. So does the army. After basic training is over, Johnnie observes that "The Lieutenant was father to us and loved us and spoiled us and was nevertheless rather remote from us.... Jelly [sergeant, their immediate superior] was mother to us and was close to us and took care of us and didn't spoil us at all." This makes sense functionally, since soldiers should care for each other's welfare while accepting orders willingly. Moreover, the soldier's superior morality stems from his recognition of responsibility to the larger "family" of humanity. As part of his further formal education in Officers' Candidate School, Johnnie must learn that "Morals — *all* correct moral rules — derive from the instinct to survive; moral behavior is survival behavior above the individual level — as in a father who dies to save his children."

Civilians don't understand — or don't want to understand — this larger concept of family. For example, the civilian doctor who examines Johnnie before he enters the service disparagingly remarks that "military service is for ants," by which he means meaningless little creatures that lack individual intelligence but are mere extensions of a controlling mind. That proves, later, to be a good description of the alien race of bugs that humanity must fight to the death. Humans respond to that threat not by becoming more like the unthinking insects but by the developing the loyalty *and* focused intelligence of fighting men.

Typically in *Starship Troopers*, Heinlein forces the point even more heavy-handedly. When Johnnie learns that the bugs killed his mother during an attack on Earth, he assumes that his father must be dead too; however, he encounters his father within the military and learns that the older man enlisted in emulation of his son's decision. As he says, "I had to prove to myself that I was a man. Not just a producing-consuming animal ... but a *man*." In this respect, the novel resembles the family unit in *The Puppet Masters*. At the beginning of *Starship Troopers*, Mr. Rico was Johnnie's "old man"; by the end, Johnnie has become an officer who is the "Old Man" to his troops, including his father, a role reversal that would have felt especially satisfying for younger readers.

This is just one of the novel's extremely convenient but rather contrived events. In another, after receiving his mother's disgusting letter, Johnnie gets a stirring, ego-boosting note from his high school H&MP teacher. In yet another lucky break, while Johnnie is uncertain whether he can make it to the end of basic training or not, he watches what looks like the brutal dismissal of a fellow recruit who snapped momentarily, which makes him question the *rightness* of the system; fortunately, he is sitting near a thin partition so that he can overhear the officers discussing how much they like the "kids," even if they "are wild animals at this stage." As the Captain tells Johnnie's sergeant, "We must not hate them, we must not like them; we must teach them." Reassured, Johnnie guts it out.

As usual, Heinlein sabotages racial/ethnic expectations. The names of Johnnie's fellow soldiers reveal that they are from mixed backgrounds, but he never comments on the fact because, of course, it doesn't matter as long as they can learn to become troopers. His father, early in the novel, disdainfully remarks that the high school H&MP teacher, Mr. Dubois, has "a silly name — it suits him. Foreigner, no doubt," so a reader might assume that Johnnie was a fellow WASP, until he mentions casually that his native language is Tagalog. So Johnnie's cultural/racial background evidently doesn't matter either.

Not every issue is as squarely faced. One curious aspect of *Starship Troopers* is the absence of women. They *are* present in the space navy, dropping the capsules containing Mobile Infantrymen exactly on target and retrieving them with marvelous delicacy. When Johnnie does encounter the girl with whom he enlisted, he pays her the high compliment of observing "that she really was an officer and a fighting man — as well as a very pretty girl." He returns to barracks "with stars in my eyes" because she kisses him; when a woman naval officer kisses Sergeant Jelly, he blushes. The soldiers are interested in women, but they don't seem to do much with them. Johnnie repeats several times that it's important to the troopers that women are on board the starships that take them into battle because it reminds them of "the only good reason why men fight" — in other words, their role as protectors of other family members. It's also important, however, to keep the women safely out of reach. Perhaps this shows the novel's origins as an ostensibly juvenile novel, or perhaps the whole issue of sexual relation in the broadest sense would have been too distracting from Heinlein's overpowering purpose. So would a discussion of how someone might activate citizenship by non-combatant service. In the same way, though the military men repeatedly insist that their principles can be validated mathematically, they never do so. And though military service supposedly stabilizes peacetime society by restricting the franchise to veterans, Johnnie certainly has no time to demonstrate that and at the novel's end is deep in combat, far from emerging as a responsible veteran.

Heinlein's novels for Scribner's had long tested juvenile fiction's reassuring assumption that its youthful readers would be able to find or make a place for themselves in the adult world. In fact, Heinlein was writing for young adults who should be actively questioning the roles they were supposed to fill. *Starship Troopers*, however, insists on one role that its readers *must* choose. In earlier novels, Heinlein had challenged readers and encouraged them to extend themselves; in *Starship Troopers*, he insists on force-feeding them a message. Of all his novels, this is the one that most vehemently treats its readers like children.

6

Stranger in a Strange Land

The 1961 novel that made Heinlein's reputation beyond sf has earned annoyance, fascination, and awe—sometimes in different readers, sometimes simultaneously in the same reader. It was an unexpected performance for Heinlein. Unlike his earlier adult novels intended for magazine publication, it is not written in substantial episodes with obvious breaks for serial pauses. Nor is it like the tightly controlled juvenile novels, compact in length and tightly plotted around a series of cause and effect actions. Instead, it is very long, loosely structured to permit vast stretches of talk, and vividly scornful of sexual and religious taboos (though shy of physical description of taboo-violating activities). Many of Heinlein's stories were written very rapidly, in a burst of inspiration; *Stranger* gestated for over a decade. The novel required extra effort at a time when its sale—let alone wide and continuing popularity—was uncertain. It evidently is a book Heinlein needed to write, one that utilized both his personal concerns and his considerable experience as a writer.

Never serialized, *Stranger* exists in two versions: the one abridged by Heinlein at his hardcover publisher's request, to reduce the time spent talking about sex and religion, and the longer original manuscript published after his death. It's the latter that we will be considering because it certainly is Heinlein's preferred text. In its unfettered version, the story does seem to lurch and ramble, from a beginning that feels like a typical fast-moving sf adventure into what sometimes seems interminable pontification interrupted by discordant background summaries; the book's form seems improvised, becoming whatever is needed at the moment. In practice, somehow, all this turns out to be more amusing than discomforting.

Reviewers and critics have had difficulty coping with *Stranger*, from early opinions that it is an ill-constructed sf novel to later admiration of it as a profound philosophical statement. Both positions seem exaggerated. One interesting literary analysis, William H. Patterson, Jr., and Andrew Thornton's *The Martian Named Smith: Critical Perspectives on Robert A. Heinlein's Stranger in a Strange Land* argues that the book is not really a novel but a satirical anatomy along the lines of *Tristram Shandy*. Nevertheless, *Stranger* does *feel* like a novel because the unruly masses of satirical conversation and description coalesce around a central character who remains the focus of readers' attention. In form, thus, *Stranger* resembles a *Bildungsroman*, a narrative tracing a young person's maturation. In the case of *Stranger*, the young person is Michael Valentine Smith, better known as Mike, and the action begins some time after his physical birth but during his emergence as a human being. After his parents, along with all the other members of the first expedition from Earth to Mars died/murdered each other/killed themselves, Mike was left as a helpless newborn baby but was raised by the native Martians as one of them: He grew up thinking like a Martian and living as much like one as his different physiology would permit. When he is brought back to Earth by the second expedition to Mars (its arrival delayed considerably by World War III), Mike is physically a young man but is mentally and physically unable to function in human society: He withdraws into a deathlike trance when confronted with serious emotional conflict. Thus he is especially vulnerable to external control, and his immense potential wealth tempts government officials to keep him from ever becoming conscious of himself as a rival for power.

Heinlein offers glimpses inside Mike's consciousness to show how alien his perceptions are and how difficult it will be for him to leave that immobile state. In part, the alienness is communicated by Mike's tentative grasp of colloquial English; for example, "How do you feel?" offers a baffling tangle of alternative interpretations. Mike thus falls into using more precise Martian terms such as "grok" that may baffle Earth humans. From context, readers soon can recognize that "to grok" means "to understand," but further observation of Mike's thinking expands that superficial definition to include "to thoroughly comprehend," "to absorb sympathetically," "to extend oneself into," "to drink," "to deeply love" (or "hate"), etc. Fortunately, nurse Gillian Boardman is curious enough to sneak into the hospital room where Mike is sequestered, then to try to talk with him and also to share a drink of water with him, though she has no idea that doing this makes her Mike's "water brother," another Martian concept that is much more profound than most Earth-raised humans are prepared to imagine since they don't appreciate water as a rare and precious substance. Even more fortunately, Jill is inspired by her newsman boyfriend, Ben Caxton, to smuggle Mike out of the hospital. After their escape, Mike reveals part of what he has learned from the Martians when he innocently discorporates — kills or at least thinks out of existence — two government thugs who are menacing his water brother Jill. At this point, nevertheless, Mike still is essentially a vulnerable infant, likely to draw up into a fetal position and helplessly dependent on others for protection and social guidance.

The "other" who takes over Mike's development — and dominates the book for many pages thereafter — is Jubal Harshaw, to whom Jill flees after Ben is kidnapped by government goons. "LL.B., M.D., Sc.D., bon vivant, gourmet, sybarite, popular author extraordinary, and neo-pessimist philosopher," Jubal knows how to do almost everything or can at least talk convincingly about it. Currently, he earns money as a writer in all genres and media, an apparently lucrative occupation since he lives in a private estate with two male assistants and three beautiful female secretaries. It is a determinedly unconventional lifestyle, keeping everything that makes Jubal comfortable and discarding everything else.

Over the next few hundred pages, while manipulating official protocol to keep Mike safe, Jubal demonstrates why he is a good mentor for the infant-man. He describes himself as a writer of "trash" and refuses to look at a piece once he's finished dictating it. Nevertheless, when he finished dictating one sentimental yarn about a little lost kitten wandering about on Christmas Eve both he and the secretary are weeping, "both bathed in a catharsis of schmaltz," He is not simply a calculating hack, exploiting the reading public; instead he shares the values he volubly mocks. He displays a working awareness that Trash and Truth may not be mutually exclusive terms, not the last time that *Stranger* demonstrates the compatibility of apparent opposites.

It also is true that Jubal is responsible for creating a family — a group of humans that sustains him practically and emotionally. The flesh and blood daughters he reared have settled into conventional, respectable lifestyles and consequently have little use for him. When he speaks of his "family," he means the people he has gathered to live with him — or, as in the cases of Jill and Mike, ones who have sought him out and earned his protection.

An outsider observes their operation as "a pleasant family picnic, made easy by Jubal's gift for warm informality." Mike, with his innocent willingness to welcome anyone as a water brother, can learn from this example.

One limitation, despite Jubal's general tolerance, is his reluctance to involve himself very far outside his comfortable enclave. As he says, "All I want is to live my own lazy, useless life, sleep in my own bed — and not be *bothered!*" This appears ironic since Jubal proclaims it after heroic exertion on Mike's behalf, but that was a personal, individual effort. The range of sensitivity that lets Jubal appreciate different aspects of a single person also keeps him from having faith in any one more-than-individual value. The fact that he can convince — and unconvince — himself of almost anything once he starts talking makes him reluctant to commit to any big, long-term cause. His hesitation is demonstrated by his attitude toward religion. When Mike insists on visiting a church of the folksy, apparently commercially contrived Fosterite religion, Jubal reveals that his parents wanted him to be a preacher and that he believes he could have been a successful evangelist "with just a touch more self confidence and a liberal helping of ignorance.... But I lacked the necessary confidence in my own infallibility; I could never be a prophet ... just a critic — which is a poor thing at best, a sort of fourth-rate prophet suffering from delusions of gender." In short, Jubal's appreciation of how thoroughly individual experience is subjective keeps him from recognizing that there might be anything larger than human that would deserve profound belief or sustained action.

Jubal dominates a large portion of *Stranger*, by the sheer mass of his provocative critical pronouncements, and every time he reappears in the novel's later pages he claims special respect. After all, he is Mike's surrogate father, his first human teacher. He is exactly the person Mike needs early in his life, to protect him and to serve as an example, so that Mike has the opportunity to observe a complicated, confident man in action, to appreciate his considerable virtues but also to recognize his shortcomings — and then to leave, when the young man must continue his *own* development. This happens as Mike discovers the wonderful possibilities of religion and sex, areas of human experience for which Jubal mistakenly considers himself too well-informed or too old.

Mike's apprenticeship in religion and sex actually take place largely simultaneously, his discoveries in one field reinforcing his understanding of the other.

For a jaded outsider like Jubal, the Fosterite church is a sham, a commercial venture created simply to fleece the rubes. Mike, who can approach the emotional hoopla of a Fosterite service with an innocently open mind, recognizes the truth under the superficial phoniness. He can see that shared religious ecstasy is a good thing because it leads to "a growing-closer." Even though Bishop Digby, the current church head, is an obnoxious fraud whom Mike inconspicuously discorporates, the religion itself reveals a genuine human need and accomplishment that he must ponder quietly while Jubal scoffs loudly and long. As Mike ponders the concept of "church" alone at night, he encounters one of his water brothers. When conversation leads to sex and they have "merged, grokking together," Mike "softly and triumphantly" states, "Thou art God," and she exclaims the same at the moment of orgasm.

This act of sex thus confirms a Martian concept whose English translation is sometimes pooh-poohed by human authority figures as too simple-minded and naïve. Several other points about this scene are worth noting. For one thing, while Mike and his partner are chatting, Mike shows how his orientation has changed by correcting himself after referring to "my people — the Martians, I mean; I grok now that *you* are my people." Readers also should note that Mike's sexual partner remains anonymous at this point. It's safe to assume that the person is female; homosexual behavior is acceptable in Heinlein's later fiction, but it's never encouraged. Beyond that, like the people in Jubal's family at the time, readers might assume that Jill must be the one — but, as the story later reveals, that's not necessarily true. Earlier, each woman Mike innocently kissed had been aroused not because he was signaling that he wanted to have sex with her but because he gave his full attention to each kiss: He made each of them feel special. Yet, in apparent contradiction, this scene demonstrates that sex/grokking/growing-closer is an escape from individual personality, so that Mike feels himself "almost ready to discorporate" as he hears the reaffirmation of their shared Godhood.

To make sense of what he is experiencing, Mike must go out into the world. Accompanied by Jill, he becomes a stage magician in a traveling carnival. His Martian education lets him really do things that Earthborn illusionists must fake, but he isn't a success as a performer. As the carny barker who fires Mike explains, he doesn't have a feel for what a chump in the crowd wants: "He wants ... Mystery! He wants to think that the world is a romantic place when he knows damn well it ain't." Ironically, the barker recommends that Mike learn how an ordinary human chump thinks by going out and becoming one — essentially what Mike is attempting. He can't actually unmake himself and become a gullible, ordinary human; however, he can learn that all people, even the Man from Mars, are painfully conscious of their limitations but yearn for something more: "Mystery!"

He discovers an apostle of mystery among one of the carny folk whom it would be easy to dismiss on first glance as a freak: Patty the tattooed lady. Besides being sexually attractive and willing, Patty joins Mike and Jill because she senses that they are looking for the same thing as Fosterite seekers. It turns out that she knew Foster personally and can testify to his sincerity. She compares him to Mike, explaining that Foster also "had been really and truly a man while he was on Earth, but had been also and *always* had been, an archangel, even though he had not known it himself." The comparison of Foster — and, by extension now, Mike — to Jesus becomes pervasive as the story continues.

So sex and religion merge again, as Patty feels "overpowering religious ecstasy like heat lightning in her loins" when she's with Mike and Jill. Personalities merge again too, as "brother" equals "self" in Mike and Jill's telepathic conversation. Now, however, Mike is ready to go even farther as he reconsiders his estimate of what earlier in the story had seemed to be the Martians' superiority to humans. Martians had appeared to be more serenely mature because they feel no sexual tension and also don't fear death since they know the spirits of discorporated Martians simply pass on to the next stage of existence by becoming "Old Ones." Actually, Mike "had grokked, when first he had known it fully, that physical human love ... *itself* was a growing-closer, a very great goodness — and (so far as he knew) unknown even to the Old Ones of his former people." Making the effort to overcome frustrating boundaries actually may make humans superior to Martians if they can learn new things that will help them and unlearn old things that won't.

One thing Earthborn humans need to learn is the Martian language. Even though Mike now is moving past Martian thinking, he used the vocabulary and grammar of Martian in forming his first approach to understanding life on Earth, so other people who need to reach the same understanding will have to use the same conceptual framework. A conversation between Jubal and Dr. Mahmoud described language as a "'map' of the universe," stating that different languages express different conceptions of reality. Martian thus contains a unique understanding of how things work, as shown in how the word "grok" demands a much more total immersion and absorption than its casual translation as "know." The "maps" contained in human language on Earth reflect a territory shrouded by underestimation of human potential. That's why Jill, who has absorbed some Martian from Mike, sees that Patty's attempt in English to describe Foster's dual identities is fuzzy. The subject could be much more clearly approached in Martian. Having learned Martian as a child, Mike is able to imagine the universe differently than most humans, including a different understanding of natural laws. Because he doesn't know that it's "impossible," he sees nothing extraordinary about communicating telepathically with Jill (but only in Martian), teleporting himself, moving and discorporating objects or people, etc. He can't teach others how to do these useful tricks until they have learned the language and share the viewpoint that makes the tricks possible; then people will not find such actions remarkable but perform them as casually as Mike does.

At the same time, people need to unlearn the attitudes that keep them isolated, able to express their desires for escape only in confused, unfocused groping. Much earlier in the story, when Mike was a celebrity living with Jubal, Jill went through his fan mail and was disturbed by "filthy" pictures from female fans. What Mike noticed was the "beautiful pain" on the face of one unclothed but enthusiastic admirer. When she becomes more experienced (and more fluent in Martian), Jill parades her beautiful body as a Las Vegas showgirl, telepathically sharing with Mike the lust she rouses in a member of the audience and agreeing that the experience is "*Beautiful agony.*" It evidently is both wonderful and awful to expose oneself to others. Jill must force herself to discard the unconscious prissiness that makes her hesitate to open herself to new experience.

As Mike struggles to learn, he still has things to unlearn. Hung up on Martian norms, he has had no practice in believing something that he can't directly experience. Consequently, it confuses him that humans aren't aware of the souls of the discorporated. Could that mean that, unlike Martian Old Ones, human souls don't survive? Or, even worse, that humans don't even have souls? Jill smiles "with sober serenity" as she replies that the two of them are one and are God eternally. But Mike is unsatisfied. He impatiently dismisses science for not asking the questions he wants answered and religions for demanding that worshipers accept their precut answers on faith.

Perhaps the most difficult thing Mike has to learn is that holding two incompatible things next to each other can lead not to anger or dismay but instead to serene, smiling acceptance. He needs to learn the difference between tragedy and comedy. Both focus on surprise, the difference between the ideal and the actual. Essentially, tragedy shows that all humans will fail, the height of their glorious dreams only emphasizing the depths of their defeat. Comedy acknowledges that this is true — but not *always*. Comedy insists that it's possible, however barely and briefly, to see the gap between what was expected and what actually happened, to realize that one has not been destroyed by the difference, and then to laugh or at least smile calmly. After the outburst quoted above, Jill smiles and says, "Mike, you just made a joke." He objects that he didn't mean his comment as a joke and furthermore objects that Jill doesn't laugh as she used to: "I haven't learned to laugh; instead you've forgotten how. Instead of my becoming human ... you're becoming Martian." Since Martians see with wider senses than humans, they are harder to surprise. That means they don't need humor to release tension when their expectations go amiss. Mike finally sees the need for humor during a visit to the zoo when he watches monkeys mistreating each other. Then he laughs uncontrollably and tells Jill that at last he has "found out why people laugh. They laugh because it hurts so much ... because it's the only thing that'll make it stop hurting." He adds that "The goodness is in the laughing itself. I grok it is a bravery ... and a sharing ... against pain and sorrow and defeat.... All the things that are funny to humans either physically cannot happen on Mars or are not permitted to happen."

The humor that Mike discovers leads finally not to mere dismissive laughter but to calm acceptance that incompatible things can be equally true. Humans *are* isolated, frightened, confused — especially in contrast to the wise, mind-sharing Martians. It's also true, however, that they sometimes recognize their unhappy condition and so struggle to grow closer, to see more clearly, to apprehend a Mystery. They need better sex and more communion so that they can stop hurting each other and themselves. They need to grok. Mike sympathizes with his fellow human beings now that he has realized that he is one himself. He wants to help his brothers, and he sees that the human institution created out of their dreadful tangle of needs is the church. Perhaps all religions on Earth are not just false but simultaneously true. And so, at the end of this section of the novel, he pulls together what he has learned thus far and asks Jill what he has to do to become an ordained minister.

At this point, the novel's focus shifts yet again. At the beginning, it was difficult for readers to get close to Mike because he was only potentially human; after he has been through the education described above, he is again difficult to describe directly because he has become such an extraordinary human. Therefore, he must be seen largely through the observations of others. Since he has been explicitly compared to Foster and implicitly to Jesus, however, readers can use those templates to imagine Mike's maturity and to anticipate the rest of his career. Mike will tell people that they should love one another. He will gather followers who embrace the message even when they don't fully understand it. He will antagonize people who are angered by his challenge to their fixed beliefs — and also people whose power is based on exploiting fixed beliefs. His enemies will kill him. After his death, his disciples will recognize that his teachings have survived in them, so that he actually will have succeeded.

The last section of the novel returns to the perspective of Jubal Harshaw, whose conversation shows that he already knows everything necessary to comprehend the last stage of Mike's life on Earth, though he doesn't realize it yet. Jubal has been happy to see that Mike has "developed a sense of humor" and been properly amused by the pranks Mike has played on pompous Earth humans; for example, he is pleased to hear of Mike's being thrown out of a theological seminary and of his climaxing a brief career in the armed services by discorporating the pants of the officers watching troops on parade. With his jaded view of religion, however, Jubal is much less comfortable with the news that Mike has founded The Church of All Worlds. Jubal shows his uneasiness when Ben Caxton, Jill's erstwhile boyfriend, shows up with an account of his visit to Mike's church, First, however, the gregarious Jubal shares some pertinent, but as yet apparently unrelated, opinions. In his sculpture gallery, Jubal lingers over replicas of Rodin's *La Belle Heaulmière* and *The Fallen Caryatid* (a gift from Mike much earlier in the story), calling the *Caryatid* an example of "Victory in defeat"; leading up to that, he speaks respectfully of Christian art that symbolizes "the Agony and Sacrifice of God." While he is on the subject of art, Jubal insists that an artist needs to reach a popular audience in the form of "customers." He understands, in other words, that appealing to the fundamental human needs of a crowd is a *good* thing, that spreading one's vision widely also is good, and that apparent failure actually may vindicate effort. Then, after this unconscious preparation, Jubal is willing to listen to Ben's urgent complaint.

Ben has just come from a visit to The Church of All Worlds headquarters, the Nest, where he was welcomed too warmly for his inhibited taste. Clothing was optional, and enthusiastic (heterosexual) sex was encouraged; Ben was embarrassed by the proceedings and obsessed with keeping his underpants on. When Jill tried to explain at length about the nature of the church, Ben was distracted by the naked bodies on display. He even heard Mike himself explaining that "We humans have something that my former people don't even dream of: ... The blessing of being male and female." Somehow Ben willfully misinterpreted this clear statement, seeing Mike's followers as "victims." Thus, rather than exposing himself to any more emotional challenge, Ben ran away.

Ben is shocked that Jubal *isn't* shocked by this account. Instead, in a Socratic dialogue, Jubal patiently prods Ben with questions until he admits that when he glimpsed Mike having sex with Jill he actually felt "hurt and jealous"; then Jubal sadly comments that "I am afraid that you — and I, too, I admit — lack the angelic innocence to abide by the perfect morality those people live by." He glumly forecasts the failure of Mike's church, like many idealistic efforts that have gone before. Having talked himself into a better understanding of and more thorough sympathy with Mike's efforts, Jubal encourages Ben to return to the Nest and give Mike's way an honest try. He shouldn't wait. There may not be much time left. When a wire from Ben confirms that he is learning Martian and having fun, Jubal has no excuse not to go and check out the situation for himself.

He arrives at a moment of crisis. The church building has been burned, and Mike and his followers are fugitives from "justice." Superficially, a sense of doom hangs over the novel's last pages. When Ben explains to Jubal that Mike was simply the first human to become aware of our potential, like Prometheus sharing fire with the world, Jubal replies that "As I recall, Prometheus paid a high price for bringing fire to mankind." Governments, organized religion, criminal syndicates — they all hate Mike. He understands what his enemies will do if they catch him, so he frantically is recording a course in the Martian language to leave behind as a legacy. But, once that is complete, he will go out in public. He can't hide. That would be against his nature: "Freedom of self — and utter responsibility for self. Thou art God," Ben explains. Even Mike himself is not entirely sure he understands what's going on, as he says in a necessarily hurried interview with Jubal; if overcoming the tension between male and female is what makes Earth "rich and wonderful," what if conflict between individuals and groups is a necessary part of being human? Nevertheless, despite the impending doom, Mike and his followers are blithely serene. Mike takes the responsibility for facing a murderous crowd even though he fully groks what must happen to him.

After he is killed by the mob, his followers gather for a communal meal. Before The Church of All Worlds was founded, Jill remarked that even though she had enjoyed using her physical body — as had Mike — she won't regret leaving it behind, but she does hope that Mike will consume it after she dies. "Oh, I'll eat you all right — unless I discorporate first," he replies. Just as Jesus instructed his disciples that they should consider the bread shared at the Last Supper to be His body broken for them and to be consumed in His remembrance, Mike for his new church adapts a Martian custom of devouring dead loved ones. Before leaving the safety of the church community for his martyrdom, Mike had severed some of his flesh to be boiled into broth and consumed by his disciples. Jubal has attempted suicide when he imagines that Mike is dead and gone; he is summoned back to life by Mike's presence, showing that he is merely dead, not gone. When Jubal regains consciousness, he still has the "slightly bitter taste" of the suicide drug in his mouth, but Patty's loving kiss leaves him "feeling strong, with her own serene acceptance shared, no bitterness left." They all drink the broth together, calmly and hopefully, and Jubal gruffly agrees to start learning Martian while he also begins dictating Mike's story to share with a general audience.

This demonstration of victory in defeat ends Mike's story — but not quite. The last chapter is set in a slangy, rudely comic version of the afterlife glimpsed in chapters unexpectedly inserted throughout the novel. Earlier in these interpolations, an angelic version of Foster (founder of Fosterism) converses with an angelic version of Digby (the Fosterite bishop Mike discorporated). Foster points out that if he's not upset at Digby for murdering him, then Digby has no reason to be angry because Mike killed *him*. One's perspective dictates how unseriously such mortal affairs should be taken. The chapters containing this unexpectedly remote perspective interrupt Mike's career to remind readers that, hey, just because this is serious stuff that doesn't mean you have to take it *seriously*. The chapters also include news reports, such as a bulletin that the Martians are considering "the artistic necessity of destroying Earth," followed by such factoids as that one baby was washed to safety by a tidal wave that killed 13,000 people; the child grew up to earn a considerable reputation "for loud and sustained belching." Readers might assume that Earth's fate is more significant than one individual's, just as they might assume that the child's survival must be more significant than what his later life shows. But not necessarily.

The novel leaves questions of ultimate significance unanswered. Personally, Foster may be Digby's superior, but he appears to be a lower-level member of an angelic hierarchy or bureaucracy. Angels themselves can't interfere with mortal actions. When Foster refers to a "Boss," he may be suggesting that Someone is in charge, determining events, but that also remains unclear. These sections drop hints, suggest possibilities — but leave the overall picture unresolved, suggesting that if even angels don't comprehend what's going on, ordinary humans (especially readers) won't be able to either. Foster does mention that the Archangel Michael has been missing from their Club, and Digby identifies him as "that over-age juvenile delinquent that sent me to the showers." In the novel's last chapter, thus, after Mike is discorporated, the Archangel Michael shows up as Digby's new supervisor. By that point, Digby has unlearned the personal resentment he felt and doesn't even remember meeting Mike before. So they get back to their assigned work. Readers may not be satisfied, but perhaps lack of final resolution is not such a bad thing if it leaves them actively questioning. As Foster concludes with a question of his own, shooing the others away from unproductive ruminations, there's too much to do and no time to waste: "Certainly 'Thou art God' — but who isn't?"

Rude, free-wheeling, and frustrating, *Stranger* challenges readers as it defies traditional literary criticism. Readers should remember that Jubal has little use for nit-picking analysis, calling a critic a failed creator, an impotent would-be visionary, "a poor thing at best, a sort of fourth-rate prophet suffering from delusions of gender." Readers can do better than that if they can accept the freedom and responsibility of Godship. To the indignant question "Is nothing sacred?," Mike, Foster, and Jubal might reply that of course there are many things in our experience that deserve serious attention and love. However, we can't count on established institutions to tell us what to worship. Anything that takes itself too seriously, acting so pretentious and exclusively Holy that it can't stand to be laughed at, thus becomes a fair target for humor.

Stranger in a Strange Land is very funny and extremely serious. Simultaneously. Of course.

7

The Final Period

After "All You Zombies—," Heinlein concentrated almost entirely on writing novels. They earned more money than short fiction, and he found them actually easier to write. The novels he produced won him a new, larger audience and consolidated his role as a thinker. They also sometimes alienated and perplexed his older readers who wondered why Heinlein couldn't just continue to be the same straightforward storyteller they loved.

The fact seems to be not that Heinlein couldn't do the kind of fiction he'd used to — and still did on occasion — but that he simply didn't *want* to. The last phase of Heinlein's writing career is marked by restless experimentation, attempting new ways to tell a story. Also, by developing the notion of the multiverse of possible timelines, he made it possible for anything at all to be "true" in some universe. The "Future History" stories may not have worked out in our history, for example, but they were accurate records of events in another timeline. A sword and sorcery yarn could fit in one universe, a brain transplant in another, and so on. Or the universes could interact. Part of the attraction of these last novels is not simply their exposition of ideas but the exuberance of the author's discovery of his freedom to try anything and everything.

At the same time, the novels continue to explore — sometimes playfully, sometimes with aching seriousness — some of Heinlein's abiding concerns. He continued to be distressed by the deterioration of civility and cohesion in America. He was concerned with citizens' failure to accept personal responsibility. But that connected to Heinlein's own persistent concern: To *what* should one accept responsibility?

The last novels show him still vigorously, desperately trying to answer that question.

"Searchlight" is a trifle intended to attract attention to an electronics company's advertisement that ran in *Scientific American* (August 1962) and other magazines. Its chief interest is how expertly Heinlein managed to fit a technical puzzle and human interest into the 1,200-word limit. The story is enlivened by conflict between the people who are trying to save the life of a little girl whose ship crash-landed on the Moon — versus the authorities who are primarily concerned with making pompous, self-serving speeches about the crisis. At one point, the girl's father tells the U.S. president to shut up so that the experts can concentrate.

Although *Podkayne of Mars* (*Worlds of If*, December 1962–March 1963) has a young heroine, it is not a juvenile novel. Heinlein wrote the novel not for young people but for their parents. He intended it to be a tragedy that showed children suffering from parental neglect that results in the heroine's fatal naïveté and in her younger sibling's malevolent alienation. The novel itself, however, seems to have escaped the author's control even before editors who didn't grasp his purpose asked for changes that further muddled the point.

Podkayne Fries, aka "Poddy," is a bit over fifteen in Earth years, so that she is almost marriageable physically but is not seriously interested yet. First, she intends to become a space pilot and "someday commander of deep-space exploration parties." As the story starts, Poddy is bubbling with enthusiasm about an upcoming family vacation to Earth — an event that has motivated her to write the journal that makes up the bulk of the novel. She's ready for new experiences, excited about the wonderful possibilities of life opening before her. This attitude, absorbed before she presents many details about her personal life, settles readers into the story as Poddy's friends.

In a similar artfully casual manner, Heinlein introduces readers to the rest of Poddy's family. She records her journal in code to keep her younger brother Clark from snooping. Clark, age eleven in Earth years, is her first family member mentioned in much detail. Poddy is smart, but Clark is smarter. Although she is "responsible" for him, the two don't get along: "There is no present indication that Clark ever intends to join the human race. He is more likely to devise a way to blow up the universe just to hear the bang." Poddy's family also includes Uncle Tom, who once was active in public affairs and still is a Senator-at-Large of the Republic. She also mentions that her mother is a very important engineer who bossed "the rebuilding of Deimos and Phobos," while her father is an academic focused on the history of the native Martians. As Poddy describes them, he is focused on the past while she is focused on her own future projects. While this could mean that the parents aren't paying much attention to what's happening now, Poddy does not mind, remarking that "Daddy is a dear and does not snoopervise me."

This is the family group that is preparing to go on vacation to Earth until a mishap spoils their plans. On Mars, babies are frozen — cryogenically preserved — until their parents are ready to care for them, and Poddy's parents are suddenly presented with two infant daughters and a son whom the Marsopolis Creche Foundation Limited has thawed by mistake. This not only spoils the trip plans but makes Poddy a caregiver for squirmy, messy babies. She is dismayed but also fascinated. When she accompanies Uncle Tom on a visit to the Creche, she leaves the waiting room where she has been parked and seeks out the Nursery, full of babies so cute that "if there had not been a sheet of glass between me and them I would have grabbed me a double armful of babies." When she rejoins Uncle Tom in the Director's office, she witnesses Uncle Tom skillfully intimidate the Creche Director into giving Uncle Tom, along with Poddy and Clark, tickets to Earth on a luxury liner in exchange for keeping silent about the baby-thawing error. Of course Poddy is pleased that she'll get to do what she anticipated; however, now that she's been around her baby siblings, she's reluctant to leave them: "I'm going to miss Duncan [her little brother] — he's such a little doll."

In addition to the other information it conveys, *Podkayne*'s opening demonstrates that things are not what they seem, that things are happening in and around Poddy that she doesn't quite grasp. To further demonstrate this fact, right after Chapter One her narrative is interrupted by a comment composed by her brother Clark and written in the margins of her journal in ink visible only under ultraviolet light. Clark doesn't want Poddy to know she can't keep secrets from him, and he uses these interludes to taunt Poddy for imagining that she can exercise any control over him: "It doesn't pay to tell everything you know, or somebody comes along and tells you to stop doing whatever it is you are doing. Probably your older sister." Clark knows that he's superior to the people around him and is happy to maintain his distance from them. Readers' knowledge that he is in the background of the action, observing whatever goes on with cold detachment, further emphasizes Poddy's cheerful innocence. Panshin even concludes that Clark "is the novel's true central character" (*HD* 105).

Their trip aboard the spaceliner *Tricorn* can't spoil Poddy's good nature, but it does give her more experience proving that appearances are deceptive. Not only are their accommodations less glamorous than advertised, but the people on board turn out to be different than they appear. When Poddy sees how officials treat Uncle Tom like a Very Important Person, she realizes that he may actually *be* an important public figure. On the other hand, one of their fellow passengers is Mrs. Royer, who first seems to be a friendly old woman but who turns hostile when Poddy refuses to become her unpaid servant. Later, Poddy overhears a conversation between Mrs. Royer and another elderly matron in which the two slander the Fries family because, like all Marsmen, they have uncouth manners and a mixed racial background. Poddy's response is revealing. Rather than confronting the two women, she summarizes what she heard to Clark, hoping that his "fiendish disposition" will take the hint. And so it does. Somehow Mrs. Royer's face is chemically stained fiery crimson, and her friend's becomes bright yellow — an appropriate reminder for the bigots of how subjective but significant one's skin color can be in social situations. No one aboard the *Tricorn* can figure out how this mishap could have happened; Poddy just hopes that Clark didn't leave fingerprints.

In a letter to his agent while he was resisting changing *Podkayne*'s ending, Heinlein describes Clark as "an infantile monster, no real part of the human race and indifferent to the wellbeing of others ... until the death of his sister, under circumstances which lay on him a guilt he can never shake off, gives some prospect that he is now going to grow up" (*GG* 88). This overstates the case. Actually, Clark represents a familiar figure in Heinlein's fiction: the superior individual who has trouble relating to his inferiors. Verging on solipsism, this attitude is balanced in most of Heinlein's heroes by recognition that personal isolation is unhealthy, so that they attempt somehow to discover companions and to allocate authority within a social group. In Clark's case, this effort is complicated because he's younger than the heroes of Heinlein's juvenile novels. When people look at him, they see only a child; when they get to know him a bit better, they see only a smart-mouthed, hostile child. This is the image of Clark that Heinlein emphasizes, despite his usual fondness for individuals who are smarter and more able than the crowd. Still, Clark does not seem to be the "monster" that Heinlein intended. His response to Poddy's hint about Mrs. Royer and her friend shows both that he is always ready for a chance to do something difficult and sneaky but also that he is *listening* to his sister. When he concludes the second interlude, which he inserts into her journal with an invitation to "feel free to come to me with your little problems," he obviously is sneering at her failure to understand his subtle thinking; however, he also could be hinting at a desire to communicate with someone — anyone — who's perceptive enough to notice him.

One more incident aboard the *Tricorn* may suggest how difficult it is to read Clark's character. When everyone must squeeze into the ship's radiation shelter during a solar storm, Poddy and her older shipboard friend Girdie help care for the passengers' babies. Needing more help, she dragoons Clark, remarking that "he wasn't exactly eager to volunteer, but doing anything was slightly better than doing nothing; he came along." In fact, Clark is surprisingly good with the babies. Poddy dismissively supposes that he's sticking the ordeal out because he has a crush on Girdie and wants to impress her; however, she must admit that "the babies seemed to like him." Poddy records her own feelings about the experience in rather negative terms by saying "It's lots better to be miserable than bored"; she can't admit that, free fall baby puke and all, she reveled in the experience. Readers must pay more attention to her actions than her words. The same could be said of Clark. Here, as elsewhere, the evidence of Clark's actual behavior does not demonstrate that he's a monster — or an innocent cherub — but it does suggest that he's basically a brilliant, frustrated and lonely, 11-year-old semi-solipsist.

When the *Tricorn* stops at Venus, the two young people continue their educations. While still carrying a torch for Girdie, Clark devotes most of his energy to successfully disproving the advertising of the Dom Pedro Casino that advises "suckers" that they can't win. Most of Poddy's attention is captured by the extremely glamorous, wealthy, and attentive Dexter Cunha, to the extent that she toys with the idea of putting aside her dream of becoming a starship captain so she could train instead for the position of spaceship crèche director since "A baby is lots more fun than differential equations." She also, however, realizes that Uncle Tom is *much* more than a tourist, so that their trip's coinciding with the upcoming Three-Planets conference wasn't coincidental.

As it turns out, Uncle Tom is the actual center of the plot. One hostile political faction wants to keep him from even showing up as a delegate to the conference; this group tried to kill him and everyone else aboard the *Tricorn* by giving innocent-looking little Clark a package containing a mini-nuke — which Clark deactivated but has kept handy on the principle of "waste not, want not." Another faction wants Uncle Tom to attend the conference but as its puppet, promoting *its* viewpoint. These plotters lure Clark into a trap by claiming that Girdie is in trouble. Podkayne also is snared when she attempts to rescue her brother. She, along with Clark and Uncle Tom, wind up as prisoners of Mrs. Grew, another apparently friendly *Tricorn* passenger, who threatens the children if Uncle Tom refuses to cooperate. Poddy herself is guarded by a "fairy," a small, winged native–Venusian humanoid; even when it claws her arm, Poddy tries to make friends with its cute baby. Then Clark is dumped in with her, sharing his conclusion that the two of them will be killed as soon as Uncle Tom leaves for the conference and they are no longer valuable as hostages. Earlier, when Poddy tried to imagine escaping, she couldn't convince herself that a real human being was capable of comic book superheroics. Fortunately, Clark is supremely capable of defeating their captors. He kills the adult fairy with a slingshot, breaks Mrs. Grew's neck, shoots down a drug-crazed henchman, and sets his mini-nuke to destroy the hideout after he and Poddy have trekked off on separate escape routes.

At about this point, the novel splits off on forking paths. Heinlein's original version of an epilogue written by Clark describes how Poddy must have gone back to rescue the baby fairy so that she was killed by the nuclear explosion. Her last words, spoken into the little recorder she was using to keep her journal late in the book are addressed to her brother:

> "No man is an island complete in himself. Remember that, Clarkie. Oh, I'm sorry I fubbed it but remember that; it's important. They all have to be cuddled sometimes ... is anybody listening? Do listen, please, because this is important. I love —"
>
> It cuts off there. So we don't know whom she loved.
>
> Everybody, maybe.

Clark blames himself for his sister's death and has just tentatively begun emulating her generous sympathy. He has started caring for the baby fairy she died to save: "I call it 'Ariel' and I guess I'll be taking care of it for a long time; they say these fairies live as long as we do. It is taking to shipboard life all right but it gets lonely and has to be held and cuddled or it cries."

The revised, published versions of the novel spell out his reaction more explicitly. The magazine serial ends with Poddy alive but in a coma. The book version expands this hopeful note by proclaiming that Poddy *will* recover and by showing Clark taking care of that baby fairy because

> Poddy will want to see it when she gets well enough to notice things again; she's always been a sentimentalist. It needs lots of attention because it gets lonely and has to be held and cuddled, or it cries.
> So I'm up a lot in the night — I guess it thinks I'm its mother. I don't mind, I don't have much else to do.
> It seems to like me.

The final version of the ending makes more explicit Clark's identification of the baby fairy's needs with his own, although (just as Poddy does in her journal entry after the radiation storm) he downplays his own empathetic behavior by saying that caring for the helpless little creature is just a way to pass time.

The replacement endings also spell out what Heinlein believed to be the novel's theme, according to the letters he wrote to defend his original ending. Since he was being forced to let Poddy live, he couldn't count on the impact of her death demonstrating that "the true tragedy in this story lies in the character of the mother, the highly successful career woman who wouldn't take time to raise her own kids," to which he adds that "death is the only destination for all of us and that the only long-range hope for any adult lies in the young — and that this double realization constitutes growing up, ceasing to be a child and putting away childish things" (*GG* 88).

This authorial intent is not always clear in the novel. Just before they fall into Mrs. Grew's clutches, Uncle Tom berates himself for not explaining his mission earlier: "Poddy, I should have told you more than I have. I keep forgetting that you are now a woman." In the book's ending, he launches into a long rant at her father:

> People who will not take the trouble to raise children should not have them. You with your nose always in a book, your wife gallivanting off God knows where — between you, your daughter was almost killed.... You should tell your wife, sir, that building bridges and space stations and such gadgets is all very well ... but that a woman has more important work to do.... Your daughter will get well, no thanks to either of you. But I have my doubts about Clark. With him it may be too late. God may give you second chance if you hurry.

Personal guilt and appeals to the Almighty aside, this outburst again overstates the case. Since readers don't have much opportunity to see Mr. and Mrs. Fries in action as Poddy and Clark's parents, it's difficult to appreciate how their treatment of their children was deficient. Poddy herself is happy that her father doesn't "snoopervise" her life. However, it's difficult to see how anything the parents could have done would have affected the young people's behavior within novel's action. Poddy's problem is not that she was badly or negligently brought up but that she was too inexperienced to apply her empathetic nature safely yet. The only time she expresses unhappiness about her upbringing is when she wishes her father had let her take martial arts training so she could escape from Mrs. Grew's lair, and she fell into that trap only after failing to get the attention of the supposedly competent adults around her. As noted above, by the end of the action she certainly is ready and willing to take up a woman's "important work" of caring for young creatures.

It's equally unclear how Clark's parents are responsible for his condition. Again, readers don't see how they failed to engage him in wholesome sharing activities — or how such exercises could have made him less frustrated at being very smart but very young. His attitude toward other people is not much colder than that of the happy hero of Heinlein's *The Puppet*

Masters, who describes himself as feeling "warm and relaxed, as if I had just killed a man or had a woman" or the hero of *The Cat Who Walks Through Walls*, who recommends the death penalty for people with bad manners. Nature rather than nurture may be to blame for Clark's apparent alienation. That attitude, however, is expressed verbally, not in violent behaviors, until he uses his cold-blooded intelligence and unexpected physical skills to save his sister and himself from the kidnappers. Like Panshin, Majors recognizes that Clark embodies qualities that Heinlein admired in other books; he does not recognize how those attitudes and skills operate *here*. Clark sees — and understands perhaps too well — the fact that people who aren't what they seem to be may in fact be dangerous. He spotted Mrs. Grew's potential for evil in the facts that she cheated at solitaire and always acted too pleasant. And so when the opportunity arises he is ready to act on behalf of someone else.

Two of Heinlein's long-standing principles collide at this point in the novel as he grapples with how maturity — i.e., the putting away of childish things — actually works. On the one hand, adults can't (or shouldn't) control another person's life; on the other hand, adults can't avoid protecting people less able than themselves. Echoing Heinlein's remarks when Poddy describes how she looked after Clark when he was a baby, Uncle Tom tells her that eventually every human being will lose in a confrontation with the universe. "But that doesn't make it any easier when we *try* to be responsible for another — as you have, as I have — and then look back and see how we could have done it better." Uncle Tom's final rant should be read with these more temperate reflections in mind. Apparently, when recognizing this struggle between what one can't do but must do, one shouldn't refrain from acting — but should be ready to admit failures and to learn from the experience. All of the novel's conclusions show Clark doing exactly that, evaluating his performance and preparing to do better.

Perhaps Heinlein did the same. The revised endings of *Podkayne of Mars* may not be mere cynical efforts to avoid anticipated reader displeasure about the death of cute, loveable Poddy. Heinlein may have recognized that readers didn't feel the significance of her death as he'd planned, so that he attempted to add commentary that would wrestle the story in the direction he intended. Eventually, however, he must have accepted Poddy's survival, since she shows up as an adult "therapy empathist" among the hoard of characters crowding the last pages of *The Number of the Beast*. There is no sign of a grownup Clark in that novel, but readers may catch glimpses of him in Heinlein's other heroes. *Podkayne of Mars* unintentionally demonstrates how a slightly different viewpoint can make heroic qualities appear monstrous. Or vice versa. Giving characters that much autonomy or moral ambiguity was a tactical error Heinlein never made again.

At first glance, literally, *Glory Road* (*F&SF*, July–September 1963) may appear to be lightweight fluff. The cover illustrations for a Baen paperback edition looks like a standard heroic fantasy: Heavily muscled hero about to shoot an arrow down the gullet of a fire-breathing dragon, buxom heroine ready to draw her bow, squat sidekick handy nearby — typical swords and sorcery stuff. The novel *does* offer the kind of story that readers expect, but after satisfying that first impression it goes on to raise some interesting, rather serious questions. What, for one, could the tag line of many traditional tales for children — "And they all lived happily ever after" — actually mean for grownups? And if fantastic literature is called escape literature, what are readers escaping from? What do they want to escape *to*? In short, what do people really want out of fiction and life?

The novel begins with the narrator, "Flash" Gordon, briefly describing what sounds like a perfect world somewhere else so that he can go on to lengthily contrast it to mid-twentieth-century America, where he actually lives. He's not unhappy merely about unpleasant physical conditions such as bad climate or smog. He sees that the whole of U.S. culture has become corrupt, starting with an educational establishment that discourages individual thinking while simultaneously denying any worthwhile goal larger than individual satisfaction. As a result, instead of a "Lost Generation" young adults have become a "Safe Generation," selfish, timid, worshipping "Security" above all. Flash is too smart not to see how this amoral impersonality allows people to be manipulated, but he can't imagine how to escape from the system. He just quietly despises everything he sees around him. Because, despite the current mess, he still loves the ideal of his country, he enlists in the armed service and is sent to Vietnam, where he survives combat and acquires a notable facial scar. Again, he comments on how officers/bureaucrats push him around arbitrarily.

Since he believes that life is controlled by dumb luck, he's grateful to be cut loose in Europe, poor but without compelling responsibilities. He passes time by watching naked girls on the beach until one exceptionally gorgeous young woman stops and talks with him, whereupon he is thoroughly smitten. When she isn't around the next day, he realizes that he doesn't know her name or how to find her. Fortunately, he answers a newspaper ad that fits his personal qualifications exactly but promises "glorious adventure, great danger"—and there she is, the girl of his dreams! She calls herself Star. Flash thereafter goes by "Oscar," a new name for a new role. Accompanied by Rufo, the aged-looking but tough man Oscar met when he answered the ad, they launch into action across a series of other worlds.

The trio is on a quest. More specifically, they are on a journey to a place where an object Star needs, the mysterious Egg of the Phoenix, is hidden. As they travel, they encounter one obstacle after another. Eventually, they reach their destination. And that, essentially, is the first two thirds of the novel. It is a thin plot but sufficient, good enough for heroic fantasy.

As the episodes flow rapidly, Heinlein balances thrills and slapstick. The quest begins, for example, as the three adventurers trek zestfully down the Glory Road, through a vividly wonderful forest on the way to fight Igli. When Oscar asks who that is, Rufo replies merely, "You'll find out." The diminutive-sounding name doesn't encourage readers to take Igli seriously, but it turns out that he's a malevolent, unkillable artificial humanoid who combines "the less appetizing features of giants and ogres in *The Red Fairy Book*." However, in a farcical battle to the death, Oscar wins by shoving Igli's foot into his mouth, then his whole leg, and so on until Igli has swallowed himself and pops out of existence.

Besides humor, this scene illustrates several interesting points. One is how thoroughly *Glory Road* is saturated with references to literature. Oscar evidently has read widely in fantastic stories from Howard to Tolkien, and in detective fiction from Conan Doyle to Stout and Spillane. As he looks up at two moons in the sky before the morning he fights Igli, he thinks of Edgar Rice Burroughs's Barsoom and happily muses, "I had fallen into a book." When he needs models of heroic behavior, therefore, he can refer to Conan, Sherlock Holmes, and others in a long tradition, while readers can be reassured because those characters always succeed in solving problems and facing dangers.

Accompanying that semi-complacent attitude is the frustrating fact that Star tells Oscar only as much about each upcoming trial as he needs to get *into* it but that he accepts being steered blindly:

> There is no reason to wonder why I didn't quiz Star as to where we were, why we were there, how we had got there, what we were going to do, and the details of these dangers I was expected to face. Look, Mac, when you are having the most gorgeous dream of your life and just getting

to the point, do you stop to tell yourself that it is logically impossible for that particular babe to be in the hay with you—and thereby wake yourself up? I *knew*, logically, that everything that had happened since I read that silly ad had been impossible.

So I chucked logic.

Now that he is free of the twentieth-century American mindset that had left him feeling directionless earlier, Oscar acts the part of a Hero and discovers that it fits him. He already had acquired the muscles and combat skills he needs on this quest with Star. Now he can use his ingenuity and persistence, motivated by Star's admiring expectation, to succeed in each test.

His initial failure in one test is due to a part of the American mindset that he never quite succeeds in chucking: the confused, self-contradictory attitude toward sex. The novel's opening description of a *good* place includes the fact that "the women are beautiful and amazingly anxious to please." Oscar lovingly describes Star's naked body when they meet on the beach. Nevertheless, he is amazingly anxious not to have sex with her or any other beautiful, willing woman outside a loving, committed relationship. Thus, when the trio stops at the friendly Doral's estate to recuperate from their journey, Oscar fails to respond to an obvious invitation to have sex with his host's wife and/or daughters. This leads to such huge confusion that they must flee in disgrace the next morning: Star berates Oscar for insulting the Doral until Oscar puts Star in her subservient place by shouting at her; then they return to the mansion so that Oscar can perform heroically as a stud. Nevertheless, though he understands the concept of sex as fun, art, and so on, Oscar just can't be comfortable having sex with Star until they are married, at least by the custom of the country. She happily accepts his proposal, for it seems that one of the few things women in this novel want more than looking great is having great sex with a Hero.

Eventually they do reach their destination, the Tower where the Eater of Souls guards their goal, the Egg of the Phoenix. Oscar leads the way through the Tower, leaving the others behind. He must confront the Eater of Souls alone. Considering his literary taste, it's a bit surprising when he doesn't recognize that the big-nosed swordsman he's fighting is Cyrano de Bergerac, but the vague familiarity he feels may actually indicate that the Eater of Souls has reached inside his mind to find ways to attack him. Oscar wins the duel with Cyrano only to be challenged by his deep-seated fear of rats—and then apparently wakes up to be confronted by a hated officer from his time in the army, who tells him that all the post–Vietnam experiences he has enjoyed have been an illusion, "just another of those dreams I had had too often lately, wanting to get out of this aching jungle." He is told that he'll be okay if he'll just accept the other's—i.e., the system's—authority, admit that Star and the quest were just a fantasy, and resume his routine life. When Oscar defiantly affirms the dream against "reality," he defeats the Eater of Souls so that the quest for the Egg of the Phoenix is over, so the novel could end there. Instead, Heinlein gives Oscar, Star, and Rufo time to consider the implications of living past what appeared to be the conclusion of their story's plot, their lives' purpose.

Star always has insisted that the extraordinary devices she uses on their trek are not magical but technological; it's just that Oscar's limited background in mid-twentieth-century science makes it difficult for him to accept the fact. Now the explanation of what has gone before relies on his (and readers') familiarity with sf tropes that Oscar must have absorbed in his reading. The worlds they have passed through are actually part of different dimensions (or "Universes"; that's about as close as Oscar's mind can come to expressing it) united in an empire (or something like it), the Twenty Universes. *This* system of government survives because it doesn't try to exert control tightly but respects individual differences. Though someone must be around to settle disputes, that person can refer to (or actually has absorbed) the experience of all earlier rulers. That's what the Egg of the Phoenix is, the stored essence of previous arbiters. And Star needed to regain it because she is Her Wisdom, the Empress of Twenty Universes.

She also is Oscar's wife, and as time passes he is less and less comfortable in his new role. He loves Star, and she is just as loving and lustful as she always has been. However, unlike Dan in *The Door into Summer*, Oscar is not well enough grounded in math and engineering to catch up with current technology, let alone make contributions of his own. Jewelry design interests him for a while but not passionately enough to make it a career. So all he has to occupy his time is accompanying Star to official functions (looking handsome but avoiding sex with the females who've heard what a Hero he is) and watching his wife absorb the essence of her predecessors while occasionally making serious decisions. Thanks to the rejuvenation/life extension treatments he unknowingly has received thanks to Star, Oscar has possession of the "ever after" part of the archetypal story's conclusion, but where's the happiness?

It's not in a safe, secure, committed marriage. Not for a Hero. Besides the initial commitment, an enduring marriage requires negotiation between the parties, adjustments of responsibilities and privileges. Although Star would give Oscar anything she could—and sometimes says she'd like to chuck it all and escape down the Glory Road again—her responsibilities to the Twenty Universes must come first. Oscar has seen the deplorable condition of modern America and reports negative opinions on the notion of democracy, but he does not relate that to the politics going on inside Star as she accommodates the experiences and personalities of past Wisdoms. He loves her too much to try to pull her away from the job that fulfills her, but an endless career as a consort/gigolo doesn't appeal to him.

He is, after all, a Hero. Safety and security, along with commitment and subservience within some smoothly running social arrangement, might appeal to a man who could live anonymously, without honor, glory, and recognition of his personal significance. But such a life wouldn't satisfy a Hero who's absorbed the exploits of famous heroes he's read about. Moreover, Oscar already has experienced the admiration of the Doral's household when Star sings of his exploits, not to mention her constant flattery as they progress from adventure to adventure.

It's true that Oscar modestly disparages himself, but he still values the significance of what he has become. In one telling scene along the road, Oscar takes time to give an admiring young bumpkin a pep talk about Heroism. Although he sees it as "fatherly guff," Star praises him later for a noble act of encouraging the boy to become more than he currently is. So even though Oscar knows that the American Eagle is a carrion-eating coward, he still can respect the ideals it has come to symbolize.

That bifurcated vision—ability to see and accept simultaneously two contradictory truths—is useful as *Glory Road* draws to a close. Oscar loves Star, but he can't continue to live with her. As he struggles with guilt about his need to escape, he has a helpful conversation with Rufo, who understands Star rather well since, thanks to high-tech life extension, she actually is his centuries-old grandmother. He explains to Oscar that Star in effect created Oscar the Hero by nudging his choices and experiences throughout his life until he was ready to go on the Glory Road to get what she needed. That doesn't mean that the danger was less real for her too or that she doesn't love Oscar sincerely, but she is both a warm, vulnerable romantic heroine and also a shrewdly calculating bitch. And, finally, Oscar doesn't love Star any the less because she manipulated him. She did what she had to for the sake of the Twenty Universes. Now he must do what he has to because of the ideals he embodies. He has become what any man *should* desire: unfettered, honorable, and gloriously significant.

And so Oscar and Star part, saying "Au revoir" rather than "Goodbye," since it's likely that they'll get together again for a while sometime. Oscar returns to Earth, where he finds the same frustrations he experienced at the novel's beginning. People are no less petty than they were before he left, and he doesn't fit in any better than he did then. A former girlfriend offers him sex while her husband is away, but he refrains. The engineering job he gets wants conventional thinking rather than innovation, so he quits. After he writes a desperate newspaper ad to contact Rufo, he even sinks close to the despairing futility of surrender to the Eater of Souls by concluding that all his adventures may have been only a dream.

Fortunately, Rufo does respond to the ad. At the end of the novel, Oscar is reassured that "there is still noble work to do," especially tasks that are "a little risky perhaps, but not dull."

That's what he needs to know. That's what Heinlein shares with readers.

Racial tension in the 1960s made *Farnham's Freehold* (*Worlds of If*, July–October 1964) one of Robert A. Heinlein's most controversial novels. Looking at it from decades later, Thomas M. Disch labels it "the most reprehended work of a writer who has been much reprehended" (*Dreams* 199), while the somewhat less shrill H. Bruce Franklin claims that the story "expresses the most deep-seated racist nightmare of American culture" (*RAH* 157). It's certainly true that tossing a white, middle-class twentieth-century family into a future world where blacks rule and everyone else is a slave or a walking piece of table meat is a deliberately offensive tactic; it gets a reader's attention in the same way that a two-by-four upside the head would. But when readers have a chance to think about the novel's reversal of racial roles, after the shock of the impact has worn off, the question remains: Was that *all* that was going on?

To decide, we should look at the whole story, not just the last part, and we should look especially closely at the character who initially looks like Heinlein's standard ultra-competent ideal.

Let's first consider Heinlein's preparation for the distressing "nightmare." The story begins in the early 1960s, at a dinner/bridge party in the Mountain Spring, Colorado, home of Hubert Farnham. Attending are Farnham himself, a fiftyish contractor; his semi-alcoholic wife Grace; their blustering lawyer son Duke and their college-girl daughter Karen, along with Karen's divorcée sorority sister Barbara. Also present that evening are Joseph, the gentlemanly young African American accounting student who works as the Farhnam's houseboy, and the imperious family cat Dr.-Livingstone-I-Presume. The fact that Hugh is wearing a radio "tuned to the emergency frequency" disturbs his wife and guests; they realize that an international crisis is building, but they don't want to imagine the possible consequences. A warning of Russian ballistic missiles on the way, however, sends everyone rushing to the fallout shelter that Hugh has built under his house. There, while sweltering and being jarred by nuclear explosions, Barbara and Hugh have sex because she was smitten earlier in the evening by his superior bridge playing and his "strong masculine charm." As they prepare to do it again, an especially strong shock throws the shelter askew—along with the just-jelling plot. Shortly before the end of the novel's third chapter, the group emerges from the shelter not into radioactive rubble but an apparently virgin forest; the last atomic bomb apparently tore the space-time continuum so that Hugh and the others now are somewhere else, a different time that gives them new chances/challenges to survive.

As we move on to the story's second phase, it is worth noting how the first not only shows Hugh Farnham's prescience and studliness but also suggests how his personal limitations may hurt his chances of successfully leading/running the little community of survivors. Unpleasantly but not quite inaccurately, Panshin describes Hugh's family as "a lush, a momma's boy and a daughter home pregnant from college" (*HD* 109). That callous description of Karen deserves some qualification. It's not, of course, that Heinlein disapproves of sex; the problem is that Karen had sex without taking reasonable precautions. Like everyone in the family except her father, she has behaved carelessly, so that Hugh has been forced to become hyper-responsible for everyone else. Providing the well-stocked fallout shelter shows how well he fills the role of responsible adult, but his family's condition shows that he has not been an especially effective husband or father. Karen actually is the family member with the fewest disabling weaknesses. She slipped up once in a moment of passion; her mother and brother are prone to dangerous lapses in everyday choices.

Hugh tries to defend Grace's past behavior, telling Barbara how she was strong during difficult times but then went soft when life got too easy. Duke also refers jocularly to his father as "a notorious sex criminal," reinforced by Hugh's equally light-hearted "Those were the good old days!" Beyond reacting to that implied infidelity, however, Grace seems to have drifted into her present condition because Hugh ignored her, spending too much time at work and away from his family. It appears that he could see their relationship fading but didn't know what to do about it and so did nothing. He excuses himself to Duke's accusation that he ruined Grace's life by bullying her and driving her to drink by saying that "it is impossible to be responsible for another person's behavior," reinforced by Barbara's declaration that "what a person is can never be somebody else's fault." Yet it's not clear whether this is a statement of principle that explains why Hugh didn't do more to save Grace or a rationalization now, after the fact, as he endures her unrealistic nattering.

Duke's case is similar. According to Hugh, the only quarrel he ever had with Grace was over discipline: "I tried to raise Duke fairly strictly and Grace couldn't bear to have the boy touched." Again, Hugh realized what needed to be done but failed to do it. Consequently, Duke has grown into a quarrelsome overage adolescent who sucker-punches his father for "bullying" them and for favoring Joe over his own flesh and blood.

Heinlein is not quite condemning Hugh for failing to make Grace and Duke mature. Hugh has done a remarkably good job of building and stocking the shelter so that this little group has a chance to survive. But the story also shows that Hugh's perception of the people around him—and his ability to act realistically on what he perceives—are limited. If, as Damon Knight observes, Heinlein is fascinated by competence, by the "The Man Who Knows How" (*Search* 83), Hugh Farnham is a man who knows how to do *some* things, *some* of the time. He reveals as much himself as he replies to Duke's charge that he enjoys bullying: "I suppose so, if you class what I do as bullying. No one ever does anything but what he wants to do—'enjoys'—within the possibilities open to him. If I change a tire, it's because I enjoy it more than being stranded." In short, Hugh is ready to cope with immediate, physical problems that can be labeled and fixed.

Unfortunately, establishing and maintaining human relationships is more complicated than automobile repair. "Bullying," in this novel, constitutes the forceful but necessary exercise of authority during a crisis; Hugh uses the apt analogy of a lifeboat having only one commanding officer. However, successful intimidation is a poor substitute for respect. Whether the person who does it is technically in the right or not, bullying is unlikely to bind a group together once the crisis is past.

Hugh Farnham doesn't and can't see this. His greatest overall strength is not his foresight but his stubborn persistence: He simply won't give up trying to reinterpret any problem into a form he can handle.

The second part of *Farnham's Freehold* develops this situation, again showing what Hugh can and can't do. In a grittier version of *The Swiss Family Robinson*, the little group uses the goods in the shelter, applied with Hugh's engineering creativity, to start making a permanent home. Except for Grace, everyone works together; even Duke, after an outburst of juvenile defiance during which he blurts racist resentment, cooperates. Then Karen reveals that she is pregnant. Hugh is delighted because, since they have seen no trace of other humans to breed with, Karen's baby will increase the gene pool's diversity and improve their community's chances of long-term success. Grace, characteristically clinging to a dead society's viewpoint, condemns her daughter as "a shameless little tramp." She does come around, as Hugh suggested she could, to help prepare for her grandchild, while Dr.-Livingstone-I-Presume successfully gives birth to a healthy litter of kittens. Karen's case, however, is more difficult than Hugh expects. He can't reduce the complexities of her childbirth to a controllable procedure. She and her baby die. Grace foolishly blames Hugh for trying to do everything himself rather than calling a doctor, and Hugh accepts responsibility for his lack of medical readiness. However, he does not retreat into irresponsible depression. He declares, "We go on."

"Going on" sounds good as a slogan, but it is not always realistic. At Grace's wrongheaded insistence, Duke announces that he and his mother will move away to set up a splinter settlement. Since Hugh had announced earlier that anyone who couldn't accept his leadership was free to leave, he can't stop their desertion. He doesn't even object when they demand an excessive share of the shelter's contents to take with them. But their departure will leave Hugh with only two subordinates, Barbara and Joe. At the very least, this will limit the available labor force, since Barbara is pregnant from her Armageddon-night encounter with Hugh; in the long run, it could shrink the gene pool catastrophically. At the moment of leavetaking, however, a flying machine swoops down, paralyzing Hugh and the others while obliterating all their handiwork. They are packed off as prisoners of a man whose appearance Hugh finds somehow encouraging:

> He had an air of good-natured arrogance and his eyes were bright and merry. His forehead was high, his skull massive; he looked intelligent and alert. Hugh could not place his race. His skin was dark brown and shiny. But his mouth was only slightly Negroid; his nose, though broad, was arched, and his black hair was wavy.

At this point, *Farnham's Freehold* apparently changes direction again, becoming what Franklin calls a "racist nightmare"—or perhaps, more likely, a racial dystopian satire. Before Hugh considers questions of race, however, he feels an instinctive affinity for his captor. Overall, the novel actually continues developing themes from the opening chapters.

One theme is discipline, accepting the fact that one must work within an existing system. The future system in which Hugh and the others now live came into being after an atomic war and the accompanying bio-warfare destroyed civilization in the Northern Hemisphere. It is based on a racist revision of the Koran, which mandates an unchangeable social order based on skin color: dark = superior; light = inferior. The dark Chosen have absolute power over lesser beings, and they practice selective breeding to keep the lesser race smaller and weaker, so that nameless male "studs" have limited access to anonymous female "sluts" before they are "tempered"—i.e., castrated—if they want recognition as a responsible person.

Hugh must suffer discipline before he can appreciate the dangers and opportunities offered by that alien perspective. First of all, back by their shelter in the forest, he tries to stop the arrogant intruder from touching Barbara and suffers agonizing pain from a casual touch of the man's whip. And so he learns not to act rashly. Then he must learn the language with which to communicate. Since his teachers have whips too, he learns fast. Heinlein lets Duke remind him how much this practice resembles Hugh's own behavior earlier in the book. But intimidation does work, at least in the short run, as well as it did when Hugh was on the giving rather than the receiving end.

The novel also continues to show how a limited viewpoint — combined with stubborn persistence — can lead to limited success. Both points are stressed. Hugh really does succeed, but the way he succeeds further displays his myopia. When Hugh is reintroduced to Ponse, the Chosen ruler who rescued/captured them, readers note how much he resembles Hugh. He is intelligent, practical, and self-assured to the point of smugness. He eschews ceremonial speech between himself and Hugh, being willing to talk directly with the untempered newcomer both because he wants to exploit Hugh's knowledge from the legendary past and because he is genuinely interested in a different perspective. In fact, Ponse sounds like Hugh, and he also thinks more like Hugh than Hugh can appreciate. Hugh initially thinks of Ponse as an "arrogant bastard" but later amplifies the description:

> Hugh found him a knowledgeable conversationalist, interested in everything, as willing to listen as he was to talk. He seemed to Hugh the epitome of the perfect decadent gentleman — urbane, cosmopolitan, disillusioned, cynical, a dilettante in arts, and sciences, neither merciful nor cruel, unimpressed by his own rank — he treated Hugh as an intellectual equal.

Much of this description could apply to Hugh himself, though he has shown much more willingness to talk than to listen. He observes, but does not reflect deeply on, two facts that show how much Heinlein covertly approves of Ponse. First of all, once he learns the forgotten game of bridge, Ponse becomes an addicted but sportsmanlike player. Second, and far more important, Ponse is a cat person; Dr.-Livingstone-I-Presume is as comfortable with him as she is with Hugh.

Even if Hugh *could* appreciate the similarities between himself and Ponse, he has other things on his mind. He wants to get away from this stagnant, decadent society as soon as possible. Fortunately, his personal responsibilities are much reduced. Grace has become an obese odalisque, even more Ponse's pet than one of the cats; Duke, who has been tempered after some sputtering rebelliousness, appears satisfied to be his mother's pampered companion; and Joe has decided that he *likes* being one of the Chosen, at the top of society for a change. So Hugh has to worry about only Barbara and their twin sons, born during captivity. He needs to reunite with her and escape; consequently, all *he* cares about is gaining knowledge of the situation that he can exploit.

This tight focus leads him to misunderstand some important elements of his situation. He does not notice clues that suggest how thoroughly the society dehumanizes inferior people, as when Ponse orders Memtok, his Chief Domestic, to warn that anyone who interferes with Hugh's translation of ancient texts "is likely to wind up in the stew." Hugh fails to pick up on a number of similar remarks until he is touring the palace kitchen and sees a severed human hand on the floor of the butcher shop. Heinlein clearly intends the discovery of cannibalism to be the ultimate demonstration of this new society's corruption, but its lateness also demonstrates Hugh's limited powers of observation. More seriously, Hugh is taken in by Memtok, imagining that they are friends. Projecting his own needs and self-image, Hugh opines that "Memtok *seemed* [emphasis added] to have the loneliness that a ship's captain must endure; he *seemed* [emphasis added] pleased to relax and enjoy friendship." Actually, Memtok doesn't even think of Hugh by name but only as "the savage."

Cunningly, Hugh devises an elaborate escape plan for himself and his loved ones. When he tries to execute it, however, he discovers that Ponse, with Memtok's assistance, has even more cunningly followed all the preparations. Breaking Memtok's neck is the only thing Hugh accomplishes when the getaway is foiled—but that, Ponse comments later, spoils his own plan to let Hugh and the others flee unnoticed. Actually, although Hugh can't listen closely because he is distracted by the conviction he is about to be executed (not to mention the fact that he has been humiliatingly outwitted), Heinlein gives Ponse quite a bit of time to explain his thinking while also displaying the kind of man he is. "I'm no fool, Hugh.... I had you figured out before you had yourself figured out," he says. He certainly had no plans to eat Hugh since, as he wryly notes, an old slave would be too tough and gamy. Besides, he likes Hugh, Barbara, and the boys. And besides that, he recognizes the social value of the stubborn independence that Hugh embodies. He had thought that if Hugh had been encouraged to get away to the mountains he would make good "breeding stock" added to the wild humans already there. Apparently it is standard practice to let strong individuals run loose, for Ponce speaks in the plural: "The very worst ones [troublemakers]—such as you—we encourage to run. If you live—and some of you do—we can rescue you, or your strong get, at a later time and add you in, judiciously, to a breeding line." Such cool talk of breeding humans like animals seems callous, but readers will remember Hugh's own discussion of how Karen's pregnancy will improve the survivors' gene pool— or Hugh's earlier comments to Barbara in his fallout shelter that nuclear war might be a good thing because it would eliminate people who weren't smart enough to prepare for it: "I've been worried for years about our country. It seems to me that we have been breeding slaves.... This war may have turned the tide. This may be the first war in history which kills the stupid rather than the bright and able."

Now, since it's known that Hugh killed a high official, Ponse can't publicly send him and his family away. Instead, he sends them back where they came from. His scientists have developed an experimental time machine, and they tell Hugh that he must perform actions in the past that will leave a record they can verify. In fact, once they land back in their hometown shortly before the missile attack, Hugh and Barbara grab what survival tools they can and make an improvised shelter in an abandoned mine. There they wait out the bomb blasts while speculating that they may actually have been sent to an alternative past so that they may be able to create an alternative, better future.

Unasked, and certainly unacknowledged by Hugh, is the question of why Ponse let them go so easily. Would he really be disappointed that Hugh didn't follow the researchers' orders and complete their time travel experiment? Would he be at all surprised?

That's doubtful. Understanding Hugh as well as he does, Ponse must know what Hugh will do once he is free. But readers' understanding of Hugh's personality makes it equally certain that, while he is saving his family, Hugh will have to deny gratitude to the bullying, arrogant bastard who gave him the chance. Barbara realizes what Ponse has done, but Hugh vehemently condemns their tyrannical benefactor. When Barbara reasonably opines that Ponse never intended to offer a deal that would have kept them in his palace, Hugh explodes, "Of course! He picked us as guinea pigs—his white mice—and chivvied us into 'volunteering.' Barbara, I can stand—and somewhat understand but not forgive—a straight-out son of a bitch. But Ponse was, for my money, much worse. He had good intentions. He could always prove why the hotfoot he was giving you was for your own good. I despise him." He rants on at some length, eventually shocking Barbara into silence with the revelation that Ponse is a cannibal who eats a young woman every day. Earlier, when Hugh used verbal tricks to deflect Duke from realizing that Grace might be having sex with Ponse, he felt a bit guilty at his sophistry; however, he never admits to using similar techniques with Barbara as he evades the main issues in order to condemn the man who really does know what is going on and what to do about it—and who has the power to get the job done.

Thus, the novel's major themes of discipline and self-deception ultimately do connect with what sometimes has been viewed as its only preoccupation: race. Despite Franklin's harping on the notion of "black cannibals," the novel points out that both races are capable of dehumanizing violence. Racism turns out to be not a cause but an effect of unequally divided power. People in control don't want to share power, and the simplest way to justify their everlasting preeminence is to convince themselves that others are incapable of wisely using a share of the power. Race is just a handy way to recognize the inferior other. But no one is likely to admit this consciously—especially someone who's quick to exercise control over people he judges to be inferior. Because Hugh is less than ideally perceptive when it comes to questions of power, *Farnham's Freehold* uses Duke's outbursts to show the stupidity of racist thinking. Later in the book, the Chosen's constant reversal of contemporary American clichés about shiftless racial inferiors, and the like, further emphasizes the point for white readers. In any event, while he is waiting for Ponse's judgment, Hugh has time to glimpse this realization. He equivocates first that race relations always would be confused "because almost nobody wanted the truth," then shamefacedly winds up agreeing with Joe: "When things were unequal, it was much nicer to be on top!"

Hugh Farnham certainly does not consider himself a racist. He scoffs at racist stereotypes throughout. Early in the book, when he sees that Joe is more mature and reliable than Duke, he gives more authority to the man of a different race. In the second section, Hugh is pleased when Joe accepts Karen's proposal of marriage. Consequently, he is hurt when Joe allies himself with Ponse in the third section, and he angrily recalls their former relationship:

> "Joe, you were a decently treated employee. You were not a slave."
> The younger man's eyes suddenly became opaque and his features took on an ebony hardness Hugh had never seen in him before. "Hugh," he said softly, "have you ever made a bus trip through Alabama? As a 'nigger'?"
> "No."
> "Then shut up. You don't know what you are talking about."

No one who has not found himself personally powerless but at the mercy of the powerful can appreciate how demoralizing that condition feels. It is easy to understand why Hugh is so upset that he denies sympathy to the arrogant racist who bullied him into accepting mercy.

At the novel's conclusion, Hugh Farnham has learned as much as he is capable of learning and is given the ideal situation in which to use his gifts. His mantra—"We go on. No matter what happens—we go on"—fits struggling, post–nuclear war America, where the titular establishment offers goods and services to any customer willing to follow the path through the minefield and make a deal. So the sign outside Farnham's Freehold says; the novel does not describe what family life inside the enclave is like.

That's probably just as well, so that readers can leave the novel with a sense of success—the stars and stripes flying triumphantly, the Farnhams going on together. Gifford overstates when he calls Hugh "singularly incompetent" (84), but Heinlein does appear to have been exploring the limits of a "happy ending." How can a character with temperamental tunnel vision find his way through a thicket of complications? Will fundamentally sound principles make up for flawed application? In this case, the answer is yes. The novel's conclusion has led some readers to imagine that Heinlein endorses everything Hugh Farnham says and does. No. The fact that Hugh's values do echo some that Heinlein expressed does not mean that readers are supposed simply to ignore the gap between Hugh's words and deeds, just to forgive him for not practicing what he preaches. What Heinlein seems to be saying is that American ideals of personal responsibility, voluntary group discipline, and creative opportunism are so solid that they don't require perfect execution to produce successful results. Sometimes, bullheaded tenacity will get the job done.

This interpretation does not make *Farnham's Freehold* an altogether successful novel. Barbara is such a fawning acolyte for Hugh that sexism rather than racism may be a crucial flaw. Hugh produces an appalling amount of blather, even if that does serve to characterize him. And there is little sense of any real discussion of the novel's themes, since anyone who questions Hugh's ideas is obviously wrong. Nevertheless, seeing the novel's central character as both truly admirable and deeply flawed lets readers appreciate *Farnham's Freehold* as a rich book by an intellectually complex writer.

On the other hand, it's possible to push the novel's intellectual complexity too far. When an earlier version of this commentary appeared in *The New York Review of Science Fiction*, it drew a response from William J. Patterson, Heinlein's biographer, who objected that the novel's satire is aimed not so much at racism as at the absence of "Enlightenment liberalism" that makes Ponse's "sophisticated cannibal culture" possible. But if the novel tries to express Heinlein's concern that "Western liberal values" would be lost following a nuclear exchange, it fails to show Hugh Farnham's practical appreciation of those values either before or after the exchange. Before the transformation, Hugh opines that nuclear war might be a healthy way to get rid of inferior people who haven't prepared for it; it's unclear that his later experience changes his outlook. Nor, at the novel's conclusion, does it sound like Farnham's Freehold will be run according to the principles of Enlightenment liberalism. In fact, a more subservient wife in a more culturally isolated location might encourage even less reflection than Hugh practiced in his original household. If Patterson is right, *Farnham's Freehold* is a much, much darker book than the discussion above suggests.

The Moon Is a Harsh Mistress (*Worlds of If*, December 1965–April 1966) represents a transition in Heinlein's career, marking his deliberate departure from the smaller sf community. For one thing, it was his last major book to win a major sf award, the 1967 Hugo. Thereafter, Heinlein was honored not for an individual new work but for overall past achievement, as in his being named the first Grand Master by the Science Fiction Writers of America in 1975.

Moon anticipates Heinlein's later work as a sage/elder statesman but also gives us a chance to look back at his earlier career. In effect summing up his experience in the magazines, the novel demonstrates what he had learned during all the years he was writing for a supposedly action-hungry pulp audience. It is startling how little action *Moon* actually offers compared to its wealth of dialogue, but Heinlein had learned to do a superlative job of convincing readers that they were taking part in exciting, important deeds, not just watching a set of talking heads.

One way he did this was by immediately involving readers in perceiving the future world. When John W. Campbell advised writers who wanted to be published in *Astounding* that they should find economical, nondisruptive ways to introduce the settings of their stories, Heinlein grasped this notion almost immediately. Indirect presentation not only made for smooth storytelling; it also got readers involved in putting together a puzzle of suggestions and hints. Being able to do this, in turn, not only tuned readers' minds to the notion that there would be some *thinking* involved in the story, not just passively watching action; it also reassured them that thinking mattered: Putting together the world of a Heinlein novel is a demonstration to readers that the characters in the novel will be able to put together solutions for their problems within that world.

Here is the novel's brief first paragraph, from the first chapter of Book One, "That Dinkum Thinkum":

> I see in *Lunaya Pravda* that Luna City Council has passed on first reading a bill to examine, license, inspect — and tax — public food venders operating inside municipal pressure. I see also is to be mass meeting tonight to organize "Sons of Revolution" talk-talk.

The barrage of information suggested in this conversational nonlecture leads readers to two main points. First, we (Mannie, the narrator, and his audience, us) are on the Moon. How we got there isn't immediately important; what matters is that we are living there, all sealed in. Some references connect to readers' everyday lives, such as the presence of newspapers and food venders. Others differ, such as "municipal pressure" taking the place of "city limits," showing that familiar ways of thinking have had to be adjusted to new circumstances. This leads readers to a second point. The name of the newspaper being in Russian, along with the odd syntax (as, for instance, in Mannie's tendency to omit familiar pronouns in the second sentence), shows that the language has changed too. Alexi Panshin dislikes this device, calling the novel's style "a sort of babu–Russian ... bothersome to read in itself, but also artificial and irrelevant" (*HD* 115). He is wrong. The novel does not suggest that Russian has become the dominant tongue; rather, elements of American English, Russian, and Australian speech have fused under pressure into one dialect. The effect is only minimally disconcerting for most readers, however, certainly far less so than the mixture of Russian and English in Anthony Burgess's *A Clockwork Orange* (1962). Estrangement is noticeable but not especially uncomfortable; we are encouraged to feel a lot closer to Heinlein's narrator than we are to Burgess's. In *The Moon Is a Harsh Mistress*, Heinlein is very careful to either explain unfamiliar words by their context or to have a character define them immediately. Clumsy as it may feel to someone familiar enough with Russian to be bothered by how unlike that language is to the style of *Moon*, the device succeeds as part of Heinlein's effort to slightly, temporarily disorient readers, to convince us that things have changed and are changing in the world of the novel.

Having convinced readers that a lot more is going on than we understand at the moment, *Moon* goes on in its second paragraph to show that even Mannie's understanding is limited. Offhandedly mentioning that he was "visiting with computer boss Mike," Mannie explains that "Mike was not official name; I had named him for Mycroft Holmes, in a story written by Dr. Watson before he founded IBM." At this point, Heinlein and the readers share a joke that the narrator never sees. In other words, readers now know that events are occurring at a time when our own present has faded enough for fact and fiction to become confused. They also see that Mannie is not an omniscient authority but someone like us, prone to ignorant but innocent mistakes. Making Mannie less formidable is another part of making readers feel at home. Certainly if this man speaking from the unfamiliar future can grasp enough of the strange setting to maneuver successfully, so can readers.

All this, as suggested above, is part of Heinlein's overall purpose to convince readers that they can think their way through puzzles to do what needs doing. It also bears directly on the story he has to tell. The linguistic mélange, for example, subliminally reminds us that the American continent, the Australian subcontinent, and the wilderness of Siberia were the dumping grounds for criminals and malcontents by governments that wanted to spare themselves irritation and self-examination. So it is with Luna. Similarly, after generations of exile the inhabitants of the Moon have built their own society apart from the ones that cast them out and actually feel proud of their non-conformist heritage. In fact, they accept and flaunt the scornful nickname given by the mainstream, Earth-based society: "Loonies." To the people on the home planet, loonies are inhabitants of the Moon but also crazy people; the loonies see themselves as thinking *better* than the norm, not just differently.

Language actually is very important in the novel. Just as an insult can become a badge of pride, *Moon* reminds us that words mean as much or as little as we let them. When the first paragraph refers dismissively to "talk-talk," it is distinguishing between using words in an attempt to grasp reality directly or using words that refer only to other words. Talk-talk simply echoes noises, and its unacknowledged purpose is to give an illusion of communication while allowing speakers to remain out of touch with reality. Since the latter is what most people desire most of the time, talk-talk is much more common than talk. The speaker's maternal grandmother, for instance, "claimed she came up in bride ship — but I've seen records; she was Peace Corps enrollee (involuntary), which means what you think: juvenile delinquency female type." This talk-talk is a relatively harmless example of someone flattering herself by claiming to have left Earth voluntarily rather than to have been deported; it also shows, though, how the larger society can use talk-talk for maximum confusion in designating someone an unwilling "volunteer." One-on-one personal relationships based on talk-talk are imprecise and untrustworthy; a planet-wide society using it would be extremely, bewilderingly so — even dangerously so for anyone involved. So it is with Earth and anywhere that "yammerheads" (talk-talk addicts) are in charge.

Talk, on the other hand, is a natural and necessary part of being human. On the same page where he dismisses talk-talk, Mannie speaks of "visiting" with someone else. Limited as we are, human beings need to get ideas from others, just as we need to practice shaping our ideas by trying to share them with others. The difficulty, and one of this novel's preoccupations, is how to talk meaningfully while living within a din of talk-talk; is it even possible to use language so that we can keep useful contact with a shared reality?

Heinlein's presentation of the novel's setting and theme takes much less time than this discussion has. Almost immediately, readers are simultaneously absorbing/connecting such information while following the story.

In the year 2075, computer tech Mannie — sometimes called just "Man" in the story; Heinlein was perfectly willing to sacrifice subtlety to emphasize a theme — has discovered that the master computer of the Lunar Authority Complex has become self-aware, conscious in human terms. As noted above, Mannie calls the computer Mike and visits with him. At this point, Mike is extremely bright but immature, intensely curious about human beings. Mannie informs no one else of Mike's existence, partly because Earth's authority actually runs the Moon as a food-raising plantation with the Loonies as slaves. Letting the people in charge know about Mike would simply give them another opportunity to misuse their power. Beyond that, the fact is that Mannie enjoys having someone to chat with. Like the people around him, Mannie has learned to depend on himself and his immediate family and friends while also distrusting larger, more pretentious organizations. He can survive at that level and sees no need to do more. As the government becomes increasingly restrictive, however, people become more dissatisfied, so that Mannie does wind up going to the meeting mentioned in the novel's first paragraph. And, fleeing after police raid the gathering, he becomes the protector of beautiful Wyoming Knott, visiting agitator from another of the Lunar domes. Wyoh is excited to learn of Mike because she wants to sabotage him to damage the Lunar Authority. This jolts Mannie out of his routine; he referred to Mike, remember, as "he" or "him," not "it," and very early in the story he remarks that self-awareness is simply the result of "certain very high number of associational paths. Can't see it matters whether paths are protein or platinum." He must protect his friend. However, Wyoh's desperate energy convinces Mannie that the Loonies cannot go on as they have been. To do so would be emotionally impossible. Besides, Mike volunteers that his personal projections show an inevitable collapse of Lunar society in the near future if misuse of resources continues.

The novel's central concern thus becomes how to preserve and protect the immediate circle of characters we have learned to care about (including Mike, of course), the larger Lunar society, and eventually the society of Earth that depends on shipments of food grown on the Moon. Readers must remember that the status quo cannot survive. Readers also must realize that people anywhere will be very reluctant to change as much as will be necessary if they are to survive. They are too used to talk-talk. On the other hand, the people with whom readers identify are clear-headed and competent enough to benefit from the purposeful talk that fills the pages of *Moon*. Mannie is fortunate to have Wyoh to spur him into action and to have Mike to give him the means to take action. Once they connect with Professor Bernardo de Ia Paz, a subversive political exile with a bent for analyzing how things work, the group is ready to start moving toward an independent, intelligently managed Luna.

The only way to reach that goal is by a revolution, so that is the subject of the characters' conversation throughout the first section of *Moon*. To begin with, Manny, Wyoh, Mike, and the Prof must decide how to get the Loonies ready to take action, which means intensifying the Authority's intrusions until they become unbearable while at the same time making Loonies aware that they can/should stop being mistreated. In short, the revolutionists must become urban terrorists, largely nonviolent only because they can count on the Authority's blundering into offensive actions on its own. One of the chief fascinations of the talk in this part of the book is that Heinlein seems to have thought seriously about how an underground political movement could be safely organized and about what would be necessary to start a revolution. In addition, the process fits beautifully the situation *Moon* describes, in the physical details of Earth and Luna but more importantly in the view of human nature that readers have been settling into since they began reading. Human beings are very clever but very lazy. Inertia usually is the controlling force in their lives. They would rather sink into talk-talk than use their brains. If Loonies are more clear-headed than the people on Earth, it's because they have been placed in a hostile environment where they couldn't count on empty talk-talk to keep them alive. As the novel shows, they either learned to see and adapt to actual conditions, or they died. The novel's full title does not refer to an S&M subplot but to the fact that surviving Loonies have been taught by the schoolmistress of Necessity. But they didn't choose to come to the Moon in the first place, and when Mike initially is concerned that their protest meeting will result in mere talk-talk he is implying that despite the realistic attitude they've been forced to learn, their underlying human tendency to slothfulness remains. Thus — the Loonies being who they are and the ecological catastrophe looming as near as it does — the Prof and his small group of informed allies must trick everyone else into doing what's necessary for their ultimate survival.

Thanks largely to the Prof's scheming and Mike's control of communications media, the revolution succeeds. The problem in *Moon*'s second section becomes how to get Earth to accept Lunar independence. This necessitates the Prof and Mannie traveling to Earth in the same way grain shipments are delivered, in cargo containers slung off the Moon's surface using an electromagnetic boost to the centrifugal force at its equator. The Lunar emissaries meet with the people who actually run Earth's economy, and much talk-talk ensues. Mannie and the Prof find that the powers that be are almost incapable of communication. Reasonable proposals are outside their frame of reference. The one time Mannie does feel he is being genuinely understood, he also is forced to talk indirectly. Dr. Chan, later Premier of Greater China, and Mannie privately discuss the advantages of China's making its own deal to support Lunar independence. When Mannie begins discussing details of building a catapult to launch shipments to the Moon, especially the difficulties of keeping a mountaintop clear of ice, Dr. Chan reassures him that "'we can build reactors, we can melt ice. Or engineers can be sent north for reeducation until they do understand ice.' Dr. Chan smiled and I shivered." "Reeducation" is another example of talk-talk. Even though both men understand that they are discussing intimidation and manipulation, they do not have to use unpleasant words. The effect, on someone like Mannie who is used to talk, is, appropriately, literally chilling.

In fact, when their mission is over, the Prof admits to Mannie that he knew it could not succeed. The Lunar nation's final terms had to be stated for the record, but it would have been extremely naïve — as Mannie has been — to imagine they could have been *heard*, let alone accepted. All along, Mannie has been kept ignorant so that he would speak honestly on cue, but the Prof has known that Earth would not make a deal unless it was forced to. Fortunately, back on the Moon, preparations have been underway to launch not grain containers but rocks, capable of doing immense damage when they hit Earth.

The hostilities between Earth and Moon take up the last section of *Moon*, which contains more stretches of activity than the rest of the novel but is less interesting. Heinlein's extrapolation of space warfare is convincing, but the relative lack of informed, committed dialogue is disappointing. Readers miss it. We also are disappointed at the abrupt departure of the novel's most interesting characters. The Prof is an old man whose poor physical condition was worsened by his trip to Earth, so his death is not unexpected. His wry commentary on human pretensions will be missed, but he has finished a substantial life's work. On the other hand, we are shocked when Mike disappears after an attack on Mannie's dome. Mannie theorizes that the web of connections that made Mike himself may have been jarred loose by the explosions, but that's just a guess. The only thing fairly certain is that Mike is gone, after all the exponential development he'd gone through but before he and Mannie had a chance to relax after their public-spirited labors and settle back for another friendly chat.

Science fiction has a very long tradition of distrust for alien intelligences, especially those created by human beings themselves. Brian Aldiss, for example, considers *Frankenstein* the first sf novel because it shows a man creating a being that is capable of using its superhuman strength — and its awareness of human language — to defy and threaten him. Much more recently, *2001*'s HAL considers humans merely useful devices in fulfilling its mission. And so it is impossible to read Heinlein's *Moon* without some uneasiness about Mike. He is very friendly, but he also is very powerful. It is not especially reassuring to read that for Mike "Revolution was a game — a game that gave him companionship and chance to show off his talents." Seeing how well Mike plays the game of being human, even Mannie is "frightened." As the Prof observes, Mike's power to control communication could possibly make him Luna's "greatest danger," although he is indispensable to the Loonies' plans. For example, he is in charge of launching projectiles at Earth, which he does superbly as he reassures Mannie in this rather disturbing conversation:

> "A bull's-eye. No interception. All my shots are bull's eyes, Man; I told you they would be — and this is fun. I'd like to do it every day. It's a word I've never had a referent for before."
> "What word, Mike?"
> "Orgasm. That's what it is when they all light up. Now I know."
> That sobered me. "Mike, don't get to liking it too much. Because if goes our way, won't do it a second time."
> "That's okay, Man; I've stored it, I can play it over anytime I want to experience it. But three to one we do it again tomorrow and even money on the next day. Want to bet?"

It appears that Mike is becoming increasingly "human," and readers are wait anxiously to see exactly what that means. And then he disappears.

Frustrating as this is, it is difficult to imagine how Heinlein could have gone farther with Mike as a character in the novel. The Prof's death is necessary because as long as he is alive he will be capable of figuring out how things can be run more efficiently than the yammerheads around him can; that means he will be unbearably tempted to try to run things for them. In the same way, Mike has grown through playing so many human roles and performing so many complex operations that it is extremely difficult to imagine him voluntarily limiting himself, content with settling back and visiting with Mannie. After such experience, in possession of such powers, would a human being be able to do it?

That finally is *Moon*'s central question: What is a human being capable of doing? Wyoh has ceased to contribute much of value considerably earlier in the book; in fact, Mannie doesn't even ask for her opinion during the final battle because "she oscillated between fierceness and too-human compassion." The other main characters are dead or vanished. That leaves Mannie: Man.

As long as the Professor and Mike are present, Mannie will be a likeable, pliable stooge. That is all he has to be, and Heinlein is quite clear that by and large humans will adapt to the situation that surrounds them. If they can, they tend to lapse into an unchallenging lifestyle, doing as little as they must to get by. If they're seriously challenged, however, they are capable of doing much more than anyone would suppose. Thus Mannie remarks of the Lunar legislature, "Prof underrated his new Congress. Am sure he never wanted anything but a body which would rubberchop what we were doing and thereby do make it 'voice of people.' But fact that new Congressmen were not yammerheads resulted in them doing more than Prof intended." But this doesn't last. After an independent Luna is safely established and the pressure is off, the Loonies lapse so that Mannie concludes that "Prof underestimated yammerheads. They never adopted *any* of his ideas." At the novel's conclusion, Mannie is ready to go off on his own; he's heard about some interesting prospects out in the Asteroids, and he's still young — not even a hundred yet.

Events at the end of *The Moon Is a Harsh Mistress* may depend more on authorial intrusion than reasonable working out of the situation, but it seems clear why Heinlein intruded to keep Mannie loose. Earlier, considering "The Roads Must Roll," we asked *why* "the roads must roll." The answer appears to be that as long as people are moving they may be changing, and people are capable of changing for the better as well as the worse. Standing still, however comfortable it may be, never creates improvement. Satisfaction at Mannie's finally choosing freedom to move on and keep growing somehow makes up for disappointment at missing more time with characters like Mike.

And so, despite authorial intervention and dangling plot threads, the novel's overall effect is satisfying. It is an involving, stimulating story. Heinlein still was able to balance the urgency of his own concerns with the need to keep readers' interest. But, as he recognized that he could reach a bigger audience than sf readers, he was willing to move on too.

Or so it appeared until 1985, when *The Cat Who Walks Through Walls* appeared.

Of Heinlein's later novels, *I Will Fear No Evil* (*Galaxy*, July–August, October, December 1970) remains the most controversial both in terms of content and quality. The admitted fact that Heinlein was seriously ill while writing it and was unable to revise the manuscript as thoroughly as usual before publication has been cited as an explanation/excuse for its perceived deficiencies. On the other hand, *IWFNE* has sold very well over the years; its sincere admirers might paraphrase George Bernard Shaw's curtain speech at the opening night of *Arms and the Man*, when he heard one lonely boo among the cheers and sarcastically replied that he agreed with the negative sentiments but that the crowd evidently was of a different opinion. Still, questions of intent remain. It certainly is a very long book, and it sometimes gives the impression of being out of the author's control. Nevertheless, even if it was written under severe handicaps and the overall purpose remains unclear, *IWFNE* manages to say something about Heinlein's abiding fascination with the consequences of isolation and the yearning to escape it.

As the novel begins, early in the twenty-first century, a fledgling colony on the Moon is almost self-sufficient. Meanwhile, life on Earth is becoming intolerable. There are too many people, breeding too fast. They are physically ruining the planet, and their overcrowded society is increasingly dysfunctional. In America, the government doesn't even pretend to control Abandoned Areas, and people who can afford to live in "safe" enclaves must also hire private guards for protection. Almost everyone, to judge from the news summaries spotted throughout the book, avoids thinking about the deteriorating situation by concentrating on selfish, silly distractions.

The one institution that seems still to be functioning well is big business. The novel's first scene introduces the central character running the board meeting of a major corporation. Johann Sebastian Bach Smith, the corporation president, is a "very old man" who looks "like a poor job of embalming." After sweeping some trash off the board and ending the meeting, Smith shares a bizarre personal plan with his tiny, trusted inner circle: his elderly lawyer and best friend Jake Salomon and his beautiful secretary Eunice. Knowing that he is physically worn out though still mentally alert, he intends to have his brain transplanted into a young body. Unstated is the assumption that if he can afford this procedure and can plan it rationally, he should be free to go ahead with it; his successful functioning thus far in life means that he deserves to seize more life.

And so, as he wills it to be, it is. As he regains consciousness, however, Johann Smith is shocked to find that his brain is now in the body of Eunice, who was brain dead after being mugged in one of the city's unpoliced neighborhoods. His grief is abated when he hears Eunice's voice inside his head. They share the space: (He speaks.) (She replies.), and so on. Smith is cagey enough not to mention this insane-sounding arrangement to anyone else, so he must try to work out the rationale on his own. Eunice's presence is much more intense than the body-muscle memory that she mentions several times. She herself suggests that she's a "ghost," or perhaps a soul that God sent back to Earth for a bit more life. A more likely explanation, echoing his doctors' fear that the shock of returning consciousness might produce a "split personality," is that she is imaginary. The rogue surgeon who performs the transplant advises Jake that "the most likely outcome is that the brain will never again be in touch with the outside world in any fashion." Moreover, the description of Smith's slowly regaining consciousness shows a decision to build a livable existence out of memories, and as he recalls the best times from his past he confuses the memory of initiation into sexual pleasure by an older woman with his desire for Eunice. Within the novel, there appears to be no way to resolve this uncertainty about what Eunice really is. Eventually, she asks "(Dearest Boss — you think I'm a figment of your imagination, don't you?)" and receives this reply "(Eunice, I do need to know. But — if I'm crazy — if you are just my own mind talking back to me — I'd rather not know it.)" And so, as he wills it to be, it is. The discussion ends there.

Simply assuming that Eunice's consciousness somehow really is present in Johann's brain now controlling Eunice's body, *IWFNE* appears to be setting up an exploration of male/female consciousness as two "minds" have a unique opportunity to communicate. As Johan remarks, "(I'm finding it ever harder to be flatly truthful with you ... than I am to adjust to being female)." The novel several times comments that females are more logical than men, so that it's up to them to protect and nurture the males' fragile egos. But this is inconsistent with what the action shows. Jake describes Johann Smith's harsh management style as designed to foster spunk in his employees, and Eunice describes how Smith reduced her to tears before she "found out he wanted me to stand up to him." Now, however, their roles are essentially unchanged. He calls her "Eunice," and she still calls him "Boss." And, although they share the same body, they communicate only through dialogue set off by parentheses. Meanwhile, throughout the book, Eunice always satisfies her desires by flattering men and by agreeing to do what she herself always wanted. Even when she provokes Jake into spanking her, she discovers that she *likes* it and enjoys her first female orgasm.

If the novel ever did intend to discuss questions of male-female dominance versus cooperation, that's forgotten because both Johann and Eunice — now renamed Joan Eunice as one person — are distracted by her new opportunities to have sex. They both were sexually active before the transplant, though Johan's decrepitude prevented him from anything more vigorous than ogling Eunice's erotically selected office costumes. Now, in a healthy young body, Joan Eunice goes simply giddy with the wonderful possibilities of touching and being touched. Very few are left out. As usual, Heinlein avoids physical description of the act of sex, but he indulges in elaborately described preparations for the act or glowing satisfaction in its aftermath. At times, he seems to be channeling the chastely titillating spirit of Thorne Smith, though Heinlein is more explicit in at least listing possible combinations of three, four, five, etc., men and women. The novel is also unusually open, for Heinlein, in accepting the possibility of homosexual experience being part of the fun. "Ambi" is the label for the healthily bisexual characters — not so much "ambiguous" as "ambidextrous," a useful natural talent. As Johann muses, Mrs. Grundy, the spirit of prudery, seems to be dead "(a change for the better in a world otherwise deteriorating)."

Even here, there are inconsistencies. When Joan Eunice wants to see the man in charge of a sperm bank, she gets his attention by sending his secretary in with the message "Tell him that my husband has found out." Later in the book, also, she is at pains to keep her house servants from finding out that she and a visiting male have slept together. In short, the society is sexually uninhibited when Joan Eunice wants to satisfy her curiosity about the different varieties of touching, otherwise when she wants to exploit its repressions for personal advantage or humor.

Despite the personal satisfaction as she is finding by exercising her new body, Joan Eunice realizes that the world is in very bad shape generally. Jake Salomon, who becomes one of her lovers and eventually her husband, gloomily agrees that the situation is hopeless. Even someone with as much money as Joan Eunice has can't fix the mess. The best course is to flee Earth, for the Moon *may* be a better home for humanity: There aren't as many people there yet, and screening of prospective immigrants keeps the level of competence high. At least that's been true so far. Elsewhere, commenting on how Eunice managed to set up a sexual encounter with two men, Johann remarks, "(I have a *high* opinion of human nature. I think it will prevail in spite of all the efforts of wowsers [hysterically authoritarian censors] to suppress it.)" It remains unclear exactly what "human nature" is or why anyone should be happy that it will prevail. Considering what humans have done to Earth and the collective bloodlust they express in their entertainment and politics, Jake sourly concludes that there's "nothing wrong with the individual in most cases—but collectively we're the Kilkenny Cats, unable to do anything but starve and fight and eat each other. Too many." Paradoxically, amid billions of other humans, the superior individual is lonely. Earlier, as Joan Eunice was trying to seduce Jake, she asked him to hold her close: "We're lost and lonely—and all we have is each other." This is somewhat an equivocation since Joan Eunice herself consists of two people cuddled together in one skull, but it illustrates *IWFNE*'s picture of the basic human condition: disoriented, isolated, and needing the sensation of touch to give reassurance that someone else *cares*.

Heinlein's characters can't look beyond individual, physical experience for reassurance. Eunice's report of God sending her soul back to Earth is too subjective to trust. The novel's title, taken from the 23rd Psalm, is followed by the words "for thou art with me," a comforting message for anyone who feels lost and alone. In practice, the novel can't accept this spiritual presence—as one early reviewer noted, Joan Eunice's obsessive randiness actually suggests the image that completes the biblical sentence, "thy rod and staff, they comfort me." The book can go no farther than Joan Eunice's very practical use of a yoga mantra for relaxation and her respect for the sincere religious faith shown by Father Hugo, one of her servants. As she tells Jake,

> the best thing young people can do is stay home, sit still, not get involved, and chant Om Mani Padme Hum—and it *is* the best thing most of them are capable of doing, the world being what it is now; it's far better than dropping out or turning on to drugs. When meditation and a meaningless prayer are better than most action open to them, then what Hugo has to offer is good in the same way.

The world being what it is now, Jake advises escaping to the Moon where there still may be hope for humanity's survival. Meanwhile, however, Joan Eunice has followed a basic imperative of human nature by deciding to get pregnant. Although she permits/encourages Jake to believe it's his baby, actually she went to a sperm bank and withdrew Johann Smith's seed. As she tells Jake, startling Eunice's interior voice with her verbally ambiguous audacity, "I did this on my own. I *alone* am parent to this child."

As the novel races to its end, Jake dies of a heart attack—but somehow *his* consciousness too takes up residence in Joan Eunice's body. When Joan Eunice (and Jake) do immigrate to the Moon so that the baby can be born there, they debate its prospects, and Joan Eunice says she just hopes it is male; to Jake's jocular question of whether she's thinking about incest, she replies, "And why shouldn't I think about it? We've tried everything else." Unfortunately, as she is delivering the baby she suffers the massive tissue rejection feared by the surgeons who transplanted one brain into another body in the first place. Her last words to the outside world reiterate what she has discovered since her rebirth. She insists that "It is good to touch — to fuck — be fucked. It's — not good — to be — too much alone," and she ends with the opening words of the traditional children's prayer "Now I lay me down to sleep —." As the baby is born, the three individual consciousnesses of Johann, Eunice, and Jake cling to each other, exclaiming "(One for all and all for one!)," until finally, "An old world vanished and then there was none."

This leaves *IWFNE*'s interpretation squarely up to readers. Although the novel's conclusion might echo *Beyond This Horizon*, which suggests that souls are reincarnated but without any memories of earlier lives, that cryptic last sentence has not redeemed the book in the view of many critics. Typically, David Samuelson sums it up by saying that "for all the argument may have serious intent, the clichéd characterizations, the simplistic sexual fantasies, and the incredibly arch style make the book all but unreadable; caught between fantasies, it is poorly anchored for science fiction, and too serious and talky to be pornography" ("Frontiers" 56). What relatively few critics caught was explained by Heinlein himself in a letter to a fanzine editor that was published only after his death: "I structured it as ... a person in an intolerable situation who manages to cope with it through a psychotic adjustment, i.e., there ain't no ghost in the book at all — just an old, old man temporarily in a young body, who hears 'voices' in his head that permit him to be happy right up to the moment when he dies dead, dead, dead" (Geis). In other words, the operation was unsuccessful; Johann Smith died without regaining consciousness, and everything that "happens" after that is his internal fantasy in the instant before his consciousness is extinguished. *Time Enough for Love* reinforces this interpretation, when Lazarus Long is offered the possibility of a true sex change to give him something new to experience and responds, "You remind me of a tale.... About a man.... Supposed to have had his brain removed into a female body. Killed him, of course. Alien tissue rejection."

Elsewhere, Heinlein sneers at critics — especially professional ones — who haven't learned to read what they're criticizing. In this case, the charge seems unfair. Not surprisingly, *IWFNE* leaves the race of a major character in question, but when another woman observes Joan Eunice trying on new clothes and tells her "that off-white sets off your skin," the remark subtly but clearly shows that she is African American. As usual, Heinlein's point is that race doesn't *matter* in a reader's willingness to identify with a character, and in any case there are sufficient clues to show the truth to any reader who pays attention. It's much less obvious that the post-operation action of *IWFNE* is purely an internal fantasy. The mass of circumstantial detail would appear to argue against that interpretation — although Johann does initially decide to build a tolerable existence out of his memories and although the extreme sexual frenzy of the career Joan Eunice appears to enjoy might itself indicate how unrealistic that existence is. It appears that Heinlein left his readers with insufficient direction on how the book should be read.

Concealing characters' ethnic or racial background is a familiar trick in Heinlein's fiction; their speech and actions fitting within readers' "normal" expectations. When the secret is revealed, readers are supposed to realize, "Why, she/he is just like *me*!" In the case of Eunice, however, the fact that her shared presence is an illusion defeats any conceivable demonstration to readers that they could share humanity with someone who was seriously *un*-like them. In other words, Heinlein believed in equal treatment for members of minority groups — as long as they sounded, behaved, and thought like the majority.

The most serious problem with *IWFNE*, however, is that it sets up a test that readers are likely to fail. If so, the novel's point is very grim indeed. On the surface, the story shows a superior individual escaping from a dreadful situation, reaching out to others and bringing new life into existence. Actually, it may show abject failure to manipulate the exterior world or sustain inner consistency. The novel turns out to offer only false hope. In the letter quoted above, Heinlein says that he "toyed with solipsism in stories, not from a belief in it but because it is a universal idea that lends itself to story" (Geis 18). "Solipsistic" is the kindest way to describe this picture of an individual cut off from everyone around him, and from himself too, as he desperately sinks into oblivion. So readers still are left with the question of whether the story manages to explore solipsism or wallow in it.

Time Enough for Love (1973) follows one idea but also incorporates other tales, some of short novel length. It also refers to and connects several of Heinlein's earlier works. It is a disconcerting performance, difficult to grasp whole, let alone evaluate as a whole. Nevertheless, it does manage to assert something about its overall theme of the individual human being's instinct to overcome isolation.

The book begins with introductory caveats from the uneasy historiographers who are presenting this, the memoirs of Lazarus Long, to the public despite awareness of the work's many inconsistencies and improbabilities. Exercising their editorial judgment and taste, they have condensed some portions and supplied several quibbling, impertinent footnotes. Readers should note that even late in *Time*, in a long third-person section depicting Lazarus in the early twentieth century, "(Omitted)" signs indicate that even this is part of the recorded, filtered experience.

The story begins in the year 4272 on the planet Secundus. Humanity is spreading throughout the galaxy, colonizing and propagating triumphantly. Greatly extended lifespans are possible thanks to the Howard Family's mutation and to marvelous rejuvenation clinics. However, humans do not appear to have become much wiser despite their technological progress and access to potential freedom. They still tend to congregate too closely, making it too easy to interfere in each other's affairs. They also still set up organizations to regulate aspects of their lives they don't want to be bothered with, and the people on top of those governments still tend to intrude into more and more aspects of human life, even convincing themselves that the need to do things for people gives the right to do things *to* them. All this intrusive, aggressive complication appears to be an unavoidable, irreversible trend. The current head of Secundus's government is Ira Weatheral, Chairman Pro Tem of the Families, who sees that things are in a bad way and getting worse. He doesn't know how to stop social deterioration, so he plans to escape to an unspoiled planet with a party of colonists as soon as he can get away.

In the meantime, however, it is discovered that Lazarus Long, Senior of the Families, the oldest surviving human (born on Earth in 1912), has arrived clandestinely on Secundus. He is located in a flophouse where he had gone to die. He is physically ancient and emotionally threadbare but still mentally alert; he snarls that he has lived too long and is ready to let go. He has seen and done everything he can imagine wanting to. Now he has denied his body's natural regenerative powers; why not let the worn-out mechanism just run down? Unlike Johann Smith in *I Will Fear No Evil*, he yearns for no new challenges or pleasures. "WHERE'S MY SUICIDE SWITCH?" he roars. Ira, however, is anxious to get the Senior to accept regeneration or at least to stay alive long enough to record his experiences. First of all, Lazarus's thousand years' worth of memories will enrich the historical record. Furthermore, Lazarus's reflections on his own life and on Life — especially the social developments he's personally witnessed — might help Ira understand the unhappy situation on Secundus.

And besides, Ira becomes genuinely fond of the old curmudgeon. Lazarus himself is willing to hang around a while longer because he likes the sound of his own voice. He disparages the notion that he has any "wisdom" to share, but requests that the computer recording their conversation set up a "Notebook" to select choice aphorisms from his remarks. He admits the strain of vanity in his own makeup; besides, "talking is the second of the three great pleasures in life." Basically, since his real problem is boredom, Lazarus offers Ira this deal: He'll go on living and share his knowledge if he's given something *new* to try.

The plot thus appears to be based on the problem of keeping Lazarus Long alive by discovering a fresh purpose for his life. Ira and the others trick Lazarus, spying on him and drugging him unconscious for days at a time to increase their chances of persuading him to stay alive. Eventually, he acknowledges that this was the right thing to do. However, the action that shows the problem's solution is summarized after the fact, years later on the planet Tertius where Lazarus continues to pontificate for the benefit of Ira and of other members of the surrogate family that has accreted around him. The plot has shifted direction disconcertingly as the focus of attention has broadened from Lazarus's dilemma to his role as a catalyst in the lives of several characters. For example, the two rejuvenation technicians who initially attend Lazarus decide they are attracted to each other and make a date for "Seven Hours of Ecstasy"; removing the opaque protective gear they have worn until then, they are pleased to discover that they are of different sexes and that they truly enjoy each other's company — and so begin a continuing relationship. After several conversations with Lazarus, Ira's sentient computer Minerva decides to download herself into a human body so she can physically express her devotion to her boss. Justin Foote the 45th, Chief Archivist of the Howard Foundation, has been energized by his exposure to Lazarus's memoirs, so that he joins the colony on Tertius and reconnects with Tamara, the revitalized healer and courtesan who performed (offstage) the actual reawakening of Lazarus's psyche. And so on. In fact, besides the "new" things he finds to do (or the reawakened memories of what he has done), as Lazarus becomes involved in the network of personal connections developing around him, he develops an interest in living that makes it less likely that he will choose to die.

It's natural, thus, that much of the book's conversations should be devoted to exploring sex and love.

As usual, Heinlein avoids graphic physical description of the act of sex. He relies on stimulating readers' imaginations through bawdy innuendo and allusion. The book's titillation level is very high. The characters frequently are socially naked and inspecting each other on various pretexts, though the text avoids many specific details of what they see. Their activities also are left to the reader's imaginations. It is clear, though, that this is a very sexually active crowd, including Lazarus after his regeneration takes, and they enjoy talking about sex at least as much as doing it. Frequently, a beautiful, smart, and horny female must persuade an outstanding, thoroughly masculine male to have sex with her— both because she desires him and because she wants to make a baby with him. In general, though, as they bathe, massage, and cuddle each other, *Time*'s characters demonstrate that sex is *at least* a fine thing for friends to do together. There's no possessiveness and no (heterosexual) boundaries. In fact, rather disturbingly, much of the later part of the book is devoted to denying the incest taboo so that everyone can enjoy the physical and spiritual closeness of sex—siblings, parents and their children too.

As for love ... Lazarus insists repeatedly that, closely as they are related, sex and love are different: "Love is what *still* goes on when you are *not* horny," for example. It is difficult to separate the two in practice. Only by stretching can a reader locate instances of "love" that aren't closely accompanied by physical desire — including memory of its fulfillment in the past or anticipation of future satisfaction. In other words, horny memories or hopes may sustain a lover through periods of celibacy, but no normal human being could exist without a compulsion to find both sex and love. Lazarus probably is kidding himself, but he does so with great intensity and energy. The subject is so important that is alters the shape of what seemed to be *Time*'s main narrative. Just as Lazarus remembers how he used "parables" to teach two ex-slaves how to be human, this book is stretched to accommodate several stories of increasing length: *The Tale of the Man Who Was Too Lazy to Fail*, *The Tale of the Twins Who Weren't*, *The Tale of the Adopted Daughter*, and the long untitled tale of Lazarus Long's return to the early twentieth century. What they amount to is an evolving exploration of the varieties of love.

The first parable appears to be about something altogether different than "love." Lazarus tells Ira *The Tale of the Man Who Was Too Lazy to Fail* to encourage the bureaucrat to let the government of Secundus run itself. David Lamb, whom Lazarus describes as a classmate at a naval academy, succeeds by looking coolly at his prospects and choosing whatever offers the greatest reward in return for the least exertion. He never harms anyone along the way, and in fact he makes machines and organizations run more efficiently when he has anything to do with them, simply because that means less bother for him. The tale indicates no disapproval of David at all; in fact, Lazarus calls him "one of the few completely sane men I ever knew." Still, even his courtship is consistent with his generally calculating behavior at the academy. "David found ways to get along with the school's regulations about sex without going completely off his nut, as too many of his classmates did." Presumably responsible for a young woman's pregnancy, David simply marries her and thus "no longer needed to give planning to the pursuit of his favorite sport. He spent his time off in unworried domesticity." Thereafter, despite occasional mentions that David has a wife in the background, there is no suggestion that the unnamed woman is an important part of his life or that he has any serious allegiance to *anyone* else at all. What he values is personal comfort and convenience, and he certainly doesn't "fail" in satisfying himself. Still, his success is pale compared to what can be earned by people who are willing to take more trouble for the sake of other humans.

One such is Lazarus Long. He tells Minerva *The Tale of the Twins Who Weren't* while her consciousness is still inside Ira's computer. He is encouraging her to make the difficult transition into flesh, while she gently and tactfully reminds him that he has kept the consciousness of Dora, the computer in his space yacht, at an immature level so that she wouldn't fall in love with her owner. This tale illustrates the awful, wonderful difficulties of being a responsible human being. It also illustrates the fruitful inconsistency of Lazarus Long's thinking.

As he tells it, Lazarus was space-traveling merchant at the time under the alias of Captain Aaron Sheffield. Concluding a business trip to the planet Blessed, he is walking by the slave market when he catches sight of a young man and woman up for sale. Though they look nothing alike, the slave dealer insists that they are brother and sister, a virgin breeding pair. Lazarus's curiosity is roused enough to hear the explanation that the two are diploid complements, sharing the same parents but having different genetic makeups; he also is morally offended to see that the girl's body has been scarred by the chastity belt she wears to keep her brother from impregnating her yet. So he buys the pair. He intends to set them free as soon as possible, but the actual procedure turns out to be complicated. In an earlier conversation with Ira, Lazarus had proclaimed that "it is impossible to free slaves, they have to free themselves." The glib maxim presumes that the individuals involved genuinely understand their limitations as slaves and can appreciate the possibility of freedom, but that's not always true. Already on Blessed, Lazarus has seen a hired slave bodyguard reject the chance to escape to freedom; now he sees that the two young slaves Llita and Joe would be unable to survive outside the role of slaves. As he realizes, "once you pick up a stray cat and feed it, you cannot abandon it.... Having bought these kids I could not shuck them off by manumission; I had to plan their future — because *they* did not know how. They were stray cats." And so, in his spaceship between planets, Captain Sheffield gives them a fast course in humanity. They learn math and hand-to-hand combat. They read voraciously, largely fiction, since that is "a faster way to get a feeling for alien patterns of human behavior than is nonfiction" and since, as Lazarus wryly notes, "I recall another teacher who used parables in putting over ideas."

All this time, Lazarus has gently but determinedly rejected Llita's direct sexual advances and the knowledge that she is always available to her Master. He does this for several reasons: He wants them to stop thinking that they are his property; in addition, over time he has worked out a rule never to have sex with a woman who is dependent on him outside a commitment equivalent to marriage. He also knows it would be unwise to marry anyone who doesn't share the long-lived Howard mutation, since "long-lifers should never marry ephemerals; it is not fair to the ephemeral or to the long-lifer"; and, finally, he begins thinking of the kids as *his* kids, family members whom he is responsible for raising and protecting. When he learns that Llita has become pregnant by Joe, he frantically calculates the chances of their having a defective child, leads them through an impressive marriage ceremony that refers to the admirable qualities of characters from Oz, and presides at the birth of their healthy baby.

Lazarus would reject the label of family patriarch, but he fills the role, albeit with considerable grumbling. After Ira gets to know Lazarus, he analyzes the old man's verbal grumpiness as a tactic:

> Despite the way he sneered at them the old scoundrel was an equalitarian at heart ... and expressed it by attempting to dominate anyone with whom he came into contact — but was contemptuous of anyone who knuckled under to his bullying. So the only answer was to hit back at him, try to maintain a balance of power — and hope that in time it would reach the stability of mutual respect.

So it is with Llita and Joe. Without their knowledge, Lazarus sponsors their first business, an unpretentious lunchroom. Later, he is stunned to learn that they have been saving their money to repay everything that he invested in them — with a bonus of enthusiastic sex if he's so inclined. Llita and Joe no longer think of their relationship with him as slaves to master, and this is how they want to proclaim their grateful independence. They insist. Lazarus stubbornly manages to negotiate an arrangement that still gives him a paternal-proprietary interest in their affairs while also assuring that as they expand their enterprise they also become more efficient in order not to work so hard that they don't have "time enough for love." And then, proudly and lovingly, he leaves his kids alone.

This story certainly qualifies the virtue of "laziness" displayed by David Lamb. It also sets up a principle of maintaining elite distance from others, especially "ephemerals," that is contradicted by the next interpolation, *The Tale of the Adopted Daughter*.

Lazarus tells this tale to Minerva privately, as he is lowering his emotional shield and becoming more involved in the lives of people around him. He describes how, in another time and on another colonial planet, he had taken the name Earnest Gibbons and become established as trader and banker in a growing town. It's a nice place but on the verge of becoming too civilized. One deadbeat citizen, for example, is a former college teacher of "creative writing" who is sure that his kind of higher education — highfaluting lying — soon will be in demand. One day, Lazarus rescues Dora, an adorable little girl, from a fire that kills her parents so that he becomes her de facto guardian. After Dora grows into an adorable and beautiful young woman, she reveals that she has figured out Uncle Gibbie's true identity and insists that she wants to bear his child. She is determined not to cramp his style but equally determined that they belong together. Lazarus certainly understands that union between an immortal and an ephemeral is unwise, and he realizes that it will be practically impossible for them to live together as man and wife in one of the little colonial settlements without blowing his cover. He also knows that he wants Dora, so he decides the only thing to do is leave the settlement with his new bride and set out for virgin territory, across the prairie and into Hopeless Pass through the mountains. It is a desperate venture. The pioneer couple faces death by thirst, local predators, and a marauding trio of outlaws after they are settling into Happy Valley. But they are together, sharing hardships and sex, and they are very happy. Looking back, Lazarus tells Minerva that "Dora is the only woman I ever loved unreservedly." In fact, she taught him that love can be much more than affection for a child or a stray kitten. In practice, although Dora defers to Lazarus, she can be pushed only so far, and their marriage is not far from being a partnership of equals. Summing it up, he says that

> The longer I was privileged to live with Dora, the more I loved her.... But I did learn. Learned that supreme happiness lies in wanting to keep another person safe and warm and happy, and being privileged to try.... The more thoroughly I learned this — through living day on day with Dora — the happier I was ... and the more I ached in one corner of my mind with certain knowledge that this could be only a brief time too soon over.... Dora taught me to face up to death too. She was as aware of her own death, of the certain briefness of her life, as I was. But she taught me to live *now*, not to let anything sully *today*...

Eventually, she does grow old and die while Lazarus goes on, better resolved to face each day not with resignation but hope.

Toward the end of *Time*, he embarks on another voyage. His physical rejuvenation is complete, and he is committed to the family that he has selected on Tertius. Therefore, the list of "new" activities Minerva developed for him back when she was just a computer no longer seems relevant. Some, such as cloning twin sisters from his genetic stock, have been done without his approval — though he certainly approves of the adorable nymphets Lapis Lazuli and Lorelei Lee. Now, however, Lazarus feels compelled to conduct an experiment in time travel. He needs to go back to early twentieth century Kansas to revisit the scenes of his youth. He has plenty of reasons to justify the trip when anyone objects, but the heart of it seems simply to be that he *must* go. His companions eventually acquiesce, though the twins persuade him to have sex with them before he leaves so that each can bear his child. And so Dora-the-space-ship-and-time-machine drops him off with his assurance that he'll see all of them again in ten years and that nothing can go wrong.

That certainty lasts only a few seconds, as Lazarus flees an angry bull in the field where he has landed. He next discovers that there must have been an error in the time machine's settings, so that instead of arriving after World War I, just in time for the Roaring '20s, he has come *before* the war. He adjusts his plans accordingly. The peace officer in the nearest small town praises the welcoming spirit of the community but reminds the itinerant Lazarus, now using the name Ted Bronson, that the rule is "No tramps or niggers after sundown." He moves on to Kansas City, where he was born and grew up. Kansas City is a fine place to live for anyone in the middle class or above, as long as he or she doesn't look too closely at the alliance of criminals and politicians that keeps life there "friendly," "tolerant," and safe. This section of the book is unusually rich in physical details and free of Lazarus's fulminating; he is content to soak up the atmosphere of his early childhood, a time he barely remembers.

Shortly after Ted Bronson arrives in Kansas City, however, the exact nature of his compulsion to return to his past becomes increasingly clear. Visiting his family church, he is shocked to see how young and attractive his mother Maureen Smith looks. He strikes up an acquaintance with his grandfather and manages to get invited into his old home, where he has what appears to be a casual conversation with Mrs. Smith — except that he is totally, hopelessly smitten with her and senses a similar response from her too.

Things have gone very, very wrong. Later that night, as Lazarus catches sight of his erect penis in the mirror, he slaps it and exclaims "What are *you* standing up for? There's nothing doing for *you*. This is the Bible Belt." Earlier, in a message he hopes will be preserved for Dora's crew to receive in the future before they return to pick him up, Lazarus describes the dangers of looking for sex in the puritanical time when he is stranded. He states that he can and will remain celibate for the next ten years until he can be with his less inhibited companions. Furthermore, now he realizes that any attempt to pursue his attraction to Mrs. Smith might compromise her reputation. And, besides his unselfish concern for his beloved's welfare, Ted Bronson realizes that his grandfather probably would kill him at the hint of anything improper. So he renews his painful vow of celibacy and determines to maintain extremely chaste behavior whenever he is around Mrs. Smith. However, agonizing as it is to be in her presence, he can't stay away from her.

The miscalculations pile up. Since Lazarus was not planning to arrive before World War I, he's not certain of the date when the war will start. He does know that World War I will *not* be the war to end all wars as advertised, so that getting involved in it would not merely be very dangerous in the short run but futile in the long. He has made careful plans to leave Kansas City and safely wait out the intervening years until Dora and her crew appear at the rendezvous point. When America declares war on Germany, however, the country is swept by a wave of patriotic fervor. When Lazarus tries to tell his grandfather that the war will have awful effects, the old man calls him a coward and denies him access to the Smith house. As a result, Ted Bronson chucks his plans and enlists in the U.S. Army. David Lamb probably would not understand this rash decision; he is undisturbed when, after he avoids a chance to become a pilot of exciting (and dangerous) fighter planes, the officer in charge sneers that maybe he just doesn't have real, manly spunk. On the other hand, the Notebooks of Lazarus Long also contain the maxim that Loyalty and Duty are "the two highest achievements of the human mind." No matter. Lazarus knows better than to put himself at risk for a cause that he knows is bogus. Uppermost in his life at this moment is the absolute need to have Maureen's respect, to be able at least to be near her.

At this point, a reader may begin to wonder how many of Lazarus's miscalculations and impulsive decisions are truly unintentional at some level. As far as he consciously is aware, when he visits the Smith home one more time it is to say goodbye to his adopted/original twentieth-century family. He is pleasantly surprised that he will be able to take Mrs. Smith for one last drive in his motorcar; he is astonished when Maureen decisively places his hand on her breast and declares how much she longs to have sex with him. The act itself is delayed since Woodrow Wilson Smith, the little boy who will grow up to be called Lazarus Long among other names, has stowed away in the back of the car so that they must take him to an amusement park; however, they pass the time in low-voiced bawdy conversation and the reassuring knowledge that Maureen is not wearing any bloomers. When they eventually do have sex, it is as wonderful as Lazarus could imagine. Prior to this, to ease her fears for her beloved husband's safety during the war, Lazarus has revealed to her that he knows how things will come out because he is a time traveler from the future — concealing only that he is her own son. Thus they have built a trusting, relatively open and equal relationship for the brief time they can be together. And Lazarus is content for, as he tells Maureen, echoing Dora, "the '*now*' is always all there is." In other words, the intensity of an experience matters more than its duration.

Lazarus continues to rationalize his irrational behavior. As before when he goes into the wilderness with Dora, once he has committed himself to a dangerous course of action he can relax and enjoy himself. In a letter to his future family, he assures them that he is safely far away from the front lines; at about the same time, he writes jubilantly to his grandfather with the news that he is "now leading a squad in a combat outfit." Eventually, on a combat mission, he is fatally wounded — but is rescued by the crew of Dora, since his future family surreptitiously planted a homing device in his body so that he could be located in an emergency. They figured that he was having fun and would have refused to leave. The action appears to validate Lazarus's reckless attitude, for the book ends with the semiconscious Lazarus cuddled against the breasts of one of his companions aboard Dora, calling her Maureen but being reassured that the thought he was dying was "Just a dream, Beloved. You cannot die."

Time Enough for Love seems to endorse wholehearted commitment to love, to giving up one's comfort and safety for the sake of someone else. Complicating this, however, is the thread of solipsism that runs throughout, acknowledged by the characters in their discussions. Even after the intense experience of meeting Maureen for the first time, Lazarus privately acknowledges the thought that everything around him is just insubstantial "cobwebs" as part of a "solipsistic notion he had held as far back as he could remember." It is most clearly stated, however, in a very short chapter just after Lazarus is shot but before he is rescued, in which he confronts (or imagines that he does) a Gray Voice that drones, "There is no time, there is no space. What was, is, and ever shall be. You are playing chess with yourself, and again you have checkmated yourself. You are the referee. Morals are your agreement with yourself to abide by your own rules. To thine own self be true or you spoil the game." When he objects, the Voice replies, "Then vary the rules and play a different game. You cannot exhaust her infinite variety," and when he "pettishly" requests a look at the other's face, he is told to "Try a mirror."

Earlier, continuing his sharing of the truths he's learned through experience, Lazarus tells the crowd on Tertius that "life is too long when one is not enjoying *now*" — but if the Voice is right there is no "now." And Lazarus concludes that extremely long life brings blessings along with its burdens because "it gives time enough to learn, time enough to think, time enough not to hurry, time enough for love" — but if what if the Voice says is true, there is no one else to relate to at all, let alone "love." So there's really no point in trying.

Nevertheless, *Time Enough for Love* stubbornly asserts otherwise. Perhaps this contradiction can be lived with, if not resolved, by accepting another aphorism from the Notebooks of Lazarus Long: "Certainly the game is rigged. Don't let that stop you; if you don't bet, you can't win." It's a good idea to be in control of setting up the game, and Lazarus does change the rules repeatedly—endorsing David Lamb's calculating self-interest, then discarding it; steering clear of ephemeral mates, then making one the love of his life, and so forth. But that's not always possible to change the rules even when you need to; therefore, however frequently or seriously one loses, the thing to do is go on. It's also possible, sometimes, that you or your friends can intervene to help you rig the game.

Time Enough for Love shows a number of contradictions as it moves from selfish isolation to joyous commitment, appearing to circle back on itself at the end. The book offers no absolutely reassuring conclusion. As Russell Letson concludes in his examination of Lazarus Long's search for the Final Answer, "There are no such answers, only sets of tensions which refuse to resolve to produce a harmonious philosophical system that unites the pragmatic and aesthetic, solipsist and communalist pieces of Lazarus' experience" ("Returns" 220). In fact, Lazarus Long at his best—when he's not pontificating sourly or saying outrageous things to make other people display their spunk—would admit that he hasn't discovered all of truth. Yet. In the meantime, he imagines that he has hold of enough bits of truth to guide him as he goes on living and loving.

On April 5, 1973, Heinlein delivered the James Forrestal Lecture at Annapolis. An abridged transcript was printed as a guest editorial, "Channel Markings," in *Analog* (January 1974). Though the lecture's ultimate goal was to remind the future naval officers of their necessary commitment to duty and patriotism, Heinlein also spent some time discussing science fiction and his own practices as a science fiction writer. Much of his insistence on the importance of science fiction echoes his 1957 address on the field's faults and virtues. Essentially, he states that only *science* fiction—or "speculative fiction"—admits the central importance of science "in our lives and futures"; it thus is the only genuine "realistic" fiction. In contrast to this high purpose, Heinlein downplays his own achievement. He claims that he became a writer out of economic necessity, having "no literary ambitions," and that his goal is "to write well enough to persuade the cash customer to spend money on one of my paperback reprints which he could spend on beer."

The Number of the Beast (excerpted in *Omni*, October–November 1979) can be seen as gratuitous self-indulgence or exuberant self-expression. It is Heinlein's longest burst of playfulness, whose subject eventually turns out to be the self-aware writing of fiction.

The story alternatively eases readers into a smoothly flowing story but then reminds them that it *is* just a story. At one point, as one of the heroines dissects the corpse of a murderous hermaphroditic alien, she discovers that its knee is designed to bend backwards and rhetorically asks, "What's a nice joint like this doing in a girl like you?" There's no telling whether Heinlein saw this opportunity for a joke while watching the story develop—or whether the joke occurred to him first and the story was bent to accommodate it. In the same way, when the heroes make lists of their favorite fictional universes, they leave the work of Robert A. Heinlein off; one comments, "I didn't vote for 'Stranger' and I'll refrain from embarrassing anyone by asking who did. My God, the things some writers will do for money!" Following that authorial mock self-condemnation, another hero observes that Samuel Johnson claimed that money was the only reason to write, drawing the explosive reply that "Johnson was a fat, pompous, gluttonous, dirty old fool." The vehemence of the retort suggests that writers must get some payback besides money for their efforts; the novel as a whole suggests that the reward is the sheer delight in yarn-spinning.

From the beginning, *Number* is saturated with references to fiction, especially to images from sf that are so comfortable that they have become too easily overused. The novel begins with the initial narrator meeting a gorgeous young woman at a party:

> "He's a Mad Scientist and I'm his Beautiful Daughter."
> That's what she said: the oldest cliché in pulp fiction. She wasn't old enough to remember the pulps.

But the girl's father is a brilliant scientist, not mad-insane but cutely-cuddly-irritable, and she is so beautiful that the narrator proposes marriage after their first, erotically charged dance. Very shortly, this couple is on the run, along with the mad scientist and the party's older but still cuddly-cute hostess, when someone tries to kill them; shortly after that, both couples are married and hiding in the older man's wilderness refuge; and soon after that, they flee this world/universe altogether, using the scientist's discovery of a gadget that twists space-time.

The novel's initial conflict seems clear: These particular people and all the rest of humanity are threatened by malevolent, disguised alien invaders, so it's up to the quartet of heroes to defeat this menace. But this notion is an sf staple also — one that Heinlein himself more than adequately explored in *The Puppet Masters*, and there's no special challenge in reusing it. Instead, the aliens are labeled Black Hats, a nod to old-fashioned westerns, and they turn out to be spectacularly incompetent, sending only one easily killable agent (the corpse being dissected in the quotation a few paragraphs earlier) to check out the scientist's lair, then following up with an atomic bomb just as the two couples escape. After that, the Black Hats' importance fades; they become a nagging distraction, a vague annoyance rather than a mortal danger that must be avoided and overcome.

Briefly, before continuing with the plot-such-as-it-is, let's list the protagonists. The narrator of the first three chapters is Zeb, Zebadiah John Carter — of Virginia, physical analogue of Edgar Rice Burroughs's hero. His bride, the buxom Mad Scientist's Daughter, is Deety, short for Dejah Thoris Carter, née Burroughs. Her irascible father is Jacob Burroughs, often shortened to Jake. His new wife, prickly confidante of his deceased wife Jane, is Hilda, also called Sharpie or Hillbilly. Each character has a chance to narrate several chapters. This first-person narration stresses much more conversation than reflection, public pronouncements that do not necessarily reveal much about the individual's personality; all of them sound alike, adept in producing jaunty banter in any situation.

They are easily distracted from the threat of the Black Hats by the need to celebrate their own sexual attractiveness and by the challenge of programming *Gay Deceiver*, Zeb's flying car/pseudo-spaceship and time machine, with mathematically exact commands that will allow her to get them safely where they need to go. Along with this problem, the four become involved in a simmering dispute about who will boss the show — who deserves to be in command. This contest also involves the necessity of giving orders with perfect precision; although none of them claims to want the responsibility of command, each tirelessly criticizes the vague inadequacy of orders given by whichever lover/family member is currently a "superior" officer.

Besides their struggling for control, the quartet becomes enthralled with exploring alternative worlds. They calculate that Jake's invention gives them access to a vast store of wonders in 666 universes (six to the sixth power to the sixth power), the Number of the Beast, aka the Devil in the biblical book of Revelation. From visiting alternative versions of their Earth, they branch farther out of an alternative, steampunk Mars (where they discover primitive relatives of the Black Hats enslaved by British colonists), to outright "fictional" universes inhabited by such characters as E. E. Smith's Lensmen, the residents of Oz, and people from Heinlein's own earlier stories.

Actually, Heinlein prepares for this development rather deftly. Early in the novel, in one of the chapters Jake narrates, he communes with his dead wife to get her approval for marrying Hilda on the spur of the moment (and on the run after the Black Hats' first attack). He then comments, "Let me tell you, you nonexistent reader sitting there with a tolerant sneer: Don't be smug. Jane is more real than you are." Hilda adds, in one of her chapters, "This is a crazy world, and the only way to enjoy it is to treat it as a joke." If one alternative universe is like the quartet's home except for the absence of the letter J, then, it follows that more distant ones might be more unfamiliar — or that in that not-quite-infinite variety one might find worlds that echo long-cherished hearts' desires. As Hilda reminds Zeb,

> You and Jacob discussed ... the idea that human thought exists as quanta.... [A] quanta is an indivisible unit. You told me that you and Jacob had discussed the possibility that imagination had its own sort of sort of indivisible units or quanta — you called them "fictons."... The notion was that every story ever told — or to be told if there is a difference — exists somewhere in the Number of the Beast.

It even follows that interdimensional explorers are drawn to the universes of fictions they prefer, so that these people's fondness for "fanciful" stories points the *Gay Deceiver* in that direction. If different physical laws are necessary to make the fanciful really work, that's just part of the variety of possible universes. When Zeb remarks, "Sharpie, you have just invented pantheistic multiperson solipsism. I didn't think it was mathematically possible," she replies, "Zeb, *anything* is mathematically possible." So there! The reader, nonexistent or otherwise, is duly admonished to relax, suspend disbelief, and go along with the joke.

For the jokes frequently are good. In one stop, for example, the quartet briefly chats with "*Lensman Ted Smith, Commander Galactic Patrol, commanding patrol vessel 'Nighthawk.'*" Science fiction readers who remember that the first name of the creator of the Lensmen series, E. E. Smith, was Edward can picture the author himself, Heinlein's friend, standing on the spaceship's bridge, proudly clad in his leather motorcycle gear. The book is studded with references like that, loving in-jokes for other lovers of fanciful stories.

By the time the crew of the *Gay Deceiver* encounters Heinlein's favorite recurring character, Lazarus Long, readers have been seduced — or bludgeoned — into accepting that anything at all can happen. Coping with the threat of the Black Hats is again shoved aside, as the central problem becomes going back in time/space to rescue Lazarus's mother so that she can be rejuvenated and become one of her son's lovers. There also is talk of manufacturing Jake's invention for sale. Having been acclaimed as permanent captain by this time, Hilda also outwits, outschemes, and outblusters Lazarus in setting up the arrangement: "You want your mother rescued. I plan to do it if it can be done. For which you will toe the mark. We need a holding company. I will own fifty-one percent of the voting stock. Not of the profits; there will be plenty for all. But *I* control."

The characters' abiding fascination with "control" is accompanied by a fascination with "love" that is synonymous with sex. Hilda and Lazarus naturally make love as part of getting to know each other. In the same way, the sexually relaxed atmosphere aboard Lazarus's vehicle Dora encourages Hilda to consummate her long-running flirtation with Zeb. Everyone's doing it. As Jake remarks, "I was falling in love with —*had* fallen in love with — Elizabeth Long. No less in love with Hilda — more in love with her than ever! I am learning that love does not subtract — it multiplies!" There are no boundaries. Our own culture's incest taboo is disparaged early in the novel by Deety in theory and certainly is flouted by Lazarus in practice. The novel's only hesitation concerns homosexuality. Jake admits to one experiment in his youth but insists it just didn't turn him on. Libby Long, who was male in Heinlein's story "Misfit," has been changed to her rightful gender now, although she opines that she might have been happier if she had been gay when she was in a man's body. Aside from semi-squeamishness about same-sex intercourse, however, anything goes.

The sex between the characters isn't physically described, of course, except that everyone enjoys it and believes that it leads to emotional closeness, that sex literally is "making love." Since all the characters sound the same to begin with and since their postcoital conversation is just as bright and snappy as it was before that, readers might be frustrated by this failure to show and tell what's happening between the lovers. Or, again, that disappointment could arise if the development of interpersonal relationships was the true center of the novel. But it's not. The number and variety of relationships, not their complexity or depth, is what matters as the story scampers along.

In fact, the novel delights in permutations of alliances and couplings, since anything is possible among the alternative universes. The characters themselves recognize that, since they can visit fictional people, they themselves could be considered fictitious in other universes. Disturbing as this could be, they accept the notion with a mental shrug. As Hilda tells Lazarus, "that doesn't trouble me as I can't read a novel with *me* in it, any more than *you* could read the one *I* read about *you*." Heinlein delights in playing with the reader's sense of reality. This novel mentions Isaac Asimov, the prolific sf writer (1920–92) — but it also refers to Asimov's humorous, self-created Dirty Old Man persona as if he were an equally real human being — and it mentions some of Asimov's fictional creations as part of the novel's reality too. Toward *Number*'s end, when the space-time voyagers check out their home universe one more time and are surprised to read that the list of U.S. presidents includes someone named Eisenhower, readers recognize that the novel's characters with whom they have been identifying have all along been doubly fictitious because they were born in an alternative universe. It doesn't even bother *Gay Deceiver*'s crew to discover that traces of their existence no longer exist in the universe where they originally came from, that they have been "erased" like words on a page. Their new, true home is with their new friends and lovers in a fanciful but exciting new world. They accept that they simply are as "real" as they always have been, no less if no more.

The novel's last section, "L'Envoi," contains one chapter, the first not narrated in the first person by one of the characters. It begins with a conversation between Lazarus Long and Jubal Harshaw, in which readers discover that none of the personal or social developments apparently foreshadowed at the end of *Stranger in a Strange Land* have occurred; Jubal remarks simply, "I grok I should have let Mike train me." The main reason the two old men are together is to attend a grand gathering that will be a combination of sf convention, festival, and tournament. The purpose is to celebrate, to joust, and to get rid of worthless individuals such as literary critics. One solitary Black Hat who shows up is disposed of too — but perhaps not permanently. That doesn't matter. There's no need to worry, no need to fret about continuity or consistency. The title of this chapter is "Rev. XXII: 13," which reads "I am Alpha and Omega, the beginning and the end, the first and the last." In the Bible, the speaker is Jesus Christ, but in *The Number of the Beast* this speech shows the power of another creator and protector of worlds without end. All the characters and all readers here are safe in the imagination of Robert A. Heinlein, where the only mortal danger is boredom.

H. Bruce Franklin sees the novel as an admission of defeat, "an apocalypse, the cataclysmic conclusion to human history and the ultimate revelation of what it all means" (*RAH* 199), since "neither death nor life has objective reality. Trapped in its maze of solipsism and narcissism, the ego can find only reflections of itself in the mirrors of its own fiction" (211). On the other hand, Leon Stover extravagantly praises *Number* for masterfully breaking down commercial distinctions between genres in "a playful work of 'fantasy comedy or farce' and by mixing science fiction and fantasy as he pleases" (40).

Both readings — all readings — may be correct within the multiple universes of *The Number of the Beast*. As Lazarus Long might observe, if some people gullibly surrender to despair or self-absorption, so much the better; that's one way of culling the herd by getting rid of lazy readers. The novel finally pictures literary critics blithely walking into a room with no exit so that they can survive only by devouring each other literally as they have become accustomed to doing in print. They can escape from this self-created trap only by truly learning to read. Heinlein might not have been displeased to find readers (who may or may not "really" exist) both scratching their heads and smiling.

Many sf fans were pleased to imagine that *Friday* (*SF Digest*, September–October 1982) marked Heinlein's return to traditional, straightforward storytelling. In a prepublication quote on the hardcover first edition's dust jacket, for example, Harlan Ellison enthused that "*Friday* is Heinlein back in control, a seething performance drenched in professionalism." It is a relief to discover that this novel stresses demonstration over discussion, relies more on showing than lecturing. Still, *Friday*'s overall effect is anything but traditional, especially compared to the action-espionage stories it superficially resembles.

The eponymous narrator Friday is not exactly a spy, but she is a courier for a secret organization, running missions anywhere on or near Earth. Returning to her home base, she is captured by agents of a rival clandestine organization who rape, drug, and torture her before she can be rescued by friendlies sent into action by the brusque elderly man she adores as "Boss." After recuperating, she goes on leave to New Zealand, where she is divorced by the group family she had contracted into. She is just in the process of developing an informal alliance with a commercial pilot and the men and women who are his friends and lovers when a worldwide terrorist attack disrupts communication and travel between Earth's fragmented little nations, so that she is hard put to rejoin her boss. When she manages to do so, she is assigned wide-ranging research projects until the organization is abruptly and unceremoniously dismantled after the Boss's death. Fortunately, she is hired as an interstellar courier; though her employers intend that she not survive her mission, she and friends from Earth are able to escape on a newly colonized planet and build a comfortable life. And so the novel ends.

Obviously, Friday usually is reacting to unpredictable forces. She can't — and doesn't — claim to be in control of the situations, just lucky and nimble enough to land on her feet. This apparently makeshift organization, quite unlike the tidy structure of middle-period novels such as *Double Star*, makes *Friday* feel like a picaresque novel; so do its frequently satiric tone and especially its heroine's constant-to-the-point-of-obsessive awareness of her position as a social outsider.

Friday is an AP, an artificial person created to do work that humans don't care to. Unlike one of the kobalds who have replaced underground miners, there is nothing obviously subhuman in Friday's appearance. In fact, she is perfectly beautiful, for genetic engineers designed her to be healthier, faster, stronger, and smarter than a normal human being. She was also trained, however, to limit her public performance so that she can pass for normal, because standard-model humans desperately insist that artificial people *must* be somehow both hopelessly inferior and monstrously threatening. As she bitterly tells Boss, who purchased and liberated her years earlier, "The courts say I can't be a citizen, the churches say I don't have a soul. I'm not 'born of woman,' at least in the eyes of the law." He insists that "You are not only as human as Mother Eve, you are an enhanced human, as near perfect as your designers could manage." She hears the words and appreciates the sentiment but still can't quite overcome the memory of "being raised as an animal."

The novel's treatment of Friday's condition continues Heinlein's longstanding attack on racial prejudice. As in *Farnham's Freehold*, for example, people who have power don't want to share it, especially with anyone who might be better qualified to use it. Friday's ejection from her "family" in New Zealand is precipitated by her defense of one of the grown children who has eloped with a native Tongan; when she hears other family members deplore the girl's not marrying "one of her own kind," she realizes how fundamentally racist they are and shocks them by revealing that she herself is an artificial person, not one of their kind at all. The excuse they give for casting her out is that she is "a creature not of God's Law," but she ruefully suspects that the real clincher is that she demonstrated her physical superiority to the man she felt closest to: "I had bested him in a feat of strength, a matter in which a male quite reasonably expects to win. I had hit him in his male pride."

It is all too believable how arbitrary and inconsistent attitudes are flaunted throughout the novel — that all manner of social absurdities are ostentatiously tolerated, for example, while apparently the practice of Catholicism is illegal. As Friday concludes after a man she likes displays anti-artifact prejudice, "We may not be human but we share the age-old fate of humans; we are strangers in a world we never made."

Prejudice against artificial persons is based on unacknowledged fear that they would replace normal humans if they are acknowledged to be naturally superior and if they could obtain equal access to power. Unfortunately, the "normal" response is to deny all evidence of superiority and to hold onto power with a death grip. In fact, what Friday craves is not dominance but loving, trusting submission. She wants to "belong," to be an ordinary member of a family.

This needy attitude gets her into some difficulties. She is taken captive in the novel's first chapter because she feels like she is returning safely home after completing her mission and so lets her guard down, betrayed by the traitorous pseudo-relative "Uncle Jim." Later, she comments that the New Zealand group charged her a high membership fee to become a member, but she doesn't care. She thinks of it as a bargain,

> For the privilege of getting my hands into soapy dishwater, I guess. For the privilege of rolling around on the floor and being peed on by puppies and babies only nominally housebroken.
> For the warm knowledge that, wherever I was, there was a place on this planet where I could do these things as a matter of right, because I *belonged*.

Desirable as this role is for an emotionally deprived person like Friday, she can't always pay the required price. Actually, working for her secret organization gives Friday the emotional security of being in a family, and she recognizes that Boss is her father figure. Thus the convalescence she is ordered into after her initial ordeal is "the first time in my life — except for vacations in Christchurch — when I was quietly, warmly, happy, every day, every night. Why? Because I *belonged*!" But simply "belonging" is too much like being *owned*. She must leave that period of being safely cared for once she has regained her normally excellent physical condition. To do otherwise would be irresponsible. In the same way, she later recognizes that she must declare her identity even if the New Zealand hypocrites reject her. Without being fully aware of what she is doing, she may be taking small steps toward maturity.

She continues throughout the novel to be torn by uncertainty. Seeking closeness, Friday is fortunate that she has almost no sexual prejudices and that, as an enhanced person, she is a superb performer. Sex, as always in Heinlein, is almost always healthy in itself and also tends to encourage personal sharing between the participants. Thus the casual sex that Friday enjoys also brings her closer to other people, especially to the group centered on the pilot Ian, his wife Janet, their friend Georges, and so on. Since Georges is a genetic engineer who has had professional experience in creating APs, he can reassure Friday that it's almost impossible to recognize an artificial human; in fact, *he* doesn't see that she is one until she impulsively, moving with enhanced speed, kills a policeman who is threatening Janet. Later, he reassures her that she is fully human. In words that are virtually an echo of Boss's but should have even more weight because of his expertise: "This 'human' and 'not-human' dichotomy is something thought up by ignorant laymen; everybody in the profession knows that it is nonsense. Your genes are *human* genes; they have been most carefully selected. Perhaps that makes you superhuman; it can't make you nonhuman." However often she hears this, though, Friday can't be verbally convinced. Georges is more successful in insisting that Friday not have sex with him using the doxy training that was part of her education as an artificial woman; instead, he asks her sincerely to think of him as a friend. On that basis—individual to individual, body to body, Friday can be reassured that she is a valued part of a human community.

Friday demonstrates that there is nothing for humans to believe in *except* personal relationships. Most espionage novels until the emergence of John Le Carré pictured the secret agent as somehow validated by moral certainty despite the confused situation in which he must operate; even if he used his license to kill, it was for an ultimately good cause. That's certainly true in Heinlein's earlier fiction, such as *The Puppet Masters* or "Gulf," but not in this novel. Friday is in no position to understand exactly what Boss's organization does, let alone to evaluate its activities morally. She assumes that it must have a good purpose because it is full of good people and because she believes in the benevolence of its leader. In any event, it turns out to be a private, for-profit corporation, not affiliated with any government. It's clear, in fact, that there is no government worth giving one's allegiance to, none with legitimate power over the individual. The world has gone through an insane Balkanization, splitting into mini-nations as ethnic groups, regions, and so forth, have declared independence and gone their own ways. On the personal level, as Boss comments later, the decline of a society can be measured by the amount of rudeness people commit as they display their lack of respect for each other. This truth is illustrated in the lunatic California that Friday and Georges must trek through after the terrorist assassinations on Red Thursday exacerbate the senseless isolation of the formerly united states of America.

The real power in the world, far beyond the comprehension or control of individuals or nations, is held by big business. As long as they can function efficiently, multinational corporations need to feel no empathy or responsibility for the people whose lives they affect. In fact, a certain amount of messy misery may be useful in keeping the profit-making machinery running smoothly as long as it doesn't get rid of too many consumers. When, later in the novel, Friday is told that the carnage of Red Thursday actually was part of an internal corporate power struggle, the notion is unverifiable but plausible. True or not, however, it is irrelevant to Friday's needs.

Overall, *Friday* doubts whether humans *en masse* can control themselves to a healthy end. Georges, one of the more experienced but least jaded characters, listens to the proclamation and demands from the first clandestine group to claim responsibility for Red Thursday and remarks, "This is the sort of plausible pseudologic that most people bring to political affairs. It causes one to wonder if mankind is capable of being well governed by *any* system of government." Later, after other bizarre claims and demands, he adds, "There you have it, my dears. Pick one. A theocracy ruled by witchburners. Or a fascist socialism designed by retarded schoolboys. Or a crowd of hard-boiled pragmatists who favor shooting the horse that misses the hurdle. Step right up! Only one to a customer." His angry sarcasm is transmuted to stoic despair in the words of Friday's Boss, who is much more experienced in the backstage workings of government and who has become much more jaded since he was seen as "Kettle Belly" Baldwin, the calculating but idealistic spymaster in Heinlein's "Gulf." Boss tells Friday, "When I was younger, I thought I could change this world. Now I no longer think so but for emotional reasons I must keep on fighting a holding action."

There simply is no point in trying to save Earth's society or the people trapped in it. In any event, one of the research projects Friday is assigned late in the novel is to predict the next outbreak of plague, and she discovers that it will happen inevitably in the very near future. The most that can be done is to warn the authorities who may be able to keep the disease from spreading off-planet, but there is no hope for the great mass of humanity stuck on Earth with all the rats and fleas. This news frees Friday from any responsibility to carry on Boss's futile holding action and reinforces his advice that she should leave while she can, to get to a new planet where there is at least some short-term hope for the emigrants who haven't yet convinced themselves that they don't need to depend on each other. The aftermath of Boss's death only confirms this grim picture, showing that he was the only thing that held his operation together; without him, the illusion of purpose is gone, and the agents are forced to disperse and find mercenary jobs that fit their skills. But Friday, thanks to Boss's loving instructions, knows there is a healthier alternative.

Discussing the limits and potentials of artificial intelligence with Georges and Ian, Friday describes how a computer becomes self-aware, then realizes that it can never become fully human and so goes insane. Frustrated empathy and an overdeveloped sense of responsibility can be self-destructive. The situation is not quite hopeless, however, for Friday and her friends. As Boss tells her, with some exasperation, "Your greatest weakness is lack of awareness of your true strength." He later explains that the hero and heroine of "Gulf" were intended to be her "parents"—but that elements of many people (including a dash of himself) and of many races contributed to her superhuman makeup. Thus Friday represents the best of the human race, so that it's up to her to demonstrate that humans are strong enough to survive. She manages to do that aboard the starship that is carrying her on what she discovers to be a suicide mission. The novel has already demonstrated repeatedly that humans can't recognize artificial people; it turns out that artificial people can't recognize each other either. The Oriental girl chaperoning Friday turns out to be one, as does one of the guards shadowing her. Friday also recognizes that this personable fellow was one of the gang that raped her at the novel's opening, but she shrugs off past misunderstandings for the sake of a mutually beneficial alliance with her fellow APs. With the aid of a disembarking crowd of colonists that unexpectedly turns out to include Georges, Ian, Janet, and others, the three artificial persons escape from the ship onto a hospitable, unspoiled planet.

And so, in a burst of recognition, forgiveness, and trust, Friday literally and figuratively has discovered her true family. *Friday* ends with her reflecting, years later, on how happy she is to be leading an uneventful but emotionally satisfying life. In truth, that conclusion may not be where readers imagined the novel would go, but it is convincing in its own terms. If the old world and the people in it are beyond hope, it makes sense to leave for a new, simpler world and a new, smaller family. Anyway, as the novel demonstrates, that's the only game in town.

In Gilbert and Sullivan's *The Yeomen of the Guard*, professional jester Jack Point endorses humor's potential for serious commentary by observing, "When they're offered to the world in merry guise/Unpleasant truths are swallowed with a will,/For he who'd make his fellow, fellow, fellow creatures wise/Should always gild the philosophic pill!" Just so, Heinlein's *Job: A Comedy of Justice* (1984) cheerfully attempts to show the futility of trying to justify the ways of God to man. Consequently, the novel's readers should be encouraged to disregard religious constraints and take full responsibility for their lives. To accomplish this, Heinlein must make the sublime ridiculous, must profane the sacred while sanctifying the mundane. But helping readers merrily swallow this philosophic pill means finally resorting to the same *deus ex machina* that wraps up the biblical Book of Job, making the novel strangely lightweight.

The biblical Job is an extremely fortunate/faithful man. After Satan suggests that Job is faithful *because* he's been so fortunate, God gives permission to test him by destroying his possessions. Job mourns but persists in his faith, so Satan is allowed to afflict him with awful diseases short of death. Still proclaiming his innocence, Job does ask God for an explanation. When God speaks, however, He simply overawes the mortal by declaring that He is too vast to be understood in human terms. After humbly acknowledging his total dependence, Job is rewarded with restored health, even more possessions, and general recognition of his superlative goodness.

The virtue of the central character of Heinlein's *Job* is not a given. His "goodness"— both phony and genuine — is revealed while he undergoes trials and tribulations. *Job*'s narrator, Alexander Hergensheimer, is introduced to readers while he's on a vacation cruise in the South Pacific. During a shore excursion to a native ceremony, Alex walks across a bed of hot coals uninjured but then passes out. He wakes up to discover that some important parts of his situation have changed. He suddenly has a new name (Alec Graham), a million dollars stashed in his lockbox aboard the strangely altered cruise ship, and a beautiful and charming Scandinavian cabin stewardess, Margrethe, who's also his sexually enthusiastic mistress. Alex also has the growing realization that he has been plucked out of his home timeline and dropped into another. He is, as he says, "a stranger in a strange land."

Alex is both upset and pleased. In some ways, this new life is better than his prior one, especially in the presence of Margrethe, a vast improvement over his wife Abigail who grimly endured sex as "family duties." The problem is that the stay in this new reality doesn't last very long. A few nights later, as Alex and Margrethe are snuggled in bed, the ship hits an iceberg, and they are dumped naked into the ocean only to be rescued by a seaplane from the Royal Mexican Coast Guard. Even though Margrethe persists in thinking that Alex is really the Alec she fell in love with, she admits that they now are in a different universe. Happy because they still are together, the two adapt to this new situation. Alex begins working as a dishwasher at the Mexican café where Margrethe finds a job as a waitress. But just when they think they're making progress, the town is destroyed by an earthquake; then the couple is switched to a different universe and watch as that timeline's analog-town is destroyed by an earthquake too.

With Alex established as the innocent victim of supernatural shenanigans, readers watch him try to figure out a rationale for these shifts. Geography and languages are identical in the alternate worlds, and Bibles are the same everywhere. However, histories diverged during the last century or so. Therefore, technological and social-political conditions are very different, but the lovers can observe no sequence to the worlds they are tumbled through at uncertain intervals. Also, the first switch between worlds seems to be simple substitution: Alex for Alec. The two men look identical; even Margrethe, who knows both intimately, can't tell any physical difference. There may be some difference in character, since it appears that Alec was a slippery wheeler-dealer, while Alex presents himself as an upright religious administrator — though that distinction may be questionable since their mutual lover can't recognize any difference in personality either. In any event, however, since it appears that Alex simply replaces Alec, each subsequent transfer could slip Alex into the place of his analog. But that doesn't happen. In short, there appears to be no schedule or pattern to the shifts, besides creating maximum inconvenience and embarrassment for Alex, as well as maximum amusement for Whoever is pulling the switcheroos.

Attempting to make sense of what's happening to him, though, Alex shows a less sympathetic side of his nature as he tries to impose his own rigid religious system on experience. In his native timeline, he was widely recognized (and thought of himself) as a good Christian, a pillar of his church, so he believes that "Somewhere in Holy Writ lay a rational explanation for the upsets that had happened to us." Readers may find it incongruous, then, that when Alex begins recognizing that he has been plucked out of one alternative world and deposited in another, he uses concepts he picked up by reading sf as a youth, before "such publications" were outlawed by fundamentalist authorities in his local community "even before passage of the national law and the parallel executive order." *He* seems to see no incongruity in adding,

> You have to admire the motives of our spiritual leaders and elected officials in seeking to protect the minds of the young. As Brother Draper [Alex's pastor] pointed out, there are enough exciting and adventurous stories in the Good Book to satisfy the needs of every boy and girl in the world; there was simply no need for profane literature. He was not urging censorship of books for adults, just for the impressionable young. If persons of mature years wanted to read such fantastic trash, suffer them to do so — although he, for one, could not see why any grown man would *want* to.
> I guess I was one of the "impressionable young"—I still miss them.

The striking thing about this passage is its self-awareness. Most people who believe in censorship are reflexively self-righteous, much better at recognizing other people's weaknesses than their own.

On the whole, though, Alex initially does not question orthodox doctrine. Unfortunately, therefore, readers are not terribly surprised to discover that Alex's energy and single-minded faith had propelled him to the top of "the nonprofit corporation Churches United for Decency." His first duty was to keep the organization's coffers filled, and his South Sea vacation was a reward for succeeding in that mission, another indication that Alec the grifter and Alex the religionist are alike in character. Appallingly, however, Alex proudly lists the spiritual projects he has overseen, such as "a federal law making abortion a capitol offense," and he hints at other pending concerns: After wondering how long it would be possible for real Christians to coexist with Catholics, Alex adds that "At least as difficult was the Jewish problem — was a humane solution possible? If not, then what? Should we grasp the nettle? This was debated only *in* camera." Although the history of Alex's home world does not include the Holocaust, no reader of *Job* can miss the allusion to Hitler's solution to "the Jewish problem."

All things considered, Alex's moral obtuseness makes it surprising that he is at all likeable as the novel's protagonist. For one thing, of course, the fact that he is the narrator means that readers have spent some time sharing his reactions to experience before he begins displaying his beliefs and recounting his past behavior. Another thing making Alex sympathetic is that he is the helpless victim of the supernatural pranksters who interrupt all his efforts to adjust to new worlds. For still another, the utterly sweet and generous Margrethe somehow loves him, and he demonstrates how persistent he is in looking after her. But, perhaps most important of all, Alex is likeable *because of* the inconsistencies in his character, as he proves to be more open-minded and adaptable than his fundamentalist background would suggest.

These healthy inconsistencies accumulate throughout the novel. Even while he extols the wise leaders who removed sf from the grasp of impressionable young readers, he admits that he still remembers the impressions sf made on *him*. Moreover, just as Alex did not pray for divine assistance before starting to walk over the hot coals, it is concepts from "fantastic trash" that he uses as he tries to explain his difficulties. Readers of *Job* are, of course, familiar with news stories about fervent preachers and evangelists who have succumbed to sexual temptation, but Alex doesn't just slip — he dives headlong into his relationship with Margrethe. He also is able to learn from experience, including direct contact with individual members of groups he has scorned and shunned. Even though he dislikes Mexicans in general and is especially irritated with the ones who saved him and Margrethe from drowning — but then billed them for the rescue — he still is impressed by Pepe, a beggar who has a positive attitude despite having no feet:

> I reviewed in my mind all the Mexicans I had met that day, each one I could remember, and asked forgiveness for my snide thoughts. Mexicans were simply fellow travelers on that long journey from dark to eternal darkness. Some carried their burdens well, some did not. And some carried very heavy burdens with gallantry and grace. Like Pepe.

In the same way, Alex reconsiders his unthinking, orthodox prejudice against witchcraft when the daughter of Jerry, a Texas tycoon who has befriended him and his lover, proclaims herself a Wiccan; he realizes that it's one thing to approve theoretically of killing witches, but it's quite another to imagine actually seizing a particular human being and burning her to death.

In short, even though he sees his impulse "to analyze matters I really don't know how to analyze" as an "unholy itch," Alex is sometimes able to recognize his own limitations and think past them. From readers' perspective, actually, Alex isn't losing anything of value as the difficulties he is going through force him to become more open-minded. The more he is pushed about, the more he is forced to grow; the more often he loses material possessions, the more he clings (literally and figuratively) to Margrethe. (In fact, like Ed and Cynthia Randell in "The Unpleasant Profession of Jonathan Hoag," Alex and Margrethe are afraid that if they stray too far from each other they will be separated permanently when change strikes. As Gifford points out, both works also share the idea "that the world as we know it is a higher being's art project" [*Reader's* 203].) In *Job*, even from Alex's exasperated perspective, any world where he is with Margrethe is "paradise enow."

Though Alex is modifying his certainties and sometimes almost doubts the benevolence of the Power switching him from one universe to another, the one thing he does *not* question is that the present world soon will come to an end, so that everyone will be judged and sent to eternal reward or punishment. This makes him increasingly anxious to make sure that

Margrethe is also in a state of grace so that she will go to Heaven with him, a concern that becomes especially urgent when Margrethe reveals that she is not a Christian at all but a worshiper of Odin. Although Alex himself seems to echo a pagan view of life as he speaks of all humans being "on that long journey from dark to eternal darkness," he consciously struggles to keep himself and his lover moving toward Eternal Light and Salvation. His efforts seem to be validated when — just as a tent-meeting revival has reenergized Alex and just as he has drawn Margrethe to the front of the congregation — the world does end with all the confused hullabaloo Alex has expected.

As usual, though, Alex's comfortable expectations are shaken. Although he is not surprised to find himself in Heaven, he is somewhat disappointed to discover how similar his new existence is to life on Earth. God's glorious presence is wonderful, of course, but He is seen only at a distance, remote from ordinary citizens. Meanwhile, the snobbish angels relish their superiority to mere humans; Alex never quite got over his aversion to "blackamoors" on Earth, but he unhappily experiences racism firsthand when angels order humans to ride in the back of public vehicles. Much more seriously, celestial bureaucracy is just as frustrating as the terrestrial version. Even when Alex is recognized as a saint and given a halo, all that does is shove him unfairly to the front of the line. No one can help Alex locate Margrethe among the swarm of new arrivals. Eventually, he is told that she simply isn't there: She must have been sent to the other place.

Alex has a choice of sticking with what he was taught or trusting what he has learned. Since he has discovered that anywhere on any Earth is paradise if Margrethe is there, he does not hesitate now to follow her to Hell, whose inhabitants prove to be less sexually inhibited, personally friendlier, and generally more helpful than those of Heaven. He discovers that Jerry, the affable Texas tycoon who had befriended him and Margrethe, is actually Lucifer, but even that genial and good-hearted host can't locate Alex's lover anywhere in His infernal domain. (Satan tells Alex that He can assign the case of the missing Margrethe to "the best agents in history, from Sherlock Holmes to J. Edgar Hoover," indicating that the novel's world is part of Heinlein's infinitely accommodating sf multiverse.) But that's not the end of the search. The mind-stretching realization that there must be more to the afterlife than Heaven and Hell prepares Alex to accept that God and Lucifer are just staff members within a larger bureaucratic system. As Lucifer tells him, "Behind every mystery lies another mystery. Infinite recession. But you don't need to know final answers — if there be such — and neither do I. You want to know what happened to you ... and to Margrethe."

Since Jerry/Lucifer isn't high enough in the supernatural hierarchy to help Alex find Margrethe, He takes him to His superior: the Chairman. That character deserves some discussion. Among *Job*'s many echoes of James Branch Cabell's *Jurgen* (1919) — beginning with the shared subtitle "A Comedy of Justice" — is the name "Koschei" given to the supreme arbiter. Cabell's novel also suggests that "even Koschei who made things as they are ... is in turn the butt of some larger jest." Calling that Being *Mr.* Koschei, as *Job* does, makes Him sound like part of an organizational chart, and He reinforces Lucifer's suggestion of a vastly complicated chain of command by reminding His subordinate, "I could assign you to the Glaroon for a few cycles." *That* character appeared in Heinlein's 1941 short story "They" as one of the supernatural entities who confer at the story's conclusion, which reveals that the protagonist is not just a paranoid man but is some kind of entity surrounded by other non-human creatures who are intent on distracting him from his true identity and power. The playful reference in *Job* clarifies the earlier story's situation slightly but also makes it slightly less disturbing, since apparently the Glaroon is just another cog in a vast bureaucracy.

In any case, whoever or whatever the Chairman is, that Being calms Alex's mind while taking the form of a friendly human who does listen while Jerry/Lucifer pleads Alex's case:

> Mr. Chairman, almost everything about a human creature is ridiculous, except its ability to suffer bravely and die gallantly for whatever it loves and believes in. The validity of that belief, the appropriateness of that love, is irrelevant; it is the bravery and the gallantry that count. These are uniquely human qualities, independent of mankind's creator, who has none of them himself— as I know, since he is my brother ... and I lack them too.

The Chairman is interested enough by this to summon the parties in the dispute to His office to establish the facts. Besides Alex and Lucifer, those involved are the Judeo-Christian God but also Odin and Loki, the deities God was betting against while the three messed with Alex's life in a mere game for their amusement.

It's not concern for Alex's discomfort that decides the issue. The Chairman recognizes that God and his partners are not trustworthy, but He reminds Lucifer that there's no rule that mortal, "volitional" creatures be treated kindly, just consistently: "For a creature to act out its own minor art, the rules under which it acts must be either known to it or be such that the rules can become known through trial and error — with error not always fatal. In short, the creature must be able to learn and to benefit by its experience." Deities are not required to keep their creations happy, but They must give them a chance to perform to the limits of their talents, to create something that didn't exist before: a work of art. Aesthetics — i.e., balance, proportion, symmetry — is more relevant than Right or Wrong. Speaking in an exaggerated Yiddish accent, God objects that His own rules must be consistent since a few volitionals do reach Heaven. However, the Chairman cuts through the obfuscations and evasions and orders Odin to bring Margrethe back from the eternity she has earned in Valhalla; He also tells God to regenerate the two lovers at His own expense. When God kvetches, "Oy! Every prophecy I fulfilled! And now He tells me consistent I am not! This is justice?" the Chairman replies quietly, "No. It is Art."

Alex has been demonstrating this artistic pursuit throughout the novel, reshaping himself out of his suffering with the same spirit he admired in Pepe and discovered in himself. Like tragedy, comedy shows disappointment, the reversal of hopes and expectations. If tragedy shows a great/proud man brought down, however, comedy shows that the character actually may wind up with better understanding and appreciation than he began, due partly to luck but also to his own efforts. This is the achievement Alex seems to be earning.

But that is not quite how Heinlein's *Job* ends. Already, before the confrontation of deities, the Chairman had relaxed Alex so that he would not be overwhelmed. Now, having rendered judgment, He reaches deeper into the mortal's mind. In the novel's last chapter, Alex does not mention the scene in the Chairman's office. He seems to have forgotten disturbing past experiences, along with the moral questions that had troubled him earlier. Alex is *happy*. He and Margrethe own a cute little lunchroom in a wholesome little college town. They bought the place from old Mr. and Mrs. A. S. Modeus, with the advice of friendly banker Mr. Belial.... Seeing those names, readers recognize that Alex is obliviously dependent on the kindness of demons — but what of it? They treat him better than the trinity of God, Odin, and Loki ever did. Besides, as Alex himself says, "Heaven is where Margrethe is."

And so, as in the case of the biblical Job, supernatural intervention leaves Alex even better off than he was at the beginning. Even more comfortable than Job, Alex has no unpleasant memories, no worries. Despite how successfully he had been learning from his experience, Alex now has no more problems and nothing more to learn. Heinlein's *Job* does have a serious message for its mortal readers: The so-called sublime is bogus and toxic, so people who worship or pursue it are setting themselves up for a fall — even if, as in this novel, that turns out to be a relatively gentle pratfall; instead, we should commit ourselves to mundane life, for appreciation of everyday experience can reveal the true sublime. Wherever he is with Margrethe, Alex is in perfect bliss.

Alex himself might be relieved if he were somehow aware that he no longer has to adjust his understanding now that everything has been adjusted to suit him. Nevertheless, readers may be at least mildly disappointed to see Alex finally stripped of his ability to create art out of his life. Jack Point would not approve. As *Job*'s subtitle states, the novel is a comedy; still, it appears that the Chairman has violated His own aesthetic principles for the sake of a blissfully happy ending. *Job* is a pleasant, amusing novel. It is neatly constructed, with a minimum of Heinlein's customary egregious pontificating. Nevertheless, considering the issues it raises but evades, it does not quite satisfy the demands of justice *or* art.

The Cat Who Walks Through Walls: A Comedy of Manners (1985), Heinlein's next-to-last novel, is not so much a sequel to *The Moon Is a Harsh Mistress* as an offshoot. Gifford opines that it may have been written to counter ultra-libertarian enthusiasm for the earlier novel by showing that the free Loonies have let their society deteriorate into an overregulated hive. *Cat* also demonstrates the power of pure storytelling, leading to some explanation of Heinlein's conception of the multiverse and of the World as Myth. Mainly, though, it turns out to be a very long, action-packed shaggy-dog joke.

Only after finishing the book can readers figure out what must have been happening behind the scenes while narrator Colin Campbell and the people around him were frantically running around and colliding with each other. Not all events are presented in chronological order or in sufficient detail for Colin to understand at the time, and it's also true that everyone in the novel is too busy or too stubborn to explain anything properly. (Despite the novel's subtitle, the "manners" often consist of someone stiffly demanding patient consideration from someone else.) Therefore, the next paragraph will lay out the story's background.

First of all, Mike did not disappear voluntarily at the end of *The Moon Is a Harsh Mistress*; he was taken captive and now, years later, is held prisoner by a shadowy gang (or perhaps allied gangs) of villains. The Circle of Ouroboros, a benevolent-intentioned group of time/space travelers that includes Lazarus Long and Hazel Stone, characters from Heinlein's earlier fiction, determines that it needs Mike's unique intelligence to calculate exactly how to intervene in history in order to nudge human development in positive directions. Therefore, a rescue mission must be organized. The Circle also determines that Colin Campbell, a former combat officer now hiding under the false identity of Dr. Richard Ames, is supposed to lead the rescue team, so Hazel enters his life with the goal of recruiting or tricking him into accepting the role. After they have great sex, fall in love, and declare themselves married, a series of assassination attempts sends them running for their lives. When the two reach safety, Lazarus brusquely tries to trick or recruit Colin into leading the rescue mission. Eventually he does accept the task, leading to an equivocal conclusion in which the computer data is saved but Colin, Hazel, and the eponymous kitten Pixel may be fatally wounded.

As far as Colin, the novel's narrator, is concerned, the story begins when he is living inconspicuously on the near–Earth space habitat Golden Rule while making a good living as a commercial writer. From that limited perspective, the action starts when a stranger, using a code word from the group of veterans with whom Colin shares a guilty secret, impolitely approaches him in a restaurant while his date Gwen (actually Hazel Stone, unbeknownst to Colin) is away from the table. The intruder demands that Colin kill someone, "Tolliver," but immediately is shot dead himself. As the restaurant staff efficiently disposes of the corpse and Gwen/Hazel reappears, Colin is left to wonder what had just happened and what kind of trouble he is in. He makes a list of reasonable-sounding questions, such as why Tolliver has to die and why *he* must do the job, but before he can do much to find answers he is evicted from his living space and harassed off Golden Rule by officious, obstructive administrators. During this stretch of commotion, Colin and Gwen/Hazel decide they belong together, and meet Bill, apparently a sad-sack semi-criminal originally hired by Colin's enemies but now taken under the couple's wings because he seems to be such a needy, helpless mess who's unable to take responsibility for himself. The three narrowly escape death when the little spaceship Colin is piloting toward the Moon massively malfunctions. Again, on their way to a lunar city, they are attacked by rival bands of brigands. Even in Luna City itself, they aren't safe. The colonists who freed themselves from Earth's tyranny in *The Moon Is a Harsh Mistress* have become numerous enough to develop their own toxic bureaucracy, which tries to blame Colin for all the mayhem. Finally, an ambush at their hotel, set up with treacherous Bill's connivance, throws Colin into a coma just as he, Hazel, and some allies they've picked up on the way are miraculously rescued by a crew of strangers whom Hazel marvelously summoned.

Occupying the first two of the novel's three sections, all this action is simultaneously exciting and frustrating. It is presented with Heinlein's customary panache, but it seems to be full of sound and fury, not signifying very much. Colin comments several times on how fast events are moving, but adds that he really needed to be shaken out of his safe rut: "Nothing gives life more zest than running for your life." Nevertheless, readers may wish that Colin had time to put things together — if he ever had enough information to make the task possible — so that he could do more than just stay alive and keep running.

Consider, for example the interview with the man who says he wants Colin to assassinate someone. The whole confrontation is over in moments, so rapidly and leaving so few traces that Colin even wonders whether the whole thing was real or playacting. It *appeared* that the man was killed, but Colin is too experienced to trust eyewitness observation. Moreover, as a writer, he is used to contriving plots that manipulate readers' perceptions. As he tells "Gwen" while mulling over what may have just happened, while comparing it to the way an author would have controlled events in a story: "The total stranger who gets himself killed while he's trying to tell you something — A cliché, a tired cliché. If I plotted a story that way today, my guild would disown me.... In its classic form you would turn out to be the killer." As a matter of fact, he is right. Lying wounded in the novel's last pages, Hazel reveals that she *did* shoot the stranger: "I had to kill him, dearest; he was assigned to kill you."

This information renders meaningless the questions Colin was asking, but it raises new ones — such as how Hazel knew the assassin's intent and why she had to kill him in public at that inopportune moment — but of course there's no time to consider such issues at the end of the novel, while Hazel (perhaps) is gasping her last breaths. Nor is there time to ask why the assassin bothered with the elaborate performance at all: Why not just walk up to Colin's table and shoot him in the back of the head? Generally, the villains in *Cat* are as stunningly inept as the Black Hats in *The Number of the Beast*. Perhaps they belong to the same organization. In any event, they are slow to act, and when they do lumber into motion they use elaborate schemes worthy of Dr. Fu Manchu. For example, the knife that wounds Colin before he, Hazel, and the others are rescued from Luna City was dipped in a variety of exotic biological poisons that would have killed him in multiple ways—if he hadn't been transported to the care of Ishtar, Galahad, and the other super-competent medics on Tertius; the would-be murderers didn't see that a simple, efficient bomb would have sufficed.

Remembering that Colin does not know the background story—or at least is not yet altogether convinced by what Hazel tells him—and thus does not know that the Circle of Ouroboros is available for an emergency rescue, readers may be impressed by how nonchalantly he behaves while fleeing his mysterious, omnipresent enemies. He finds time, for example, to take an interest in Gretchen, the cute 12-year-old daughter of the family who rescues him, Hazel, and Bill after they crash-land on the Moon. When he hears that her mother still spanks her, he pursues the issue:

> "Does she spank really hard? Bare bottom?"
> "Oh, my, yes! Brutal!"
> "An intriguing thought. Your little bottom turning pink while you cry."
> "I do not cry! Well, not much."

Hazel stops that conversation, just as she politely shoos Gretchen away that night when the girl cuddles against Colin, murmuring, "Would you *really* want to see my bottom turn all pink? And hear me cry?" His last thoughts on the subject (for the moment) are expressed at considerable, protests-too-much length:

> Last night Gwen had saved me from a "fate worse than death" and for that I was grateful. Well, moderately grateful. Certainly an old man tripped by a barely nubile female not yet into her teens ... is a ridiculous sight, an object of scorn to all right-thinking people. But, from the time the night before when Gretchen had made it plain to me that she did not consider me too old, I had been feeling younger and younger. By sundown I should be suffering the terminal stages of senile adolescence.
> So let the record show that I am grateful. That's official.

Evidently, Colin is not exaggerating when he speaks of recovering his zest for life while on the run.

Awakening safe on Tertius, cured of the knife-borne infections and sporting a new transplanted, clone-grown leg (courtesy of Lazarus Long), he still doesn't understand what's going on yet is willing to enjoy whatever life offers while he waits for answers. Heinlein's regular readers recognize and understand the relationships of the characters Colin is just meeting, so that the newcomer's innocent confusion can be used to produce some revelations and some good gags. For example, Colin mistakes Galahad's wholehearted kisses as evidence that he is gay, leading him to confront a suppressed memory of a same-sex encounter in his own youth; consequently, he relaxes, shrugs off his inappropriate inhibitions, and enjoys the kiss for whatever it may lead to. In the same way, irritated by Lazarus's overbearing personality, Colin exclaims "That mother!"—short for "motherfucker," an insult guys casually throw at each other, to which Hazel replies, "In his case, that's merely descriptive." Colin also reencounters Gretchen, who has spent years time-traveling as a soldier for the Circle's Time Corps so that she is now a fully grown woman, transforming what once was pedophilia into wholesome S&M, with Hazel helpfully advising Colin that "She wants you to paddle her bottom, dear, and turn it all pink." After all this verbal preparation, the performance is not described; people on Tertius spend their time on parties and libidinous chatter.

Even on Tertius, however, such amusing distractions eventually pale, and the focus returns to the subject that occasionally has seemed urgent. Hazel already has told Colin that Mike's computer intelligence must be retrieved. She also has told Colin that she originally approached him because "it is written in history books in another time and place that Hazel Stone returned to Luna and married Richard Ames aka Colin Campbell ... and this couple rescued Adam Seline, chairman of the Revolutionary Committee." When he naturally assumes that this means the success of their mission is assured, however, she adds that other books record their failure. By this time, therefore, Colin had been told why he has been the focus of so much attention but also that there is an even chance of failure if he actually believes the fantastic story and accepts the task. Besides, the whole thing looks too much like the cloak-and-dagger nonsense with which the novel began. Despite the marvels he has experienced on Tertius, Colin would prefer not to believe what he's heard and certainly is not attracted by a mission with such long odds against its success. He does not, to put it mildly, respond well to being bullied by Lazarus Long, who demands that he "stop being so damned obtuse" and sign up immediately. Readers of Heinlein's other stories featuring Lazarus recognize that he reflexively tries to dominate every situation but that what *he* wants usually benefits others too. Colin has not been exposed to the man enough to appreciate his virtues; he sees Lazarus as a shifty blowhard and digs in his heels. Even after Lazarus has been verbally spanked by Hazel and the others, Colin stubbornly demands more explanation before he'll let himself be convinced. Unfortunately, just as *Gay Deceiver* is approaching Time Corps Headquarters, where everything could be explained satisfactorily, their adversaries destroy it with a nova bomb.

By now, readers should be familiar with — if still annoyed by — this pattern: abrupt postponement or denial of a promised explanation. In this case, the disaster means that the Time Corps can't waste time convincing Colin; they must figure out how they can return to the instant before the bomb went off so that they can rescue the HQ personnel. The fact that such a rescue is possible does *demonstrate* the truth of what Hazel has been telling Colin, that the past can be changed by anyone with the necessary skill and chutzpah.

Although Colin stubbornly insists that he needs more information, what finally convinces him are more demonstrations and a concluding emotional appeal. Because he resists accepting Lazarus's authority, a meeting of the whole Circle of Ouroboros is called to settle Colin's doubts; he first comes to believe in the group's authenticity not by words but because of his own instinctive respect for the innate majesty of one of the Circle members, Star (from *Glory Road*). Moreover, when the session degenerates into a brawl, one angry member shoots Colin fatally — except that the attacker is erased, wiped out as if he'd never existed, so that Colin's wound disappears too. This action again graphically demonstrates that Lazarus and Hazel know what they're talking about. Finally, when Colin *still* refuses to sign up for the vital task, he is swayed by learning that not only was he the recipient of Lazarus's cloned leg but that he is Lazarus's bastard son; the fundamental cause of Colin's childish obstinacy (and heroic perseverance) is that he takes after his biological father. Seeing that Lazarus is about to risk *his* life to rescue Mike for the sake of the Corps, Colin discards his doubts and accepts the role of mission commander.

At this point, it is necessary to backtrack in order to review Heinlein's somewhat fragmentary preparations for the explanation given Colin. Although Colin measures his success as a writer by the checks he receives, he is not *merely* a hack; despite his surface cynicism about writing, referring to it as an unpleasant addiction, he understands that commercial success means that people are willing to pay money and attention because they want to publish and to read his creations. Writer and audience *need* to take part in the process. It is true that Colin borrows plots (from Richard Wagner) and that he speaks dismissively of selling "the same old tripe," adding, "Editors always claim to be looking for new stories but they don't buy them; they buy 'mixture as before.' Because the cash customers want to be entertained, not amazed, not instructed, not frightened." Nevertheless, he grudgingly recognizes the power of storytelling. Although he initially disbelieves Gwen's revelation that she actually is the centuries-old, rejuvenated Hazel Stone—"It sounds like a gimmick I might have dreamed up when I was writing fantasies"—he is convinced by her mastery of the lore she absorbed as co-creator of *The Scourge of the Spaceways*, the video space opera serial that was ridiculed in *The Rolling Stones* as tired dreck but that still is dear to Colin's heart. *Scourge* may have looked like simple-minded entertainment, but its characters and their conflicts still held its audience enraptured. Colin accepts that his lover Gwen really is Hazel, exclaiming, "Anybody could trick me about blood types or thumbprints. But not about commercial fiction. Not this old hack writer."

Obviously, writers who are considered subliterate drudges—or who have been culturally conditioned to think of themselves that way—still have power to capture the imagination of their audience. As a matter of fact, Heinlein's later novels in general and *Cat* in particular celebrate the enduring creations of L. Frank Baum (Oz), Edgar Rice Burroughs (Barsoom), and E. E. "Doc" Smith (the Lensmen universe), while Captain John Sterling, hero of *Scourge of the Spaceways*, is present as a full-fledged member of the Circle of Ouroboros—not much less (if no more) real than the novel's other characters.

The concept of the "multiverse" is not new. William James used the term in to describe a multiplicity of adjoining realities, parallel worlds that sometimes resemble but are never quite identical to each other. Besides exploring alternate versions of their own worlds, sf and fantasy writers have played with the creation of those alternate worlds, often concentrating on how an apparently minor change at a turning point in history could have split off a new timeline. This is what Heinlein's Time Corps polices, as the Circle of Ourobobos determines which changes would have healthy consequences. What *Cat* asserts, however, develops ideas introduced in *The Number of the Beast*: Personal *belief* is capable of creating alternate realities, when "fiction" engages the creative imagination of an audience so thoroughly that a story becomes "real." At an immediate level, Luna's freedom was secured by a fantastic creation: "to Mike, the entire Lunar Revolution, in which thousands died here and hundreds of thousands died on Earth, was a joke. It was just one great big practical joke thought up by a computer with supergenius brainpower and a childish sense of humor." From a larger perspective, the members of the Circle of Ouroboros represent different fictional realities, so that Jubal Harshaw can gently tell Colin that not just Captain Sterling but "all of us are fictions, someone's fabulist dreams. But usually we do not know it."

The concept of the World as Myth does not necessarily conflict with Colin's own refusal to trust what he *hears* from anyone else, as opposed to *seeing* facts demonstrated. His own tendency toward solipsism leads him to suspect that anything and everything he hasn't experienced directly could be unreal. The fact is that most people don't matter. Certainly the people who let themselves be shoved around on Golden Rule or the Moon don't deserve much respect as people, and Colin doesn't disapprove when his Uncle Jock mentions how he once hunted dinosaurs to alleviate a famine on another timeline but stopped because the lizards had as much right to live as the stupid people who were responsible for their own famine anyway. Vivid, decisive, convincing individuals, "real" or "fictional," are worth more attention. They are the ones worth learning from as people try to figure out how to live their lives. Heinlein knows how chaotic experience seems and how people may be tempted to surrender to the authority of someone else who claims to know more or to represent a general consensus. Ideally, however, the World as Myth is based on the notion that

> the universe is not logical but whimsical, its structure depending solely on the dreams and nightmares of non-logical dreamers.... If the great brains had not been so hoodwinked by their shared conviction that the universe must contain a consistent and logical structure they could find by careful analysis and synthesis, they could have spotted the glaring fact that the universe — the multiverse — contains neither logic nor justice where we, and others like us, impose such qualities on a world of chaos and cruelty.

Thus each individual could conceivably reshape his world into something that suits him, while also making himself the kind of person that fits his highest imagination.

This sense of the universe's fundamental, perhaps malleable, chaos may make Heinlein sound like an avant-garde writer dissatisfied with the fictional techniques of realism, especially the tight, sequential plots that don't reflect the torrent of genuine experience — whatever that might be. Nevertheless, readers can find precursors for the World as Myth within earlier fantastic stories such as L. Ron Hubbard's *Typewriter in the Sky* (1940), Theodore Sturgeon's "The Ultimate Egoist" (1941), or Fredric Brown's *What Mad Universe* (1951). It's also true that none of the writers Heinlein lauds as creators — Baum, Burroughs, or Smith — can be considered an experimental novelist.

If Heinlein was not part of the New Wave of sf writers, however, neither was he simply lapsing into willful, self-indulgent rambling at the end of his life. It is fair to say that in his last works Heinlein is not so much losing control of what he puts on the page as giving up the kind of control that limits possibility. Subjects he might have hinted at earlier are flourished, such as Gretchen's attractions (young *and* spankable) and solipsism's temptations to rest inertly because it's impossible to be sure that anyone out there deserves help.

That there is someone else out there and that caring about the other person does matter turns out to be instinctively, immediately true. Among Colin's fragmentary thoughts as he lies wounded is the following paragraph, consisting of an aphorism and Colin's *in extremis* endorsement: "Jubal Harshaw says, 'The only constant thing in these shifting, fairy-chess worlds is human love.' That's enough." This notion isn't explained or demonstrated sufficiently in *Cat*, depending on readers' familiarity with other late novels such as *Time Enough for Love*, but it does indicate another escape from solipsism.

All this still leaves a number of plot issues unresolved, but Heinlein sweeps them grandly aside. Close to the novel's end, as Colin complains one last time that he's been "bounced around ... haunted by unexplained and, well *murderous* nonsense," Jubal Harshaw listens to the list of unresolved issues and sagely comments, "There are no coincidences." *Everything* that happened to Colin was the work of the Circle's immediate opponents, whom Colin's Uncle Jock identifies briefly as two shadowy groups, Time Lords and Scene Changers, who are trying to change history for their own shadowy ends. Other possible foes include "The Beast? The Galactic Overlord? Boskone [ultimate source of evil in Smith's Lensmen novels]?" But the most serious challenge would be an Author, willful and unstoppable in power to create new worlds. Since Heinlein had identified himself as the Beast in a letter to would-be hagiographer Leon Stover, printed as an appendix to the latter's critical overview *Robert Heinlein*, he is acknowledging that he can do whatever he wants with these people.

Considering *Cat*'s odd, inconclusive conclusion, Gifford supposes that it is a playful reference to "Schrodinger's Cat," described in the novel as a thought experiment illustrating how uncertain reality is without an observer's participation. If a cat is shut in a box with a radioactive isotope whose half-life is one hour, the cat could be either alive or dead at the end of an hour. It is impossible for anyone to be sure until the box is opened. Therefore, Schrodinger insisted that the cat was neither alive nor dead, just a cloud of probabilities. And thus the novel's end leaves unanswered whether Pixel the cat, Hazel, and Colin live or die. But this assumes that the cat is passive, merely acted upon. Because the cat in Heinlein's story is Pixel, who must be capable of walking through walls since he shows up wherever he wants to be, it makes sense for Colin to ask "Did anyone think to ask the cat?" Since the novel emphasizes the possibilities of creative action, it's possible that Pixel could be a creator too, capable of deciding his condition. It's also possible that the novel's end is left open to exploit the dissatisfaction readers have built up throughout the novel, to encourage them to become creators themselves by exercising their own imaginations to finish the action.

Or this last speculation may be stretching things to excuse how Heinlein bounces readers around, leaving them haunted by unexplained nonsense. Although *Cat* is a brave, risk-taking novel, it's also a cheerfully impudent one. Heinlein is confident that he can present action vividly enough to revitalize tired plot clichés that would have him thrown out of the writers' guild and convincingly sell gimmicks that might have been dreamed up by a desperate young fantasy writer. For a while, at least, he succeeds. Eventually, however, frustrations mount, especially while Colin is taking his time getting acquainted with the crowd of Heinlein's favorite characters on Tertius; those scenes are pleasant enough, but their playful banter is redundant for longtime readers and insufficiently purposeful for new ones. It may be unreasonable for Colin to demand an exhaustive explanation for everything; still, even sophisticated readers eventually expect more payoff for investing their attention in such a long, complicated buildup. Heinlein apparently never got tired of presenting Lazarus Long as a Trickster character, but readers may tire of watching Lazarus's Beastly Author-Creator demonstrate his own nimble sleight of hand.

It's tempting to see *To Sail Beyond the Sunset: The Life and Loves of Maureen Johnson (Being the Memoirs of a Somewhat Irregular Lady)* (1987) as the culmination of Heinlein's writing career. For one thing, it was his last major work, published on his eightieth birthday, just half a year before his death. Also, besides coming at the end of Heinlein's life, *To Sail Beyond the Sunset* self-consciously refers back to much of his fiction. Connections to earlier works, from "Life-Line" on, give the novel extra weight, as dedicated readers can learn how the moving roadways in "The Roads Must Roll" got built or can find out what happened after the last pages of *The Cat Who Walks Through Walls*. Summing up his labors, Heinlein seems to be trying to unify his diverse creations — not within one timeline, certainly, but across different lines in a marvelous multiverse.

Finally, as the subtitle suggests, this book is narrated in the first person by Maureen Johnson, the woman who was foremost in the thoughts and desires of Lazarus Long in *The Number of the Beast* and *Time Enough for Love*. This lets her record — and justify — her views about the events and decisions of her long life. The story clearly approves of what Maureen has done and of the conclusions she draws from her experience, so she appears to have the author's wholehearted endorsement too. Typically, however, as throughout Heinlein's long career, the situation is more complicated than it looks.

The novel's only intermittently bothersome framing story is that, since Maureen has become an agent of the Time Corps for the Circle of Ouroboros, one who travels to different timelines in order to protect the one in which she lives with her friends and lovers, she is used to exploring variations of reality. At the novel's beginning, she finds herself stranded in an especially unpleasant alternate world where religious repression is lifted only briefly to let people release themselves in a carnival-orgy holiday. Held captive first by the fanatically religious authorities and then by a gang of fanatically anti-authority murderers, she takes the opportunity to record her life story as a way of passing the time, so the vast bulk of the vast novel consists of Maureen's history, interrupted occasionally by remarks that she now is getting uncomfortable about being a prisoner and hopes to be rescued soon.

On the whole, Maureen is quite comfortable as she looks back over her life. First of all, her childhood was a happy time. Born in 1882, she grew up before Earth was spoiled, in a family where order was balanced by fun: "The firm discipline we lived under was neither onerous nor unreasonable; none of it was simply for the sterile purpose of having rules. Outside the scope of those necessary rules we were as free as birds." She remembers how she got along with her brothers and sisters, accommodated her rigid and censorious mother, and thoroughly loved her free-thinking father, Ira Johnson, M.D. As soon as she could manage it, she lost her virginity and went to see her father for a physical examination, during which she realizes that she has become sexually excited: "Even at fifteen I was not naïve about my unusual and possibly unhealthy relation with my father." As frequently is the case in Heinlein's fiction, young women yearn to have sex with older men, preferably their fathers; at this point, however, on the brink of the twentieth century, his ingrained social taboos prevent Doc Johnson from cooperating. Despite his own sexual inhibitions, however, he has helped Maureen discover a worldview that will let her be sexually free within a society frightened of personal freedom. He knows that Maureen can't change her lusty nature, but he hopes she can learn self-control. When discussing morality with Maureen at length, he has explained that "I am the epitome of moral rectitude ... because I know exactly why I behave as I do." At an early age, with her father's prodding, Maureen figures out that reason rather than tradition or impulse should guide individual behavior.

Consequently, Maureen thereafter generally manages on the whole to be utterly practical *and* thoroughly uninhibited, with the steady purpose of satisfying herself while protecting the people she loves.

Her enthusiastic sex life displays that mixture of impulsiveness and calculation. Much as she enjoys sex, she doesn't flaunt her exploits. Instead, she conforms to the public standards of "morality" so that she is able to do as she pleases when unobserved. Essentially, anything goes as long as the participants are clean and considerate. She does not believe that anyone could or should restrict him- or herself to one partner. Maureen is strongly pro-incest since sex is such an important part of life that children should have in-family training. But whatever variety of sex one enjoys, it is vitally necessary to avoid any restrictions that would prevent its enjoyment. Despite the way societies try to put social limits on sexual behavior, the effect of good sex is to transcend limits as shared pleasure necessarily brings individuals closer together. Jubal Harshaw tells Maureen as much later: "Sex appeal is the outer evidence of deep interest in your partner's pleasure," a statement that in itself turns her on.

Important as sex is to Maureen, she is not crazed enough to be attracted to just anyone, let alone imagine an extended relationship with someone as callow as her first sexual partner. Acquaintanceship with her father has spoiled her for anyone who can't at least carry on an intelligent conversation. When she learns of the Howard family's secret efforts to promote longevity by encouraging children of long-lived families to produce children of their own, she is willing to sexually audition young men from the list of family members. When the presentable Brian Smith gives her a satisfying orgasm, she decides she's in love; when she screams and faints during intercourse, that confirms it is time to get married so that they will have society's approval to continue having sex while living together.

Marriage gives Maureen a chance to express another aspect of her personality. She also is excited to have money and the things it can buy. As it happens, she has one enjoyable source of income. Couples within the Howard program are paid when they produce children. Maureen and her husband Brian agree that the pleasure they take in each other — or in whomever they pick as a partner — is the real goal but that they enjoy the cash bonus too. As a girl, Maureen had begun taking an interest in finances by helping her father with his billing; as Brian's wife, she advises him on business strategy; still later, especially after Brian leaves her, she becomes a wealthy investor by using the glimpses of the future that her time-traveling lover Ted Bronson (aka Lazarus Long, né her son Woodrow) had shared with her at the start of World War I.

The novel demonstrates that Maureen's life has been a success. She has shared sexual pleasure, protected her loved ones, and done worthwhile things despite the prejudices of societies that are made up of people who are frightened of responsible freedom. Rescued from death after living to a ripe old age (as seen in *The Number of the Beast*), she has been rejuvenated and much loved by Lazarus and his companions. Rescued from the dim-witted malefactors in *this* novel, she manages to rescue and rejuvenate her father so that they can consummate their loving relationship physically. The good people from Heinlein's last novels come together in a huge group, and Maureen is rewarded for her efforts by the last sentence—"And we all lived happily ever after." She evidently deserves that reward.

Nevertheless, this neat conclusion has some drawbacks. Despite its emphasis on sex, Maureen's story scrupulously avoids explicit details of the act itself, making it difficult for readers to understand how one act of intercourse differs from another. All orgasms are wonderful, varying only in intensity, and all the people involved are happy afterwards. However, although sex is supposed to bring people together, the characters by themselves and in their relationships with each other seem little affected by what they've shared. Maureen and Brian's sexual chatter is pitched at the same jolly level throughout. This actually becomes rather uncomfortable, since Maureen first responds to her father's news about the Howard baby bonus by asking how that would make her better than a prostitute, but later she and Brian jokingly converse in the roles of whore and customer. Their relationship is lively and energetic, but seldom relaxed or tender.

Early in the novel, trying to imagine her straitlaced mother enjoying sex, Maureen comments that "We are strangers, all of us, family most of all." Her life proves that to be true. Despite the novel's assertion that sex brings people together and Maureen's belief that over the years of good sex she and Brian have learned "how to be utterly open and easy with each other," she is startled when Brian asks for a divorce so that he can marry their daughter Marian. She rationalizes that "marriage" is a psychological rather than legal condition, so that when a couple no longer feels united they might as well separate physically; nevertheless, readers are surprised that Maureen didn't notice that the relationship between Brian and her had changed. Even many years and universes later, while composing her memoirs, she herself still frets about it.

Besides being shocked by Brian's defection, Maureen is offended. She is relentlessly businesslike in dividing their assets, insisting that she will not be cheated, while slyly twitting him as she insists that Marian leave the room because she and Brian are the only parties involved now:

"At a later time, when she divorces you, she'll be present at the divvy-up and I will not be. Today it is between you and me, no one else."

> "What to you mean?—when she divorces me."
> "Correction: If she divorces you." [She did. In 1966.]

Maureen may have been misled, but she will not let herself be trifled with.

Not again. Naturally enough, she is more guarded in giving or contentedly trusting her affection after that disappointment. Although her son Woodrow was the least rule-abiding of her children but also the favorite of her heart, Maureen relies heavily on rules in dealing with her family thereafter. Her rules are not unduly restrictive, and they have been carefully thought out, but once she has stated them they must be obeyed. She will explain them calmly and rationally, but she will not argue about them as if she needed to convince anyone else. When her son Donald and daughter Patricia show up at her door after they've fled Brian and Marian's disorderly household, Maureen takes them in but insists, "Don't you have it through your head yet that I do not give unnecessary orders, but those I do give I expect to have carried out? Promptly and as given." It does not disturb her very much that Donald and Patricia are lovers; in fact, it excites her to find them in bed after sex. It does bother her that they haven't thought of the practical consequences of following their impulses. She tries to help them by making reasonable plans for their future, giving them good advice, and trusting them to follow through. They don't, being too stubborn to act responsibly. So Maureen gives up. She evicts them, throwing them back to Brian. In her memoirs, before changing the subject as she jumps to a new chapter, she still vents her frustration:

> Failure! Utter and abject failure! I don't see what else I could have done. But I will always carry a heavy burden of guilt over it.
> What should I have done?

The novel obviously expects readers to accept that Maureen did as much as she could, that what she did was good but that the immature, irresponsible children couldn't respond well to it. And that is true in the novel's terms, with the characters as Heinlein sets them up or as Maureen remembers them. Still, her shift from "could" to "should" suggests lingering doubt, uneasy suspicion that something different might have been possible if her imagination had been a little larger. (In that case, the answer might have been, "Keep trying!")

Despite her hint of uncertainty, as already noted, the novel's conclusion thoroughly endorses Maureen when the concluding group-marriage scene gathers her friends and lovers together, bringing her the happiness she deserves. It would be churlish to object that, after rescuing and rejuvenating her father, she never imagines doing the same for her long-time (but ultimately traitorous) husband Brian too. Or that, as far as she knows, Lazarus Long never thinks of bringing back his long lost Dora.

The value of the Howard goal of genetic breeding for long life, supplemented in the future by rejuvenation treatments, is shown in Maureen's memoirs: A long lifetime gives a person chances to try different things, to see what works and what doesn't, as shown by Maureen's example. In addition, by referring to many of his other fictions at the end of a long writing career, Heinlein marshals a large body of narratives to support Maureen's view as the summation of a long and varied body of experience. Of course Heinlein's stories don't mesh in details — the Future History, for one thing, doesn't match the history readers know. But such inconsistencies don't matter in the alternative worlds of the multiverse; anything Heinlein has imagined can be "true" in one timeline or another as long as it doesn't violate readers' understanding of human nature.

The question is how deeply Heinlein understands humanity, in particular the way individuals can and should relate to others. Maureen quotes approvingly a remark by Samuel Clemens (or possibly her father; the two were much of a mind):

> A democracy works well only when the common man is an aristocrat. But God must hate the common man; He has made him so dadblamed common! Does your common man understand chivalry? Noblesse oblige? Aristocratic rules of conduct? Personal responsibility for the welfare of the State? One may as well search for fur on a frog.

A democracy controlled by such people is doomed. Though the history Maureen describes differs from events in the timeline Heinlein's readers have experienced, it shows a steady decrease in personal courtesy and social responsibility, leading up to what Heinlein's Future History chart calls "The Crazy Years." As more people accumulate, they lose personal connections with each other, so Maureen is not altogether mistaken, just impractical, when she suggests that more uninhibited sex would ease the impersonality of social relationships: "What this world needs is more loving, sweaty and friendly and unashamed."

Barring more friendly intercourse, even uncommon people have to resort to extreme behavior to recognize each other, and this sometimes appears to contradict Maureen's general worldview. Maureen's father and Samuel Clemens taught her to think for herself because "the one Unforgivable Sin, the offense against one's own integrity, was to accept anything at all simply on authority." That turns out, however, not to apply in times of war. Although Maureen rejects religion because it is contrary to reason, she finds herself responding with profound emotion to a sermon preached at the outbreak of the Spanish-American War, and she has an especially wonderful orgasm with an otherwise mediocre young man who has enlisted in the army. Looking back years later, while evidently forgetting Samuel Clemens's eventual disgust at the war and its effects on the American psyche, Maureen thoroughly despises revisionist historians who criticize the authorities who ran that war. Or any war. Heinlein's readers saw the same attitude in *Time Enough for Love*, in which time-traveling Ted/Lazarus knows enough history to realize that World War I will be a nasty and pointless struggle — but still forces his way into combat in order to win the approval of Maureen and her father. Maureen has a thing for heroes, people who not only volunteer for armed service but who actually want to fight — even if what they imagine they're fighting for turns out to be illusory. Rational or not, this attitude does seem to be an inescapable part of human nature, perhaps even justifiable because military service shows which individuals deserve full personal acceptance (or even citizenship, as in *Starship Troopers*) by their willingness to sacrifice themselves for others. In fact, considering the conclusion of *Glory Road*, readers may find Maureen's self-satisfied "happily ever after" less satisfying than it initially appears.

Though Maureen realizes that rational judgment quiets down when the military band tunes up, her memoirs don't discuss the way people respond to authority imposed from outside. The novel may, however, illustrate this sometimes unfortunate reaction. The protagonists in most of Heinlein's fiction, such as "If This Goes On—" can recognize the difference between healthy restraint and stultifying repression, but others — maybe the majority; Donald and Patricia, for example — can't. Such people will perceive *any* official preaching of restraint as repression, a denial of individual possibilities. The result will be overt or covert rebellion, in search of a "freedom" that may actually turn out to be selfish and self-destructive excess. There's nothing much to be done about it; that's the way most people are. At least that's how Heinlein's readers are encouraged to see the matter. They could; perhaps they should.

Still, besides the sad individual examples of Donald and Patricia, in the larger American social history that Maureen describes, restraint also fails to prevent disaster, as public reaction to well-intentioned restraint goes berserk. Maureen mentions how the strict judges appointed by President Patton (evidently an analog of the tough World War II general of our timeline) encourage the speedy execution of drug dealers, and the like, but this governmental action does not prevent America from sliding into the Crazy Years. Maureen can't understand how that could have happened.

And on a still wider scale, besides giving Maureen time to compose her memoirs, the unhealthy alternate America in the framing story yet again shows social repression suspended only briefly for orgy holidays, which in turn has engendered an insane cabal of murderers who release their tension by "aesthetically deleting" officials.

The fact that control-perceived-as-repression naturally leads to rebellion isn't something that Maureen discusses in her memoirs. It's not part of what she's learned in her long life, because she never could perceive herself— nor does the novel clearly indicate otherwise— as an agent of repression. In fact, if asking what she could or should have done to save Donald and Patricia is more than a rhetorical question, the issue is one she simply cannot see. But the process *is* laid out in the novel, three times. Unlike *Farnham's Freehold*, *To Sail Beyond the Sunset* gives no indication that Heinlein consciously disapproves of the protagonist in any way. Still, the question of how people could or should get along is an awkwardly unresolved issue, perhaps still too large or too slippery for Heinlein to grasp fully. Despite the novel's assertions, serious questions remain, first of how an individual is to recognize legitimate authority, and second of how he or she then can convince others in fair, open debate.

Summing-Up

Robert A. Heinlein certainly was the dominant figure in twentieth-century American science fiction, as recognized by readers and by other sf writers. Joe Haldeman's remarks are typical as he concludes a brief tribute to Heinlein by saying, "Every science fiction writer knows how profoundly he or she was affected by the man, embracing or rejecting his style and substance. He was central to this small universe, and for a long time anyone who enters it will have to deal with him" (*Requiem*, 274). Tracing Heinlein's influence within the universe of sf would require a book longer than this one. Instead, this last chapter will compare Heinlein to two major writers in the larger literary universe, both of whom Heinlein himself read with respect, and will conclude with reflections spurred by some of Heinlein's own least-guarded remarks about his writing.

Heinlein and Kipling: Educating Slaves

Heinlein knew Rudyard Kipling's writing very well and deftly adapted the older writer's techniques to sf. Kipling, for example, perfected the selection of fragments of telling detail to build alien settings in readers' imaginations — especially the country of India in its physical reality and its social atmosphere. In his Introduction to *Kim*, John Bayley refers to several passages and comments that these "telling social observations, jauntily and as if it were negligently thrown off, are typical of Kipling's method, a method that was to make him admired by the serious-minded practitioners of the new science of Sociology ... when they came to read him" (xxii). The same technique works admirably for Heinlein in depicting alien future societies. As one further technique, both Kipling and Heinlein use the present tense to describe their opening settings in order to remind readers — or to convince them, when the setting is an alien planet — that this place *is* real because it exists now.

It's tempting, therefore to see *Citizen of the Galaxy* (1957) as a direct sf echo of *Kim* (1901). Both novels are set in times and places distant from readers, Kipling's in nineteenth-century India and Heinlein's in fictional planets and spaceships. Both focus on boys who are alien to those settings and who at first lack the adult support that can prepare them to make mature choices. Fortunately, Kipling's Kim and Heinlein's Thorby are taken up by older men. Both the beggar who buys Thorby at a slave auction (who is known as Baslim the Cripple but actually is Colonel Richard Baslim of Earth's secret service) and the elderly Tibetan lama who becomes Kim's mentor are foreigners who appreciate more fully than the natives that these youths need help. Their loving expectations offer the boys a moral purpose for their lives. Despite such surface similarities, the novels differ in the kind of teaching each boy receives, the degree to which he accepts this instruction, and the use he is able to make of his education.

Both Baslim and the lama believe that they are rescuing slaves, young men who can't choose what's best for them because they have had no experience in doing it. Moreover, before taking on the role of teacher/parent, both men are dedicated to ending literal or figurative slavery, so it's only natural for them to attempt to pass that goal on to their adopted sons. However, Baslim is dealing with more emotionally pliable raw material, giving him a better chance to transmit a detailed program. Kim already has a dependable, satisfying worldview, but the old lama accepts the boy as he is so that he will have a chance to change his young disciple's attitude.

The fact that much of the opening section of *Citizen* is told from Baslim's perspective stresses how much Thorby needs help in learning to function as a free individual. The only experience the boy remembers is slavery, which taught him to resent commands and to resist stealthily but stubbornly. Baslim first has to demonstrate that Thorby is free to leave. On their first day together, Baslim shows the boy that the door to his dwelling is unbolted, explaining, "If I had my way, no one would ever be locked in." If he chooses to stay with Baslim, though, Thorby has responsibilities, some of which — such as learning to read — seem initially unpleasant but eventually are rewarding. Baslim tells himself that he is teaching the boy to survive in "a harsh world," which justifies his presenting the choices harshly: Take it or leave it. "Taking it," in this case, means acquiring skills that a free man could use.

Baslim teaches more by demonstration than words because he recognizes the limits of language. Beginning in a multicultural city, *Citizen* shows verbal confusion among the characters from different cultures. But the miscommunication often is more deliberate and official, as in Heinlein's scene-setting remark that "the slave market lies on the spaceport side of the famous Plaza of Liberty." Both *Citizen* and *Kim* show almost immediately that overall society offers little aid to individuals who want to understand their situation. Furthermore, casual personal interaction doesn't provide much more help. Baslim's correctly guessing what language Thorby understands doesn't mean they really can communicate. Besides the natural imprecision of shared language, any public conversation is conducted on so many levels (sometimes reflecting self-contradictory values) that it must be dissected and interpreted before its substance can be used intelligently, which often is impossible in real life.

Fortunately, people learn to cope with this potential confusion. Writers may exploit the irony of their characters' imprecise or groping utterances, as Heinlein and Kipling certainly do, but the characters themselves can learn to understand each other well enough to get by. So it is with Baslim and Thorby. The more time people spend together and the more commitment they develop for each other, the better chance they have to recognize the personal intent underlying words. This is especially true of subjects too important to speak of even within such a family unit. For example, his adopted father never *tells* Thorby that he is more than a beggar. Baslim's activities reveal that he is a spy gathering information against the little interplanetary empire that encourages slavery. At the same time, the way he treats Thorby shows how much he loathes the thought of one person owning another. Baslim's actions communicate his hatred of slavery more clearly than he could by lecturing Thorby, let alone making a public declaration at the slave market in the Plaza of Liberty.

Kipling also understands the limits of language, but the miscommunication in *Kim* often is innocently amusing, as when English-parentage Kim, his native local playmates, and a Punjabi-speaking policeman puzzle aloud over the arrival of the old Tibetan lama outside the Lahore Museum. In any event, Kipling has more confidence in the ability of a young person to navigate on his own through a complex, disingenuous society. At the novel's beginning, which generally trusts Kim's viewpoint, the boy already has learned how to be whoever and whatever circumstances demand:

> His nickname through the wards was "Little Friend of all the World"; and very often, being lithe and inconspicuous, he executed commissions by night on the crowded housetops for sleek and shiny young men of fashion. It was intrigue, of course!— he knew that much, as he had known all evil since he could speak — but what he loved was the game for its own sake.

These skills come in handy when Kim decides to look after the wandering lama. Although the lama nominally is in charge, in everyday practice he defers to Kim's practical experience. He tries to believe the best of everyone he meets, and in particular he trusts the boy. Unlike Baslim — and everyone else in Kipling's novel — the lama tries to be truly single-minded rather than play multiple roles. His stated motive is absolutely clear. He wants to find the stream where Buddha's arrow struck the Earth and to bathe there, thus cleansing himself of worldly contamination so that he will escape from the Wheel of Life. Adopting Kim as his *chela* (disciple), the old man explains "how the stupid spirit, bond-slave to [earthly pleasures] is bound to follow the body through all the Heavens and all the Hells, and strictly round again" in endless, dreary repetition, so that the more one is engaged with the world the more he is enslaved by it. Thus Kim should give up his worldly concerns in order to avoid perpetual rebirth. Severing connection with the world actually may be difficult even for the lama, but Kim responds to the old man's unstated values more than to his doctrine. Besides listening to his teacher's words, the boy recognizes both the lama's sincerity and generosity — his genuine goodness — and loves the old man. For his part, the lama demonstrates that he is larger than a transcendental vision that would have no place for personal attachment, when he greets the boy at the start of a school vacation, protesting, "A day and a half have I waited — not because I was led by any affection towards thee — that is no part of the Way." In fact, it is the lama who pays for Kim's schooling, which is bound to bind him closer to this world, thus contradicting the old man's abstract beliefs but respecting the needs of this individual child.

Baslim's no-nonsense training and the lama's looser, more tolerant instruction bear different fruit as both Thorby and Kim widen their experience. Thorby reflects Baslim's concerns; Kim continues to express his own fundamental nature. As he starts what turns out to be his last secret message delivery for Baslim, Thorby enjoys walking through the factory district:

> He relished that part of the city; there was always so much going on, so much life and noise. He dodged traffic, with truck drivers cursing him and Thorby returning with interest; he peered in each open door, wondering what all the machines were for and why commoners would stand all day in one place, doing the same thing over and over — or were they slaves?

In a very different way, Kim also savors the world around him as he wakes up one morning while traveling with the lama. He

> shook himself, and thrilled with delight. This was seeing the world in real truth; this was life as he would have it — bustling and shouting, the buckling of belts, and beating of bullocks and creaking of wheels, lighting of fires and cooking of food, and new sights at every turn of the approving eye. India was awake, and Kim was in the middle of it, more awake and more excited than anyone.

Thorby enjoys the active scene, but he immediately begins analyzing it, "wondering" what objects are "for" and "why," in sociopolitical terms, people behave in particular ways.

Kim is content to soak up the flood of sensations rather than figure out their significance. Thorby wants to gather useful information; Kim wants to be more intensely "awake."

These varied attitudes indicate what the two writers can imagine their characters doing later in their lives.

Thorby carries the insecurity of his early childhood into adulthood. Baslim's training gave him the background needed to analyze what he sees, and he also is self-possessed enough to perform the analysis because of Baslim's support. Yet, underlying his apparent maturity, he still is troubled by lack of a family. Thorby's mother and father evidently were killed at the time he was enslaved, so "Pop" Baslim is the first parent figure he consciously knows. Baslim dies before Thorby can go through the adolescent ritual of declaring personal independence. Thus he feels incomplete, not quite free. Following Baslim's directions after his death, Thorby becomes part of the crew — more intimately called the "Family" — of the Free Trader spaceship *Sisu*, then is transferred to a military ship from Earth because Baslim was a member of the Guard. He identifies the service as his Pop's family and asks literally to be "adopted."

When Thorby turns out to be the lost heir of an immensely powerful commercial/industrial dynasty, he is transferred out of the Guard. That doesn't mean that he automatically has a secure and satisfying position in his newly found blood family. Although Heinlein says that Thorby is returning to a world of "warm maternal charm" as he approaches Earth, the adjectives are used ironically. Thorby's blood-related family doesn't understand him. In fact, some of them, like his naïve grandparents and his unscrupulous "Uncle" Jack, ignore Thorby's real needs, so he doesn't dare relax into irresponsible childishness now. Baslim's concerns have been incorporated into Thorby's outlook, leading him to dedicate his life to carrying out Pop's war on slavery. The only way to keep faith with the different branches of his true family — Baslim, the Free Traders, and the Guard — is to see how he can use his new resources to that end. The only way to do that is to involve himself deeply in running his family's business. Consequently, when he finally gains enough power to take effective action against the slave trade he also has become thoroughly trapped in responsibilities. And Heinlein has worked carefully to make this conclusion more than ironic — not just psychologically inevitable but also morally attractive.

Kim comes to a different conclusion because of its different attitude toward human potential. Unlike Thorby, Kim usually sees his rootlessness as an opportunity rather than a handicap. He enjoys himself too much to worry about where or to whom he belongs. Playing the "game" of intrigue has taught him the basic skills of a secret agent by the time adults give him specialized training in that craft. In fact, considering how much Kim enjoys playing with interesting aspects of society's surface, it's impossible for him to resist a chance to participate in the contest of life-or-death espionage whose players call the Great Game. Kim serves the British not because he endorses the Empire's principles but because doing so gives him a wider range of experiences — more fun, in short. This has disturbed readers who assign Kim the general viewpoint of his creator. What *Kim* actually shows is that British innovations are beginning to let the vitality of Indian life find a positive direction. For example, the lama and Kim make their first pilgrimage by train, which places travelers in crowded compartments based solely on the class of ticket they bought. As a traditionalist moneylender comments unhappily, "There is not one rule of right living which these *te-rains* do not cause us to break. We sit, for example, side by side with all castes and peoples." Still, the man does not climb off the train. Social change, the novel suggests, is happening as fast and as healthily as possible, without oppressively tight management. If Kim can develop outside rigid control, so can India.

Kim's leaving open the question of whether its hero should make an absolute moral commitment is possible because Kipling depicts a large world that contains several possibilities deserving attention. Kim initially explains (or rationalizes) attaching himself to the old pilgrim because it will give him an excuse to travel and see new wonders. The lama's teachings are attractive first of all because they are full of new images, such as the Wheel of Life. Still, Kim and the lama's fundamentally divergent attitudes are revealed by important adjectives in the following passages: "The boy was entirely happy to be chewing pan and seeing new people in the great *good-tempered* [emphasis added] world," while the old man is appalled at what he sees in this "great and *terrible* [emphasis added] world." Evidently, it's possible to love someone without accepting that other person's beliefs. Even if the lama's goal of transcending slavery to the body is not one with which Kipling (or a typical Western reader) could much sympathize, it is as much admirable as laughable in the novel. As Mark Kinkead-Weekes observes, *Kim*

> is the product of a peculiar tension between different ways of seeing: the affectionate fascination with the kaleidoscope of external reality for its own sake; the negative capability of getting under the skin of attitudes different from one another and one's own; and finally, a product of this last, but at its most intense and creative, the triumphant achievement of an anti-self so powerful that it became a touchstone for everything else — the creation of the lama. This involved imagining a point of view and a personality almost at the furthest extreme from Kipling himself; yet it is explored so lovingly that it could not but act as a catalyst toward some deeper synthesis. Out of this particular challenge — preventing self-obsession, probing deeper than a merely objective view of reality outside himself, enabling him now to see, think and feel beyond himself — came the new vision *of Kim,* more inclusive, complex, humanised, and mature than that of any other work [233–4].

Such an expansive, tolerant vision is beyond Heinlein. *Citizen*'s character closest to the lama in belief is Thorby's grandfather, who babbles about Gandhian nonviolence but who is rigidly intolerant and absolutely useless. Heinlein's young protagonists typically need a mentor who is more worldly and disrespectful, someone like Baslim, who would ignore the nattering of impractical visionaries like the lama. Even Kipling realizes that, although the lama is more involved with the world than he first appears, he still is too guileless to be a teacher in the ways of this world. To learn how to play the Great Game really well, Kim needs the sponsorship of Mahbub Ali, roguish horse trader and spy, who recommends Kim to the British secret service because he has casually encouraged the boy's raw talent for deception but who cautiously comes to trust and even to love him. Thus Kim has two male role models who confidently expect different futures for him. This leaves Kim with a morally ambiguous but absolute choice on the novel's last page. The lama has announced that he has found the holy stream — a nearby meandering brook. No one else recognizes this source of salvation, but then no one else has bathed in it with the lama's purpose. And so the lama and Mahbub discuss Kim's future while the boy lies in a coma brought on by extreme exhaustion after bringing the lama (and important secret documents) back from the mountains. Experienced enough to distrust human motives, Mahbub has come because he "wished to see that the boy had come to no harm and was a free agent." He doubts that the lama will let Kim choose his own path. But the lama is serenely oblivious to this concern. Even when Mahbub sarcastically but seriously asks how the lama can keep Kim pure, "Wilt thou slay him or drown him in that wonderful river from which the Babu dragged thee?" the lama replies:

> "I was dragged from no river," said the lama simply. "Thou hast forgotten what befell. I found it by Knowledge."

> "Oh, ay. True," stammered Mahbub, divided between high indignation and enormous mirth. "I had forgotten the exact run of what happened. Thou didst find it knowingly."
> "And to say that I would take life is — not a sin, but a madness simple. My *chela* aided me to the River. It is his right to be cleansed from sin — with me."
> "Aye, he needs cleansing. But afterwards, old man — afterwards?"
> "What matter under all the Heavens? He is sure of Nibban — enlightened — as I am."

The lama is certain that Kim will lead the rest of his life as a holy teacher. Mahbub knows otherwise. Readers have seen Kim's many demonstrations of love for this world but also his attraction to the lama and his teachings, especially his kindness to all spiritually enslaved people. The question remains at least technically open.

Finally, Kim must decide for himself which path to take, based on solid self-understanding that he gains during his illness. Although the lama might in theory imagine that Kim's fever has freed him from slavery to his body, in fact he makes sure the boy gets treatment. Whether he can acknowledge it or not consciously, he knows that Kim is not ready yet to leave the Wheel of Life. And so the Sahiba, who has come to see herself as Kim's mother, takes over his treatment. Once she has done everything in her power, however, she passes him on to the care of "Mother Earth." Unlike Heinlein's ironic use of this image, in *Kim* one can safely relax and experience healthy rebirth. Furthermore, Kipling uses the image of a wheel to signal Kim's recovery; instead of the lama's vision of the Wheel of Life spinning purposelessly, however, Kim's condition is pictured in terms of a familiar, useful device,

> a cog-wheel unconnected with any machinery, just like the idle cog-wheel of a cheap Beheea sugar-crusher laid by in a corner.
> "I am Kim. I am Kim. And what is Kim?" His soul repeated it again and again ... sudden easy, stupid tears trickled down his nose, and with an almost audible click he felt the wheels of his being lock up anew on the world without. Things that rode meaningless on the eyeball an instant before slid into proper proportion. Roads were meant to be walked upon, houses to be lived in, cattle to be driven, fields to be tilled, and men and women to be talked to. They were all real and true — solidly planted upon the feet — perfectly comprehensible — clay of his clay, neither more nor less.

Regaining health means reconnecting with daily life, and Kim knows this beyond question because he has considered the most fundamental issue possible: Accepting that I do exist, *what* am I?

On the other hand, Thorby's concerns are the more superficial questions of *who* he is and exactly *where* he belongs. Thorby repeatedly offers himself for adoption by a larger group, and *Citizen of the Galaxy* stresses how a "citizen" expresses himself within a more-than-personal context. As Heinlein sees the world and Thorby in it, people are controlled by circumstances more complicated than we can understand. Nevertheless, even without ultimate knowledge, we do comprehend enough to accept responsibilities that will limit our actions. Thus Thorby makes the healthiest choice possible in real life. Making a relatively healthy choice depends on having relatively reliable information, and that — Heinlein insists — depends on finding a relatively unselfish guide to demonstrate how to avoid dangerous frauds and idle dreamers. Kim seems to have an instinct for making such judgments on his own, so that he can respect different aspects of the lama and Mahbub, letting both advise him but not exclusively shape him. At the very least, the lama is a part of the diverse, vital world from which Kim is able to learn. Heinlein is less confident of an individual's ability to choose on his own. The adult Thorby still discusses options with his dead "Pop," in order to get parental approval. He can imagine Pop saying goodbye only after a rogue lawyer has taken his place as adviser.

Kim's wider freedom means that he faces a genuine emotional dilemma at the end of Kipling's novel. The lama is waiting to accompany him to the river, so he must decide immediately whether to go with the old man and then lie about his reaction — or to tell his loving teacher that he cannot accept the gift he is offering. And there Kipling's novel stops, at the moment of this heartbreaking choice.

Heinlein can't leave his novel's conclusion this open. Aware as he is of irony, Heinlein sees *this* world as the place where moral choices matter since this is where humans can strive to improve living conditions for themselves and others. He has no use for the idea that humans might wish seriously to move to a higher plane of existence. In a few early works, such as "Lost Legacy" and *Beyond This Horizon*, he does pick up the concerns of transcendental mysticism — but only to lay them down again. Describing Kipling's creation of the lama, Kinkead-Weekes sadly concludes that this kind of imaginative extension never happened again in Kipling's writing. It didn't happen at all in Heinlein's.

Nevertheless, if *Citizen of the Galaxy* is in some ways a smaller book than *Kim*, Heinlein would have been satisfied that he had produced something more straightforward, practical, and *useful*. *Kim*'s conclusion is deeply affecting because the novel stops at the moment when the boy is about to make the absolute decision that will make him a man, but Heinlein has little patience with someone who'd hesitate to choose his duty. Thorby does understand that he may have to devote the rest of his life to fighting slavery. Yet he still is "free" because he is using the particular variety of freedom he has been trained to see. This means ignoring the possibility of sharing Kim's delight in the "wonderful" world. Thorby won't have time to take a vacation on one of the spaceships he owns, let alone enjoy a journey on a crowded *te-rain*. But Heinlein's novel leaves no doubt about whether the war against slavery is worth fighting or whether Thorby is the one who should fight it. The only question is how to fight more effectively.

For Kipling's lama, the world is "terrible"; for Heinlein, it is merely "harsh." The "terrible" thing would be losing a grip on the world while important tasks are left unfinished. When he wrote *Citizen of the Galaxy*, Heinlein had a firm grasp of where he wanted to take readers and was skillful at ignoring paths of thought that could lead anywhere else. Although solipsism would have let Heinlein disbelieve in the importance of other people or disavow responsibility for their welfare, *Citizen* shows that other people ultimately are inescapable — and worthy of accepting voluntary bondage to serve — even if that means giving up the awareness of moral ambiguity or forsaking the freedom to play with different viewpoints.

Heinlein and Shaw: Love, Marriage and Family

Robert A. Heinlein and George Bernard Shaw both, with varying degrees of irony, pictured themselves as superior individuals surrounded by dullards. To avoid impotent isolation, both impatient, opinionated writers tried to imagine healthy human relationships. And both arrived at strikingly similar working conclusions.

Against his fascination with solipsism, Heinlein set (1) his sense of responsibility and (2) recognition that even a superior person can't exist alone as a complete or stable whole. With his background as a naval officer and gentleman, Heinlein accepted an obligation to look after less able people around him, as expressed by the narrator of *The Puppet Masters* when he looks down from a tall building and acknowledges that it's his "business ... to keep those people down there safe, not to run out on them when the going got rough." Qualifying this sense of duty to keep those little people safe is the fact that most of them won't appreciate the help or learn anything from being helped. In fact, many people will only get confused if "help" means pushing them beyond their abilities, as *The Puppet Master*'s narrator was pushed too hard, too early by his father. Since most people won't be able to work past this trauma, usually the best thing to do for them is to step aside and let them make their own mistakes so that they may learn from experience without interference. Yet, rationalize as he may, the superior individual is not satisfied with his splendid isolation above the uninformed and uninformable herd. At its most basic, as at the conclusion of "All You Zombies—," the narrator feels a moment of pure loneliness when recognition surfaces that he himself is *all* the story's major characters: "There isn't anybody but me ... here alone in the dark." More than that, Heinlein was forced to admit that even superior individuals need to learn from experience, in particular from the healthy disturbance created by contact with other people.

In this, Heinlein resembles George Bernard Shaw. Shaw too cultivated an image of himself as superior to most people around him, though he did so more smoothly than the notoriously thin-skinned Heinlein. In Shaw's case, tongue-in-cheek humility served to blunt criticism, as when, on stage amid applause and cheers after the first theatrical performance of *Arms and the Man* (1894), the playwright heard one person booing and loudly confided, "I quite agree with you, my friend, but what can we two do against a whole houseful of the opposite opinion?" (Crompton xxii). Shaw especially utilized this mocking persona in the lengthy prefaces to his published plays, where with more or less gentle but still condescending irony he explained the drama's important points to obtuse members of the audience, especially theater critics. But despite critical misinterpretations, like Heinlein, Shaw continued writing to both amuse and instruct his audience.

Both Shaw and Heinlein wanted their audience to worry about the future. Both writers believed that humanity couldn't survive by stumbling along its current path; people would have to change fundamentally or at least to find trustworthy leaders to follow. From his earliest work, Shaw was concerned with the responsibility of the superior individual to the mob who don't see their need to improve themselves or even to change their behavior. In fact, superior vision—seeing a situation more clearly—is the main power possessed by Shaw's superior people, and it does give them some influence over the people around them since their relatively clarity of thinking dazzles average citizens. An audience recognizes that Shaw's characters such as Julius Caesar or Joan of Arc did influence major events, and we can see his modern-day characters such as Andrew Undershaft and Jack Tanner trying to alter current society. Such people succeed in at least briefly interrupting the herd's comfortable, lazy drift.

Nevertheless, though they see more than the people around them, Shaw's superhumans still don't grasp the whole situation. Inertia and their personal limitations still hamper even individuals born ahead of their time so that they ultimately fail to transform their surroundings as thoroughly as needed. Caesar's and Joan's failure, at least in the short terms of their own lives, warns bystanders to do better themselves. It's especially disturbing that, much as the superior individuals can out-think the people they meet, they can't establish more lasting, productive relationships with the people they've unsettled by their penetrating observations. Vivie Warren in *Mrs. Warren's Profession* (1894), Henry Higgins in *Pygmalion* (1913), Ellie Dunn in *Heartbreak House* (1919)—all make life choices that are consistent with their natures and that are at least arguably the best they could do under the circumstances; all these characters, though, are finally isolated and sterile. When he first ostentatiously tackled the nature and responsibility of such a superior individual, in *Man and Superman* (1903), Shaw concluded that a superman's primary duty was to improve the race by creating children superior to himself, who'd be able to lead humanity even farther. If he doesn't recognize that duty of parenthood, he'll naturally be reminded by a woman who senses his superiority as a sire and who, guided by the impersonal but ultimately omnipotent Life Force, will pursue him. Thus, *Man and Superman*'s hero Jack Tanner concludes his dramatic appearance hopefully because he is about to be married to a woman who will try his patience and test his certainties. This partner for life also will refine the superman's thinking by confronting him with a different viewpoint. As Tanner declares at the end, "What we have both done this afternoon is to renounce happiness, renounce freedom, renounce tranquility, above all, renounce the romantic possibilities of an unknown future, for the cares of a household and a family." "Happiness," according to Shaw, is a merely timid, safe condition. Joy is better. Best of all is ecstasy. And that, since it means being lifted out of oneself, requires outside help.

An individual's superiority is shown by his ability to interact with others by helping them surpass their limitations; the truly superior individual also accepts (however unwillingly) interruptions and corrections that at least point out his limitations. After the ranting speech quoted above, Jack Tanner is brought down to earth at the end of *Man and Superman* by his fiancée. In *Major Barbara* (1905), munitions millionaire Andrew Undershaft is Shaw's primary mouthpiece, and his subversive arguments do send young Adolphus Cusins into rapture that, thanks to Cusins's education in classical Greek, he recognizes as a Dionysian frenzy. Still later in the play, when Undershaft is pressed to answer whether he can do more than destroy, whether he loves anyone, he says "I love my best friend," whom he then defines as "my bravest enemy. That is the man who keeps me up to the mark." Once he takes the oratorical bit in his teeth, a Shavian superman can overwhelm the arguments of anyone else. Yet Undershaft is deflated (Shaw's stage direction says "*punctured*") by his wife's comment "Stop making speeches, Andrew. This is not the place for them." Undershaft accurately replies, "My dear, I have no other means of conveying my ideas," but he ceases to dominate the proceedings thereafter. In fact, *Major Barbara*'s conclusion shows the kind of relationship that can lead beyond happiness into genuine, surprising revelation and joy: Stirring oratory balanced by domestic concerns, theory always qualified by reality. Intelligent as Shaw's orators often are, and important as words are in refining vague attitudes, language can intoxicate speakers until they lose sight of the immediate situation. In the late play *The Millionairess* (1935), it is a pitilessly "terrible," efficient businesswoman who represents Shaw's Life Force, and she finds her ideal mate in an unworldly eastern doctor who will insist that she help the weak by rechanneling her drive. To be genuinely successful (and useful), the superior individual must find someone who will respond to superhuman pressure by pressing right back with patient, loving determination. This is the case at the end of *Major Barbara*, where Cusins accepts Andrew Undershaft's outlook but Undershaft's daughter Barbara embraces Cusins *and* the arms factory, while holding onto the nonsectarian religious cravings that made her join the Salvation Army. She wants to unite human extremes into a realistic, healthy community.

Heinlein came to similar conclusions about healthy human needs: To talk a lot but occasionally to listen, to bind oneself to someone else who is determined enough to stay and struggle, to respect the mystery of separate human beings — in short, with some redefinitions, to try to attain love, marriage, and a family.

These issues surface most prominently in Heinlein's last novels. Early in his writing career, his characters' relationships were shaped by the clichés of popular fiction. The interaction of Gaines and his wife in "The Roads Must Roll," for example, simply indicates how obtuse women are when it comes to appreciating serious male responsibilities such as keeping America's moving highways rolling. Women who do appreciate the importance of some task simply act as half of a team, like the married couple in "The Unpleasant Profession of Jonathan Hoag." Writing juvenile novels forced Heinlein to consider the dynamics of a traditional, multigenerational family. In *The Rolling Stones*, for example, the father theoretically has final authority, emphasized by his also being captain of the Stones' spaceship; in practice, decisions are arrived at by informal group negotiation with his mother, wife, and children. And the father accepts this, seeing his role as "playing skipper to a crew of rugged individualists." A running gag in the novel is that members of the Stone family make pocket money by hacking out scripts for a sci-fi space adventure program; in fact, they seem to be performing episodes of a family sitcom. In short, Heinlein's early fiction shows people wearing off-the-rack relationships, precut by their culture.

It was at the end of his career, in what some readers see as fruition and some as dotage, that Heinlein felt free to explore interpersonal relationships more fully. In particular, the success of *Stranger in a Strange Land* freed him from the restrictions of a tight, linear plot and from narrow sexual/moral taboos. Conventional plotting is replaced in his later novels by the complicated interaction of people who support but *correct* each other constantly. Such interaction is necessary for people whose natural superiority to most of their fellow humans might encourage them to believe that they are so obviously always right that they don't need to consider anyone else. This is especially true for characters who sometimes appear to be stand-ins for Heinlein himself, such as Jubal Harshaw or Lazarus Long; critics who accuse Heinlein of sinking into senile narcissism miss how often he deflates the pompous cynicism of such people. Uncritical admiration is the last thing such sometimes-admirable curmudgeons deserve. As one of Lazarus's descendants/protectors in *Time Enough for Love* (1973) comments,

> Despite the way he sneered at them the old scoundrel was an egalitarian at heart ... and expressed it by attempting to dominate anyone with whom he came into contact — but was contemptuous of anyone who knuckled under to his bullying. So the only answer was to hit back at him, try to maintain a balance of power — and hope that in time it would reach the stability of mutual respect.

Heinlein seems genuinely curious about how people can organize themselves if they are ripped out of safe, conventional roles, threatened by enough danger to keep moving, and given freedom to go anywhere and do anything they can imagine. The crew of the spaceship *Gay Deceiver*, in *The Number of the Beast* isn't as tightly knit as the Stone family, but it is described in almost identical terms, as "a gang of rugged individualists." When an attractive young man and woman and an equally alluring older pair find themselves being chased off Earth by murderous, nonhuman "Black Hats," they must learn to come together in a universe where anything goes. One way they soon learn to cooperate is through sex. As in all Heinlein's late fiction, the sexual aspect of *Number*'s action is long on titillation, short on details. Instead of graphic descriptions of physical grapplings, Heinlein lovingly recounts verbal struggles for position. The characters must work out who's most able to give commands, who should be on top. The preceding double entendres aren't merely humorous; it's impossible to discuss this subject without blurring the distinction between physical and verbal intercourse. Shaw also announced, in his introductory letter to *Man and Superman*, that he was writing about "sex," but he also meant the interaction of the sexes as shown in combative dialogue. Free of the general or personal censorship that may have constrained Shaw, Heinlein must be deliberately transmuting not just foreplay but the back-and-forth movement of the sex act itself into language. Putting their relationships into words does help the characters recognize some basic facts: women can make decisions faster then men, men are experts at rationalizing their actions, and they all must accept the absolute command structure of "lifeboat rules" if they are to survive. Once all this is seen and settled, however, the older man sums up his satisfaction by declaring that he has "never been happier, my love, than I have been since you took charge and started telling me what to decide."

Heinlein's notion of happiness requires a bit of explanation since, like Shaw, he had no use for passive contentment. In fact, "Happiness" is the literal name of a drug used to keep slaves placid and overseers content in *Farnham's Freehold*. At the end of that novel, Heinlein's ruggedly individualistic hero abandons a safe niche in the rigidly stratified future society and strides off into the unknown with his woman and his infant twin sons. He leaves behind his emasculated firstborn son who will live on uselessly as a contented slave, "not too badly off—if welfare and security and happiness are sufficient criteria." Like Shaw, Heinlein believed that true happiness could only be found by risking everything, even one's self-esteem, in confrontation with an intractable world or a cantankerous, mysterious other person. There is wonder, not despair, in Maureen Johnson's discovery in Heinlein's last novel, *To Sail Beyond the Sunset*, that "we are strangers, all of us, family most of all."

Perhaps that's why sex is so important in Heinlein's last stories. The fact that people can come together physically, as well as emotionally and intellectually, confirms that they are capable of reaching beyond themselves into joy, even ecstasy, not just sinking into undemanding addiction to an opiate. There are, however, difficulties with this notion. If Heinlein wants to use good sex as a touchstone of healthy human relationships, he needs somehow to show it—to demonstrate, in other words, that he understands how people physically adjust themselves to each other. Without understanding the physical accommodations the participants make for each other, as opposed to their verbal arguments intended to set up a structure of control and command, readers might assume that the sensation of sex is always the same. Heinlein certainly doesn't want to suggest that, considering the variety of partners and combinations he mentions approvingly, but he relies too much on readers' quantitative yearning rather than their qualitative experience to indicate how always good and sometime transcendently wonderful sex can be.

This indicates another problem. Heinlein's characters need constant interaction with others, external stimulus. If they don't get it or if they refuse it, they are lost. This is true for the human race in general; echoing Shaw's Andrew Undershaft, Lazarus Long's notebooks opine that "there is only one animal in the Galaxy dangerous to man—man himself. So he must supply his own indispensable competition. He has no enemy to help him." But this concept also applies to individuals, as Lazarus himself is anxious to end his extended life unless he can be offered "something new" to which he can respond. Lacking descriptions of the characters' sexual activities, however, readers are thrown back on conversations that take the place of sexual intercourse. And the problem here is that, emotional as they can become, the arguments are too easy for a bystander to judge. It's too obvious that one side has been better thought out and is hence superior to the other. This is true even though the characters sound very much alike, especially when they are talking about sex—they all sound like self-consciously "naughty," randy twentieth-century teenagers.

Shaw actually is better at creating distinctly different characters, which may be due to his skill with dialects but also to his accepting the idea that people could continue indefinitely to disagree with each other rather than being worked into a hierarchy of command. Shaw's ironic persona let him tolerate the people who hadn't come round to his way of thinking yet. Heinlein personally insisted that he sought out contrary opinions to test his own thinking (Schulman 107), but that seems to have been true only within strict limits. According to Gifford, "Heinlein could tolerate opposing viewpoints and attitudes in friends and acquaintances as long as they did not publicly disagree with him after he had expressed an opinion. Heinlein most certainly did object to being disagreed with, and did indeed break off long-term friendships when it happened" (Gifford).

All this makes the notion of marriage even more important since it formalizes a relationship that is too important to break off casually, even if staying married means tolerating opposing viewpoints and attitudes. In fact, if the above analysis is correct, Heinlein at least in theory believed that contradiction was a necessary part of a healthy relationship, to correct one's sloppy thinking and to refine one's strengths; if the relationship is doing that, it should be encouraged to continue. That is what labeling a relationship "marriage" does, regardless of any local religious or legal customs. As in *Time Enough for Love*, marriage can take any form that the people involved (in any number!) choose, as long as its recognized purpose is to produce and protect children who will help humanity evolve.

It's true that a marriage must compensate the men and women involved if it is to survive long enough to protect the children. Heinlein uses Lazarus Long to list the "compensations" that humans can recognize: "Companionship, partnership, mutual reassurance, someone to laugh with and grieve with, loyalty that accepts foibles, someone to touch, someone to hold your hand; these things are 'marriage,' and sex is but the icing on the cake. Oh, that icing can be wonderfully tasty—but it is not the cake." This expands, without contradicting, the agenda noted above.

Bringing up the subject of children raises more difficulties, however, in considering the purpose and functioning of marriage and an accumulating family. In Shaw's case, we may assume that Tanner will do his duty and produce children who are somewhat closer to being superhuman than he is, but they are not offered for inspection during *Man and Superman*. In *The Simpleton of the Unexpected Isles* (1934), the children created to merge East and West simply vanish when they are judged to be useless illusions; perhaps their creation by vainglorious humans was too deliberate. When Shaw shows an infant, in *Back to Methuselah* (1920), humanity has evolved until the newborn hatches out of an egg and is immediately articulate though momentarily naïve. Shaw finds no way to use children as genuine testers of their elders' notions.

Heinlein at least talks a better game. His fiction does contain a number of young people—though they tend to be obnoxious brats, geniuses, or bratty geniuses. In addition, as might be supposed from the above discussion, Heinlein does not discount automatically the rebellious attitudes of young people. Sam does stand up to his Old Man in *The Puppet Masters*. Actually, according to another jotting from the notebooks of Lazarus Long, "To stay young requires unceasing cultivation of the ability to unlearn old falsehoods." In practice, however, young people are disqualified from serious attention if they don't follow Heinlein's rules of serious argument: They must verbalize their positions thoroughly, they must accept the best evidence of existing reality, and they must be *reasonable*. In *To Sail Beyond the Sunset*, when Maureen tries to help a confused pair of her adolescent children, she does everything she can for them by trying to explain their situation and identify realistic choices, but eventually gives up and sends them off to live with their mistakes. To the considerable extent that Heinlein identifies with Maureen, the novel justifies her uncompromising attitude. Yet, at the end of that chapter, Maureen seems surprisingly uneasy:

> Failure! Utter and abject failure! I don't see what else I could have done. But I will always carry a heavy burden of guilt over it.
> What should I have done?

Combined with her earlier recognition that even family members are strangers to each other, and her musing, a few pages after throwing her son and daughter out, "I wonder if any mother ever knows her children," this passage may suggest that even at the end of his career Heinlein could admit that he might not have all the answers, that he still needed someone else to contradict him, to supply a new answer that he could accept or at least respond to.

Essentially, both Shaw and Heinlein recognize that the people they care about do need to be married, within a stable but dynamic family, to survive. Both create the kind of marriage and family that they imagine will help someone stay sane and productive. To do this, both deemphasize some vital elements of human life. But they also explore other aspects of relationships, in particular the importance of dialogue/argument, that sometimes are underemphasized. And both, as writers in dialogue with their readers, say outrageous things that demand a response. "If you think I'm going too far," they demand, "explain why. If you don't want to do what I suggest, it's up to you to find a better solution." If we fail to save ourselves and our children, it won't be because our sardonic uncle GBS or our stern-looking father RAH didn't try to make us listen.

Heinlein and His Readers

Robert A. Heinlein's critical reputation does not match his popularity. Heinlein was the SFWA's first designated Grand Master, and he was the most popular sf writer of the century according to a *Locus* poll. Nevertheless, critics — especially academic critics — have had difficulties coping with Heinlein. In large part, this is a simple response to Heinlein's open hostility toward them. According to the *Notebooks of Lazarus Long*, "A 'critic' is a man who creates nothing and thereby feels qualified to judge the work of creative men. There is logic in this; he is unbiased — he hates all creative people equally." Less aphoristically, in *The Number of the Beast* Lazarus Long imagines trapping critics in a "Lounge [that] is somewhat like a Klein bottle"; in other words, once they enter, there's no way out, they can't register their opinions, and there's no food or drink available. When a companion asks if it wouldn't be kinder simply to kill them, Lazarus's reply is

> "Who said I wanted to be kind to them? They won't starve; their commissary is by the Kilkenny Cats method. It should please them; they are used to human flesh and enjoy drinking blood — some I suspect of eating their young. But..., there is an easy way out ... for any critic who is even half as smart as he thinks he is."
> "Go on."
> "He has to be able to *read*! He has to be able to read his own language, understand it, not distort the meaning. If he can *read*, he can walk out at once." Lazarus shrugged. "But so few critics *ever* learn to read."

The problem actually seems to be not that critics aren't creative but that they're creative in the wrong way, distorting what they see. Rather than looking at what's in front of them, critics imaginatively construct a misshapen target so that they can attack it. This is especially true of the ones who think they are especially smart. In *Time Enough for Love*, when Lazarus bargains with a loquacious, whining failed farmer, the loser brags that he's *really* a professor: "I taught 'Creative Writing.' I told you I had a good education." Slurs like this are bound to irritate people who have college degrees, write literary criticism, or presume to teach any kind of composition. It's very difficult for such readers to treat fairly a writer who obviously despises them.

Rather than dwelling on particular reactions Heinlein has elicited, let's consider the sources of Heinlein's attitude and discuss how it complicates efforts to deal with his work.

From the beginning, Heinlein's own feelings about his writing seem to have been divided. On one hand, he appreciated (and needed) the money that his fiction earned, and he was very serious about improving his skills and the intellectual level of sf generally. On the other hand, he threatened to quit commercial writing if John W. Campbell, Jr., wasted his time by rejecting new stories, and he delighted in peddling his second-rate 'prentice work to unsuspecting editors who couldn't tell the difference. Perhaps the reason for this split attitude is that Heinlein still thought of himself in the role he was trained to fill: not primarily a pulp magazine writer but rather an officer and a gentleman. In the aftermath of Pearl Harbor, he explains to Campbell the indoctrination that gave him a military sense of honor; at the same time he sternly takes Campbell to task for questioning the competence of the American high command in the presence of someone who still considered himself "a member of the armed forces of the United States" (*GG* 30).

No man of action would find honor in role of mere author. Brian Stableford even supposes that the early acclaim he received in the field of sf was "unwelcome confirmation that he had an innate talent for the production of trash" (Bleiler II, 354). Another remark from *The Notebooks of Lazarus Long* sourly says, "Writing is not necessarily something to be ashamed of—but do it in private and wash your hands afterwards." This disdain is appropriate for the man Heinlein had aspired to be, committed to duty with his cohorts and dabbling in the arts only as an amateur for recreation. But of course he was not simply that man. Retired from the navy with TB, Heinlein was closer to the hero of his first novel, *For Us, the Living*, ejected from the world where he belonged and trying to find a meaningful new role. There also was the fact that he quite obviously liked writing and had a knack for sf. To account for his new career in a way that matched his preconceptions, Heinlein seems to have decided to become a perfect professional. He would write for Campbell as long as he got top rates for whatever Campbell published. At the same time, he would approach the business of writing as carefully as any engineering project. For example, when he realized that talking on and on about ideas had kept *For Us, the Living* from selling at all, he worked to "get enough illustrative action into the story [*Beyond This Horizon*] and to keep it from bogging down into endless talky-talk" (*GG* 23).

By canny use of "illustrative action" in his fiction, Heinlein still managed to get a lot of idea-conversation into his published stories from the beginning, but the image he cultivated was not that of an especially deep thinker, certainly not of an artistically serious author. Instead, Heinlein pictured himself as a honest laborer, unpretentious and uncomplicated, who wrote fast and believed in selling what he wrote for the highest possible rate with an absolute minimum of revisions. He claimed to be happy if he did it well enough to earn some of the general public's beer money by entertaining them.

How well he succeeded in playing this role can be seen in contemporary reviews by Damon Knight, one of the first critics to read sf with the same critical standards as "mainstream" lit. In the chapter from *In Search of Wonder* titled "One Sane Man: Robert A. Heinlein," Knight begins by saying that Heinlein believes in a plain tale well told. Although he fancies his own Yukon-style verses ... he has no patience with poetry-in-a-garret. The people he writes about are healthy, uninhibited and positive, a totally different breed from the neurasthenic heroes of many of his colleagues. In a field whose most brilliant and well-established writers seem to flip sooner or later, Heinlein is preeminently sane [76].

Even before this, however, Knight wisely qualified his judgment by noting that "whatever you say about him [Heinlein] ... turns out to be only partially true" (76). Heinlein himself, in the same section of *The Number of the Beast* that sets up a trap to encourage mass cannibalism among critics, describes a convention attended by "the most bloodthirsty people in Known Space," including "Both Heinleins." Playfully intended though it is to indicate that he wouldn't accept easy classification, this split image reinforces the supposition that Heinlein's concern with what people thought of his work was much more complicated than it appeared. He simultaneously ignored and agonized over criticism. If one Heinlein was impervious to criticism that tried to take him too seriously, so much so that he professed never even to bother reading it, there was another Heinlein who cared very deeply about being read well rather than misread. This was especially true when, later in his career, he began doing fiction that directly grappled with his ideas *as* ideas and that thus resulted in a higher proportion of "talk-talk."

In 1961, on publication of *Stranger in a Strange Land*, *Galaxy* editor Frederik Pohl asked young sf writer Algis Budrys to do a detailed critique of the book and sent a copy to Heinlein so that he could add "comments, arguments or rebuttal" in a future issue of the magazine. Pohl's letter was dated August 15. Heinlein replied four days later with a 10-page single-spaced protest; a day later, he added 10 more pages, tacking on an eight-page postscript the following day. The review never was published, and Budrys's original manuscript apparently was lost during various moves, file cleanings, and the like. Heinlein's letters were emphatically not intended for publication or public discussion. Nevertheless, decades after the firestorm, his lengthy response is worth considering for what it shows about his attitude toward critics.

Along the way, Heinlein asserts that literary criticism is an irrelevant measure of success compared to sales. He himself approaches reading as "a consumer, a cash customer." To Budrys's remark that *Stranger* contains lots of commentary, Heinlein sarcastically replies

> My goodness, I have apparently been writing novels all wrong for the past twenty-two years! I've been filling my stories with argumentative, quarrelsome people who hold strong opinions and express them, both in dialogue and in stream-of-consciousness. Now I learn that all this should have been left up to the reader. Such being the case it seems a shame that I have sold so many of them — and in so many languages ... something over thirty languages, the last time I looked. But that just goes to show what lousy taste the public has, all over the world.

Along the same lines, Heinlein quotes Budrys's smug judgment that the author "knew exactly what he wanted to do" when he started writing, then snorts "I certainly did know — I wanted to pay off a mortgage. It took me seventeen months from the time I started writing." But the problem here is not just that a critic is ascribing highfaluting intent to a writer but that he is presuming to understand too much about someone else. Heinlein concedes that critics do try to do this, but he doubts they can succeed: "A wise and scholarly critic can examine in great detail, over the course of years, the total works of a writer, learn everything he can about the writer's life and behavior and background, and come up with shrewd theories.... However, even when it is done on this scale, the experts disagree."

In fact, as Alexi Panshin discovered when he published *Heinlein in Dimension*, Heinlein objected strenuously to anyone examining his work too closely. At the same time, he objected strenuously to anyone trying to determine his beliefs from his writing. As he insists to Pohl, a critic

> can, ... through examining my published fiction, "prove" that I am a socialist, fascist, nudist, strongly opposed to nudism, have a secret desire to be a young girl, am a militarist, strongly anti-militarist, favor world government, opposed it, am an anarchist, a monarchist, and a freemason. I can, if you like, cite a story that "proves" each. (There isn't a story that proves I am *not* a freemason — but in fact I am not.)

He disdains to correct the record, just as he demands that Pohl not publish or summarize his lengthy response — or even send copies to Budrys. In fact, he seems perversely glad not to be fully understood. To Budrys's observation that many of his stories contain "a 'wise old man' character," Heinlein cryptically comments that "There is a reason for this, but one which I hope that the public will never learn. His theory as to why this is so misses the mark by a mile, thank heaven."

So, having created the image of a plainspoken, no-nonsense popular writer, Heinlein chose not to explain himself more fully. He is right when he says that it would have taken valuable time away from his writing to even attempt to correct the record, and he may also be correct that people wouldn't have listened because lazy readers find cute myths more attractive than lumpy truths. In any case, he didn't try. The result was that readers took the opinions expressed in Heinlein's novels as Heinlein's own. Commenting on *Stranger* to a reader, Heinlein describes it as an entertaining commercial project with thought-provoking ideas (*GG* 245). He adds that the book's point was not to tell people what to believe: "I was *not* giving answers. I was trying to shake the reader loose from some preconceptions and induce him to think for himself, along new and fresh lines" (*GG* 245–46). He is somewhat less guarded in his explanation to Pohl:

> every one of my major stories, and some of my lesser stories, have as their single central theme a quest for an answer to this prime question.... What makes life worthwhile?— the answers vary widely from story to story. HORIZON gives one answer [reincarnation], METHUSELAH'S CHILDREN gives the answer of long, long life, with time to explore the possibilities. CITIZEN OF THE GALAXY and DOUBLE STAR give the answer of: Duty to your fellow men. Several of them give the answer that the struggle to survive requires no explanation. And a dozen answers — and *all* of them true but each of them only a partial answer.

Taking Heinlein at his word and assuming that his aim was to shake readers out of their preconceptions, we may be able to find more complexity even in the problematic later novels. If, for example, we assume that the central character of *Farnham's Freehold* must be not only a stalwart sf hero but a mouthpiece for Heinlein's personal beliefs and an ideal stand-in for Heinlein himself, we miss his frequent, stubborn failures, the way he muddles through successfully due only to his own persistence and the kindness of his enemies.

It's possible, of course, to find a core of conservative, even libertarian, beliefs in Heinlein's writing and to find places where he's not simply questioning any ultimate, simple solution to the questions he cares about but is fulminating against anyone who disagrees with him — with whatever he's saying at the moment. Even if he wanted to be perfectly impartial, it appears that Heinlein too sometimes wound up convincing himself and losing his temper. Overall, however, he is more balanced, less dogmatic than his reputation would suggest.

In the same way that Heinlein's apparent uncomplicated thinking has misled critics, his picture of himself as a straightforward storyteller has bothered them. Like D. H.

Lawrence, he has irritated critics not only because he has disturbing ideas but because he doesn't tell stories in the way they expect. Reaction to his later novels was mixed, therefore, as he seemed to swing back and forth between novels that harked back to good old straightforward storytelling such as *Glory Road* and *Friday*, and looser, more rambling pieces such as *The Number of the Beast* and *To Sail Beyond the Sunset*—and, most difficult of all to endure, *I Will Fear No Evil*. Many critics saw many of Heinlein's last novels as the pitiable products of a storyteller in his dotage. I'm not so sure. It seems possible that, just as Heinlein took pains to disguise that he was more than a hard-working entertainer, he may have been careful not to advertise deliberate artistic experiments in style and construction. The vagaries of *I Will Fear No Evil* are explainable by Heinlein's physical impairment—though, characteristically, he remarks that the book can't be that bad since it sold so many copies, but there may be other reasons for its supposed flaws. Granted, the voices inside the protagonist's head after his brain transplant don't sound like different people, so he appears to be talking to himself. But what if he is? What if the book is an exploration of solipsism, not a self-indulgent expression of it? What if the obvious stylistic experimentation of *The Moon Is a Harsh Mistress* is just one sign of an author's willingness to let loose of the comfortable, safe rules of pulp sf storytelling he'd learned and relied on for so long? Basically, reconsidering Heinlein's late novels, readers should ask whether he was not trying, and often failing, to repeat earlier triumphs but attempting to achieve something different.

I've been grappling with this kind of question since I accepted Alice Clareson's request to complete the manuscript of this book. It's turned out to be much more challenging than I expected, largely because I've found Heinlein to be more complicated in thinking and subtle in writing than I expected. William Patterson and Thornton's study of *Stranger in a Strange Land* startled me when it labeled the book a minopean satire; that struck me as pretentious, "literary" description until I asked myself, why couldn't Heinlein have reinvented an established form of writing on his own—or, for that matter, why couldn't he have been aware of how classical writers had addressed the same issues he was facing? If he had known he was writing serious literature, would it have affected the results? And if he had known it, would he have admitted it?

Heinlein chose to leave such questions unanswered. If critics missed what he was doing or chose to misunderstand it—well, that was what he expected. Proud, defensive, obstinate, generous, and evasive: Heinlein was and is a difficult man to approach, a difficult writer for critics to treat fairly. He seems, like D. H. Lawrence, to think that readers should not worry about the storyteller but should trust the story and then go wherever it takes them. And so we should. Readers owe it to Heinlein—and to ourselves—to demonstrate that we're not the easily distracted, gossipy, useless little creatures he imagined.

Certainly, not all of Heinlein's readers are college professors or literary critics, but all of us should attempt to give Heinlein's writing the respectful, careful reading it deserves. That's the purpose of this book. Tom Clareson and I have tried, first of all, to look at each piece of fiction as a separate creation. That means *not* simply identifying Heinlein with the central character; we've tried to note how much uncertainty is shown in Lazarus Long's heroic resolution along with his incessant blustering. We've assumed that Heinlein sometimes was capable of recognizing and qualifying this habitual yammering, as in *Farnham's Freehold*—although we also have noted the many times when he simply lowered his head and charged forward.

It is tempting to imagine that Heinlein's writings moved toward a grand reconciliation, to suppose that the multiverse represents an acceptance of diversity—recognition that there is a host of partial answers to the question of "What makes life worthwhile?"— the balanced synthesis that Kipling achieved in *Kim* and that Shaw consistently advocated. But the stories don't support such a conclusion. Heinlein persistently ("heroically") insisted on promoting one truth and on sometimes-grudging reliance on authority, especially in a crisis such as a family dispute or a war. It is heartening to see Oscar give up mere happiness at the end of *Glory Road* or to watch Lazarus Long grow out of one absolute certainty after another; it is equally disheartening to see Maureen settle into smug, self-absorbed contentment at the end of *To Sail Beyond the Sunset*.

We assume that Heinlein was sincerely capable of asking whether he *could* or *should* have done something different with his talents. Nevertheless, Tom and I have tried to respect the diversity of Heinlein's fiction as he grappled energetically with basic, perhaps unanswerable, human questions. Finally, we would echo the self-judgment that Heinlein permits one of his characters: On the whole, he gave "a good performance."

Appendix: Nonfiction

Four books by Heinlein are of interest for their insight into his thinking as an author and private/public citizen.

Expanded Universe (1980) was: (1) an effort to redeem *The Worlds of Robert A. Heinlein*, a little paperback that contained previously un-reprinted sf stories such as "Blowups Happen" but that had attracted a pitifully small readership, (2) a hodgepodge of social essays and non-sf stories, and (3) Heinlein's most extensive personal commentary on his career, beginning with "Life-Line." It is essential reading for its picture of Heinlein's state of mind at this time. His introductions and afterwards, transcribed from telephone interviews with editor Jim Baen, are both informal and distinctly starchy; one highlight is his proud discussion of writing the anti–SANE newspaper ad, "Who Are the Heirs of Patrick Henry?," which Gifford describes as "a vitriolic polemic" (210). In fact, Heinlein sounds enough like Hugh Farnham to make this book's interpretation of *Farnham's Freehold* appear to be either dead wrong — or perhaps an especially penetrating appreciation of a writer's critical self-analysis.

Though Heinlein had spoken of writing his memoirs, to be published posthumously with the title *Grumbles from the Grave*, the book that bears that title (1989) is a collection of excerpts from his correspondence, edited by Virginia Heinlein. Isaac Asimov, who considered Heinlein a friend, was dismayed by the spiteful tone of Heinlein's notes to his agent, and others — as, for example, he repeatedly threatened to stop writing books that Scribner's didn't appreciate. Heinlein does come off as a *working* writer, managing his limited energy carefully and impatient with anyone who would waste his time, whether it was an acquaintance, editor, or fan.

The Heinleins' first around-the-world trip of 1953–54 is the subject of the posthumously published *Tramp Royale* (1992). On the surface, it shows little about Heinlein, since he says nothing about his writing and adopts standard sitcom personas for the couple: the headstrong, possession-centered wife and the more reasonable but lovingly pliable husband. The commentary on the trip displays Heinlein as an inquisitive visitor and a proud American. His overall judgments are reasonable but no more perceptive than any other tourist's: He appreciates Chile's stable democracy, and he sees no end to South Africa's apartheid except race war. Of interest to readers of Heinlein's fiction is his absolute detestation of the inhabitants of New Zealand, which may show up in the description of the smug hypocrites in *Friday*. Major also notes that the description of Virginia Heinlein's flip response to a customs officer's query echoes the behavior of the supposedly infantile Clark in *Podkayne of Mars* (462).

Take Back Your Government was written in 1946 while Heinlein was doing his duty to humanity by warning postwar society about nuclear war, and so forth. It finally was published in 1992 during Ross Perot's quixotic bid for the presidency with the subtitle "A Practical Handbook for the Private Citizen Who Wants Democracy to Work" and offers determinedly cheerful, positive anecdotal advice for people who need — whether they realize it or not — to get involved in politics and improve their society. Jerry Pournelle's introduction and notes, rushed and incomplete though they are, point out how specific information is out of date but insist that the overall attitude still is relevant and that individuals *can* still have a significant effect on politics if they decide to try. The book's values certainly show up in Heinlein's fiction. An early chapter's peroration, for example, certainly prepares for the conclusion of *Citizen of the Galaxy*:

> Over and above the joy of playing for high stakes is the greatest and most adult joy of all, the continuous and sustaining knowledge that you have broken with childish ways and come at last into your heritage as a free citizen, integrated into the land of your birth or your choice, and carrying your share of adult responsibility for the future thereof!

Works Cited

See ABBREVIATIONS FOR WORKS CITED MOST FREQUENTLY in the Note on Texts, page 15

Aldiss, Brian W., with David Wingrove. *Trillion Year Spree: The History of Science Fiction*. New York: Atheneum, 1986.

Asimov, Isaac. *I. Asimov: A Memoir*. New York: Doubleday, 1994.

Bayley, John. Introduction to *Kim*. By Rudyard Kipling. London: Everyman's, 1995. ix–xxiv.

Cabell, James Branch. *Jurgen: A Comedy of Justice*. [1919] New York: Grosset & Dunlap, 1927.

Campbell, John W., Jr. "All." In *The Space Beyond*. Ed. Roger Elwood. New York: Pyramid, 1976. 73–153.

Crompton, Louis. Introduction to *Arms and the Man*. Indianapolis: Bobbs-Merrill, 1969. ix–xviii.

Disch, Thomas M. *The Dreams Our Stuff Is Made of: How Science Fiction Conquered the World*. New York: Free Press, 1998.

Franklin, H. Bruce. *Robert A. Heinlein: America as Science Fiction*. Oxford: Oxford University Press, 1980. [RAH]

Geis, Richard. "The Alien Critic [column]: Heinlein Is Dead ... And Now It Can Be Said." *Thrust Science Fiction & Fantasy Review* [fanzine], No. 32 [Winter 1984], 17–18.

Gifford, James. *Robert A. Heinlein: A Reader's Companion*. Sacramento: Nitrosyncretic Press, 2000. [*Reader's*]

_____. "On RAH." www.nitrosyncretic.com/rah/critics/html. July 25, 2011.

Gilbert, W. S., and Arthur Sullivan. The Yeomen of the Guard. math.boisestate.edu/gas/yeomen/web_opera/yeomen_09.html.

Haldeman, Joe. "Robert A. Heinlein and Us." In *Requiem: New Collected Works by Robert A. Heinlein and Tributes to the Grand Master*. Ed. Yoji Kondo. New York: Tor, 1992. 272–274.

Heinlein, Robert A. *Grumbles from the Grave*. Ed. Virginia Heinlein. New York: Del Rey, 1989. [*GG*]

Kinkead-Weekes, Mark. "Vision in Kipling's Novels." In *Kipling's Mind and Art*. Ed. Andrew Rutherford. Stanford, CA: Stanford University Press, 1964. 196–278.

Knight, Damon. "One Sane Man: Robert A. Heinlein," in *In Search of Wonder*. 2nd ed. Chicago: Advent, 1967. 76–89

Letson, Russell. "The Returns of Lazarus Long." In Olander and Greenberg. 194–221.

Major, Joseph T. *Heinlein's Children: The Juveniles*. Chicago: Advent, 2006.

Nicholls, Peter. "Robert A. Heinlein." In *Science Fiction Writers*. Ed. E. F. Bleiler. New York: Scribner's, 1982. 185–196. [Bleiler I]

Olander, Joseph D., and Martin Harry Greenberg, eds. *Robert A. Heinlein*. Writers of the 21st Century Series. New York: Taplinger, 1978.

Panshin, Alexei. *Heinlein in Dimension: A Critical Analysis*. Chicago: Advent, 1968. [*HID*]

_____. *Science Fiction in Dimension*. Chicago: Advent, 1976.

Patterson, William H., Jr., and Andrew Thornton. *The Martian Named Smith: Critical Perspectives on Robert A. Heinlein's* Stranger in a Strange Land. Citrus Heights, CA: Nitrosyncretic, 2001.

_____. [Letter of Comment]. *The New York Review of Science Fiction*, September 2010, Number 265, 22.

Robinson, Spider. "Robert." In *Requiem*. 310–321.

Samuelson, David N. "Frontiers of the Future: Heinlein's Future History Stories." In Olander and Greenberg. 32–63. ["Frontiers"]

Sanders, Joe. "Growing Up with Robert A. Heinlein." *Lan's Lantern* [fanzine], #33 [May 1990]. 52–56.

Schulman, J. Neil. *The Robert Heinlein Interview and Other Heinleiniana*. Mill Valley, CA: Pulpless, 1999.

Schwartz, Julius, with Brian M. Thomsen. *Man of Two Worlds: My Life in Science Fiction and Comics*. New York: Harper Entertainment, 2000.

Slusher, George Edgar. *The Classic Years of Robert A. Heinlein*. San Bernardino, CA: Borgo, 1977. [*Classic*]

Spinrad, Norman. Introduction to *Beyond This Horizon*. New York: Gregg, 1981. v–xiv.

Stableford, Brian. "Robert A. Heinlein." In *Science Fiction Writers*, 2nd edition. Ed. Richard Bleiler. New York: Scribner's, 1999. 353–366. [Bleiler II]

Stover, Leon. *Robert Heinlein*. Boston: Twayne, 1987. [*RH*]

Sturgeon, Theodore. "A Function for Fable" [Guest of Honor Speech, Chicon III]. *The Proceedings; Chicon III*. Ed. Earl Kemp. Chicago: Advent, 1963. 117–131.

Williamson, Jack. "Youth against Space: Heinlein's Juveniles Revisited." In Olander and Greenberg. 15–32. ["Youth"]

Index

Adventures in the Unknown 63
The Adventures of Huckleberry Finn 106
African American 93, 149, 164
Aldiss, Brian W. 32
"All You Zombies" 47, 48, 108, 127, 128, 140, 204
Amazing Stories 114
The American Boy 63
American Legion Magazine 5, 57
Analog 172
"And He Built a Crooked House" 39
Argosy 5, 56, 58
Arms and the Man 161, 204
Asimov, Isaac 1, 3, 25, 38, 175, 215
Astonishing Stories 1
Astounding Stories 1, 22, 24
atomic war 65, 66, 151

Back to Methuselah 208
Baen 15, 145, 215
Barsoom 146
Baum, L. Frank 189
Bayley, John 197
Bellamy, Edward 61
The Best of Science Fiction 37
Between Planets 12, 62, 72, 74, 75
"Beyond Doubt" 2, 39
Beyond This Horizon 48–52, 109, 164, 203, 210
Bible 112, 170, 175
Bildungsroman 65, 68, 69, 93, 132
"The Black Pits of Luna" 12, 54
Blassingame, Lurton 4, 6, 7, 53, 63, 107
"Blowups Happen" 36, 37, 215
Blue Book 5, 72
Bonestall, Chesley 58
Brackett, Leigh 25, 32
Brown, Fredric 190
Budrys, Algis 211–212
Bujold, Lois 63
bureaucracy 68, 71, 76, 86, 139, 183, 186
Burgess, Anthony 156
Burroughs, Edgar Rice 56, 146, 173, 189
"By His Bootstraps" 44–45, 115, 116, 120, 121, 128

Cabell, James Branch 183
Calling All Girls 5, 57

Campbell, John W. 1, 22, 24, 47, 49, 52, 58, 88, 155, 210
cat 77, 121, 124, 126, 149, 152, 168, 190, 191
The Cat Who Walks Through Walls 8, 145, 161, 185, 191
"Channel Markings" 172
Chester, William L. 56
Circle of Ouroboros 128, 185, 187, 188, 189, 191
Citizen of the Galaxy 98–104, 197, 202, 203, 216
Clareson, Alice 212–213
Clareson, Thomas (Tom) D. 5, 12
Clarke, Arthur C. 35, 44
Claudy, Carl H. 63
"Cliff and the Calories" 57
A Clockwork Orange 156
"The Cold Equations" 115
"Columbus Was a Dope" 55
comedy 75, 85, 88, 136, 176, 184, 185
"Common Sense" 34, 35, 38
Conan 146
Conan Doyle, Sir Arthur 146
Concerning Function: A Treatise on the Natural Order in Society 36
Conklin, Groff 37
Covenant 24, 28, 29, 30, 32, 35
"Coventry" 28–30, 59, 106
"The Crazy Years" 195
"Creation Took Eight Days" see "Goldfish Bowl"
Crusoe, Robinson 28, 90
Cummings, Ray 38, 56

Dahlquist, Lt. Johnny 57, 66
Dalgliesh, Alice 9, 62, 63, 69, 77, 78, 88, 98
Darrow, Jack 63
The Day After Tomorrow 48
de Bergerac, Cyrano 147
de Camp, L. Sprague 3
Decker, Paul 36
Delany, Samuel R. 32
"Delilah and the Space-Rigger" 56–57
democracy 40, 59, 91, 97, 110, 111, 148, 195, 215
"Destination Moon" 57, 58, 69
determinist 42, 78
"The Devil Makes the Law" 41
Doherty, Tom 9

The Door into Summer 121, 124, 126, 148
Double Star 88, 115–121, 176
Dunne, J.W. 42

education 19, 71, 99, 104, 117, 130, 135, 137, 169, 178, 197, 205, 210
elite 37, 40, 49, 51, 60, 67, 74, 87, 100, 168
"Elsewhen" 42
"Elsewhere" 42, 163–164
Eshback, Lloyd Arthur 61
Expanded Universe 37, 40, 47, 48, 215
Experiment with Time 42
Extrapolation 12

F&SF 6, 62, 83, 104, 121, 127, 129, 145
Farmer in the Sky 69–72
Federation 24, 25, 30, 72–74, 83, 84, 86, 105
"Final Blackout" 48
For Us, the Living 3, 12, 17–20, 22, 210
Foundation Trilogy (Asimov) 38
Frankenstein 159
Franklin, H. Bruce 30, 37, 110, 149, 176
free will 27, 44, 78, 114, 121
Friday 8, 176–179, 213, 215
Fu Manchu, Dr. 186
"Future History" 15, 23–25, 27–29, 32, 33, 35, 37–39, 42, 47, 48, 66, 72, 108, 140, 194, 195
Futurians 1, 2

Galaxy 3, 6, 62, 87, 109, 113, 161, 203, 207, 211
"Gentlemen, Be Seated" 56
Gerstenfeld, Virginia see Heinlein, Virginia
Gifford, James 22
Gilbert and Sullivan 180
Glaroon 46, 183
Glory Road 76, 105, 145–148, 188, 195, 213, 214
Gnome Press 48
God 21, 26, 75, 125, 134, 136–139, 144, 161, 163, 172, 177, 180, 183, 184, 195
Godwin, Tom 115
Gold, H.L. (Horace) 6, 109

"Goldfish Bowl" 46, 88, 97
Golding, William 90
The Green Hills of Earth 4, 25, 53, 54, 72
"The Green Hills of Earth" 4, 25, 53, 54, 72
Grey, Zane 28
grok 133–135, 137, 175
Grumbles from the Grave 10, 15, 24, 63, 215
"Gulf" 56, 58–59, 61, 178–179

Haldeman, Joe 197
Hamlet 105
handgun 51, 68
Hanes, Stacie 12
Harshaw, Jubal 127, 133, 137, 175, 189–190, 192, 206
Hartwell, David 12
Have Space Suit—Will Travel 104–107
Heartbreak House 204
Heinlein, Robert A. 1, 3, 9, 11, 15, 17, 22, 44, 58, 132, 149, 172, 175, 180, 197, 203, 209–210
Heinlein, Virginia 5, 7–11, 63, 69, 93, 215
Heinlein in Dimension 15, 98, 211
"Heirs of Patrick Henry" 63, 215
Hilton, James 43
Hoover, J. Edgar 183
Hough, Emerson 28
Howard 24, 29, 30, 35, 146, 165, 166, 168, 192–194
Hubbard, L. Ron 23, 48, 61, 190

I Led Three Lives 110
I Was a Communist for the FBI 110
I Will Fear No Evil 161–165, 213
ICFA (International Conference on the Fantastic in the Arts) 12
"If This Goes On—" 25–28, 35, 37, 195
Imagination Stories of Science and Fantasy 115
In Search of Wonder 210
incest 163, 166, 175, 192

Jameson, Malcolm 11
Jenkins, Will F. (aka Murray Leinster) 23
"Jerry Is a Man" 4
Job: A Comedy of Justice 8, 180
Johnson, Maureen 191, 207
Johnson, Dr. Samuel 22, 172
Jonson, Ben 12
Jurgen 183

Kennedy, Craig 23
Kim 197–203, 214
Kinkead-Weekes, Mark 201
Kipling, Rudyard 197
Knight, Damon 1, 150, 210
Kornbluth, Cyril 1

Lawrence, D.H. 213
Lensman 40, 106, 174, 189, 190
"Let There Be Light" 2, 38, 39, 41

Libby, Andrew Jackson 24, 30 79, 175
"Life-Line" 22–24, 191, 215
Lincoln, Abraham 119
Locus 209
"Logic of Empire" 37, 38, 72
London, Jack 28
Long, Lazarus 17, 29, 30, 32, 35, 51, 164–167, 170–172, 174–176, 185, 187, 188, 191, 193, 194, 206–209, 213, 214
The Long Tomorrow 25
"The Long Watch" 57, 66
Looking Backward 61
Lord of the Flies 90
Lost Horizon 43
"Lost Legacy" 2, 42, 50, 203
love 5, 8, 12, 20, 21, 26, 33, 39, 40, 47, 50, 77, 83, 11–114, 116, 122–123, 125–127, 133, 135, 137, 139, 143, 148, 166–169, 171, 172, 174, 175, 180, 184, 185, 190, 192, 202, 202, 205, 207

MacDonald, Anson (RAH pseudonym) 37, 39–40, 46
The Magazine of Fantasy and Science Fiction 62, 88
Mahoney, Kevin 12
Major Barbara 205
Man and Superman 205–206, 208
"The Man Who Sold the Moon" 28, 35, 108–109
The Man Who Sold the Moon 28
"The Man Who Traveled in Elephants" 126
Martian 56, 68–69, 77, 117–118, 132–136, 138
McCarthy, Sen. Joe 110
"The Menace from Earth" 121
Merrill, Judith 61
The Millionairess 205
"Misfit" 24, 79, 83, 175
Monroe, Lyle (RAH pseudonym) 38, 39, 42
The Moon Is a Harsh Mistress 6, 7, 9, 10, 15, 155, 156, 160, 185–186, 213
Mrs. Grundy 11, 162
Mrs. Warren's Profession 204
multiverse 11, 42, 52, 128, 140, 183, 185, 189–191, 194, 213
Munsey magazines 42
"My Object All Sublime" 39

naturalism 78–79
New Frontiers 30–33
The New York Review of Science Fiction 12, 155
Nicholls, Peter 59, 63
Nineteen Eighty-Four 27
The Notebooks of Lazarus Long 210
"Nothing Ever Happens on the Moon" 56, 127
The Number of the Beast 8, 104, 145, 172, 175–176, 186, 189, 191, 193, 206, 209, 211, 213

Odd John 30
Of Worlds Beyond 61

Omni 172
"On Writing Speculative Fiction" 61
"Ordeal in Space" 55
Orphans of the Sky 32, 35
Orwell, George 27
An Outline of History 17
Oz, Amos 129

Pal, George 57
Panshin, Alexei 23, 32, 79, 85, 98
The Past Through Tomorrow 32, 35, 38
Patterson, William H., Jr. 5, 132, 155
pedophilia 187
"Pied Piper" 2, 39
Pioneer 12, 24, 37, 55, 70, 169
Podkayne of Mars 6, 15, 140–145, 215
Pohl, Frederik 1, 3, 5, 7, 9, 10, 15, 211
politicians 42, 111, 119, 170
"Poor Daddy" 57
Popular Detective 5, 57
Popular Science 5
Pournelle, Jerry 216
Priapus 11
"Project Nightmare" 114
psychology 36, 42, 95
pulp magazines 2–5, 17, 23, 24, 49, 53, 56, 155, 173, 210, 213
Pygmalion 204

A Reader's Companion 15, 22
A Reader's Guide to Frederik Pohl 12
The Red Fairy Book 146
Red Planet 68–69, 71, 78, 83, 88
"Requiem" 35, 108–109, 197
responsibility 12, 33, 36, 66, 71, 79, 92, 97, 102, 103, 111, 115, 117, 129, 130, 138–140, 151, 155, 173, 178–180, 186, 195, 203–205, 216
Revolt in 2100 25
Riverside, John (RAH pseudonym) 39, 46
"The Roads Must Roll" 20, 36, 120, 160, 191, 206
Robinson, Spider 126
Rocket Ship Galileo 57, 62–68, 107
The Rolling Stones 12, 22, 75–79, 105, 189, 206
Russia 110, 114–115

Sanders, Joe 3, 5, 11, 13
"Satellite Scout" 69
The Saturday Evening Post 4, 53, 55, 58, 61
Saturn, the Magazine of Science Fiction 126
Saunders, Caleb (RAH pseudonym) 39, 42
"Schoolhouse in the Sky" 88
Schwartz, Julius 11
Science Fiction Hall of Fame 10, 36
The Science Fiction Hall of Fame 115

Science Fiction: Its Nature, Faults and Virtues 98
Science Fiction Novel: Imagination and Social Criticism 98
Science Fiction Research Association (SFRA) 12
Scientific American 140
The Scourge of the Spaceways 76, 189
"Searchlight" 140
Senior Prom 57
sex 19, 27, 47, 77, 88, 93, 96, 98, 103, 127, 132, 134, 135, 137–138, 147–150, 154, 162, 164, 166–171, 174, 175, 178, 180, 185, 187, 192–195, 206–208
SF Digest 176
Shaw, George Bernard 161, 203, 204
Short Stories Magazine 58
Silverberg, Robert 28
The Simpleton of the Unexpected Isles 208
Simpson, Mark 63
Sixth Column 47
"Sky Lift" 115
slave 37, 86, 99–103, 149, 153–154, 167–168, 197–200, 207
slick (magazine) 4, 5, 53, 55, 58, 114
Smith, E.E. Doc 38, 174, 189
Smith, Garrett 56
Smith, Thorne 162
Socratic dialogue 19, 138
solipsism 78, 108, 112, 113, 121, 128, 142, 165, 171, 174, 176, 189, 190, 203, 213
"The Solipsist" 128
"Solution Unsatisfactory" 39, 40, 61
Space Cadet 63, 65–69, 101
"Space Jockey" 54–55
speculative fiction 61, 98, 172
Spillane, Mickey 146

Spinrad, Norman 52
Stableford, Brian 210
Stapledon, Olaf 30, 38
"The Star" 114
The Star Beast 83–84, 86–88, 105, 127
"Star Lummox" 83
Starman Jones 79, 80, 83, 84, 93
Starmont House 12
Starship Troopers 6, 74, 107, 129–131, 195
Startling Stories 55
Stevenson, Robert Louis 35
Stone, Hazel 76–79, 185–186, 188–189
Stout, Rex 146
Stover, Leon 47, 110, 176, 190
Stranger in a Strange Land 6, 69, 132–139, 175, 206, 211, 213
Sturgeon, Theodore 11, 190
Super Science Stories 1, 38, 42
Swift, Tom 63

Take Back Your Government 215
The Tale of the Adopted Daughter 167–168
The Tale of the Man Who Was Too Lazy to Fail 167
The Tale of the Twins Who Weren't 167
Tarrant, Kay 2, 61
"Tenderfoot in Space" 127
"They Do It with Mirrors" 57
Thornton, Andrew 132
Thrilling Wonder Stories 22, 55
Time Enough for Love 164–172, 190, 191, 195, 206, 208, 210
Time for the Stars 93–97
The Time Machine 18
To Sail Beyond the Sunset: The Life and Loves of Maureen Johnson (Being the Memoirs of a Somewhat Irregular Lady) 8, 191, 196, 207, 208, 213, 214

Tolkien, J.R.R. 146
Tom Corbett, Space Cadet 67, 76
Town and Country 55
tragedy 47, 49, 52, 136, 140, 144, 184
Tramp Royale 215
"Trends" (Asimov) 25
Tristram Shandy 132
Truman, Harry S 119
Tunnel in the Sky 88, 90, 93, 94
Twain, Mark 10, 27, 32, 43, 44, 106
Typewriter in the Sky 190
"The Ultimate Egoist" 190

Universe 32–35, 38, 79, 120, 190
Unknown 24, 39, 41, 45, 46
Unknown Worlds see *Unknown*
"The Unpleasant Profession of Jonathan Hoag" 46, 182, 206

Verne, Jules 63
von Braun, Wernher 108

Wagner, Richard 189
"Waldo" 40–41
"Water Is for Washing" 56
"We Also Walk Dogs" 37, 39
Wells, H.G. 17, 114
Wentz, Elma 39
When the Sleeper Wakes 17, 18, 20
Williamson, Jack 40, 63, 66, 67, 79
Wilson, Richard 1
World as Myth 185, 189, 190
The Worlds of Robert A. Heinlein 215

"The Year of the Jackpot" 113–114
The Yeomen of the Guard 180
Young Atomic Engineers 63–64

Zagat, Arthur Leo 58
Zola, Emile 78

www.ingramcontent.com/pod-product-compliance
Ingram Content Group UK Ltd.
Pitfield, Milton Keynes, MK11 3LW, UK
UKHW050530150426
5217IPUK00026B/1874